Glenn Niemeyer
Jeremy Poteet

Extreme Programming with Ant

Building and Deploying Java™
Applications with JSP™, EJB™, XSLT,
xDoclet, and JUnit

SAMS

201 West 103rd Street, Indianapolis, Indiana 46290

Extreme Programming with Ant
Building and Deploying Java™ Applications with JSP™, EJB™, XSLT, xDoclet, and JUnit

Copyright © 2003 by Sams Publishing

International Standard Book Number: 0-672-32562-4

Library of Congress Catalog Card Number: 2003102955

Printed in the United States of America

First Printing: June 2003

05   04   03   4   3   2   1

Trademarks

Warning and Disclaimer

Associate Publisher
Michael Stephens

Acquisitions Editor
Todd Green

Development Editor
Sean Dixon

Managing Editor
Charlotte Clapp

Project Editor
Andy Beaster

Copy Editor
Margaret Berson

Indexer
Johnna Dinse

Proofreader
Kay Hoskin

Technical Editors
Ed Goodwin
Jeff Linwood

Team Coordinator
Cindy Teeters

Interior Designer
Gary Adair

Cover Designer
Aren Howell

Page Layout
Stacey DeRome
Michelle Mitchell

Contents at a Glance

Table of Contents

About the Authors

Jeremy Poteet has more than 15 years experience in software development. He has led numerous Java development and XP projects and has incorporated Ant at several customer sites. He has been involved in every aspect of the software development process, with team sizes ranging from 1 to more than 100. Jeremy is a CISSP and the Chief Technology Officer at Technology Partners, Inc., a consulting company specializing in application development and security, located in Chesterfield, Missouri. He can be reached at `jpoteet@tech-partners.com`.

Glenn Niemeyer is a consultant with Technology Partners Inc., consulting firm based in Chesterfield, Missouri. He has a Master of Science in Electrical Engineering from the University of Missouri, and 15 years of experience in software development. Glenn joined Technology Partners in 1996, and has been a technical team leader and project leader on a number of software development projects. He is also active in the area of Application Security. Glenn can be reached at `gniemeyer@tech-partners.com`.

Dedications

Jeremy Poteet: To my wife Sandy for being my best friend and our three boys, Michael, David, and Johnny, who are really excited that Daddy is writing a book about bugs.

Glenn Niemeyer: To my wife Sandy, and my two children, Melissa and Michael, who mean so much to me.

Acknowledgments

Jeremy Poteet: First I have to thank my wife Sandy for putting up with the long hours and missed family time. Also, my three boys, Michael (5) and the twins (3) David and Johnny, for bringing Daddy a Mountain Dew whenever he needed it. Thanks to Greg Nichols, the president of Technology Partners, whose patience and flexibility allowed this book to be completed. A special thanks to Kevin Bridges, who taught me how to be a professional in this business and first got me interested in build and deployment processes. I'd also like to thank Glendon Deal, my first mentor, who modeled many of the concepts that continue to impact my career today.

Glenn Niemeyer: I first want to thank my family: Sandy my wife, and Melissa and Michael, who have been patient and supportive throughout this project. I'd also like to thank Greg Nichols, the president of Technology Partners, for his contribution and assistance in this effort. I also want to acknowledge Kevin Bridges, David Levine, and Steven Veit, for the help and friendship they have given me.

We Want to Hear from You!

As the reader of this book, *you* are our most important critic and commentator. We value your opinion and want to know what we're doing right, what we could do better, what areas you'd like to see us publish in, and any other words of wisdom you're willing to pass our way.

As an Associate Publisher for Sams, I welcome your comments. You can email or write me directly to let me know what you did or didn't like about this book—as well as what we can do to make our books better.

Please note that I cannot help you with technical problems related to the *topic* of this book. We do have a User Services group, however, where I will forward specific technical questions related to the book.

When you write, please be sure to include this book's title and author as well as your name, email address, and phone number. I will carefully review your comments and share them with the author and editors who worked on the book.

Email: feedback@samspublishing.com

Mail: Michael Stephens, Associate Publisher
            Sams
            201 West 103rd Street
            Indianapolis, IN 46290 USA

For more information about this book or another Sams title, visit our Web site at www.samspublishing.com. Type the ISBN (excluding hyphens) or the title of a book in the Search field to find the page you're looking for.

Introduction

The *Extreme Programming* (*XP*) methodology is a lightweight development process that is focused on delivering quality software by using iterative processes that maintain simplicity and provide continuous feedback on the state of the process. By gaining continuous feedback and factoring this information into decisions, XP processes enable a team to steer an XP project to successful completion. Because of the iterative nature of XP, it's desirable to automate many of the processes. One tool that is ideally suited for use with XP is Apache Ant.

Ant is a tool that permits users to create build, test, and deployment processes by defining them in XML. Ant has a broad set of built-in capabilities, but it is also extensible in several ways. Users can create their own custom tasks in Java that will plug into Ant. Ant also supports the *Bean Scripting Framework* (*BSF*) and allows scripting code written in languages like JavaScript and Python to be included in a build process.

In this book, we'll follow the course of a project that implements XP processes with Ant. Throughout the project, some typical and even some unusual problems and challenges are encountered, and solutions are developed that can be applied to most projects. We'll first demonstrate how to create typical build, testing, and deployment processes that would be suitable for many projects. We also demonstrate a number of ways to extend Ant. The book provides numerous examples of custom tasks, including Java code and the buildfile XML, for extending Ant. Some of the custom tasks include developing ways to detect missing unit tests, creating Unified Modeling Language (UML) diagrams during a build, and integrating tools like Oracle SQL*Loader and NoUnit. We also demonstrate the creation of a custom logger that will create encrypted mail messages for use over an unsecured network. The use of the BSF engine in Ant for incorporating JavaScript or Python into an Ant buildfile is also demonstrated. Ant can also be integrated with Integrated Development Environments (IDEs). We also discuss how to structure Ant build, test, and deployment processes to be used on a larger scale, for a department or even an entire enterprise. All examples in this book are written for use with Ant 1.5.3.

Even if you're not using XP, this book will still be a useful guide for applying Ant to your build and deployment processes.

Who Should Read This Book?

This book is suitable for developers, technical project leaders, and system architects. It offers practical advice for implementing an Extreme Programming project using automated processes with Ant, and seeing it to successful completion. As a developer, you should be comfortable with writing XML and Java code, and have some appreciation of the challenges faced with building, testing, and deploying software. As a developer, technical team leader, or architect, you should welcome learning and applying new technologies and methodologies.

How This Book Is Organized

This book contains 11 chapters that build upon one another. An ongoing story line follows a fictitious project called eMarket that is being implemented with XP. We outline the problems and needs of the eMarket team along the way in each chapter, and then discuss the problems that will be solved in their overall build, testing, and deployment process. Finally, each section demonstrates the details of implementing the technique under consideration, with examples. This includes XML for buildfiles, Java code for extending Ant, and the integration of third-party tools into their process.

Chapter 1 discusses the XP methodology, and why Ant is a good choice for XP projects.

In Chapter 2, the basics of Ant are discussed, and using it as part of the initial spikes that are performed as part of XP. We cover how to implement basic XP processes with Ant's built-in capabilities.

Chapter 3 discusses many aspects of unit testing and revision control, and integrating these into your XP process.

Chapter 4 covers the creation of the first complete build process, including automatic generation of documentation, beginning with Javadoc and the use of doclets. We also discuss more advanced aspects of unit testing and version control.

In Chapter 5, we develop the nightly build process. Chapter 5 shows how to use Loggers and Listeners, how to create a completely clean build process that pulls everything from revision control, compiles, unit tests, and generates automated reports and metrics about the build results for the project team members and leaders. We also show how to integrate the CruiseControl tool for unattended continuous builds.

Chapter 6 moves into the creation of deployment processes. In this chapter, the project must be deployed to test servers. Basic Ant archiving tasks are examined. We also show how to use third-party tools for the automatic creation of deployment descriptors for Web applications, Enterprise JavaBeans (EJBs), and JavaServer Pages (JSP) Tag Libraries (taglibs).

In Chapter 7, we consider the challenges to an XP project when more developers are added to the project. This chapter focuses on how to modify the build process to cope with the shift in responsibilities. The focus here is how to keep the project from deteriorating into chaos when more people are added. We introduce a number of tools that can be integrated into an Ant build process for enforcing project standards. This includes IContract, Jalopy, Checkstyle, and PMD.

Chapter 8 considers moving an application into production and some of the problems that must be overcome. This covers the automatic generation of several CVS reports, and the generation of release notes. We also cover some techniques to increase the efficiency of a code generation step, execute a remote build on another server, and load data into a database as part of a production deployment. We develop a custom Ant task to integrate Oracle SQL*Loader into our deployment process.

Chapter 9 deals with a company reorganization, and the fact that the team must accommodate some new demands. We discuss the use of Ant with the NetBeans IDE. The Styler tool is introduced for advanced multi-stage pipelined code generation. We cover the Anteater functional testing tool, which is a derivative of Ant. A custom task is developed that will find classes that are lacking a unit test class. This chapter also shows how to insert scripting code (with JavaScript) into an Ant buildfile using Ant's Bean Scripting Framework (BSF) engine.

In Chapter 10, we discuss a commercial software development team that decides to adopt the XP process being used by eMarket. We discuss some of the changes that have to be made to handle their needs. For example, they're releasing JAR files, and need to obfuscate their JARs so that they can't be reverse-engineered. This is added to the Ant build process. We cover the use of the NoUnit tool from SourceForge to get insight into code coverage of unit tests. We add some features to increase the efficiency of the build.

Chapter 11 discusses the use of the Ant processes we've developed in an enterprise-wide fashion. The build files are refactored to be suitable for this. We also create a custom task to permit the automatic generation of UML diagrams from a Java code base. The Cactus Web application-testing framework is covered here, as well as some specific Ant tasks for starting and stopping a WebLogic server. Also we create a custom MailLogger, called the EncryptedMailLogger, that performs encryption using Gnu Privacy Guard (GPG) encryption of the build results prior to e-mailing. This is to support teams that need to send results via e-mail over the Internet.

Appendix A covers where to get Ant, how to decide between a source or binary distribution, and how to install Ant after you've downloaded it.

Appendix B discusses ways to extend Ant, with numerous examples. You will learn how to write Custom Tasks, Loggers, Listeners, Mappers, Selectors, Filters and Input Handlers, and see examples of each of these. You will also learn some principles of creating custom components, the lifecycle of a task, and how to write tasks that accept nested elements. Also you'll see how to use Ant's logging system in your custom components.

Appendix C previews what can be expected with Ant 2. This includes some of the compatibility issues that will occur between Ant 1 and 2, and some of the practices you can adopt to ensure that your transition to Ant 2 will be as smooth as possible.

Appendix D summarizes the buildfiles that are created in this book. Throughout this book, we follow an XP project that is continually improving the build and deployment process with Ant. This appendix provides a single place to find the cumulative buildfile changes that occur throughout the book.

Appendix E provides a summary of all of the tools that were used in this book, along with their version numbers.

Special Elements

This book contains a number of special elements. Story elements throughout the book track the progress of the eMarket development team and their use of XP. Sidebars show how to install tools that are used in conjunction with Ant. Finally, numerous examples and code listings show how to implement the concepts discussed. Many of these examples and source code can be directly applied to most projects with very little modification.

Source Code and Updates

You can download all the code files and examples discussed in this book at Sams' Web site: www.samspublishing.com. Simply type the book's ISBN (0672325624) into the "search" window, press Enter, and you'll be taken to a page with links to the code files. There, you will also find updates to the book, and corrections if necessary.

1

XP and Ant

Extreme Programming (XP) is a software development methodology for delivering quality software while maintaining a focus on customer satisfaction. *Ant* is an open-source tool from the Apache Project for creating build and deployment processes. In this book, you will learn how to implement effective XP processes by using Ant.

What Is XP?

XP development is iterative in nature, and delivers quality software through continuous automated testing and integration. XP development demands simplicity. It means refactoring code that is working to eliminate duplicate or redundant code. It is a focus on the here and now, not on what might be needed a week from now. XP emphasizes constant communication between customer and developers, as well as between developers. In fact, in XP, the customer is part of the team. XP is similar to the just-in-time inventory practices in manufacturing.

Characteristics of XP

XP maintains a focus on customer satisfaction. In XP, the customer is part of the team. That means that the customer has visibility and plays an important role in the overall plan. The customer drives the implementation and releases through writing user stories and participating in the Release Planning meetings. Because software is developed iteratively in XP, a working system is always available with some level of functionality. The customer can always view this working system and assess the state of the project or make changes in the system requirements (user stories). That also means that if the customer pulls the plug on the project, he or she will have something of value to show for the investment made to date.

XP emphasizes teamwork. Developers work in pairs on production code, and they communicate with each other. The customer, or at least a customer representative, is co-located with the development team to answer questions that naturally arise. Everyone on the development team works in different areas of the system, and everyone has ownership of the code. The XP methodology facilitates teamwork and requires trust among the team members.

Using XP adds agility to a project. Because of XP's emphasis on simplicity, quality, and testing, an XP project can more easily adapt to unforeseen circumstances than other heavier-weight methodologies can. In fact, XP expects the unexpected. That's why there is the emphasis on delivering functionality as it's needed, and testing and integrating continuously. Developers are always implementing user stories and delivering functionality as it's needed.

In XP, integration problems are caught early. This is because XP is iterative. Builds, unit testing, integration, and acceptance testing are done continuously. You don't have to go through months of coding followed by a death-march type of integration cycle. Integration is easier because it's happening all of the time. If someone starts to diverge on a meaningless tangent in code development (which is unlikely with pair-programming, and the emphasis on implementing stories), the miscue is caught early, before it has a major impact on schedule.

The Core Values in XP

The heart of XP is its four core values:

- Communication
- Simplicity
- Feedback
- Courage

Communication

Communication is critical to the success of any XP project. That means effective communication between developers, and between the development team and the customer. XP expects that the customer, or a representative of the customer, should be co-located with the development team. This encourages and increases communication and is part of the just-in-time nature of XP. Formal communication occurs between the customer and developer during the Release Planning and Iteration Planning meetings.

Communication occurs between developers during pair-programming. It also occurs between customer and developer when a developer has a question and is able to get a timely response because she can just go talk face-to-face with the customer. Getting timely answers to questions increases the overall quality and success of the project. If a developer has to wait for a document, or a message to be returned, he will probably do one of two things: Either he will guess at the answer or go on to something of lower priority. Neither action is desirable. Although an e-mail dialogue can occur, face-to-face communication is better because it's easier to convey information and to judge how well the recipient understands it.

Simplicity

Simplicity is often harder to achieve than complexity. It requires a commitment to achieve simplicity. In XP, this means that we don't code things that we think we might need at some point down the road. Developers code what is needed to meet the current requirements. As a development team, we strive to maintain a simple design. It also means that we have a constant focus on refactoring to eliminate redundant code. If after a piece of code is developed, a simpler approach becomes apparent, rewrite the code. Because much of the cost of software is in the maintenance, doing this will actually save time and money in the long run. Also, you won't be afraid to change parts of the system or to refactor classes because of the emphasis on continuous testing in XP.

Another aspect of simplicity is in maintaining coding standards. If code is written in a consistent style, it's much easier for anyone to pick up a piece of code and understand it. Maintain standards for naming variables, methods, and classes. Be consistent in the use of capitalization, braces, and indentation. All of this adds to reducing the complexity and the associated cost of building and maintaining software.

Feedback

Feedback is achieved in XP through frequent and thorough automated testing. Testing includes unit tests and acceptance tests. XP emphasizes the need to write your unit test for a class before you write the class. You then write the class to pass the unit test. By doing this, a team builds up a large suite of unit tests very rapidly. This practice will more than pay for itself as the project progresses, by preventing catastrophic mistakes that are costly to debug and fix. This also helps to maintain the focus on how a class will be used, and guides the developer into creating only what is needed.

Consider the importance of feedback. For example, no one would open a word processor, disconnect the monitor, and then type a document. The constant feedback provided by seeing the results of our actions on the monitor helps to reduce mistakes. It doesn't eliminate them entirely, but it does help prevent us from going too far off on some tangent. The feedback provided in XP by constantly running automated unit tests each time a build occurs will also help to reduce mistakes. Running automated tests frequently will also eliminate much of the pain normally experienced during the integration and testing cycles of most projects, because problems will be detected early.

There's another reason for testing frequently. When a developer is working on an area of code, that is what is foremost in her mind. The best time to test code is right after it's been written, while the developer remembers exactly what she was doing. If testing is postponed until a week or two after the code was written, and a developer has moved on to other areas, testing and bug fixes will be more difficult. There is a certain amount of ramp-up time to remember what was done and why. Using iterative cycles of unit testing and acceptance testing reduces this problem.

Courage

If you have never used XP before, using this methodology for the first time might seem a bit daunting. It does require courage to get started. Courage in XP means that the customer is not afraid to tear up a user story card if it doesn't fit, and to rewrite it. As a developer, have the courage to refactor code even though it's working, but is unwieldy. Don't hesitate to throw away unneeded code or to rewrite an algorithm because you now see a simpler way to do it.

Courage also means being willing to ask questions when you don't understand something. Talk to the customer when you need more information about a story. Don't fear the pair-programming aspect of XP when writing production code. This is all part of the courage required to implement XP.

Increased Productivity

XP developers are highly productive. First, they are implementing user stories that have the most business value, as determined by the customer. They are doing what is important first. They are not spending time on functionality that is of questionable value. In XP, there is less chance that something just implemented will be useless because it was done months in advance, and the requirements changed after it was implemented. Second, XP developers create high-quality code because they are continuously testing and refining their code. Far less time is spent chasing after bugs whose cause is obscure.

The XP Process

In XP, the customer drives the development priorities. The process starts by the customer developing *user stories* that describe the operation of the system. User stories should be written on index cards, so they can be shuffled around, marked up, or even torn up. A user story might say something like: "When the user finds an item they want to buy, they can add it to their shopping cart, and continue shopping." A user story should be something that a developer can implement in about a week. Of course, the customer has no way of knowing what a week's worth of work is for a developer. So it's the developer's responsibility to ask the user to break up a story into smaller stories if it's too big, or to combine small user stories into an appropriate sized story.

The user stories form the system requirements, and the customer gets to drive the order and priority of implementing those stories. When the developers look at the user stories, some concerns may arise about how to implement a story or the technology that may be used. In such cases where things are fuzzy, and therefore risky, the answer is to write a *spike*. The spike is intended to be throw-away code, so it doesn't get developed with the same rigor as production code. The intent is to test and perform a proof-of-concept for something specific. This will allow a more accurate estimate of the time required to implement a particular user story. The phase where customers are writing stories and developers are experimenting with spikes is considered the *exploration phase* of the iteration.

THE PHASES OF AN ITERATION

Releases are composed of iterations. A release should contain about three iterations, and each iteration should be about one to three weeks in duration. XP divides the activities within releases and iterations into three phases: exploration, commitment, and steering.

The *exploration phase* is for information gathering. It involves collecting user stories, determining the requirements of the system, and performimg spikes.

In the *commitment phase*, the developers take the story cards and estimate the difficulty of each task. Here is where stories might be combined or broken up to create work units of the correct size. Then a release or iteration planning meeting is held to plan the work. At this point, the user stories for the upcoming release or iteration are chosen, based on their business value.

The *steering phase* encompasses the rest of the iteration or release. Steering occurs by gathering project feedback and then taking corrective action based on that feedback. It is a process of continuous course corrections, much like steering a car. Steering is a very important part of the XP process, because it's done continuously. Some traditional forms of project management may go weeks or months without serious corrective action based on feedback. It's easy for projects like this to go astray. In XP, software is tested and integrated many times per day. Continuous steering ensures that the project will stay on track.

The next step is the Release Planning meeting. The customer and the development team meet and go over the user stories that the customer would like to have in the first release. The developers divide into groups and go over the user stories, assigning a difficulty rating, or points to each story. The harder a story is to implement, the more points it gets. This is also the opportunity for developers to ask the customer questions about stories. The developers attempt to estimate how many points they can get done in an iteration, and therefore, how many stories can be implemented in the first iteration. If it's not possible to accomplish everything in the first iteration that the customer wants, it's up to the customer to decide what the priorities are. The customer makes that decision based on the business value of each story, and its estimated difficulty. It's important to plan small, frequent releases, to put new capability into the hands of the customer as quickly and as often as possible.

XP projects typically work in 3- to 4-week cycles called *releases*. At the end of each release, new functionality in the form of an incremental release is delivered to the customer. Each release is broken up into *iterations*, which typically are a week long. At the start of each iteration, an Iteration Planning meeting occurs with the development team and the customer. The customer will present each user story in detail, and permit the developers to ask questions about it. The developers in turn will discuss the technical aspects of implementing the story, and put them up on a board. At the end of the meeting, developers sign up for tasks and make commitments for completing those tasks.

Iterations

After each Iteration Planning meeting, and within each iteration, developers will meet for short design sessions. The tools might include Class-Responsibility-Collaborator (CRC) cards or some Unified Modeling Language (UML) sketches, to get a good idea of what objects are involved, and how they will collaborate.

When the team starts to actually develop code, developers will pair up. The pairs are not permanent arrangements, but arranged to address some particular phase of development. Any given developer might pair with several different people during the course of the work day. When writing code, the pair first writes a unit test that will test the aspect of the class that they're going to implement. Then the class is written, compiled, and tested. Writing the unit tests and classes can be iterative in itself. For example, the unit test may be written to test one method of the class, and then that method is implemented in the class. Then another unit test may be written to test the next method of the same class, and then the second method added. The point is to make incremental changes and test often. Because of the frequency of unit testing, it's imperative that unit testing be automated. In this book, we'll show you how to automate unit tests and make them part of your build process. Also, by having automated unit tests, it will become immediately apparent if a developer makes a code change that breaks something.

At any point when code compiles and passes unit tests, it can be committed to the revision control repository. When this happens, it will be integrated and tested in the overall system. XP relies on a process of continuous integration. This means that the entire system is built on a regular basis, perhaps many times per day. The purpose is to catch problems and inconsistencies as quickly as possible, while they're still easiest to fix. As part of the integration build, tools are used to check for compliance to coding standards, and metrics can be generated. This book also covers the use of open-source third-party tools for accomplishing these tasks, and how to integrate them with Ant as part of the build and deployment process.

Prior to delivering a release to the customer, automated acceptance tests are run. If any of these fail, the bugs are fixed, and the code is rebuilt and tested again. If you plan small releases, functionality can be added incrementally, and quality maintained, while delivering new functionality to the customer on a frequent basis.

The Need for Speed

Working in an iterative methodology like XP means that a development team will be performing builds, unit testing, and integrating many times per day. These tasks need to happen as accurately and rapidly as possible to increase the project velocity. Also, these processes need to be repeatable. That's why these processes must be automated into a repeatable build, testing, and deployment process.

Creating an automated process provides another advantage by enforcing a discipline in the thought process. When creating an automated build process to perform a task, you as a developer are forced to think through all the details with greater stringency than you would if you simply documented a procedure. A written procedure doesn't have to compile or execute, and it's easy to miss a step or make a mistake. Certainly, the written process can be tested by users and debugged. Conversely, an automated procedure is not guaranteed to be bug-free. But even with a well-debugged written procedure, as complexity increases, so does the likelihood of human error when following it.

In short, an automated process means less drudgery for the developer and fewer errors. That translates into increased speed. In the spirit of XP, it's mandatory to automate as much as possible to reduce the developer workload and the likelihood of errors each time a process is carried out. Any task that must be repeated on a frequent basis should be automated.

Sharing the Knowledge

Another advantage that results from automating a process is that the whole team gets to share the benefit of the knowledge of the developer who created the process. It also preserves that knowledge for the team. When you've validated that an automated procedure works correctly, you only have to make it available to other developers to ensure that this procedure will then be run consistently by all users.

This can shield the development team from having to know the details of every product in the development environment. This is accomplished by developing Ant rules that handle the details of certain complex tasks. When the team size gets larger, it's unlikely that everyone will have an in-depth knowledge of every aspect of the system, such as the revision control system, for example. Suppose you're using Concurrent Versions System (CVS). Most developers will probably know how to perform basic operations, such as how to do an update, how to check out a module, and how to commit changes to the revision control system. However, they might not understand the nuances of branching or tagging. Perhaps your deployment process requires the developer to deploy Enterprise Java Beans (EJBs) to an EJB container, such as JBoss. This can be a complex task to get right every time, especially when you're under the pressure of a deadline. But if you develop the right rules in your build and deployment tool, the developers won't need this level of knowledge.

Also, as team size increases, it's likely that not every developer will perform certain operations, such as branching, in the same way, even with a written procedure. This could be because of simple human error or a miscommunication. By creating rules in a tool such as Ant to perform development tasks such as revision control access or EJB deployment, you've abstracted the details of the underlying tool.

If you've created the necessary rules in your build process to perform all the tasks that your development team needs to perform for a function such as revision control, it's possible to change the underlying service while maintaining the same procedures for the development team. This really follows the spirit of good object-oriented (OO) design practices at a developer interface level. It's considered a good practice in OO design to "program to an interface, not an implementation" so that your design is not tied to a particular implementation. By abstracting the details of tasks such as EJB deployment or revision control, your team won't have to learn a new set of procedures if the underlying tool changes.

Ant and the XP Process

Ant is an open-source Java-based build tool that enables users to rapidly develop build and deployment processes by configuring an XML file. It's actually a framework that enables a developer to write an XML file that executes a series of actions, where Ant controls the main thread of execution. Ant is ideally suited for implementing XP. It provides the framework needed to set up automated builds, testing, and integration. Ant is also extensible, so if it doesn't have a required capability, the feature can easily be added. There is also an abundance of third-party tools that integrate easily with Ant. It's also possible to integrate tools that weren't designed for use with Ant (examples will be given throughout this book).

The role that Ant fulfills in build processes is analogous to the role that a tool such as InstallShield plays in installation programs. If you're developing an installer for a Windows-based product, using a product for building installers enables you to rapidly configure a very professional-looking installation. Certainly, you could write your own installer from scratch, but it would be time-consuming, with little value added. In the same manner, you can write your own custom build processes, but the question to ask is, "Am I adding value to the project by writing my own build tool?" Most likely, the answer is no. If the real goal is to reduce workload by creating a reliable, repeatable build process, it makes sense to use an off-the-shelf product.

Ant can be used to create a regular automatic build, such as a nightly build. It's a good practice to have such a process in place to routinely build and test the code that has been checked into the revision control system. Another recommended practice is to set up an account that is not associated with any particular developer and then have the build performed under that account. This detects problems caused by differences in the developer's respective environments, such as differences in environment variables.

Why Choose Ant?

Many choices exist for build and deployment processes besides Ant. What advantages does Ant have over other products? What advantages does Ant have over using nothing at all? Some of the options we'll consider in this chapter are make, various Integrated Development Environments (IDEs), and even custom in-house solutions (or proprietary solutions). We also consider why Ant is better than relying on a written process and performing the steps manually.

A major advantage of Ant over many other build tools is that it's platform-independent. Ant is written in Java. Therefore, it can be run on any operating system that has a Java Virtual Machine implementation, which is pretty much every platform. Additionally, Ant has the same logical behavior across platforms. This eliminates the need for special handling of conditions in your build process based on various operating systems that you must support. For example, if you want to create a directory tree, you specify the structure in your XML file. Ant takes care of the differences between operating systems, such as the use of a backslash in Windows but a forward slash on UNIX-based systems. Ant also has properties that can be referenced (like constants). You don't have to be aware of the operating system (unless you use the <exec> task, which enables you to make an operating-system–specific call).

Make is probably the most serious direct competitor of Ant. First, we should give make its due respect. Make was a tremendous step forward at its inception, enabling developers to create a file for command execution management that could be used to create a repeatable process. Many developers grew up on make and have successfully used it on numerous projects. Also, some common ground exists between make and Ant. Both (Gnu) make and Ant are free software, so cost is not a barrier for choosing either tool. Both can be used to create a build process and are basically platform-independent.

So, why do we consider Ant to be a superior alternative? The biggest advantages of Ant over make are its use of a standard syntax (XML), its rich feature set, and its extensibility. To the uninitiated, make syntax can be very cryptic, whereas XML is more intuitive and self-documenting. In fact, most developers are either familiar with XML or should become familiar with it in the near future.

As the Ant Web site (ant.apache.org) points out, make also has various quirks, such as the infamous tab problem. Probably every make user has had to debug a makefile problem that was caused by an unfortunate (and invisible) space in front of a tab in the file. A space in front of a tab in a makefile breaks the make process, and it's not always obvious that the problem is a space before the tab. In addition, different varieties of make have slightly different behaviors. Certainly, this problem can be circumvented by standardizing on a particular variety of make, such as Gnu make.

The other advantages mentioned are the rich feature set and extensibility of Ant. Substantial functionality is built into Ant in the form of core and optional tasks. If

Ant doesn't have a built-in capability that you require, it's extensible in several ways. First, you can write your own functionality (tasks) in Java and plug it into Ant. Second, you can use the Bean Scripting Framework (BSF) scripting engine embed scripting code written in other languages (such as Perl, Python, JavaScript, and shell scripting) directly in your build process. Ant also has the ability to execute an operating-system–specific command, so it's also possible to integrate legacy scripts into an Ant process, easing the migration to Ant from proprietary processes.

Another reason for selecting Ant is that it uses current technology. Developers like to do work that will enhance their marketable skills. They generally don't like to work with technology that is perceived as outdated or as a dead end. It's easier to attract talented people to a project that uses leading-edge technology.

Finally, Ant is open source. This means that you can become a developer for Ant yourself and contribute to it. This also means that others have developed third-party add-ons for Ant. For more information about external tools and tasks for Ant, check the following URL:

```
http://ant.apache.org/external.html
```

Try doing a search on the Internet for a task that fits your requirements. If Ant doesn't already have a capability that you need, you might do a little research before writing your own; someone might have already solved the problem for you. In addition, you can post questions about Ant at mail lists or discussion forums to seek help from the user community. For more information about this, check the Apache Web site at

```
http://ant.apache.org/mail.html
```

In fairness, make is a better choice than Ant in some situations. Ant is definitely Java-centric. In fact, it's written in Java. Although it's not imperative for a user of Ant to know Java, it is helpful. Some of the tasks, such as the commands to invoke the Java compiler (javac) or to create Java documentation (javadoc), simply are oriented toward Java. No built-in commands exist for invoking a C or C++ compiler: These can be added through BSF scripting, by writing an Ant task in Java, or by simply using the <exec> task of Ant to execute a command in the native operating system.

Projects that are being developed in C or C++ might be better candidates for make. If the development team has no experience with Java or with XML and is already very familiar with make, the cost of surmounting the learning curve might be not be worth the expense. Another situation in which make might be appropriate is a project with legacy makefiles. If these work well and can be easily maintained, there might not be a compelling reason to shift to Ant. In fact, unless using make actually causes a problem in terms of usability or maintenance, it doesn't make sense to rewrite a well-tested process. However, if a team has no experience with either make or Ant, we recommend Ant as the build and deployment tool of choice.

Build Alternatives

Some projects elect not to have any formal automated build process. They rely on a developer manually performing a known set of steps for each iteration of the build cycle. Here are some of the pitfalls of this approach. The process must be well documented and communicated to all members of the team. That's certainly true whether or not an automated process is used. However, when a process is automated, changes can be made behind the scenes that don't affect the interface or the way a developer uses the tool. When that's the case, users are shielded from the details of the implementation. They only need to know if there is a change in the manner in which a procedure is run. Suppose that part of your build and deployment process is to deploy Enterprise JavaBeans into an EJB container. If the build tool has a rule for EJB deployment, developers need only to invoke that rule. Suppose that the team decides to change the EJB container product. It's then possible to change the underlying implementation of the rule for EJB deployment without changing the way in which developers invoke it. In this way, the development team is shielded from the changes in EJB deployment procedures because they're automated.

The level of complexity in a manual process is greater than that of an automated process. Because of the increased complexity, the probability of an error occurring in the execution of the task increases. Someone might miss a step, or changes in the procedure might not be communicated effectively throughout the group. Certainly, no tool can solve a lack of effective communication. But again, as the complexity of any procedure increases, the probability that an error will occur also increases. A problem created by missing even a single step in a procedure (such as forgetting to copy a DLL or a JAR file) is often the nastiest type of problem to track down. When the problem is finally found and corrected, nothing of value has been added to the project. Correcting a bug that results in a code change usually improves the product and definitely adds value. By contrast, time spent tracing a bug caused by a procedural error is time wasted.

An automated process removes some of the mundane work and leaves time for the fun and enjoyable work, such as design work and product enhancement. These are the activities that also help the company's bottom line, which is to produce a useful product. Effort spent performing mundane, repetitive tasks that the computer could perform is a waste of the development team's time and talent.

A complex manual process is not a repeatable process. Even if the same person performs the process each time, there's no guarantee that the results will be the same. Certainly, the quality of the outcome is likely to vary among individuals. By configuring a build process, you can debug the process once and then use it repeatedly.

A manual process is also fatiguing because it adds to the overall workload of project team members. If getting a procedure correct under normal circumstances is difficult, it's even more difficult when the team is under pressure, which is often the case in development projects. The time when people are under the most pressure is the time when they're most likely to make a schedule-killing mistake in a procedure. Repeatedly performing a procedure that could be automated is mentally fatiguing and adds to the likelihood that mistakes and schedule slips will occur. It's part of a vicious cycle.

Another downfall of manual build and deployment processes is that they require each team member to have specialized knowledge of the process. When a team member leaves the project, that knowledge is lost. The time and training required to bring new team members up to speed on the procedures increases with the level of complexity of the procedures. Automating those procedures reduces the learning curve for new team members. This also permits team members to develop areas of expertise instead of requiring everyone to be an expert in everything.

No project is too small to have some level of automated processes in place.

Custom and Proprietary Solutions

Some of the disadvantages of custom and proprietary build processes are really true of any proprietary solutions. Most developers we know really don't like to work on them. In fact, most developers prefer to develop skills that they can take with them to the next assignment. Learning the details of an in-house product that's not used anywhere else is generally not appealing. The consequence is that it could be difficult to attract qualified people to the project if it's seen as a technological dead end. Also, with a proprietary solution, you're virtually guaranteed to have to train new members to the project in your methodology. Ant is becoming a widely used tool, so it's possible to hire someone with a working knowledge of the tool.

It might be argued that custom scripts written in a standard scripting language, such as Perl, shouldn't be considered a custom solution. Certainly, it's true that the language itself is a standard and that it's possible to hire people who are experts in it. But there is a downside to choosing a proprietary solution to your problem. Creating proprietary solutions when off-the-shelf solutions exist is generally a bad idea. When using an off-the-shelf tool, you gain the benefit of numerous hours of development, debugging, and testing by the producers and customers of the tool. On the other hand, a proprietary solution requires your team to pay for all the initial development and debugging. Proprietary solutions also require your team to pay for the ongoing cost of maintenance, which includes fixing bugs and adding new features. With an off-the-shelf solution (especially a free open-source tool), the cost of development is amortized over a much larger customer base, making it more cost-effective. In short, a quality off-the-shelf solution will probably be quicker and cheaper to implement and maintain over the life cycle of the project.

Another advantage of Ant is that the buildfiles are written in XML, which is fairly self-documenting. With scripting, unless the writer used meaningful variable names and comments, the script could be fairly obfuscated and unmaintainable. This isn't necessarily the case all the time; it's just that Ant XML files in general are more likely to be easily maintained than custom scripts. Also, just because you have custom scripts doesn't mean that you have to throw them away to use Ant. Ant has a BSF scripting engine capability that enables you to integrate existing scripts.

Integrated Development Environments (IDEs)

Various IDEs on the market help a user with the development process. Most include the capability to define a project's build requirements to facilitate a well-configured repeatable build process. Many also include a lot of other features, including a symbolic debugger, visual graphic design tools, and testing features. Here are some aspects of relying on an IDE for your build process to consider.

One of the disadvantages of relying on an IDE for your build process is that it might tie you to the platform on which your development work is being done. Many Java IDEs are written in Java and, therefore, are platform-independent. If your IDE isn't platform-independent and you must support multiple platforms, you might find that you are maintaining more than one build process. This can be problematic because it's difficult to keep multiple processes in sync. It's also common to experience problems with infrequently used build processes because of changes in the surrounding environment. Another problem when relying on the IDE's build environment is that if you're forced to change IDEs, you must redevelop your build and deployment process. Depending on the complexity, this could be time-consuming.

Another problem with IDEs is that the environment must be set up for each developer. We have worked on projects with more than a hundred developers using an IDE. Sometimes problems are caused by subtle differences in the configuration of development environments among developers. These problems can be difficult to track down.

IDEs are definitely useful. Fortunately, with Ant and IDEs, it's not an all-or-nothing choice. One of the features of Ant is that it can be integrated into many of the IDEs that are now available. This gives you the benefits of both products. You can use the IDE for code development and debugging tasks, and you can use Ant to achieve a common enterprise-wide build process. In Chapter 9, "Company Reorganized—Working with a New Subteam," we delve into the techniques of integrating Ant with a popular IDE.

Summary

Ant is an open-source build and deployment tool that enables users to rapidly configure platform-independent build processes. Because Ant is written in Java, it's supported on any platform that has a Java Virtual Machine implementation available, which is nearly everything. It uses XML, which is a technology that is familiar to many developers. Because XML is fairly intuitive and self-documenting, Ant processes tend to be fairly readable and easy to maintain. Ant has an extremely rich feature set and can be extended when a unique or proprietary function is required. It has a gentle learning curve, and developers can easily put together a useful XML file with very little Ant experience.

But Ant also is a powerful tool that an advanced developer won't quickly outgrow. Because Ant is open-source, it's possible to obtain extensions to it from third-party sources. Ant also offers the possibility of extension by writing custom Java classes or using scripting languages and Ant's BSF scripting engine. If all else fails, a user can always shell out to the native operating system to perform a specific function. Because of these features, developers will never find themselves painted into a corner.

Ant offers numerous advantages over other possible choices for build environments and tools, such as make or various IDEs. Because many IDE products support Ant, users can leverage the power of the IDE while still using Ant.

Admittedly, in some situations, other solutions might be preferable. For one thing, Ant is Java-centric. Although it's not imperative to know Java to use Ant, it is useful. A situation in which another solution might be preferable arises when a development team already has expertise in another technology and has no experience with Ant, Java, or XML. Another case might be a project with a legacy build system that has been thoroughly debugged and works well. In such a case, it might not be justifiable to scrap the current build system in favor of a new one. However, when starting a new project, especially a Java-based project, or when the current build system is difficult to maintain, we believe that Ant should be the tool of choice.

The Scope of This Book

Throughout this book, we'll follow a group in a fictitious company called Networks Byte Design, which is implementing a project using XP. The primary focus will be on the details of how they implement their processes with Ant. But following the project should also provide other insight into the implementation of XP.

This is a book about how to implement XP processes with Ant. This book does not discuss topics such as how to effectively refactor code. It is intended to be a practical guide about implementing the repeatable build, testing, and deployment processes that XP requires, by using Ant. It does cover topics that have to do with automating processes, including

- Compiling code

- Packaging

- Automating unit tests

- Automating acceptance tests

- Generating deployment descriptors in the build process
- Creating a continuous build process
- Creating distributed build and deployment processes
- Maintaining project standards (such as coding standards)
- Generating metrics about the code
- Generating documentation
- Use of third-party tools

This book will also show how to extend Ant by writing custom components in Java and by using the BSF scripting capability in Ant. Included are a number of custom components written in Java that you can download from the Sams Web site and apply to your project.

2

Creating Initial Spikes

The first step in launching this XP project is to get the customer writing user stories. On this project, the customer is a marketing group in Networks Byte Design, Inc. User stories are usually written on index cards, and each story will describe some aspect of the system. It's the job of the development team to take those stories and make sure they contain the right amount of work. The development team will also assign difficulty points to the stories. In preparation for the Release Planning meeting, the development team will look over the stories and form ideas about how the system should be implemented. They will use a spike to test certain areas that seem to pose risk or are just an unknown. In doing the spike, they will gain insight and confidence in their estimates of how to implement the user stories.

Story

Networks Byte Design, Inc. develops a variety of hardware and software solutions for analyzing a network for bottlenecks. Although their products have done well in direct sales, the company president is pushing the company to develop new markets. One of the areas the company is focusing on is to develop an e-commerce presence to market and sell their product line over the Internet.

Networks Byte Design, Inc. has decided to embark on a new project called "eMarket." The eMarket project is the company's new e-commerce solution for marketing and selling their products online. This is the company's first attempt at a product like this, so there are a large number of risks associated with pulling off the solution. The launch of the eMarket project must be on time as it is slated to be one segment of an overall marketing push, which has been carefully laid out to give Networks Byte Design the maximum visibility possible.

Sandy McPherson has been named the Project Manager for eMarket. She in turn has selected Michael Walden as the Lead Developer. In addition to experience as a lead developer, Michael also has experience as an architect. Sandy has met with Michael prior to his acceptance of the position as lead developer, and emphasized the importance of delivering eMarket on time. She explains that schedule slips will cause a ripple effect on other projects that Networks Byte Design has slated, and will have an adverse effect on the business. They also discuss some of the higher-risk aspects of the project. After some consideration, Michael and Sandy decide that the eMarket project be developed using the Extreme Programming methodology (XP). Using XP will help them to keep the project on schedule and mitigate risk, by allowing them to perform smaller incremental releases. It will also give Sandy regular feedback on the state of the project, so that she can keep the management well informed.

Story

The customer has created the user stories, and the developers have had a chance to go over them. They've asked the customer to break down some stories that were too long into smaller stories, and have combined some very small stories into larger stories. The user stories include items like "User must be able to put selected items into a shopping cart for purchase at the end of the session." As the group reviews the stories from the customer, and sorts through them, they begin to have some questions about the technical aspects of implementing these stories.

The development team begins to form ideas about how the application will be developed. They plan to implement the site in Java with servlets and JSPs. Because Oracle is used heavily within Networks Byte Design, they choose to use Oracle as the database. They also plan to use Enterprise Java Beans (EJBs) to implement the business logic, avoiding direct database access by the servlets. This will also help with distributing the application later. Michael has some technical concerns about the project. In order to help him to decide which approach to take in a few areas, he decides to have some spikes built.

Lisa Berreta and Scott Jenkins are developers on the project. They begin the work of implementing the classes for this particular spike, and will need to compile the code on an iterative basis. They could simply compile from the command line, but the group has decided to set up a build process from the start. The intent is to develop and enhance the build process throughout the project. The team has selected Ant as the tool for build and deployment processes. The first task is to develop an Ant build process that will simply compile a set of Java classes and put them into a JAR file. Another developer on the team, Jeff Franklin, has signed up to make the initial implementation of the Ant buildfiles. Jeff starts by creating an Ant buildfile that will meet the simple requirements for creating the spikes.

Introduction to Ant

Ant provides a framework that enables developers to rapidly configure processes for all phases of the software life cycle. An Ant build process is described in an XML file, called a *buildfile*. The buildfile is used to configure the steps necessary to complete a build process. Users also can control the behaviors of Ant throughout the build process by means of various options, properties, and environment variables. This includes parameters such as the volume of information generated during a build, its form, and its destination. It's even possible to cause certain actions to happen, such as sending an e-mail notification when a build completes.

Ant has a gentle learning curve, which makes it easy to create a useful tool without extensive knowledge of Ant. In this chapter, we examine some of the fundamental concepts of Ant. To help you become familiar with Ant basics, we'll begin by showing you how to write a simple buildfile. At this point, you should have completed the Ant download and followed the installation instructions in Appendix A, "Installing Ant."

This chapter covers basic concepts of Ant. The purpose of Ant is discussed, and the constructs that Ant provides are examined. After reading this chapter, you will understand what a buildfile is and how it's constructed, and some of the fundamental concepts in Ant.

Elements of a Buildfile

Ant is directed to perform a series of operations through a buildfile. A buildfile is analogous to a makefile for make, and it is written in XML. Buildfiles are composed of projects, targets, and tasks. These constructs are used to describe the operations that a buildfile will perform when Ant is invoked. Projects, targets, and tasks have a hierarchical relationship, in which a buildfile describes a single project. Within the single project are one or more targets. Targets are composed of one or more tasks. Figure 2.1 illustrates the relationship of projects, targets, and tasks within a buildfile. In this section, we examine these elements and how they are used to create a buildfile. We also examine how a developer can control the order in which operations are performed.

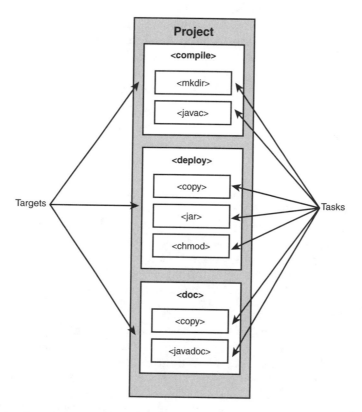

FIGURE 2.1   A project comprises one or more targets, which themselves comprise one or more tasks.

Projects

A *project* is a set of operations to be executed to perform a build process. A project can be any length and provides a way to logically group a set of operations to be completed. A buildfile can have only one project. The operations within a project are called *targets*. Targets can have interdependencies and also can be executed on a conditional basis. Each target is made up of tasks. *Tasks* are the building blocks that come with Ant, which a user can assemble into a useful process.

The first step is to construct the basic framework of the buildfile, named build.xml. The buildfile can be called anything you like, but there's a reason for using the name build.xml. By default, Ant searches for a file by this name if no other buildfile name is passed to it at invocation. If the file is named something else, simply pass the name on the command line with the -buildfile option. The first line of the build.xml file is a standard line that defines the XML version, and it is required by the XML parser: <?xml version="1.0" ?>. Next, the project needs to be added. The <project> tag has three possible attributes that can be defined: name, default, and basedir. As of Ant 1.5.3, only the default attribute is required, but for completeness, we'll define all three in this project. Adding the project results in the following buildfile:

```
<?xml version="1.0" ?>
<project name="myproject" default="test.ant" basedir=".">
</project>
```

This buildfile, which is self-documenting, contains the project myproject with a default target of test.ant. If no default target is defined in the buildfile, Ant will search for a default target called main. Finally, the basedir is defined to be the current working directory from which Ant is invoked. The basedir is the directory that Ant uses to perform all directory calculations. Relative directories within the XML file are specified in relation to the basedir. The basedir can also be an absolute path in the file system. This buildfile won't work yet because the test.ant target has not been defined.

Recall that in XML the tags must be balanced. The start tag, <project>, must be matched with the closing tag, </project>, or the shorthand notation for a closing tag (a slash at the end of the tag name) must be used. So, <project></project> is equivalent to <project/>. Within an XML tag, an attribute is defined with a key/value pair of the form *key=value*, as in: <tag attribute1="value1" attribute2="value2">. In general, all the attributes supported for any given tag might not be required. Because we will need to add additional tags within this project for tasks, the closing tag </project> is used instead of the shorthand notation.

Targets

A *target* is a set of steps to be executed together as a unit. A target is made up of tasks, which we'll cover later. A target tag has five attributes:

- `name`
- `depends`
- `if`
- `unless`
- `description`

The `name` attribute is simply the name assigned to the target to refer to it, and this attribute is required. The `depends` attribute is used to define a dependency by one target on one or more other targets. The `description` attribute enables you to create a descriptive comment. The attributes `if` and `unless` are used to define conditional execution on a target.

If execution of a target fails, the buildfile can be configured to either continue execution of the remaining targets or to stop the build process. With a target, however, if any step fails, the rest of the target is abandoned. So, the execution of a target is not an atomic operation. It's unlike a database transaction in which the entire set of operations either succeeds or can be automatically rolled back to a consistent state. If a target fails in the middle of a set of steps, it leaves everything in that state. As a user, you can design your targets to leave the system in a consistent state. This is important to keep in mind when defining targets that might do things that require transaction-like behavior, such as updating a database or copying a set of files or libraries to a deployment location. You'll want to design your project and targets in such a way that if a failure occurs, the system will not be left in a corrupted state.

So far, the buildfile defines a project called `myproject`, specifies the default target as `test.ant`, and defines the working directory, or `basedir`, as the current directory. Now you'll add a target called `test.ant` because that's what you defined your default target to be. The default target is simply the target to be executed if no particular target is specified at Ant invocation. It's common to name a specific target to execute when running Ant. To provide correct default behavior, you either need to provide a target called `main` or to define a default target in the project line and implement that target. The following code shows the initial, but incomplete, buildfile:

```
<?xml version="1.0" ?>
<project name="myproject" default="test.ant" basedir=".">

    <target name="test.ant" description="A simple build file to test ant.">
    </target>

</project>
```

The file is syntactically correct, but it doesn't do anything useful yet. To accomplish some work, the target needs to be populated with one or more tasks.

Tasks

The constructs that make up an Ant target are called *tasks*. Tasks are predefined operations that Ant can perform. The actual task implementation is a Java class. The behavior of any given task is configured within the buildfile through attributes of the task.

Ant has two categories of tasks:

- Core tasks
- Optional tasks

Core tasks cover fundamental operations that are common to most build and deployment processes. This includes tasks such as <delete>, <copy>, <move>, and <tar>. In general, optional tasks tend to be more specialized or specific to a software product, although this is not entirely the case.

The *optional tasks* include items such as <ftp> and <telnet>. However, most optional tasks have to do with a specific software product, such as <junit>, or a procedure, such as EJB deployment. Another note about optional tasks is that they are included in a separate .jar file (optional.jar) from the core tasks (ant.jar). Beyond these differences, optional tasks and core tasks are used in the same manner; Ant makes no distinction between the two in terms of their use within the buildfile.

Ant is also extensible. If you have a requirement for a task that doesn't exist in Ant, you can write your own task and plug it into your build process. It's also possible to plug in scripts written in scripting languages, such as Perl and Python, using the BSF scripting capability. Techniques of extending Ant are covered throughout this book. Because Ant is extensible, third-party tasks that other developers have written are available to all users. As a last resort, you can make an operating-system–specific call with the <exec> task. The <exec> task might break platform independence, but it's always an option.

For this first example, the buildfile echoes the phrase, "Ant is working correctly" to the terminal from which Ant is running. You'll use the Ant <echo> task, which is used to write to a file or to the standard output. There's often more than one way to do things in Ant, and this is true of the <echo> task. The message for the <echo> task can be defined through the use of the message attribute or can be embedded between the <echo> start and end tags. Using the message attribute will result in the buildfile shown in Listing 2.1.

LISTING 2.1   Simple Buildfile That Prints a Message When Run

```
<?xml version="1.0" ?>
<project name="myproject" default="test.ant" basedir=".">

    <target name="test.ant" description="A simple build file to test ant.">
        <echo message="Ant is working properly" />
    </target>

</project>
```

If the embedded message tag is used instead of the `message` attribute, the buildfile will be as shown in Listing 2.2.

LISTING 2.2   Alternate Form of the Buildfile from Listing 2.1 with the Message Embedded Within the `<echo>` Tags

```
<?xml version="1.0" ?>
<project name="myproject" default="test.ant" basedir=".">

    <target name="test.ant" description="A simple build file to test ant.">
        <echo>Ant is working properly</echo>
    </target>

</project>
```

In this situation, the choice of using an attribute or a nested element is largely a matter of choice. In the case of the <echo> task, the tag approach would be preferable to setting an attribute if the message had quotation marks in it. In a tag, the quotation marks wouldn't have to be protected as they would be when setting the `message` attribute (with message inside quotation marks). If multiple elements need to be added, embedding them inside tags is the required method. If only a single parameter needs to be set, it might be easier and more readable to set an attribute. Either way, these two buildfiles are logically equivalent. We realize that, in terms of XML and the structure of a DOM document that would be created as a result of parsing these files, the two are not structurally the same. But in terms of Ant behavior, the two files are equivalent.

To run this buildfile, all that's required is to change directories to the location of the buildfile and run Ant. Several things should be noted about running Ant with this buildfile. First, the buildfile name may be explicitly passed to Ant on the command line with the `-buildfile` option, as in this example:

```
ant -buildfile mybuildfile.xml
```

If no buildfile name is given on the command line, Ant looks for a file named
`build.xml` in the directory where it's invoked. Another option is to use the `–find`
option. This option causes Ant to look for the buildfile (either the default or the one
you defined) in the current directory. If the file isn't found, the parent directory is
searched next. The process continues up the directory tree until the file is found or
the base directory is reached. The `–find` option can be used with or without the
`–buildfile` option. This might be useful, for example, in an emacs editor command
to invoke a compilation. The `–find` option enables the developer to execute the
`build` command from anywhere inside the source code tree (assuming that the
buildfile is at the top level of the source code directory structure).

If you specified the buildfile to be used and the target to execute, you would run Ant
with the following line:

```
ant -buildfile build.xml test.ant
```

However, because you have the correct defaults in place, you can run the buildfile by
simply typing this:

```
ant
```

The result of running this buildfile is the following output shown in Listing 2.3.

LISTING 2.3   Output from Running the Buildfile of Listing 2.2

```
% ant
Build file: build.xml

test.ant:
    [echo] Ant is working properly

BUILD SUCCESSFUL
Total time: 1 second
```

Ant Command-Line Options

Ant has several command-line options. Run this command:

```
ant -help
```

to see a list of possible command-line arguments, as shown in Listing 2.4.

LISTING 2.4   Output Resulting from Running the ant -help Command

```
% ant -help
ant [options] [target [target2 [target3] ...]]
Options:
  -help                    print this message
  -projecthelp             print project help information
  -version                 print the version information and exit
  -diagnostics             print information that might be helpful to
                           diagnose or report problems.
  -quiet, -q               be extra quiet
  -verbose, -v             be extra verbose
  -debug                   print debugging information
  -emacs                   produce logging information without adornments
  -logfile <file>          use given file for log
    -l      <file>                    ''
  -logger <classname>      the class which is to perform logging
  -listener <classname>    add an instance of class as a project listener
  -buildfile <file>        use given buildfile
    -file    <file>                   ''
    -f       <file>                   ''
  -D<property>=<value>     use value for given property
  -propertyfile <name>     load all properties from file with -D
                           properties taking precedence
  -inputhandler <class>    the class which will handle input requests
  -find <file>             search for buildfile towards the root of the
                           filesystem and use it
```

The projecthelp option will print information about your build file in a nice summary, which includes the main targets and subtargets. Listing 2.5 shows an example from running ant -projecthelp on the ant project.

LISTING 2.5   Output Resulting from Running the ant -projecthelp Command on the Build File Used to Build ant

```
% ant -projecthelp
Buildfile: build.xml
Main targets:

 test.ant  A simple build file to test ant.

Default target: test.ant
```

As you might expect, the -version option simply prints the version of Ant in use. The -quiet option will suppress debugging information, whereas the -verbose option results in more voluminous output.

The -logfile option causes Ant's output to be written to a logfile, rather than to the standard output of the terminal from which Ant is run. This is especially useful if Ant is being invoked from a cron job on a Unix system as part of a nightly build. The -logfile option can also be used in conjunction with the -listener and -logger options. The -logger and -listener options give some additional capabilities to monitor and report build results.

The -buildfile option, as previously mentioned, permits you to specify a build file other than the default build.xml. The -find option, which was also previously mentioned, causes Ant to search up its directory tree for the build file. The -D option allows properties to be specified from the command line, as discussed in the section on properties.

Using an Ant Initialization File

Invoking Ant runs a wrapper script for a specific operating system, which starts a Java Virtual Machine (JVM) that runs the Ant Java code. Ant's behavior can be altered by setting environment variables that are passed from the wrapper script to the JVM. Environment variables can also be set in platform-dependent files, which are called by the Ant wrapper scripts. When running Ant on a Unix-based platform, such as Linux, Solaris, Mac OS X, and Cygwin, the Unix wrapper script for Ant will look for the file ~/.antrc before invoking Ant in the JVM. The wrapper script for Windows platforms looks for %HOME%/antrc_pre.bat before invoking Ant in the JVM, and %HOME%/antrc_post.bat after running Ant.

Let's look at the environment variables that can be set in a configuration file to alter the behavior of Ant. The environment variable JAVACMD can be set to the full path name of a Java Virtual Machine of your choice. If this isn't specified, the default value is JAVA_HOME/bin/java(.exe), which is probably fine for most users. The purpose of the environment variable ANT_OPTS is really to contain options to pass to the JVM. So any argument that is valid for the JVM that you are using can be set in the ANT_OPTS environment variable. You can run the java -help command to determine the valid arguments for this option. Multiple arguments can be passed to the JVM by enclosing them in single quotes. For example, if you wanted to print the version of the JVM you're using, and set the maximum heap size to 500 Mbytes, you could set the following in your Ant initialization file, as shown here:

```
ANT_OPTS='-showversion -mx500m'
```

Running ant will result in the following output:

```
% ant
java version "1.4.1"
Java(TM) 2 Runtime Environment, Standard Edition (build 1.4.1-24)
Java HotSpot(TM) Client VM (build 1.4.1_01-12, mixed mode)

Buildfile: build.xml

test.ant:
    [echo] Ant is working properly

BUILD SUCCESSFUL
Total time: 2 seconds
```

Finally, the environment variable ANT_ARGS can be used to set any of the command-line arguments discussed in the last section. If the same command-line arguments are being used each time you run ant, you can set this variable in the init file to avoid having to type them in each time. You could also write your own script or batch file to run Ant with the necessary command-line options. So for example, you could set ANT_ARGS=-find, and this would cause Ant to perform the directory search for your build file that was mentioned in the previous section.

Because Ant is a Java program, you could also elect to run the Ant classes directly, and avoid the wrapper scripts directly. This implies several configuration requirements. The Ant classes (in ant.jar) must be in your CLASSPATH. Also, the JAR file(s) for your XML parser must be included in the CLASSPATH. Finally, any JAR or ZIP files required for the Java Development Kit (JDK) must also be in your CLASSPATH.

Running the Ant classes directly could be very useful if you wanted to invoke Ant from another Java program. By using the Java classloader and invoking the class directly within Java, you avoid the need to shell out to run the wrapper scripts, which would be an expensive operation. This also has the advantage of maintaining platform independence in your application.

A Basic Project-Management Buildfile

Let's now turn our attention to a useful example. The eMarket project team first needs to create a buildfile to compile a set of Java source code. They would proceed with the following approach. First, the basic syntax of a buildfile is put in place, which is the XML definition line followed by the project-definition tag. Next, create a target named compile to perform the action of compiling a set of Java source code files. As part of the compile target definition, a description will also be provided. Remember that descriptions will be printed when Ant is run with the -projecthelp option. The opening and closing tags of `<target></target>` will also be added because additional lines of XML are going to be added within the target to specify the tasks to perform. The project definition needs to be modified to define a default target, because there is no target called `main` (the standard default target). The build-file so far will look like this:

```xml
<?xml version="1.0" ?>
<project name="eMarket" default="compile" basedir=".">

    <!-- compile target -->
    <target name="compile" description="Compile all of the source code.">
    </target>

</project>
```

Within the `<compile>` target, a task needs to be added to actually compile the Java source code. For this purpose, the core Ant task `<javac>` is needed. The `<javac>` task compiles Java source code and deposits the class files in the specified directory structure. The source and destination directories are set with the `srcdir` and `destdir` attributes. The `srcdir` attribute defines the directory in which the beginning of the source code directory tree is found. The eMarket's Java source code files are found in the directory `/usr/projects/eMarket/src`. The Java compiler should look for Java source code beginning at the src directory and below. The attribute `srcdir` should then be defined as `srcdir="/usr/projects/eMarket/src"`. In this case, there are no subdirectories below `src`. However, there could be a directory structure below the `src` director that corresponds to a package structure such as `com/networksByteDesign/etc`, and the `<javac>` task would pick them up and compile everything in and below the `src` directory.

The `<javac>` attribute `destdir` is the destination directory where the compiled Java class files should be deposited. Using this attribute will also result in the classes being compiled into a directory tree that matches Java package structure, as if you had compiled with the -d option of the Java compiler. Using the `destdir` attribute also has another advantage. If the source code directory structure follows the Java package structure, Ant optimizes the compilation. It scans the Java source files and the destination class files, and compiles only those source files that don't have a corresponding class file or that have a class file whose timestamp is older than the source file.

As a first pass for a spike, the eMarket team just compiles the class files into the same directory as the source code. With these changes in place, the buildfile is now complete enough to actually perform useful work. The buildfile for the eMarket project team's spike is shown in Listing 2.6.

LISTING 2.6   Buildfile to Compile a Set of Java Source Files in a Specified Directory

```xml
<?xml version="1.0" ?>
<project name="eMarket" default="compile" basedir=".">

    <!-- compile target -->
    <target name="compile" description="Compile all of the source code.">
        <javac srcdir="/usr/projects/eMarket/src" />
    </target>

</project>
```

When the buildfile of Listing 2.6 is run, the resulting output is shown in Listing 2.7.

LISTING 2.7   Output Resulting from the Execution of the Buildfile of Listing 2.6

```
% ant
Buildfile: build.xml

compile:
    [javac] Compiling 7 source files

BUILD SUCCESSFUL
Total time: 2 seconds
```

This buildfile is simple and yet still performs a useful function. The purpose of using Ant is to build a tool that will save time and labor, and that also will make a process repeatable. The result is a reliable, repeatable process that can be enhanced to perform additional functions.

Using Properties

The buildfiles written so far have had project specifics such as pathnames hard-coded into the attributes of the tasks. It is preferable to collect these hard-coded values into parameters in one place. Ant permits this through the use of *properties*, which are name/value pairs.

Properties can be defined in several different ways. They can be specified explicitly within the buildfile. They can be read from a properties file, passed in through the command line, or even picked up through environment variables. Properties set by Ant also are available for use within the buildfile. All the operating system properties are available, such as the operating system name (os.name), the user's home directory (user.home), and even the version of the Java runtime environment (java.version).

Besides operating system parameters, Ant has some built-in properties of its own that are available, such as the version of Ant being used (`ant.version`) or the absolute path of the `build.xml` file (`ant.file`). By defining and using properties, it's possible to collect environment-specific characteristics into a single location, which makes maintenance easier. This is basically the equivalent of defining constants in a program, rather than scattering hard-coded constants or string literals throughout the source code. Also, properties are immutable. Unlike variables in code, after a property's value is set, it cannot be changed.

So, to begin with properties, let's modify the buildfile file to explicitly define a property for the directory names. Currently, the path is hard-coded in only one place, but as the file is changed during the course of development, it will most likely get referenced in multiple places. It's simply a good practice to define properties from the start. It's easier to avoid bugs caused by mismatches in hard-coded values. Properties can be defined outside targets, which causes them to be evaluated before any targets are executed. We prefer to define properties in a block at the top of the buildfile, just before the first target. After a property is defined, it's referenced with the notation ${*propertyName*}. In Listing 2.8, the property `dirs.source` is created to specify the absolute pathnames of that directory's. The task that uses this pathname has also been modified to pick up the value from the property.

LISTING 2.8   Buildfile with the Path for the Java Source Code Moved to a Property

```xml
<?xml version="1.0" ?>
<project name="eMarket" default="compile" basedir=".">

    <property name="dirs.source" value="/usr/projects/eMarket/src" />

    <!-- compile target -->
    <target name="compile" description="Compile all of the source code.">
        <javac srcdir="${dirs.source}" />
    </target>

</project>
```

Story

While writing one of the spikes, Scott realizes that he made some changes that he now regrets. He wishes he could go back to a previous version of some files. Because the code wasn't in version control, he's unable to do that. He has to reimplement some of the code he had previously written. Although it's not a huge setback, it does cost him time and needless effort. The development team discusses this and decides that they would like to start using version control for spikes as well as deliverable code. Even though a spike is intended to be a throwaway, it's advisable to keep the source code in version control while it's being developed. The only problem is that the development server with the source code repository isn't ready yet, and won't be ready for a while, so the group needs a stopgap measure. After some discussion, they decide to implement a simple backup solution in Ant using tar files. A story is written to implement a backup system using compressed tar files. John and Lisa sign up for that task and begin to implement it.

With this in place, the developers will be able to retrieve a previous version if needed. Through the use of this temporary backup method, the team is protected from accidental overwrites or deletions of files. Also, the spike will still be retrievable later in the project if anyone wants to review what was done. Finally, all of the files can be added to CVS when the server and CVS repository are finally ready.

Ant contains tasks for running the archiving utilities tar, zip, and gzip. The eMarket team has decided to create a simple backup scheme using these tasks, to create a time-stamped backup of the source code. Although CVS isn't all that difficult to set up, it's possible that a team may be using a different product that has licensing restrictions, and the team must wait for the development server to be set up. Another reason for using this target might be due to restrictions for checking in code. For example, on most of our projects, we establish team rules that state that no code can be checked into version control on the main branch until it compiles and has been successfully unit tested. Although the code being modified may not meet those standards, a backup may be helpful before making certain modifications. This section will show how a stopgap backup system could be created using some of the tasks available in Ant.

Let's begin by developing a simple target to perform a backup of our source code directory. The backupTar target will create a date/time-stamped tar file containing the contents of the source code directory. This can be used as a snapshot of the current source code regardless of whether the code can be checked into version control. First, a target has to be defined. Also, because this is a target intended to be called directly when running Ant, it should be given a description as shown here:

```
<target name="backupTar"
        description="Backs up all source into a tar file.">
```

Next, the backup directory should be created using the core <mkdir> task. In order to create a robust target, we don't assume that the required directory already exists, but guarantee it with the use of this task. The <mkdir> task will create the directory if it does not exist, or it will do nothing if the directory already exists. Using <mkdir> ensures that the backup target will perform correctly regardless of whether the directory initially exists or not. With the addition of the <mkdir> step, we now have the following:

```
<!-- backupTar target -->
<target name="backupTar"
        description="Backs up all source into a tar file.">

    <mkdir dir="${dirs.backup}" />
</target>
```

With the <mkdir> task, the directory to be created is defined with the dir attribute. Rather than hard-code the backup directory name, we set a property at the start of the buildfile. Remember that properties are immutable, so they can only be set once. Also, properties can use other properties in their definition, provided that the included property has already been defined. Using an undefined property won't cause Ant to fail, but will give unexpected results. The property definition for dirs.backup looks like this:

```
<property name="dirs.backup" value="${user.home}/backup"          />
```

The use of properties is the same concept as using defined constants in code, rather than hard-coding values throughout a program. In the backupTar target, we follow the same practice of using properties as in the creation of the backup directory. The destfile is the one required parameter and points to the tar file being created. There are a variety of ways to indicate the files that should be included in the tar file. We are going to simply set the source directory as the basedir to back up the entire directory. From there, we can specifically include or exclude certain files, with the includes or excludes attributes. For example, suppose this target were going to be used to make intermediate backups of code before it was ready to be committed to CVS. If we're using it in a directory that was checked out from CVS, and has the CVS subdirectory, we might want to specifically exclude this directory from the backup. This could be done by excluding all CVS directories with the pattern "**/CVS". The pattern "**" matches any directory hierarchy of directories, or file names. So the expression "**/CVS" will exclude any directory named "CVS" regardless of its absolute path. This means that /usr/projects/eMarket/CVS would be excluded, as would /usr/projects/eMarket/src/CVS, if these directories existed.

The gzip compression utility can then be used to compress the tar file. The gzip compression utility can be invoked through the <gzip> task, or by using the compression attribute of the <tar> task, specifying "gzip" as the compression method. Doing this will create a gzipped, tar file. The target definition now looks like this:

```
<!-- backupTar target -->
<target name="backupTar"
        description="Backs up all source into a tar file.">

    <mkdir dir="${dirs.backup}" />

    <tar tarfile="${dirs.backup}/${backupFile}"
         basedir="${dirs.source}" compression="gzip" />

</target>
```

The `backupFile` property value still needs to be defined. This could be hard-coded to a filename, but the downside of this is that our backup file will be overwritten each time the target is executed. That means there would be no way to retrieve anything earlier than the last backup. A preferable solution would be to create a file with a timestamp in the name, to guarantee uniqueness, and not overwrite earlier versions of the backup. This is accomplished by using the `<tstamp>` task, which sets the `TSTAMP` and `DSTAMP` built-in properties of Ant. By calling the `<tstamp>` task, the `TSTAMP` is set to the current time, in the format of "hhmm", and `DSTAMP` is set to the current date, in the format "yyyyMMdd". By combining the `TSTAMP` and `DSTAMP` properties into another property, a unique filename based on a timestamp value can be constructed, as shown here:

```
<property name="backupFile"
          value="${ant.project.name}_${DSTAMP}${TSTAMP}.tar.gz" />
```

Adding this to our target, it now looks as shown here:

```
    <!-- backupTar target -->
    <target name="backupTar"
            description="Backs up all source into a tar file.">

        <mkdir dir="${dirs.backup}" />

        <tstamp />
        <property name="backupFile"
                  value="${ant.project.name}_${DSTAMP}${TSTAMP}.tar.gz" />

        <tar tarfile="${dirs.backup}/${backupFile}"
             basedir="${dirs.source}" compression="gzip" />

    </target>
```

The final step is to use the `<echo>` task to print a message indicating that the target has completed successfully. This message will display on the screen or in a log file depending on how the Ant rule is executed. The completed `backupTar` target is added to the buildfile for the eMarket project, and the result is shown in Listing 2.9.

LISTING 2.9 The eMarket Project Buildfile with the `backupTar` Target Added

```
<?xml version="1.0" ?>
<project name="eMarket" default="compile" basedir=".">

    <property name="dirs.source" value="/usr/projects/eMarket/src" />
    <property name="dirs.backup" value="${user.home}/backup"          />
```

LISTING 2.9   Continued

```xml
<!-- compile target -->
<target name="compile" description="Compile all of the source code.">
    <javac srcdir="${dirs.source}" />
</target>

<!-- backupTar target -->
<target name="backupTar"
        description="Backs up all source into a tar file.">

    <mkdir dir="${dirs.backup}" />

    <tstamp />
    <property name="backupFile"
            value="${ant.project.name}_${DSTAMP}${TSTAMP}.tar.gz" />

    <tar tarfile="${dirs.backup}/${backupFile}"
        basedir="${dirs.source}" compression="gzip" />

    <echo message="Backup file ${backupFile} has been created." />

</target>

</project>
```

Story

Scott and Lisa did a nice job of implementing the backupTar target to create a compressed tarball of a code snapshot, with a timestamp in the name. The only problem with this target is that it leaves the backup on each developer's local machine. The major problems are that the developers' desktop machines are not backed up, and that this approach leaves backup files scattered across the development team's desktop machines. This makes it difficult for developers to be aware of what backups are available, or to share backups if they need to. The development server with revision control is still not available, which is why the team is using the backupTar target. However, there is a server used primarily for storing and sharing documents that is backed up on a nightly basis. So, another task will be to copy the compressed tar files to the document storage server as part of the buildfile. Scott and Lisa work on this task and implement a solution using Ant's <ftp> task.

Next, let's examine how to add a task to FTP the backup file to another server. In order to do this, an additional target will be created that will make use of Ant target dependencies. The next section explains why.

Target Dependencies

Currently, each target in the buildfile is standalone in that it doesn't require another target to execute first. As other targets are added, the order in which targets are executed may become an issue. In our buildfile, a target will be added that will FTP the gzipped tarball to another server that gets backed up. We could create a target that replicates the backupTar target, and then does the FTP. But this unnecessarily increases the size of the buildfile, and more importantly, it creates maintenance problems. If for some reason we wanted to create zip files instead of gzipped tarballs, we would have to change this in more than one place. A better solution is to create a new target that does only the FTP step, and make it dependent on the backupTar target. This way, if the ftp target is executed, it will first execute the backupTar target, and create the backup archive.

Any target can be defined as having a dependency on one or more other targets. By defining dependencies on targets, it's possible to ensure that all the targets in a project get executed in an acceptable order. When Ant encounters a list of dependencies in a target, it attempts to execute them from left to right, if that's possible. However, if those targets have additional dependencies, that might not be possible. Look at the example shown in Listing 2.10.

LISTING 2.10   Buildfile to Demonstrate Target Dependencies

```xml
<?xml version="1.0" ?>
<project name="targetDependencies" default="tgt_1" basedir=".">

<target name="tgt_1" description="target 1">
    <!-- tasks here -->
</target>

<target name="tgt_2" depends="tgt_1" description="target 2">
    <!-- tasks here -->
</target>

<target name="tgt_3" description="target 3">
    <!-- tasks here -->
</target>

<target name="tgt_4" depends="tgt_3, tgt_2, tgt_1">
    <!-- tasks here -->
</target>

</project>
```

In this example, the final target is `tgt_4`. By default, Ant attempts to execute the target dependencies in the order listed in the target. If we were to execute a target with no dependencies, such as `tgt_1`, it simply executes. If we execute a target with a single dependency, `tgt_2`, Ant will determine that `tgt_1` needs to execute first. So `tgt_1` will execute followed by `tgt_2`. In the case where there are multiple dependencies, as in `tgt_4`, Ant attempts to execute the targets from left to right in the dependency list. Ant starts with `tgt_3`. Because `tgt_3` has no other dependencies, it executes. Then Ant moves to `tgt_2`, but it has a dependency on `tgt_1`. So Ant will execute `tgt_1`, followed by `tgt_2`. Then Ant moves to the last target in the list, `tgt_1`. However, `tgt_1` already executed, so Ant won't run it again. The output from running `tgt_4` looks like this:

```
% ant tgt_4
Buildfile: build.xml


tgt_3:


tgt_1:


tgt_2:


tgt_4:


BUILD SUCCESSFUL
Total time: 1 second
```

It's best to avoid introducing artificial dependencies. For example, if `tgt_2` really doesn't depend on `tgt_1`, leave off the dependency. Sometimes it's tempting to daisy-chain a series of targets like `compile`, `unittest`, and `javadoc`, where `unittest` depends on `compile`, and `javadoc` depends on `unittest`. In fact, maybe `javadoc` only needs to depend on `compile`. Introducing unneeded dependencies only complicates matters unnecessarily. If a user wants to run `javadoc`, they shouldn't be forced to run unit tests unnecessarily. So use the minimum number of dependencies possible, and let Ant sort it out.

The `<ftp>` task uses a nested element called `<fileset>` to define the file or set of files to be transferred. Before continuing with the FTP-based `backupAdvanced` target, let's discuss filesets and directory-based tasks.

Directory-Based Tasks

The `<javac>`, `<tar>`, and `<ftp>` tasks are examples of what are called directory-based tasks. A *directory-based task* is defined as any task that operates on a set of files or directories in a directory-tree structure. In the case of Java source code, the directory structure matches the package structure that the `<javac>` task will navigate to perform its job. Other examples of directory-based tasks include `<copy>`, `<delete>`, `<chmod>` (performs a `chmod` on UNIX platforms), and `<tar>`. In each case, the task enables a user to perform some operation on a set of files or directories. When performing an operation such as `<tar>` or `<ftp>` on a set of files or directories, you might want to include certain items while excluding others.

Some directory-based tasks can use either filesets or attributes within the task tag to describe the set that they operate on. Consider the core task `<delete>`, for example. It has attributes for defining the file and directory of interest. The attribute can be used when you want to delete a certain file or all the files down a directory tree. This is fine when the name and path are known in advance. Suppose that a README file gets generated from an XML file as part of the build, and you want to remove it each time you perform a build. That file exists in the directory `/usr/build/docs`. Because the filename and location are static, and there is only one of them, you could use the following rule in your `build.xml` file to remove the file:

```
<delete file="/usr/projects/eMarket/src/README"/>
```

The `file` attribute can be a filename, a filename with a relative path, or a full-path filename, as shown in the preceding example. The `dir` attribute can be used if you want to delete all the files and directories down a directory tree. If, instead of deleting only the README file, you wanted to delete all the files and directories below `/usr/projects/eMarket`, including the `docs` directory itself, you could specify the following rule:

```
<delete dir="/usr/projects/eMarket"/>
```

Ant would proceed to delete everything below `/usr/projects/eMarket`, including the `eMarket` directory. Sometimes you want to include certain files or directories and exclude others. Also, you might want to include or exclude certain types of files (for example, include all the files ending with the `.class` extension). Ant provides a number of ways to accomplish this through the use of constructs such as patterns, filesets, dirsets, file lists, and so on. Let's examine some of these features of Ant and how to use them in the build process.

Patterns, Filesets, and Dirsets

Ant provides constructs for defining groups of files and directories in a standard way across different Ant tasks. These constructs consist of filesets, dirsets, and patterns. Filesets and dirsets enable a user to include or exclude specific files and directories. Patterns are used within filesets and dirsets to define rules for selecting or ignoring certain types of files and directories. By using these constructs, it becomes possible to deal with groups of files in a task without having to explicitly list the names of the files. Because the files aren't explicitly named, that also means that when new files are added to a directory, it's not necessary to modify the buildfile to accommodate the additional files. Filesets and dirsets use patterns to describe the set of entities a task is to operate on.

Patterns

An Ant *pattern* is used to describe the set of files or directories for use in a directory-based task. Patterns behave essentially like wildcards in DOS and UNIX. If you wanted to designate all the Java class files in a directory, you would use the pattern `*.class`, which is the same way you would designate those files on a UNIX- or Windows-based platform. Similarly, to refer to all Java source files in a directory, you would use the pattern `*.java`. However, if you want to refer to all the class files down a directory tree that end with the `.class` extension, regardless of the directory they are located in, a simple `*.class` is not sufficient. Ant patterns provide a special double asterisk (**) wildcard, which matches directory structure. It matches any directory name and any number of directory levels. Suppose the following directory structure existed beginning at the `usr/projects/eMarket/src` directory:

```
com/networksByteDesign/biz

com/networksByteDesign/util/base

com/networksByteDesign/util/adv

com/networksByteDesign/gui
```

Class files would exist in each of the leaf directories (`biz`, `base`, `adv`, and `gui`), and you want to refer to the class files in each of these directories. In this situation, simply apply the double asterisk pattern to match the directories down the directory tree. The pattern `**/*.class` matches the class files in any of these directories, not just the leaf directories. That means that if there are class files in the directory `networksByteDesign`, it matches those also. If you want to match only the class files below the `util` directory in the `base` and `adv` directories, the pattern could be modified to the following: `**/util/**/*.class`. This now matches any directories that have "util" in the pathname, which includes `util/base` and `util/adv` but excludes `biz` and `gui`.

Filesets

A *fileset* is a construct for defining a group of files down a directory tree. A fileset permits the inclusion of some files and exclusion of others, through the use of nested `<includes>` and `<excludes>` elements. These elements contain lists of patterns to be included or excluded. Some directory-based tasks have attributes that can be used to describe target files (and directories), but filesets provide a consistent way to define sets of files across tasks. In the Ant documentation, sometimes these types of attributes are listed as deprecated, but other times they're not. For example, as of Ant 1.5.3, the `<delete>` task has deprecated attributes for `includes` and `excludes`, which use patterns. However, the `<tar>` task also has attributes for `includes` and `excludes`, which are not yet deprecated. Filesets are a clean, consistent way to define groups of files. Because that's the direction Ant appears to be heading, filesets are recommended over attributes in directory-based tasks.

For the `<ftp>` task, the eMarket team wants to include a certain directory, and will simply FTP everything in that directory. This requires the following fileset definition:

```
<fileset dir="${dirs.backup}" />
```

where the `${dirs.backup}` property is set earlier in the buildfile. In this case, there are no special includes or excludes requirements, so this fileset construction will meet the needed requirements.

Adding the backupAdvanced Target

Let's now create the target to FTP the backup file to another server. In order to use the FTP task, you will need to build Ant using the optional FTP task, or include the optional JAR file in your classpath. Also, the `netcomponents.jar` file is required for FTP (and for telnet), and can be downloaded from `www.savarese.org/oro/downloads`. The Ant documentation provides a table of dependencies for optional tasks, and the additional JAR files that are required to run them. This table can be found at `http://ant.apache.org/manual/install.html#librarydependencies`.

By making the `backupAdvanced` target dependent on the `backupTar` target, we ensure that the backup file has been created prior to the FTP process to move the file to the server. If you're familiar with the FTP program, the `<ftp>` task follows naturally from it. FTP (file transfer protocol) is a program commonly used to transfer files from one computer to another. In order to connect to the target machine, FTP requires the user to provide a login and password. After you're connected, you can send or receive files from the target computer. The default values for the `ftp` task are to send files in binary mode, which is required for the compressed backup file.

There are several attributes of the `<ftp>` task that will need to be set. The `server` attribute defines the name or IP address of the server that FTP will connect to. The `remotedir` attribute is the name of the directory to `cd` to after connecting. The `userid` and `password` are just as the names say, the userid and password to give when connecting. Finally, we need to define the file, or set of files to be transferred. This is done by plugging in the `<fileset>` definition created earlier in the discussion of filesets. When the target is added to the buildfile, it is as shown in Listing 2.11. This target invokes the `backupTar` target and FTPs it to a backup server.

LISTING 2.11   The eMarket Buildfile with the backupAdvanced Target Added

```xml
<?xml version="1.0" ?>
<project name="eMarket" default="compile" basedir=".">

    <property name="dirs.source" value="/usr/projects/eMarket/src" />
    <property name="dirs.backup" value="${user.home}/backup"        />

    <!-- compile target -->
    <target name="compile" description="Compile all of the source code.">
        <javac srcdir="${dirs.source}" />
    </target>

    <!-- backupTar target -->
    <target name="backupTar"
            description="Backs up all source into a tar file.">

        <mkdir dir="${dirs.backup}" />

        <tstamp />
        <property name="backupFile"
                value="${ant.project.name}_${DSTAMP}${TSTAMP}.tar.gz" />

        <tar tarfile="${dirs.backup}/${backupFile}"
            basedir="${dirs.source}" compression="gzip" />

        <echo message="Backup file ${backupFile} has been created." />

    </target>

    <!-- backupAdvanced target -->
    <target name="backupAdvanced"
            depends="backupTar"
            description="Moves backup files to remote server">

      <ftp server="127.0.0.1" remotedir="ftpFiles"
          userid="sjenkins"    password="s1Nd!32W">
        <fileset dir="${dirs.backup}" />
      </ftp>
```

LISTING 2.11   Continued

```
        <delete dir="${dirs.backup}" />

    </target>


</project>
```

Story

After completing the backupAdvanced target, Scott realizes that there is a security concern with the target. Hard-coding his login ID and password will violate the company's security policy by giving out his login ID and password, and allowing other developers to use it. Scott and Lisa decide they need to change the target to get rid of the hard-coded userid and password. In addition to modifying the buildfile, Scott will also need to change his password because Lisa now knows it.

Entering a User ID/Password at Runtime

Entering the user ID and password at runtime is actually a simple change to implement. Ant provides the <input> task, which provides a means for prompting the user for additional information at runtime. Here is an example of the use of the input task to prompt the user to enter their user id, and store their response in the property ftpUserID:

```
        <input message="Please enter ftp user id:"
               addproperty="ftpUserID" />
```

By adding input tasks to the target, the user can be prompted to enter their user ID and password. Those entered values can then be stored in properties, and used in other tasks later in the buildfile. There's one more consideration. Although the ftp task will provide a fairly understandable error message if the user does not provide a login or password, our target could do some basic error checking that would make it a little more usable. What should Ant do if the user doesn't supply either or both of these values? In order to make the buildfile exit gracefully, the <condition> element can be used to check for the presence of an attribute. Here's an example of the use of this element:

```
        <condition property="noFTPUserID">
            <equals arg1="" arg2="${ftpUserID}" />
        </condition>
```

What this does is check if the property ${ftpUserID} (arg2) is empty (arg1). If the <equals> condition is true, <condition> sets the property noFTPUserID. Remember that properties are immutable, and can only be set once. After this check is completed, a <fail> construct is encountered that looks like this:

```
<fail if="noFTPUserID">You did not enter your ftp user id.</fail>
```

If the property noFTPUserID was set by the <condition> check, the build will print the message You did not enter your ftp user id., and then exit gracefully. If this property is not set, the buildfile drops through and continues execution. This also illustrates how to achieve conditional programmatic logic in a buildfile. But again, remember that properties are immutable and can be set only once, so you can't reset them like variables in a program. Listing 2.12 shows the modified buildfile that has the hard-coded personal information removed, and now uses the <input> task for this information It also has the conditional logic to test that the userid and password were set.

LISTING 2.12 Buildfile Using the <input> Task to Prompt for User ID and Password, and <condition> to Fail the Build If User Doesn't Provide This Information

```xml
<?xml version="1.0" ?>
<project name="eMarket" default="compile" basedir=".">

    <property name="dirs.source" value="/usr/projects/eMarket/src" />
    <property name="dirs.backup" value="${user.home}/backup"        />

    <!-- compile target -->
    <target name="compile" description="Compile all of the source code.">
        <javac srcdir="${dirs.source}" />
    </target>

    <!-- backupTar target -->
    <target name="backupTar"
            description="Backs up all source into a tar file.">

        <mkdir dir="${dirs.backup}" />

        <tstamp />
        <property name="backupFile"
                    value="${ant.project.name}_${DSTAMP}${TSTAMP}.tar.gz" />

        <tar tarfile="${dirs.backup}/${backupFile}"
            basedir="${dirs.source}" compression="gzip" />

        <echo message="Backup file ${backupFile} has been created." />
```

LISTING 2.12   Continued

```
    </target>

    <!-- backupAdvanced target -->
    <target name="backupAdvanced"
            depends="backupTar"
            description="Moves backup files to remote server">

        <input message="Please enter ftp user id:"
               addproperty="ftpUserID" />

        <condition property="noFTPUserID">
            <equals arg1="" arg2="${ftpUserID}" />
        </condition>

        <fail if="noFTPUserID">You did not enter your ftp user id.</fail>

        <input message="Please enter ftp password:"
               addproperty="ftpPassword" />

        <condition property="noFTPPassword">
            <equals arg1="" arg2="${ftpPassword}" />
        </condition>

        <fail if="noFTPPassword">You did not enter your ftp password.</fail>

        <ftp server="127.0.0.1" remotedir="ftpFiles"
             userid="${ftpUserID}" password="${ftpPassword}">
            <fileset dir="${dirs.backup}" />
        </ftp>

        <delete dir="${dirs.backup}" />

    </target>

</project>
```

Story

In order to cover the group, Scott and Lisa make an additional change to set up a cron job to do nightly backups of the development teams working directories. After making modifications to the backupInteractive target, Lisa realizes that they could refactor the targets so that the same target could be used by the development team, or the cron job.

As a final step, let's say we decide to use this target for multiple purposes. Some projects have a fictitious user account to perform team-related tasks. For example, we have a user called "cronus" on a project that performs tasks such as team builds, cron jobs, and so on. Suppose the eMarket team wants a target that a user could utilize interactively, but could also be used as a background task by the general purpose account "cronus."

To achieve this capability, we need to split the backupAdvanced target into two targets. The first is shown in Listing 2.13.

LISTING 2.13   The backupAdvancedInternal Target Has Been Designed to Be Used
Interactively or in a Cron Job

```
<!-- backupAdvancedInternal target -->
<target name="backupAdvancedInternal"
        if="ftpLogin">

    <ftp server="127.0.0.1" remotedir="ftpFiles"
        userid="${ftpUserID}" password="${ftpPassword}">
        <fileset dir="${dirs.backup}" />
    </ftp>

    <delete dir="${dirs.backup}" />
</target>
```

The second part for use in a background task is shown in Listing 2.14.

LISTING 2.14   backupAdvancedBackground Target

```
<!-- backupAdvancedBackground target -->
<target name="backupAdvancedBackground"
        depends="backupTar"
        description="Moves backups to server with hardcoded login/pwd">

    <property name="ftpLogin"    value="" />
    <property name="ftpUserID"   value="cronus" />
    <property name="ftpPassword" value="f#8jW9t3s!" />

    <antcall target="backupAdvancedInternal" />
</target>
```

Because this buildfile uses the <antcall> task, let's digress for a moment to look at the purpose of <antcall>. This task is used to invoke other targets within a buildfile. When calling another target, all of that target's dependencies will be evaluated and executed. With <antcall>, it's possible to have properties set to a different value. Remember that properties are immutable, and can't be reset throughout a buildfile. The exception, however, is with <antcall>. If the inheritAll attribute is set to false, properties will not be passed to the target invocation, and can be reset within that target. Putting Listings 2.13 and 2.14 together with the other needed parts of the buildfile yields the buildfile in Listing 2.15.

LISTING 2.15   Buildfile Containing a Backup Target That Can Be Used Either
               Interactively or in a Background Task

```xml
<?xml version="1.0" ?>
<project name="eMarket" default="compile" basedir=".">

    <property name="dirs.source" value="/usr/projects/eMarket/src" />
    <property name="dirs.backup" value="${user.home}/backup"        />

    <!-- compile target -->
    <target name="compile" description="Compile all of the source code.">
        <javac srcdir="${dirs.source}" />
    </target>

    <!-- backupTar target -->
    <target name="backupTar"
            description="Backs up all source into a tar file.">

        <mkdir dir="${dirs.backup}" />

        <tstamp />
        <property name="backupFile"
                  value="${ant.project.name}_${DSTAMP}${TSTAMP}.tar.gz" />

        <tar tarfile="${dirs.backup}/${backupFile}"
            basedir="${dirs.source}" compression="gzip" />

        <echo message="Backup file ${backupFile} has been created." />

    </target>

    <!-- backupAdvancedInteractive target -->
    <target name="backupAdvancedInteractive"
            depends="backupTar"
            description="Moves backups to server with supplied login/pwd">
```

LISTING 2.15   Continued

```
    <input message="Please enter ftp user id:"
           addproperty="ftpUserID" />

    <condition property="noFTPUserID">
        <equals arg1="" arg2="${ftpUserID}" />
    </condition>

    <fail if="noFTPUserID">You did not enter your ftp user id.</fail>

    <input message="Please enter ftp password:"
           addproperty="ftpPassword" />

    <condition property="noFTPPassword">
        <equals arg1="" arg2="${ftpPassword}" />
    </condition>

    <fail if="noFTPPassword">You did not enter your ftp password.</fail>

    <property name="ftpLogin" value="" />

    <antcall target="backupAdvancedInternal" />
</target>

<!-- backupAdvancedBackground target -->
<target name="backupAdvancedBackground"
        depends="backupTar"
        description="Moves backups to server with hardcoded login/pwd">

    <property name="ftpLogin"    value="" />
    <property name="ftpUserID"   value="cronus" />
    <property name="ftpPassword" value="f#8jW9t3s!" />

    <antcall target="backupAdvancedInternal" />
</target>

<!-- backupAdvancedInternal target -->
<target name="backupAdvancedInternal"
        if="ftpLogin">

    <ftp server="127.0.0.1" remotedir="ftpFiles"
         userid="${ftpUserID}" password="${ftpPassword}">
```

LISTING 2.15   Continued

```
        <fileset dir="${dirs.backup}" />
    </ftp>

    <delete dir="${dirs.backup}" />
  </target>

</project>
```

Story

After two days, Lisa and Scott have completed the spike, and have verified to Michael's satisfaction that the selected pattern will solve the necessary problems. Jeff has taken the buildfile through several rounds of changes, and has a solid basis on which to start the build process for the upcoming series of development iterations. The team is now ready to move into the release planning phase of the project.

Summary

The Ant build and deployment tool by the Apache Project is an ideal choice for any software project that is being developed with the Extreme Programming methodology. XP is a heavily iterative process, with an emphasis on testing and repeatability. Manual processes really won't do on an XP project. Complex manual processes are neither fast or repeatable with any level of confidence.

Ant provides a framework for rapidly implementing repeatable build, testing, and deployment processes. Also, Ant is written in Java, and works on just about every operating system platform available. If there's a JVM for an operating system, Ant will run on it. Ant has a great deal of capability built into it that will meet most projects' needs. For the instances where a project requires some unique capability that Ant doesn't have, Ant offers extensibility. New capability can be added into Ant by writing custom components that will plug into the framework. If you're not a Java developer, Ant offers the alternative of extending it by incorporating scripting code in a familiar scripting language directly in the buildfile, and executing it with its BSF scripting capability. And if all else fails, Ant will let you shell out to the native operating system and run a command.

By selecting Ant, an XP development team can reduce much of the risk and overhead associated with building, testing, and deploying software. And that translates into an increased probability of project success.

3

The First Iteration

Ant can play an important role in testing. By integrating testing into the build and deployment process, it becomes easier to implement and enforce ease-of-use considerations and compliance with testing standards. Development teams will see a marked improvement in quality and can more easily stick to delivery schedules. Ant plays a key role in merging the testing process with the build process, to provide a seamless integration of the often-divergent processes.

Story

Networks Byte Design, Inc., has embarked on a project to implement eMarket, their new e-commerce solution for sales and marketing. The core project team has been assembled and is developing the product using XP. So far, the eMarket project team has collected user stories written by the customer, decided on a high-level architecture, and implemented spikes to reduce the risks associated with the technical design decisions. Sandy, the project leader, schedules a *release planning* meeting between the development team and the customer to sort out the user stories in order to create a *release plan*.

At the meeting, the developers listen to the customer present each story. The development team divides into smaller groups and assigns a point value to each story to indicate its expected difficulty. During the meeting, some user stories are torn up and rewritten, some are discarded entirely, and a few new stories are added.

The development team returns the stories to the customer with their initial estimates and anticipated velocity. After seeing the estimates, the customer begins to define the priorities. The customer determines the order in which the stories should be implemented, based on the business value and time required to complete the story. The result of the meeting is that the first release plan is developed, which was created to get the stories with the highest business value completed first.

The customer has selected the stories that she wants to have completed in the first iteration, and puts them at the top of the stack of all the stories. The developers and customer go over the user stories, and the development team discusses the technical aspects of the stories and the tasks that need to be completed. Finally, the developers sign up for tasks for this iteration.

Sandy is concerned with the customer's uncertainty about requirements related to workflow and usability. She directs the team to focus on the user interface so that the customer can have an early look at the proposed design and workflow.

Michael, the lead developer, decides that for the first iteration, they will use dummy business objects that have their interfaces developed as needed, but will just return hard-coded data for the time being. The real implementation of the business objects will occur in later iterations.

Having completed the first release plan and iteration plan, the group begins work on the first iteration, which is to begin implementing the Web interface and mocking up the business objects. Each pair of developers will write a unit test that tests the functionality that they are about to implement. That is followed by the required class implementation. As new functionality is added to each class, the unit test is first modified before adding the new functionality to the class. The developers must run their unit tests each time they build their code. To do this efficiently, they need to modify the buildfile to handle unit testing. JUnit, a free open-source tool that integrates easily with Ant, is selected as the team's unit-testing tool.

The expense of fixing a bug also generally increases as you move along the development cycle. A bug caught during development is less expensive to fix than a bug caught during testing. The cost rises dramatically when a bug must be fixed in a product that has already shipped. The sooner bugs can be detected and fixed, the less money they cost to fix.

Testing is an important aspect of every development project. Unless the software can meet the minimal standards for usability, reliability, performance, requirements, and overall quality, it might never make it to a production system. All the work spent in planning, design, and coding will go to waste if the intended audience never uses the system.

With all the emphasis on testing, it would seem that the various forms of testing would be a major aspect of most software-development projects. Unfortunately, many projects start out with good intentions but rarely follow through with those plans. Most people agree on the importance that testing should play in the project, but testing often is conducted toward the end of the project, when the schedule for testing becomes severely compacted, sometimes to the point of becoming ineffective.

To attempt to combat this trend, newer development methodologies, such as XP, emphasize testing early and often in the process. Many of the techniques for testing in these methodologies are not new; they are simply changes in the frequency and schedule of testing procedures. Emphasis is placed on unit testing, in which developers test the smallest components of the system. These new concepts are not miracle cures or silver-bullet solutions, but they can help ensure that the software being developed has been designed and coded with testing in mind.

Benefits of Automated Testing

Automated testing brings a number of benefits. For one, the tests are repeatable. When a test is created, it can be run each time the testing process is launched. Automating testing reduces the fatigue of performing testing manually, which leads to more consistent results. Also, because the tests are automated, they're easy to run, which means that they will be run more often. As new bugs are discovered and fixed, tests can be added to check for those bugs, to ensure that they aren't reintroduced. This increases the overall completeness of testing.

Automating the testing process can be as beneficial as automating the build process. The testing process is based on the concept of being repeatable, which requires an automated or, at the very least, well-documented process. Some of the benefits of automated testing are that it

- Is a repeatable process

- Uses a consistent approach

- Follows a documented process

- Frees up developer-hours for more profitable tasks

- Is expandable and flexible, with changes in code propagated to the testing procedure faster and more efficiently

- Negates the fatigue factor as development deadlines approach because automated tests will eliminate the stress and workload of manual testing on developers

Some drawbacks are worth mentioning, of course. Some features don't easily lend themselves to automated testing. For example, sometimes automation-testing software can be used to test complex GUI applications, but often these applications must be tested by hand.

Automated testing is not a panacea for all problems, but it can contribute to an efficient and effective software development process. Integrating a testing tool into Ant that wasn't designed to be executed from Ant can require additional work. This can be accomplished by extending Ant, using BSF scripting, or using the <exec> task to launch another tool. If the test will be run frequently, the effort is worth the benefits gained in ease of testing.

Because it's a repeatable process, automated testing achieves an important part of the testing process by making it possible to conduct regression testing, to retest the same scenario again. How many bugs reported by testing teams cannot be duplicated by the developers? How many bugs are fixed, yet the tests that are run to check the fixes are insufficient or different from the original tests? These are the types of issues that regression testing helps address, and this is why the benefit of repeatable tests is so high.

Consistency issues are easiest to observe in teams with multiple testers and developers, but even a single tester would rarely conduct the same tests the same way each time. Automating the process maintains consistency from one run of the test to the next, regardless of how much time passes between the two runs of the tests or who is executing the tests.

The best kind of documentation is documentation that does not have to be written and yet is guaranteed to be correct. In a nutshell, that is a description of a self-documenting system. The goal is to create readable code. When the programmer clearly defines the testing goals for the test, someone who comes along later can easily understand the purpose of the test. This documentation does not have to be written; it is a beneficial side effect. The code is guaranteed to be correct because the tests have been executed under certain conditions and passed. Basically, tests should be as self-documenting as possible. Most developers don't like to comment the code that's going into the product. They're even less likely to comment the unit tests that accompany the product code because they know that the unit-test code won't go into the product. By developing readable code, the need to heavily comment the unit tests is greatly reduced.

By automating the testing process, the computer will usually execute the testing process in less time than it takes a tester to perform manually. Although the code will take the same time to execute, the prep time and interpretation of the results will be quicker with the automated process. Also, because this is a repeatable test, the automated approach becomes even more beneficial when the tests must be run multiple times. People get tired of conducting the same tests repeatedly, and will make mistakes, but the automated processes run consistently each time. Again, manual testing has its place; the advantage of automated testing is that it can easily catch many of the problems before manual testing even begins.

Benefits of Integrating Testing into Ant

Beyond the benefits of automating the testing process in general, integrating the testing process into the Ant build process has additional benefits:

- The integrated testing process is likely to be used.

- Integrated testing stresses the importance of testing early and often.

- Enforcement of testing standards is easier.

- Testing is consistent over every version of the software project.

By including the testing process inside the Ant build process, the likelihood that the process will be used increases enormously. If the process is as simple as performing a task that the developers do many times a day, many of the typical excuses for skipping the process are eliminated. If a process precludes the developers from executing it, the benefits of the process can never be realized.

Another benefit of placing the testing process inside Ant is that it enforces the idea that testing is part of the development process, not just something to be done by a testing group prior to shipping. Testing is conducted at many levels to test various aspects of the application. By including testing throughout the process, bugs can be found earlier, fewer mistakes are repeated, and problems are found closer to the time when they are introduced.

Finally, including testing in the Ant process provides for easier enforcement of the testing standards. Ant targets can be developed to ensure that all classes have a unit test created for them. We will look at techniques for accomplishing this in Chapter 9, "Company Reorganized—Working with a New Subteam," and Chapter 10, "Additional Teams Adopt the XP Process." The Ant build process can enforce the stipulation that tests must be run at certain points, such as before deployment. Ant also can enforce that all tests must pass before moving on to subsequent steps. By allowing Ant to enforce these standards, the development team is freed up to focus on developing production-quality code.

Types of Automated Testing

A variety of different types of automated testing can be conducted, and Ant can be used to integrate most, if not all, of them. These tests can be used to check the quality of every aspect of the project. Some of the types of testing that can be automated as part of the Ant build process include

- Unit—Verifies that certain parts of the code are working properly. It is not an overall system test.

- Functional—Used to test the usability of the system. This type of testing is also known as "black box testing" because the testing is conducted with no knowledge of how the code was implemented.

- Acceptance—Used to determine if all of the requirements have been met. These are the requirements defined by the customer in the form of user stories.

- Regression—Verifies that previously working parts of the system are still working after changes have been made.

- Performance—Verifies that the components of the systems meet the stated requirements for speed.

- Load—Stresses a system to test how it will behave under heavy use. A system that works well with one user may completely break down with several hundred or more users. Load testing helps to evaluate how well a system holds up under heavy use.

If your project is not using any form of automated testing currently, we highly recommend it. A great sense of accomplishment comes when a job has been done well. Testing allows success to be quantified and measured. By automating the test, you have the added benefit of being able to easily repeat the test.

In this chapter, we focus on *unit testing*. Unit testing is an important part of the XP process. Of all the types of automated testing, this is the one that should get the most use because developers should be running these tests at least daily, if not more frequently. Developers should also be writing new tests for all new code that they write and all changes that they make. It has been our experience that this also is an area of testing that many teams overlook or do not adequately implement. An organization might have experience with integration or performance testing, but unit testing often falls by the wayside.

What Is Unit Testing?

A *unit* is defined as the smallest piece of functionality that can stand alone. In C++ and Java applications, a unit generally is seen as equivalent to a class. If the class has been well designed and deals with a distinct object, the one class equals one unit test is a good rule of thumb. Unit tests are one of the many concepts in Ant in which consistency in conventions is important and can reduce the effort required to automate the process.

As an example, let's consider a simple class with a method that adds an object to the end of a list. Without unit testing, you probably would have performed some basic testing to make sure that the object was added to the end of the list, not to the beginning or somewhere in the middle. Unit testing provides the confidence that the method will do the proper thing, no matter what the input is. For example, consider what the sample method would do if the inputs were as follows:

- The object is null.
- The list is empty.
- The list is null.
- The list has exactly one item.

These are the types of tests that often are not conducted. At some point, a section of code that calls the sample class might be modified so that the list can be empty. The application no longer operates correctly, but the bug is more difficult to locate because what appeared to be working code that has not been changed is now broken. Rightly so, the focus is placed on the new code that was written rather than the code where the bug actually exists. By ensuring that the code can properly deal with all types of inputs, this method can be used in a variety of circumstances. It will be unlikely that the code is hiding a dormant bug, which always seems to appear at the worst possible time.

Test First Design

Unit testing has become such an important part of the development process that it is a central focal point of XP. In XP, you actually write your unit tests first, and then write the code. This is known as Test First Design.

Test First Design is a required practice in XP. The premise of Test First Design is that quality software can be designed and implemented by using the following iterative process. First, test for a condition that we want our software to fulfill. Initially, this test will fail. Second, write the code necessary to make the test pass. Finally, the code should be refactored periodically. Code can be refactored with confidence because unit tests are in place to detect any problems we may create, and to let us know when we have working code. This process is performed in a series of short iterations that will lead to an effective design. This also helps the developer to stay focused on implementing only what is needed.

Without the benefits that unit testing provides, development methodologies such as XP would not be possible. Even if your team is using a more traditional development methodology, unit testing can provide the same level of benefits and should be regarded as a critical part of all software development.

NOTE

In XP, unit tests are written first, and then the code they are designed to test follows. This is known as Test First Design. Writing tests first places the emphasis on how the class will be used, and therefore on coding only what is needed. This is also a good strategy for fixing bugs because it catches the presence of the bug immediately. Then write the code to pass the unit test. This way, you'll add to the overall suite of unit tests that are run, and you will catch the bug if it's ever reintroduced. You'll also ensure that your unit test works correctly.

JUnit

Although many techniques can be used to implement unit testing, the most popular tool for Java development is JUnit. This tool provides a framework for developing unit tests, which fits very nicely into the Ant build and deployment process. You can find JUnit, along with a lot of documentation and add-on tools, at www.junit.org.

INSTALLATION OF JUNIT

To install JUnit, follow these steps:

1. Download JUnit from

    www.junit.org

2. Add the `junit.jar` file to your `CLASSPATH` or to the Ant `lib` directory. Because JUnit is an optional task, the `optional.jar` file that ships with the Ant distribution must be in the Ant `lib` directory as well.

Sample Class

Let's take a look at how to incorporate JUnit into your development process and seamlessly integrate it into the Ant buildfile. Listing 3.1 is a sample Java class for which you will create a JUnit unit test. This is a simple class with a constructor, along with setter and getter methods. This class is a simple domain object to store the information about a single sales item in the eMarket application.

LISTING 3.1   Sample Class for Use with JUnit Unit Test

```
/*--------------------------------------------------------------------------
  File: salesItem
  --------------------------------------------------------------------------*/


package com.networksByteDesign.eMarket.inventory;

public class salesItem
{
    /* ================================================================
       salesItem Constructor
       ================================================================ */

    public salesItem(int id, String name)
    {
        mId          = id;
        mName        = name;
    }


    /* ================================================================
       getId
       ================================================================ */

    public int getId()
    {
        return mId;
    }


    /* ================================================================
       setId
       ================================================================ */

    public void setId(int id)
    {
        if(id <= 0)
        {
            throw new IllegalArgumentException("Id must be a valid id #");
        }

        mId = id;
    }
```

LISTING 3.1   Continued

```
/* ================================================================
   getName
   =============================================================== */

public String getName()
{
   return mName;
}

/* ================================================================
   setName
   =============================================================== */

public void setName(String name)
{
    if(name == null || name.length() == 0)
    {
        throw new IllegalArgumentException("Name must be populated");
    }

    mName = name;
}

private int    mId   = 0;
private String mName = null;
}
```

Sample Unit Test

Let's create a unit test to demonstrate how JUnit hooks into Ant. Listing 3.2 is the JUnit test that was written to test the sample class shown in Listing 3.1. We have included tests for both the constructor and the setter method. The getter method is tested as part of the other two tests. This JUnit class also includes a main() method for running the unit test from the command line.

LISTING 3.2   JUnit Test for Sample Class in Listing 3.1

```
/*----------------------------------------------------------------
  File: salesItemTest
  ----------------------------------------------------------------*/
```

LISTING 3.2   Continued

```
package com.networksByteDesign.eMarket.inventory;

// Internal libraries
import  com.networksByteDesign.eMarket.inventory.salesItem;

// Third party libraries
import  junit.framework.Test;
import  junit.framework.TestCase;
import  junit.framework.TestSuite;

public class salesItemTest extends TestCase
{
    ////////////////////////////////////////////////////////////////////////
    // salesItemTest(String)
    ////////////////////////////////////////////////////////////////////////

    /**
     * <p>
     * This is the constructor for the <code>salesItemTest</code>
     * class.  It calls the super class and configures the instance.
     * </p>
     *
     * @param testName the name of the test to construct
     *
     * */

    public salesItemTest(String testName)
    {
        super(testName);
    }


    ////////////////////////////////////////////////////////////////////////
    // main(String[])
    ////////////////////////////////////////////////////////////////////////

    /**
     * <p>
     * This is the mainline for the <code>salesItemTest</code>
     * class.  It runs the test suite that has been established.
```

LISTING 3.2   Continued

```
 * </p>
 *
 * @param args any command line arguments to the test program
 *
 * */

public static void main (String[] args)
{
    junit.textui.TestRunner.run(suite());

}


//////////////////////////////////////////////////////////////////////
// suite()
//////////////////////////////////////////////////////////////////////

/**
 * <p>
 * This is the static method that defines the specific tests that
 * comprise the unittest.
 * </p>
 *
 * @return the test suite that has been established
 *
 * */

public static Test suite()
{
    TestSuite suite = new TestSuite();

    // test constructor()
    suite.addTest(new salesItemTest("testConstructor"));
    suite.addTest(new salesItemTest("testSetter"));

    return suite;
}



//////////////////////////////////////////////////////////////////////
// testConstructor()
//////////////////////////////////////////////////////////////////////
```

LISTING 3.2   Continued

```
/**
 * <p>
 * Test for constructing a salesItem object
 * </p>
 *
 * */

public void testConstructor()
{
    int    id      = 123;
    String name    = "Router";

    // Does "happy path" work?
    salesItem test1 = new salesItem(id, name);
    assertEquals("Happy Path id test failed",   id,   test1.getId());
    assertEquals("Happy Path name test failed", name, test1.getName());

    // Is negative id handled?
    try
    {
        salesItem test2 = new salesItem(-123, name);
        fail("Expected exception was not thrown");
    }
    catch(IllegalArgumentException e) {}

    // Is zero id handled?
    try
    {
        salesItem test3 = new salesItem(0, name);
        fail("Expected exception was not thrown");
    }
    catch(IllegalArgumentException e) {}

    // Is empty string handled?
    try
    {
        salesItem test4 = new salesItem(id, "");
        fail("Expected exception was not thrown");
    }
    catch(IllegalArgumentException e) {}
```

LISTING 3.2   Continued

```java
        // Is null string handled?
        try
        {
            salesItem test5 = new salesItem(id, null);
            fail("Expected exception was not thrown");
        }
        catch(IllegalArgumentException e) {}
    }


    ///////////////////////////////////////////////////////////////////
    // testSetter()
    ///////////////////////////////////////////////////////////////////

    /**
     * <p>
     * Test for setter for the salesItem object
     * </p>
     *
     * */

    public void testSetter()
    {
        int      id   = 123;
        String   name = "Router";
        salesItem test = new salesItem(456, "Another");

        // Does "happy path" work?
        test.setId(id);
        assertEquals("Happy Path id test failed",   id,   test.getId());

        test.setName(name);
        assertEquals("Happy Path name test failed", name, test.getName());

        // Is negative id handled?
        try
        {
            test.setId(-123);
            fail("Expected exception was not thrown");
        }
        catch(IllegalArgumentException e) {}
```

LISTING 3.2   Continued

```
        // Is zero id handled?
        try
        {
            test.setId(0);
            fail("Expected exception was not thrown");
        }
        catch(IllegalArgumentException e) {}

        // Is empty string handled?
        try
        {
            test.setName("");
            fail("Expected exception was not thrown");
        }
        catch(IllegalArgumentException e) {}

        // Is null string handled?
        try
        {
            test.setName(null);
            fail("Expected exception was not thrown");
        }
        catch(IllegalArgumentException e) {}
    }
}
```

The unit test has two test methods: testConstructor() and testSetter(). These two tests were added to the test suite in the suite() method. When each test method is called, JUnit will call a setup() method if there is one. The optional setup() method can be used to perform one-time activities needed for the test such as instantiating a certain class, or making a database connection. Next the testConstructor() method is called. Within this test method, several tests are run to verify correct behavior of the tested class under all different conditions. Correct behavior is checked with various assertXXX() methods, such as assertTrue(). The assertXXX() methods can be used to check expected values and fail the test if the expected values aren't received. In our example of a unit test, the setter methods should throw an IllegalArgumentException if the parameter is invalid. If the exception is not thrown, we call the fail() method to indicate that the test has not performed as expected and has failed. Finally, if we had implemented the optional teardown() method, it would be called after the test method completed. teardown() is used to clean up after a test, such as closing a database connection. The cycle repeats for the next unit test. In the JUnit test class, the `suite()` method is used to add unit test methods to the suite of tests to be run. There are two ways to add tests. The first way is shown here:

```
public static Test suite()
{
    TestSuite suite = new TestSuite();

    // test constructor()
    suite.addTest(new salesItemTest("testConstructor"));
    suite.addTest(new salesItemTest("testSetter"));

    return suite;
}
```

In this approach, each unit test is explicitly added in the `suite()` method. With this approach, each new unit test must be added as it is created. The other technique is to make use of the fact that JUnit uses Java reflection. If we name all of our unit test methods starting with "`test*`", we can add all of the tests with one statement, as shown here:

```
public static Test suite()
{
    TestSuite suite = new TestSuite(salesItemTest.class);
    return suite;
}
```

The advantage to the second technique is that you don't have to add each new unit-test method into the `suite()` as it is created. With the first approach, you have more control over which tests are run, in case you want to temporarily turn some of them off while debugging a problem.

Command-Line Unit Testing

Before we hook JUnit into Ant, let's begin by running the unit test interactively at the command line. We first need to compile both the sample class and the unit test, using the `<compile>` target. In order to run the unit test at the command line, `junit.jar` must be in the CLASSPATH. Listing 3.3 shows the output of running the unit test at the command line.

LISTING 3.3   Output of Running Command-Line JUnit Test

```
% java com.networksByteDesign.eMarket.inventory.salesItemTest
.F.
Time: 0.033
```

LISTING 3.3 Continued

```
There was 1 failure:
1) testConstructor(com.networksByteDesign.eMarket.inventory.salesItemTest)
   "Expected exception was not thrown"

FAILURES!!!
Tests run: 2,  Failures: 1,  Errors: 0
```

Simple JUnit Target

Of the two tests run, one failed. The constructor does not have the same level of checks as the setter, and it contains a bug if the object is constructed with a null or empty String. Before fixing this problem, let's hook the unit test into Ant, to see how failed tests are handled.

Listing 3.4 is a unittest target that simply calls the JUnit class shown in Listing 3.2. This is about as simple as a unit-testing target can be.

LISTING 3.4 Simple unittest Target

```xml
<?xml version="1.0" ?>
<project name="eMarket" default="compile" basedir=".">

    <property name="dirs.source" value="/usr/projects/eMarket/src" />
    <property name="dirs.backup" value="${user.home}/backup"        />

    <!-- compile target -->
    <target name="compile" description="Compile all of the source code.">
        <javac srcdir="${dirs.source}" />
    </target>

    <!-- unittest target -->
    <target name="unittest"
            description="Run the unit tests for the source code.">
        <junit>
            <test
              name="com.networksByteDesign.eMarket.inventory.salesItemTest"
              />
        </junit>
    </target>
</project>
```

As you can see, this target simply calls the unit test just as we did from the command line. In Chapter 4, "The First Complete Build Process," we will change this task to include sets of tests rather than listing each test individually. The output of this target appears in Listing 3.5.

LISTING 3.5   Output of Simple `unittest` Target with Broken Test

```
% ant unittest
Buildfile: build.xml

unittest:
    [junit] TEST
            com.networksByteDesign.eMarket.inventory.salesItemTest FAILED

BUILD SUCCESSFUL
Total time: 2 seconds
```

Although running the `unittest` target shows the test class that failed, the output does not tell which test within the class failed or contain other useful information. If we fix the class by having the constructor call the setter rather than setting the member variable directly, all the unit tests should pass. Listing 3.6 shows the output when all tests pass. As you can see, there is no output from the target.

LISTING 3.6   Output of Simple `unittest` Target with No Broken Tests

```
% ant unittest
Buildfile: build.xml

unittest:

BUILD SUCCESSFUL
Total time: 2 seconds
```

haltonfailure/haltonerror

Let's begin enhancing the `unittest` target by looking at what happens when you run multiple tests. JUnit has a concept of failures and errors. Failures are tests that do not pass, but in anticipated ways. For example, the sample unit test had a failure because we checked to make sure that a particular exception was thrown.

Errors are unanticipated problems. An exception that is thrown but not caught by the class or the test is a common occurrence of this. Errors are considered failures as well.

The JUnit task has two attributes for determining how Ant should behave if a failure or error occurs:

- `haltonfailure`

- `haltonerror`

If these attributes are set to yes, the build fails if a unit test experiences a failure or error.

Listing 3.7 shows a unit test run with `haltonfailure` set to no. Even though a test fails, the subsequent tests are still run.

LISTING 3.7   Output from Unit Test Run with `haltonfailure` Set to No

```
% ant unittest
Buildfile: build.xml

unittest:
    [junit] TEST com.networksByteDesign.eMarket.inventory.salesItemTest FAILED
    [junit] TEST com.networksByteDesign.eMarket.inventory.customerTest FAILED

BUILD SUCCESSFUL
Total time: 1 second
```

Listing 3.8 shows the same test run, but with `haltonfailure` set to yes. Notice that when the first test fails, the build ends. No further tests are run, and no opportunity exists to clean up after the test.

LISTING 3.8   Output from Unit Test Run with `hailtonfailure` Set to Yes

```
% ant unittest
Buildfile: build.xml

unittest:

BUILD FAILED
file:/usr/projects/eMarket/build.xml:15:
    Test com.networksByteDesign.eMarket.inventory.salesItemTest failed

Total time: 1 second
```

Sometimes you want the build to fail, but not until you have cleaned up after the unit test. In this case, you can use the attributes `failureproperty` and `errorproperty`. If you supply a property name to these attributes, the property will be set automatically if a failure or error occurs. Your Ant target can check these properties after cleaning up, to determine whether the build should be halted. Listing 3.9 shows an example of how `failureproperty` can be used.

LISTING 3.9   Example of Using `failureproperty` to Clean Up After a Failed Test

```xml
<?xml version="1.0" ?>
<project name="eMarket" default="compile" basedir=".">

    <property name="dirs.source" value="/usr/projects/eMarket/src" />
    <property name="dirs.backup" value="${user.home}/backup"        />
    <property name="dirs.temp"   value="/tmp"                       />

    <!-- compile target -->
    <target name="compile" description="Compile all of the source code.">
        <javac srcdir="${dirs.source}" />
    </target>

    <!-- unittest target -->
    <target name="unittest"
            description="Run the unit tests for the source code.">
        <junit haltonfailure="no" failureproperty="unittestFailed">
            <test
             name="com.networksByteDesign.eMarket.inventory.salesItemTest"
             />
            <test
             name="com.networksByteDesign.eMarket.inventory.customerTest"
             />
        </junit>

        <antcall target="cleanupUnittest" />
        <fail if="unittestFailed" message="One or more unit tests failed."/>
    </target>


    <!-- cleanupUnittest target -->
    <target name="cleanupUnittest">
        <delete>
            <fileset dir="${dirs.temp}">
                <include name="*${ant.project.name}.test" />
            </fileset>
        </delete>
    </target>
</project>
```

The unittest target makes use of the <antcall> task. The <antcall> task is used to invoke another target within the same buildfile. Doing this creates another instance of a project. All of the properties in the current project will be passed to the new project unless the inheritAll attribute is set to false. The nested <param> element can also be used with <antcall> to pass new property values.

The <fail> task is used to inform the Ant build process that the build should fail and provide an appropriate message. In this case, we use the if attribute of the <fail> task to only cause the build to fail if the unittestFailed property is set. This allows us to cause the build to fail, but provide appropriate cleanup code prior to the failure.

printsummary

By default, Ant displays only the tests that fail or have an error. Although this is often desirable, some feedback on how things are progressing can be helpful when the unit testing process takes a long time. Listing 3.10 shows the output of the unittest target when multiple tests are run. As you can see, two classes are shown in the unittest section of the output.

LISTING 3.10   Build Output with Multiple Unit-Test Classes

```
% ant unittest
Buildfile: build.xml

unittest:
    [junit] TEST
            com.networksByteDesign.eMarket.inventory.salesItemTest FAILED
    [junit] TEST
            com.networksByteDesign.eMarket.inventory.customerTest FAILED

cleanupUnittest:
    [delete] Deleting 2 files from /tmp

BUILD FAILED
file:/usr/projects/eMarket/build.xml:26: One or more unit tests failed.


Total time: 2 seconds
```

To show the output from the tests being run, whether the tests fail or not, use the printsummary attribute. When this attribute is set to yes, all tests are summarized in the build output. Listing 3.11 shows the output using the same classes as in Listing 3.10. A third class is now visible. This class was being tested before, but because the tests passed, it was not visible. Setting the printsummary attribute shows all tests regardless of whether they pass or fail.

LISTING 3.11   Build Output with `printsummary` Set to Yes

```
% ant unittest
Buildfile: build.xml

unittest:
    [junit] Running com.networksByteDesign.eMarket.inventory.salesItemTest
    [junit] Tests run: 2, Failures: 1, Errors: 0, Time elapsed: 0.03 sec
    [junit] TEST
            com.networksByteDesign.eMarket.inventory.salesItemTest FAILED
    [junit] Running com.networksByteDesign.eMarket.inventory.customerTest
    [junit] Tests run: 2, Failures: 1, Errors: 0, Time elapsed: 0.015 sec
    [junit] TEST
            com.networksByteDesign.eMarket.inventory.customerTest FAILED
    [junit] Running com.networksByteDesign.eMarket.inventory.companyTest
    [junit] Tests run: 2, Failures: 0, Errors: 0, Time elapsed: 0.169 sec

cleanupUnittest:

BUILD FAILED
file:/usr/projects/eMarket/build.xml:31: One or more unit tests failed.

Total time: 2 seconds
```

Using the `printsummary` attribute, you see not only all the classes, but also the number of tests run, how many failures and errors occurred, and the time elapsed for each test. You might want to experiment with both approaches and see which style works best for your team.

`showoutput`

If your classes make use of logging, whether with a logging tool such as log4j or a simple `System.out.println()`, that information can be displayed by running the unit tests. By setting the `showoutput` attribute, any information written to `stdout` and `stderr` is displayed in the unit test's output. Listing 3.12 shows the sample class with a logging statement in each setter method.

LISTING 3.12   Sample Class with Logging Statement

```
/*-----------------------------------------------------------------
  File: salesItem
  ----------------------------------------------------------------*/

package com.networksByteDesign.eMarket.inventory;
```

LISTING 3.12   Continued

```java
public class salesItem
{
    /* ======================================================================
       salesItem Constructor
       =================================================================== */

    public salesItem(int id, String name)
    {
        mId         = id;
        mName       = name;
    }

    /* ======================================================================
       getId
       =================================================================== */

    public int getId()
    {
        return mId;
    }

    /* ======================================================================
       setId
       =================================================================== */

    public void setId(int id)
    {
        System.out.println("ID = " + id);

        if(id <= 0)
        {
            throw new IllegalArgumentException("Id must be a valid id #");
        }

        mId = id;
    }

    /* ======================================================================
       getName
       =================================================================== */
```

LISTING 3.12   Continued

```
    public String getName()
    {
        return mName;
    }

    /* ===================================================================
       setName
       =============================================================== */

    public void setName(String name)
    {
        System.out.println("Name = " + name);

        if(name == null || name.length() == 0)
        {
            throw new IllegalArgumentException("Name must be populated");
        }

        mName = name;
    }

    private int    mId   = 0;
    private String mName = null;
}
```

Listing 3.13 displays the output of the unittest target with showoutput and printsummary set to yes. This can be useful in debugging or when you create your nightly unit test process, later in this chapter.

LISTING 3.13   Output from unittest Target with showoutput Set to Yes

```
% ant unittest
Buildfile: build.xml

unittest:
    [junit] Running com.networksByteDesign.eMarket.inventory.salesItemTest
    [junit] ID = 123
    [junit] Name = Router
    [junit] ID = -123
    [junit] ID = 0
    [junit] Name =
    [junit] Name = null
```

LISTING 3.13   Continued

```
[junit] Tests run: 2, Failures: 1, Errors: 0, Time elapsed: 0.034 sec
[junit] TEST
        com.networksByteDesign.eMarket.inventory.salesItemTest FAILED
[junit] Running com.networksByteDesign.eMarket.inventory.customerTest
[junit] Tests run: 2, Failures: 1, Errors: 0, Time elapsed: 0.009 sec
[junit] TEST
        com.networksByteDesign.eMarket.inventory.customerTest FAILED
[junit] Running com.networksByteDesign.eMarket.inventory.companyTest
[junit] Tests run: 2, Failures: 0, Errors: 0, Time elapsed: 0.186 sec


cleanupUnittest:


BUILD FAILED
file:/usr/projects/eMarket/build.xml:32: One or more unit tests failed.
Total time: 2 seconds
```

Formatter

The `<junit>`JUnit task provides formatter classes to facilitate the handling of the output from unit tests. These classes listen to all of the output and act as both filters and formatters in presenting the final output. A formatter can be added by using the nested formatter tag inside the `<junit>` task. Three basic formatters are provided by the `<junit>` task:

- Plain

- Brief

- XML

It's also possible to develop custom formatters. The following target shows how the formatter is set.

```
<!-- unittest target -->
<target name="unittest"
        description="Run the unit tests for the source code.">
    <mkdir dir="${dirs.test}"/>
    <junit haltonfailure="no"
           printsummary="yes"
           showoutput="yes">
        <formatter type="brief" usefile="true" />
        . . .
    </junit>
</target>
```

Plain Formatter

Plain is a flat-file text format that provides information about both the tests that failed and those that succeeded. If the output does not need to be parsed by another process and information on successful tests is desired, this is probably the formatter type to select. Listing 3.14 shows the output of a unit test run with the formatter set to plain.

LISTING 3.14   Sample JUnit Output File with JUnit Task Set to Plain Formatter

```
% ant unittest
Buildfile: build.xml

unittest:
   [junit] Running com.networksByteDesign.eMarket.inventory.salesItemTest
   [junit] Tests run: 2, Failures: 0, Errors: 0, Time elapsed: 0.025 sec
   [junit] Testsuite: com.networksByteDesign.eMarket.inventory.salesItemTest
   [junit] Tests run: 2, Failures: 0, Errors: 0, Time elapsed: 0.025 sec

   [junit] Testcase: testConstructor took 0.017 sec
   [junit] Testcase: testSetter took 0 sec
   [junit] Running com.networksByteDesign.eMarket.inventory.customerTest
   [junit] Tests run: 2, Failures: 1, Errors: 0, Time elapsed: 0.113 sec
   [junit] Testsuite: com.networksByteDesign.eMarket.inventory.customerTest
   [junit] Tests run: 2, Failures: 1, Errors: 0, Time elapsed: 0.113 sec

   [junit] Testcase: testConstructor took 0.003 sec
   [junit]     FAILED
   [junit] Expected exception was not thrown
   [junit] junit.framework.AssertionFailedError:
           Expected exception was not thrown
   [junit]     at com.networksByteDesign.eMarket.inventory.customerTest.
                   testConstructor(Unknown Source)
   [junit]     at sun.reflect.NativeMethodAccessorImpl.
                   invoke0(Native Method)
   [junit]     at sun.reflect.NativeMethodAccessorImpl.
                   invoke(NativeMethodAccessorImpl.java:39)
   [junit]     at sun.reflect.DelegatingMethodAccessorImpl.
                   invoke(DelegatingMethodAccessorImpl.java:25)

   [junit] Testcase: testConstructorTestcase: testSetter took 0 sec
   [junit] TEST com.networksByteDesign.eMarket.inventory.customerTest FAILED
   [junit] Running com.networksByteDesign.eMarket.inventory.companyTest
   [junit] Tests run: 2, Failures: 0, Errors: 0, Time elapsed: 0.033 sec
```

LISTING 3.14   Continued

```
[junit] Testsuite: com.networksByteDesign.eMarket.inventory.companyTest
[junit] Tests run: 2, Failures: 0, Errors: 0, Time elapsed: 0.033 sec

[junit] Testcase: testConstructor took 0.003 sec
[junit] Testcase: testSetter took 0.001 sec

cleanupUnittest:

BUILD FAILED
file:build.xml:80: One or more unit tests failed.

Total time: 2 seconds
```

Brief Formatter

Brief is the same as the plain formatter, except that detailed information on successful tests is filtered out. If the output does not need to be parsed by another process and detailed information only on failed tests is desired, this is probably the formatter type to select. Listing 3.15 shows the output of a unit test run with the formatter set to brief.

LISTING 3.15   Sample JUnit Output File with JUnit Task Set to Brief Formatter

```
% ant unittest
Buildfile: build.xml

unittest:
    [junit] Testsuite: com.networksByteDesign.eMarket.inventory.salesItemTest
    [junit] Tests run: 2, Failures: 0, Errors: 0, Time elapsed: 0.005 sec

    [junit] Testsuite: com.networksByteDesign.eMarket.inventory.customerTest
    [junit] Tests run: 2, Failures: 1, Errors: 0, Time elapsed: 0.007 sec

    [junit] Testcase: testConstructor(com.networksByteDesign.eMarket.
                                      inventory.customerTest): FAILED
    [junit] Expected exception was not thrown
    [junit] junit.framework.AssertionFailedError: Expected exception was not
                                      thrown
    [junit]      at com.networksByteDesign.eMarket.inventory.customerTest.
                    testConstructor(Unknown Source)
    [junit]      at sun.reflect.NativeMethodAccessorImpl.
                    invoke0(Native Method)
```

LISTING 3.15   Continued

```
[junit]     at sun.reflect.NativeMethodAccessorImpl.
                invoke(NativeMethodAccessorImpl.java:39)
[junit]     at sun.reflect.DelegatingMethodAccessorImpl.
                invoke(DelegatingMethodAccessorImpl.java:25)


[junit] TEST com.networksByteDesign.eMarket.inventory.customerTest FAILED
[junit] Testsuite: com.networksByteDesign.eMarket.inventory.companyTest
[junit] Tests run: 2, Failures: 0, Errors: 0, Time elapsed: 0.001 sec


cleanupUnittest:

BUILD FAILED
file:build.xml:82: One or more unit tests failed.

Total time: 2 seconds
```

XML Formatter

The XML format provides the most information and should be used whenever the output will be parsed by another process, such as an XSLT to generate an HTML report. However, because some constructs are illegal in XML, the output from your unit tests may be filtered to prevent the inclusion of information that would invalidate the XML file. Listing 3.16 shows the output of a unit test run with the formatter set to xml. The XML formatter can be used to supply the test results in XML to the <junitreport> task, which provides HTML reports and is discussed in Chapter 5, "Creating the Automated Nightly Build."

LISTING 3.16   Sample JUnit Output File with JUnit Task Set to XML Formatter

```
% ant unittest
Buildfile: build.xml

unittest:
    [junit] <?xml version="1.0" encoding="UTF-8" ?>
    [junit] <testsuite errors="0" failures="0"
            name="com.networksByteDesign.eMarket.inventory.salesItemTest"
            tests="2" time="0.169">
    [junit]   <properties>
    [junit]     <property name="dirs.temp" value="/tmp"></property>
    [junit]     <property name="java.vm.version"
                        value="1.4.1_01-12"></property>
```

LISTING 3.16   Continued

```
[junit]      <property name="java.io.tmpdir" value="/tmp"></property>
[junit]      <property name="os.name" value="Mac OS X"></property>
[junit]      <property name="ant.home"
                         value="/usr/software/ant/"></property>


...


[junit]   </properties>
[junit]   <testcase name="testConstructor" time="0.0050"></testcase>
[junit]   <testcase name="testSetter" time="0.0"></testcase>
[junit]   <system-out><![CDATA[]]></system-out>
[junit]   <system-err><![CDATA[]]></system-err>
[junit] </testsuite>
[junit] <?xml version="1.0" encoding="UTF-8" ?>
[junit] <testsuite errors="0" failures="1"
           name="com.networksByteDesign.eMarket.inventory.customerTest"
           tests="2" time="0.027">
[junit]   <properties>
[junit]      <property name="dirs.temp" value="/tmp"></property>
[junit]      <property name="java.vm.version"
                         value="1.4.1_01-12"></property>
[junit]      <property name="java.io.tmpdir" value="/tmp"></property>
[junit]      <property name="os.name" value="Mac OS X"></property>
[junit]      <property name="ant.home"
                         value="/usr/software/ant/"></property>


...


[junit]   </properties>
[junit]   <testcase name="testConstructor" time="0.0070">
[junit]     <failure message="Expected exception was not thrown"
                     type="junit.framework.AssertionFailedError">
             junit.framework.AssertionFailedError:
               Expected exception was not thrown
[junit]       at com.networksByteDesign.eMarket.inventory.customerTest.
                 testConstructor(Unknown Source)
[junit]       at sun.reflect.NativeMethodAccessorImpl.
                 invoke0(Native Method)
[junit]       at sun.reflect.NativeMethodAccessorImpl.
                 invoke(NativeMethodAccessorImpl.java:39)
[junit]       at sun.reflect.DelegatingMethodAccessorImpl.
                 invoke(DelegatingMethodAccessorImpl.java:25)
```

LISTING 3.16   Continued

```
[junit] </failure>
[junit]    <system-out><![CDATA[]]></system-out>
[junit]    <system-err><![CDATA[]]></system-err>

...

[junit] </testsuite>

cleanupUnittest:

BUILD FAILED
file:build.xml:82: One or more unit tests failed.

Total time: 4 seconds
```

Direct Output with the `usefile` **Attribute**

Another attribute of the formatter tag is `usefile`. Normally, all information published by a formatter is sent to a file. Especially in the case of the XML formatter, where later processing is planned to take place, this file-based approach is usually the best way. However, if the intent is to provide feedback directly to the user or to add the information to a build log, setting `usefile = "no"` will send the formatter information to the screen instead.

The files created by the `<formatter>` are named `TEST-<the name of the class>.txt` for plain and brief and `TEST-<the name of the class>.xml` for xml. The filename for the `companyTest` class would be `TEST-com.networksByteDesign.eMarket.inventory.companyTest.txt` or `TEST-com.networksByteDesign.eMarket.inventory.companyTest.xml`.

Alternative `TestRunner`s

JUnit uses a class called `TestRunner` to execute the individual tests and display the results. JUnit provides alternative `TestRunner` classes to meet the needs of various users. All of the tests we have been running use the `textui` `TestRunner` as can be seen in Listing 3.17.

LISTING 3.17   The Output from Running a Unit Test Using the `textui` `TestRunner`

```
% java junit.textui.TestRunner
      com.networksByteDesign.eMarket.inventory.salesItemTest
.F.
Time: 0.006
```

LISTING 3.17   Continued

```
There was 1 failure:
1) testConstructor(com.networksByteDesign.eMarket.inventory.salesItemTest)
   "Expected exception was not thrown"

FAILURES!!!
Tests run: 2,  Failures: 1,  Errors: 0
```

Ant offers an AWT TestRunner that provides a graphical user interface to the test results. This can be used by calling java junit.awtui.TestRunner com.networksByteDesign.eMarket.inventory.salesItemTest and can be seen in Figure 3.1.

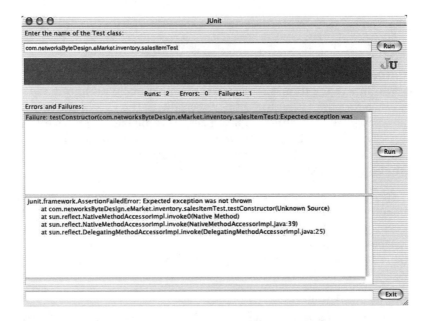

FIGURE 3.1   The AWT TestRunner provides a graphical user interface for the test results.

Ant also offers a Swing version of the TestRunner, which provides a more modern graphical interface. This can be used by calling java junit.swingui.TestRunner com.networksByteDesign.eMarket.inventory.salesItemTest and can be seen in Figure 3.2.

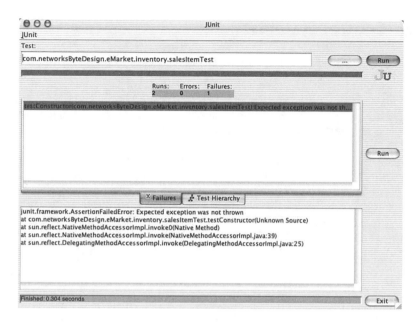

FIGURE 3.2   The Swing version of the TestRunner provides a more modern graphical interface.

Forking Unit Tests

It's possible for unit tests to have undesirable side effects on the build process. For example, if someone put a condition in their code that called System.exit(), this could cause the entire build process to exit. We would rather have just the unit test fail, but the entire build process continues to completion. Ant provides a way to insulate the build process from unintended side effects caused by unit testing, by allowing unit tests to be forked into their own JVM. There are several reasons why you might want to fork the JUnit tests into a separate process:

- As just discussed, forking will isolate a unit test from the build process. If the unit test caused a condition that prompted the process to exit, this would prevent the build process from exiting because the unit test is executing as a separate process.

- Forking will allow the JVM to take advantage of a multiprocessor platform.

- Forking unit tests into separate processes can also insulate them from picking up side effects that might occur in the build process. For example, if a unit test modifies the state of a singleton class, another unit test running in the same JVM might execute differently than if the singleton's state had never been altered.

Version-Control Systems

Story

On Wednesday of the second week of the project, the development server finally became available. Until now, the developers had been doing all work on their local desktop machines, and transferring files between one another for compiling and testing. This includes the initial spike tests as well as development of production code. One of the developers on the team is John Reynolds, who is a Java developer and has expertise in CVS. Michael asks John to set up their CVS repository, and to pair with Jeff so that Jeff can learn more about setting up CVS. Jeff in turn will be able to teach John more about using Ant. The two will work together to define the necessary targets in the buildfile to handle their CVS needs. Because Jeff has completed the unit testing targets for the buildfile, he begins adding some targets that they will definitely need: perform a CVS update and perform a clean build.

After the CVS repository is set up, the developers are able to add and commit their code to the repository, and begin controlling their code in CVS. Michael sets the requirement that code committed to CVS must compile and pass its unit tests.

No matter what the size of the development team is, version control plays an important role in the process. At one level, you can think of version control as a part of an automated backup process. Beyond that basic level, version control enables development team members to work in conjunction with each other, regress to earlier versions, and treat a group of files as a single unit. We believe that it's important at the outset to set up a version-control practice. Version control is one of those areas that isn't as interesting as architecture or design, and it can easily be neglected. This is exactly why we think it's important to set up such a system initially; that way, it isn't postponed or neglected entirely.

CVS Access and Logins

Ant supports several version-control systems, either natively or through the use of optional tasks. The version-control system called *Concurrent Versions System* (CVS) is used by Ant's developers to manage the Ant source code and is the version-control system that is the most integrated with Ant. CVS is widely used in both open-source and commercial software development, and it is available on most platforms. Although we focus on CVS here, the concepts demonstrated in this book can be applied to almost any revision-control system.

CVS Login

CVS has a repository that contains the revision history of each of the files. The location of this repository typically is referred to as CVSROOT. Usually, an environment variable named CVSROOT is set, and CVS commands implicitly make use of it to determine which repository to act on. The value of CVSROOT also can be passed as a parameter to CVS commands.

Most CVS tasks in Ant behave in the same manner as their CVS command-line counterparts. If the CVSROOT environment variable is set, the Ant tasks pick it up automatically. CVSROOT also can be set as an attribute on the CVS tasks. The one exception is the <cvslogin> task, which requires CVSROOT to be set as an attribute because it ignores the environment variable.

From a user's viewpoint, logging into CVS is not a step that takes place every time the developer accesses CVS. When a user logs in to CVS, a local password file, typically named .cvspass, is created. This file is used to authenticate the user on subsequent calls to CVS. So, the CVS login command doesn't actually log in the user, as most systems do, but it creates the password file in preparation for later CVS commands. Therefore, entering an invalid password when logging in does not do anything. The result is seen only when the first CVS command is run. Listing 3.18 shows the cvsLogin target.

LISTING 3.18   cvsLogin Target

```
<!-- cvsLogin target -->
    <target name="cvsLogin">
        <input message="Please enter CVS password:"
               addproperty="cvsPassword" />

        <condition property="noCVSPassword">
            <equals arg1="" arg2="${cvsPassword}" />
        </condition>

        <fail if="noCVSPassword">You did not enter your CVS password.</fail>

        <cvspass cvsroot=":local:/usr/local/cvsArchive"
                 password="${cvsPassword}" />
    </target>
```

This target begins by incorporating the concepts from the backup tasks, where the <input> task was used to obtain the cvsPassword from the user. If no password is entered, the task fails with an appropriate error message.

Next we call the cvspass task to set the cvsroot and password attributes. The other optional attribute is passfile, which defaults to .cvspass if not overridden.

In reality, the cvsLogin target rarely is called because, in most installations of CVS, the login process is an operation that takes place once per user per machine. However, if users move from machine to machine, or if new users frequently are added, the frequency of logins could increase tremendously. Even if logging into CVS needs to happen more frequently, this step should occur naturally during the build process.

A Custom Task to Check for Required Input Parameters

Story

After a number of changes to the buildfile have been made to check that mandatory parameters are set, it becomes apparent to the developers that there is a lot of replication throughout the buildfile to check for required input parameters. Besides being sloppy, this replication creates a maintenance problem. The development team agrees that a pair of developers should write a custom task to clean this up and consolidate this functionality into one place.

The buildfile has grown to include a lot of constructs to verify that mandatory parameters are set. Recall from Chapter 2, "Creating Initial Spikes," that properties are immutable and can't be used like ordinary variables in a scripting language. Because of this, we wind up setting a number of temporary parameters to check for required input, and the buildfile becomes unwieldy. Also, whenever we want to require parameters in a buildfile, we wind up rewriting the same XML. The team decides to create a custom task that handles required input. This consolidates the checking of required input into a single task and also enables them to write and debug this code once. Listing 3.19 shows the custom task RequiredInput, which extends the Ant Input task. The Input task is not an abstract base class listed in the Ant documentation as a task specifically intended for extension, but there's also no reason why other tasks in Ant can't be extended.

A Task class in general has private attributes, public setter methods for each attribute, and a public execute method. When the task executes, the Ant framework calls the setter method for each attribute that is set in the XML tag. Then the public execute method is called to do the actual work. Appendix B, "Extending Ant," explains the general procedure for writing a custom task as well as methods for setting nested elements.

One of the problems faced in writing this task is that it's necessary to know the value of the attributes of the Input class, but they're private and the derived class doesn't have access to them. The way around this problem is to override the setter classes. Each setter method calls the base class's setter method (such as super.methodname()) and then stores the value of the attribute in the class. This grants access to a copy of the attribute values in the derived class.

When the RequiredInput task executes, it checks the boolean values to determine whether all the required attributes have been set. If they haven't, the value of the unpopulated attribute is false. The execute method then throws an Ant BuildException, which fails the build and prints an error message indicating which required parameter hasn't been set. This task is shown in Listing 3.19, which extends the Input task and simplifies the process of checking for mandatory parameters.

LISTING 3.19   A Custom Task for Checking for Required Input

```
package com.networksByteDesign.util;

import org.apache.tools.ant.BuildException;
import org.apache.tools.ant.taskdefs.Input;

public class RequiredInput extends Input
{
    /**
     * Defines the name of a property to be created from input. Behavior is
     * according to property task, which means that existing properties
     * cannot be overridden.
     *
     * @param addproperty Name for the property to be created from input
     */
    public void setAddproperty (String addproperty)
    {
        super.setAddproperty(addproperty);
        propertyName     = addproperty;
        havePropertyName = true;
    }


    /**
     * Returns the property that gets set during the build run.
     * @return The property being set.
     */
    public String getProperty()
    {
        return propertyName;
    }


    /**
     * Sets the Error Message which gets displayed to the user during
     * the build run.
     * @param errorMessage The error message to be displayed.
     */
    public void setErrormessage (String errorMessage)
    {
        this.errorMessage = errorMessage;
        haveErrorMessage  = true;
    }
```

LISTING 3.19   Continued

```java
/**
 * Returns the Error Message which gets displayed to the user during
 * the build run.
 * @return The error message to be displayed.
 */
public String getErrormessage()
{
    return errorMessage;
}


/**
 * Actual test method executed by ant.
 * @exception BuildException
 */
public void execute () throws BuildException
{
    if (!havePropertyName)
    {
        throw new BuildException("Missing attribute propertyName",
                                location);
    }

    if (!haveErrorMessage)
    {
        throw new BuildException("Missing attribute errorMessage",
                                location);
    }

    super.execute();

    if(getProject().getProperty(propertyName).trim().length() == 0)
    {
        throw new BuildException(errorMessage, location);
    }
}

private String  propertyName     = "";
private String  errorMessage     = "";
private boolean haveErrorMessage = false;
private boolean havePropertyName = false;
}
```

Appendix B describes the integration of a custom task in detail. One method of hooking a custom task into an Ant buildfile is to declare a mapping between the classname and the taskname with a `<taskdef>` tag, as shown here:

```
<taskdef name="requiredInput"
        classname="com.networksByteDesign.util.RequiredInput"/>
```

Afterward, all that's required is to put the classfile in your system CLASSPATH, and then run the buildfile. There is an alternate, more "permanent" way to integrate a task, which is described in Appendix B.

Listing 3.20 shows the custom `RequiredInput` task hooked into our `cvsLogin` target.

LISTING 3.20   RequiredInput Task Hooked into Build File

```xml
<?xml version="1.0" ?>
<project name="eMarket" default="compile" basedir=".">

    <taskdef name="requiredInput"
            classname="com.networksByteDesign.util.RequiredInput"/>

    <property name="dirs.source" value="/usr/projects/eMarket/src" />
    <property name="dirs.backup" value="${user.home}/backup"        />
    <property name="dirs.temp"   value="/tmp"                       />

    <!-- cvsLogin target -->
    <target name="cvsLogin">
        <requiredInput message="Please enter CVS password:"
                      addproperty="cvsPassword"
                      errorMessage=" You didn't enter your CVS password."/>

        <cvspass cvsroot=":local:/usr/local/cvsArchive"
                password="${cvsPassword}" />
    </target>

    <!-- compile target -->
    <target name="compile" description="Compile all of the source code.">
        <javac srcdir="${dirs.source}" />
    </target>
</project>
```

CVS Initialization

Now that we have refactored our Ant buildfile to deal with required input tasks, let's make the CVS login process transparent to the user. Because the CVS login is typically a rarely used target, we'd like to make sure it handles the login when it is necessary but doesn't get in the way of normal usage.

To accomplish this, we'll take a look at the <available> task. The purpose of the <available> task is to allow a specified property to be set if a particular resource, such as a file, a class, a directory, or a JVM system resource, exists. In this case, you can make the CVS login process transparent by looking for the .cvspass file. If it exists, you proceed normally. Otherwise, you prompt the user for the CVS password and create the .cvspass file. Listing 3.21 shows the cvsInit target.

LISTING 3.21   cvsInit Target

```
<!-- cvsInit target -->
    <target name="cvsInit">
        <available file="${user.home}/.cvspass"
                   property="cvsAlreadyLoggedIn" />

        <antcall target="cvsLogin" />
    </target>
```

Next we modify the cvsLogin task to check for the cvsAlreadyLoggedIn property. Instead of using the if attribute as before, we use the unless attribute, which has the opposite effect. These changes are shown in Listing 3.22.

LISTING 3.22   cvsLogin Target (Revised)

```
<!-- cvsLogin target -->
    <target name="cvsLogin" unless="cvsAlreadyLoggedIn">
        <requiredInput message="Please enter CVS password:"
                       addproperty="cvsPassword"
                       errorMessage=" You didn't enter your CVS password."/>

        <cvspass cvsroot=":local:/usr/local/cvsArchive"
                 password="${cvsPassword}" />
    </target>
```

Now we can make all CVS targets depend on cvsInit, which ensures that the user is logged in if he has not previously done so. If a user already has logged in, the cvsLogin task will be bypassed.

The CVS Task

Now that you have handled the initial access into CVS, you can turn your attention to the <cvs> task itself. In its simplest form, the <cvs> task is simply a pass-through mechanism to the cvs command itself. All the CVS commands and options can run through the <cvs> task as well. Listing 3.23 shows the output from calling cvs --help-command. For additional information about CVS and a list of CVS commands and options, see www.cvshome.org/docs/manual/cvs.html.

INSTALLATION OF CVS

To install CVS, follow these steps:

1. Download CVS from

   http://www.cvshome.org

2. CVS is available for a number of different platforms. Be sure to check the installation instructions for your specific platform.

3. The CVS manual can be found at:

   http://www.cvshome.org/docs/manual

LISTING 3.23   Output from the cvs --help-command

```
% cvs --help-command
CVS commands are:
        add          Add a new file/directory to the repository
        admin        Administration front end for rcs
        annotate     Show last revision where each line was modified
        checkout     Checkout sources for editing
        commit       Check files into the repository
        diff         Show differences between revisions
        edit         Get ready to edit a watched file
        editors      See who is editing a watched file
        export       Export sources from CVS, similar to checkout
        history      Show repository access history
        import       Import sources into CVS, using vendor branches
        init         Create a CVS repository if it doesn't exist
        log          Print out history information for files
        login        Prompt for password for authenticating server.
        logout       Removes entry in .cvspass for remote repository.
        rdiff        Create 'patch' format diffs between releases
        release      Indicate that a Module is no longer in use
        remove       Remove an entry from the repository
        rtag         Add a symbolic tag to a module
        status       Display status information on checked out files
```

LISTING 3.23   Continued

```
      tag         Add a symbolic tag to checked out version of files
      unedit      Undo an edit command
      update      Bring work tree in sync with repository
      watch       Set watches
      watchers    See who is watching a file
(Specify the --help option for a list of other help options)
```

CVS Checkouts

The first command we'll look at is the CVS checkout command. This command is used to retrieve a set of files from CVS into a new workspace. As with all CVS commands, you can configure a multitude of options and parameters to meet your specific needs. This book is not intended to be a tutorial on CVS, so we simply pick from some of the more common sets of options.

One of the advantages of using Ant for your build and deployment process is that you can easily check Ant buildfiles into version control, and you can track revisions of your buildfile as well. On many of our projects, the Ant buildfile had more revisions than the source code as we enhanced our build and deployment process throughout the lifecycle of the project. In fact, the buildfiles used as examples throughout this book were maintained in a CVS repository. The issue with keeping the Ant buildfile under version control is that it creates a circular dependency. To run a target on an Ant buildfile, you first must check the workspace out of version control. When the workspace has been checked out, the need for an Ant target to check out a new workspace is negated.

However, if the Ant file is contained in a separate workspace from the rest of the source code, a checkout target for pulling a particular release of the source code makes perfect sense. You will apply this technique later in the book when application deployment is discussed. For example, we have an application that has its installation CD built with Ant. The Ant buildfile checks out a copy of Tomcat and JBoss from CVS and includes it as part of the installation.

If you are familiar with other revision-control systems but not with CVS, there is an important distinction in the concept of checkout. In revision-control systems such as the Revision Control System (RCS), the Source Code Control System (SCCS), and Clearcase, checking out a file usually means retrieving a copy of it with the intent of modifying it. This means that the file is locked in the repository, preventing others from modifying the file until the person who locked the file releases the lock. By contrast, in CVS, checking out means pulling a copy of the source code, but not necessarily with the intent to modify any of it. Also, the checkout command can be used to pull code based on some criteria such as a tag, all the latest versions on the main branch, and so on. The important distinction here between CVS and other revision-control systems is that the term checkout doesn't mean that the repository is locked for modification, as it implies in most other revision-control systems.

The concepts presented so far will assist you in building robust, reusable targets that can be used interactively by a developer, but also as part of an unattended build and deployment process.

Listing 3.24 shows the cvsCheckout Target. This target depends on cvsInit, which ensures that the user has previously logged in to CVS, either through the Ant rules or through CVS directly.

LISTING 3.24   cvsCheckout Target

```
<!-- cvsCheckout target -->
    <target name="cvsCheckout" depends="cvsInit">

        <requiredInput message="Please enter CVS module:"
                       addproperty="cvsModule"
                       errorMessage="You didn't enter a CVS module." />

        <requiredInput message="Please enter working directory:"
                       addproperty="dirs.working"
                       errorMessage="You didn't enter a working directory"/>

        <mkdir dir="${dirs.working}" />

        <cvs package="${cvsModule}" dest="${dirs.working}" />
    </target>
```

As with the backup targets, the user is prompted to provide the name of the module to check out from CVS, as well as the directory in which to place the checked-out code. Modules are a convenient way in CVS to group files and directories that are logically related. If the module or working directory is not properly entered, the target fails.

```
<mkdir dir="${dirs.working}" />
```

We then create the working directory in case it does not exist. As you learned earlier, if it does exist, the default behavior is to do nothing.

```
<cvs package="${cvsModule}" dest="${dirs.working}" />
```

Next, call the cvs task, passing the module that you want to check out in the package attribute and the working directory in the dest attribute. The default command for the <cvs> target, if no command is supplied, is to check out a new workspace; for the purposes of this discussion, you do not need to be concerned with the cvs options passed to the checkout command.

The end result of the cvsCheckout target is a checked-out CVS module in the directory of your choice. As with the backup process, you can break the interactive part of cvsCheckout into a separate target so that you can produce an unattended version as well.

CVS Updates and Commits

Now that we have checked out a version of the source code, we need a way to pull the latest changes that other developers on the team are checking in. In CVS, this is done through the use of the update command. As with the checkout command, all CVS commands and options can be used in the command attribute of the cvs task. We must add the attribute to the new target because we relied on the default value for the checkout target.

The following code shows the cvsUpdate target. The module name is not required because CVS looks in the ${dirs.source} to find the information it needs regarding the CVSROOT and the module where the source code is mastered. The update command displays a list of files that have been changed, updated, or added since the last update. For example, a ? in front of the filename indicates that this is a new file, an M indicates a modified file, and a C indicates that changes you have made conflict with other changes made to the same file and that CVS cannot resolve the conflicts automatically. Information on the meaning of each of the flags, as well as how to work with issues such as conflicts, can be found on the CVS Web site.

```
<!-- cvsUpdate target -->
<target name="cvsUpdate" depends="cvsInit">
    <cvs command="update" dest="${dirs.source}" />
</target>
```

In CVS, putting your changes into the repository is done with the commit command. This is analogous to the concept of checkin with other revision-control systems. Committing changes is straightforward. CVS prompts you to enter a comment describing the changes, which is always a good practice to follow. CVS attempts to use your default editor for the entering of the comments (the value of the EDITOR environment variable in UNIX, for example). The following code shows the Ant task for committing changes to CVS.

```
<!-- cvsCommit target -->
<target name="cvsCommit" depends="cvsInit">
    <cvs command="commit" dest="${dirs.source}" />
</target>
```

If you would rather use the <input> task for adding comments as you have been doing, just add the appropriate tasks, as shown in Listing 3.25.

LISTING 3.25   cvsCommit Target (Revised)

```
<!-- cvsCommit target -->
    <target name="cvsCommit" depends="cvsInit">
        <requiredInput message="Please enter your CVS comment:"
                        addproperty="cvsComment"
                        errorMessage=" You did not enter a CVS comment."/>
        <cvs command="commit -m ${cvsComment}" dest="${dirs.source}" />
    </target>
```

In this case, we are enforcing a team policy in the build process rather than relying only on verbal and written policies and procedures. If the developer does not enter a cvs comment, the commit process will abort. If a comment is added, commit is called, with the –m flag passing the comment as a parameter.

The cvsUpdate and cvsCommit targets work fine until two developers change the same file. Even if the changes are not in conflict, if one developer does not call cvsUpdate before cvsCommit, cvsCommit will fail. Although the error message will indicate what went wrong, it is better to change cvsCommit to be dependent on cvsUpdate.

```
<target name="cvsCommit" depends="cvsUpdate" description="">
```

If the changes are in conflict, the update will indicate this and the commit will fail with an appropriate error message. This rule will check in all your changes with the same comment. Depending on your team standards, this might not be appropriate. However, if you make small, logical changes to the source code, this approach can be a best practice. By concentrating on the reason for the change rather than the specific code changes, which can be easily gleaned from a comparison of the two versions, a reviewer of the comments can better understand the motivation for certain changes.

Basic Deployment

Story

During the course of testing, the team is expending effort by manually copying the class files to a directory for deployment on the app server. Scott and Lisa decide to automate the process. They add a simple deploy target to the buildfile that will copy the required class files and JAR files to the correct directory. This will save time and effort because they are now having to deploy on a frequent basis.

A full deployment can be a complex process in which to fully automate the steps. The team is taking the correct approach in creating a simple process and adding the complexity only as needed. The deployment target described in Listing 3.26 will simply jar up the class files and copy the JAR file and all JSP pages to the deployment directory.

LISTING 3.26   Simple Deployment Target

```xml
<?xml version="1.0" ?>
<project name="eMarket" default="compile" basedir=".">

    <taskdef name="requiredInput"
             classname="com.networksByteDesign.util.RequiredInput"/>

    <property name="dirs.source" value="/usr/projects/eMarket/src"         />
    <property name="dirs.backup" value="${user.home}/backup"               />
    <property name="dirs.temp"   value="/tmp"                              />
    <property name="dirs.deploy" value="/usr/projects/appServer/eMarket" />

    <!-- compile target -->
    <target name="compile" description="Compile all of the source code.">
        <javac srcdir="${dirs.source}" />
    </target>

    <!-- deploy target -->
    <target name="deploy" description="Simple deployment of the app">
        <jar jarfile="${ant.project.name}.jar">
            <fileset dir="${dirs.source}" includes="**/*.class" />
        </jar>
        <copy file="${ant.project.name}.jar" todir="${dirs.deploy}" />
        <copy flatten="true" todir="${dirs.deploy}">
            <fileset dir="${dirs.source}" includes="**/*.jsp"/>
        </copy>
    </target>
</project>
```

Our <deploy> target begins by creating a JAR file containing all of the class files. The JAR file will be named with the name of the project, which in our case will create a JAR file called eMarket.jar. The file will be copied to the deployment directory.

The <deploy> target then goes on to copy all JSP pages to the deployment directory. Notice the flatten attribute in the <copy> task. When this attribute is set, the directory structure from the source is not preserved. So, even if the JSP pages are scattered in various subdirectories, they will be copied directly into the deployment directory.

Story

The group reached the end of the first iteration and their stories are complete. Also, because the buildfile is able to perform the needed requirements, Jeff and John decide to refactor it to clean it up. The development team and the customer get together and look over the user interface. As expected, the customer makes some changes in the user stories. At the iteration planning meeting for the second iteration, Sandy, Michael, the developers, and the customer meet again to have another look at the user stories. Once again, the customer sets the priorities based on business value, and the plan is created for the next iteration.

Summary

In this chapter, the team began their first iteration. We've seen the first unit test and hooked JUnit into the Ant build process. We've used attributes such as `haltonfailure`, `propertyfailure`, `printsummary`, `showoutput`, and `fork` to tune the unit-testing process to meet the team's needs.

We have also introduced the use of CVS as the version control system. We have gone through the process of logging into CVS, and performing a checkout, update, and commit. We also developed a custom task to simplify the use of the `<input>` task.

Finally, a simple deployment target was developed that handled the creation of a JAR file along with copying the necessary files to the deployment directory

The First Complete Build Process

Generating Documentation

Documentation is one area that is often neglected in a project, but it's also an important part of the project deliverables. Even when documentation is created as part of a project, it's often out-of-date with the actual state of the project. Because of these factors, it's important to make updating the documentation a part of the project build process.

Story

The eMarket project, an e-commerce solution for sales and marketing at Networks Byte Design, Inc., is nearing the end of the first development release cycle. The team has made progress with creating unit tests and implementing code for the Web interface.

In fact, the team has developed enough of a code base that it's getting awkward to search though the code for API information. They need to start generating documentation on a regular basis for their code. Generating documentation manually is an option, but it's likely to be out of sync if the team relies on a manual process. Two of the developers, Lisa and Scott, decide to modify the buildfile to produce basic Javadoc as part of the build.

Generating Javadoc

When considering Ant for documentation generation on Java projects, the type of documentation that comes immediately to mind is Javadoc. The Javadoc tool by Sun Microsystems ships as part of the JDK, parses Java source code and special comments within the code, and generates API information in the form of HTML. Ant has a core task, <javadoc>, that is used to invoke the Javadoc tool to produce the HTML containing the API. One interesting thing to note about the <javadoc> task, as mentioned in the Ant documentation, is that the <javadoc> task is run in a separate JVM than the Ant thread of execution. This is because the Javadoc process calls System.exit() upon completion. If it weren't run in a separate JVM, Ant itself would exit upon completion of <javadoc>.

Only a few attributes are required to run <javadoc>. The remaining attributes (and there are many) are used to tune the behavior of <javadoc>. According to the Ant documentation, the following must be defined to set up a minimal build target for <javadoc>:

- The destdir where the Javadoc HTML will be deposited (this isn't necessary if using a doclet).

- One of the following:

  - The sourcepath attribute

  - The sourcepathref attribute, a reference to a path defined elsewhere

  - The sourcefiles attribute, a comma-separated list of source files

  - A nested <sourcepath>, <fileset>, or <packageset> element

---

NOTE

A *doclet* is code written in Java that implements the doclet API by Sun Microsystems. Its purpose is to create documentation of Java source code in HTML from special tags embedded in the source code. Doclets are used with Sun's Javadoc tool, provided as part of the Java Development Kit. Because doclets conform to the doclet API, it's also possible to write your own doclets or to obtain third-party doclets and use them as part of your documentation process. By doing this, you can customize the type of documentation that is generated when using Javadoc.

Javadoc Examples

Ant 1.5.3 doesn't work with just a sourcepath value unless you also include a list of package names. Let's look at some examples using these constructs. Listing 4.1 shows the most straightforward approach, using sourcepath, destdir, and packagenames.

The packagenames attribute is simply a comma-separated list of Java package names to be included in the generated Javadoc. The Ant <javadoc> task also permits you to define a list of one or more package names. In this case, the sourcepath is expected to be the path up to the start of the directory structure corresponding to the package structure. Also, the directory structure must follow the package structure.

If a package contains subpackages, a wildcard can be used to pick the subpackages also. So, setting the packagename attribute to com.networksByteDesign.eMarket.inventory generates Javadoc for the package com.networksByteDesign.eMarket.inventory only, whereas using com.networksByteDesign.eMarket.* picks up com.networksByteDesign. eMarket.inventory and other subpackages, such as com.networksByteDesign. eMarket.util and com.networksByteDesign.eMarket.presentation.

In Listing 4.1, the source directory is specified up to the directory containing the Java files.

LISTING 4.1   A Buildfile for Simple Generation of Javadoc

```xml
<?xml version="1.0" ?>
<project name="eMarket" default="compile" basedir=".">

   <taskdef name="requiredInput"
            classname="com.networksByteDesign.util.RequiredInput"/>

   <property name="dirs.source" value="src"         />
   <property name="dirs.backup" value="${user.home}/backup"                />
   <property name="dirs.temp"    value="/tmp"                              />
   <property name="dirs.deploy" value="/usr/projects/appServer/eMarket" />
   <property name="dirs.doc"      value="docs"                             />

   <!-- compile target -->
   <target name="compile" description="Compile all of the source code.">
       <javac srcdir="${dirs.source}" />
   </target>

   <!-- javadoc target -->
   <target name="javadoc" description="Generates javadoc for the source.">
       <mkdir dir="${dirs.doc}"/>

       <javadoc sourcepath="${dirs.source}"
                destdir="${dirs.doc}"
                packagenames="com.networksByteDesign.eMarket.*" />
   </target>
</project>
```

Nested <filesets> can be used to specify the files to be generated, as shown in the target of Listing 4.2.

LISTING 4.2   The Use of a Nested Fileset to Specify the Files to Be Included in the Javadoc

```
<!-- javadoc target -->
<target name="javadoc" description="Generates javadoc for the source.">
    <mkdir dir="${dirs.doc}"/>

    <javadoc destdir="${dirs.doc}">
        <fileset dir="${dirs.source}">
            <include name="**/*.java"/>
        </fileset>
    </javadoc>
</target>
```

NOTE

The following `<fileset>` construct includes all Java files down the directory. If you want to include only certain files or specifically exclude certain files, you can use the `include` and `exclude` elements of `<fileset>`. Here's an example showing how to include only certain files:

```
<!-- javadoc target -->
<target name="javadoc" description="Generates javadoc for the source.">
    <mkdir dir="${dirs.doc}"/>

    <javadoc destdir="${dirs.doc}">
        <fileset dir="${dirs.source}">
            <include name="**/*.java"/>
            <exclude name="**/*Test.java"/>
        </fileset>
    </javadoc>
</target>
```

Another way to use `<javadoc>` is to define the `sourcepathref` attribute. This attribute is used to refer to a previously defined path. Listing 4.3 shows an example of a path definition that is referred to in the `<javadoc>` task. Normally, you would define a path if it will be used more than once, but for the purpose of illustration, the path is defined and used once, as shown in Listing 4.3.

LISTING 4.3   The Use of a Path Reference Construct with `<javadoc>`

```
<?xml version="1.0" ?>
<project name="eMarket" default="compile" basedir=".">

    <taskdef name="requiredInput"
             classname="com.networksByteDesign.util.RequiredInput"/>
```

LISTING 4.3   Continued

```
<property name="dirs.source"  value="/usr/projects/eMarket/src"      />
<property name="dirs.backup"  value="${user.home}/backup"           />
<property name="dirs.temp"    value="/tmp"                          />
<property name="dirs.deploy"  value="/usr/projects/appServer/eMarket" />
<property name="dirs.doc"     value="docs"                          />

<path id="path.doc">
    <pathelement path="${dirs.source}"/>
</path>

<!-- compile target -->
<target name="compile" description="Compile all of the source code.">
    <javac srcdir="${dirs.source}" />
</target>

<!-- javadoc target -->
<target name="javadoc" description="Generates javadoc for the source.">
    <mkdir dir="${dirs.doc}"/>

    <javadoc destdir="${dirs.doc}"
             sourcepathref="path.doc"
             packagenames="com.networksByteDesign.eMarket.*" />
</target>
</project>
```

The <javadoc> task also can use the <packageset> element. This element is a form of a <dirset> and is used to specify the directories to search for Java source code. Listing 4.4 shows an example using the <packageset> element within <javadoc>.

LISTING 4.4   Example of the Use of `packageset`

```
<!-- javadoc target -->
<target name="javadoc" description="Generates javadoc for the source.">
    <mkdir dir="${dirs.doc}"/>

    <javadoc destdir="${dirs.doc}">
        <packageset dir="${dirs.source}">
            <include name="**"/>
        </packageset>
    </javadoc>
</target>
```

If the list of packages to include is extensive, another solution is to use the packageList element of <javadoc>. A packageList also can be used when you want to generate the list from another process or custom task and then run <javadoc> against the packages in that list. Listing 4.5 shows the use of packageList. Simply set the attribute packageList to point to a file containing the names of packages.

LISTING 4.5   Example Showing the Use of the packageList Attribute of <javadoc>

```
<!-- javadoc target -->
<target name="javadoc" description="Generates javadoc for the source.">
    <mkdir dir="${dirs.doc}"/>

    <javadoc sourcepath="${dirs.source}"
             destdir="${dirs.doc}"
             packageList="eMarketPackages.txt" />
</target>
```

The file eMarketPackages.txt, used in the buildfile of Listing 4.5, contains the list of package names:

```
com.networksByteDesign.eMarket.inventory
com.networksByteDesign.spike
```

NOTE

Some tasks, such as <javadoc> and <sql>, have the option to read information from a file. This is a convenient way of passing dynamically generated lists to a task. Simply have your process or custom task write its output to a file. Then pass the filename to the task through the attribute that accepts files. In the case of <javadoc>, the packageList can be used to read the list and execute <javadoc>.

Use of Doclets

Using a doclet with the <javadoc> task is fairly straightforward. The following is an example showing the use of a doclet with the <javadoc> task in a simple target:

```
<target name="doclet.example ">
<javadoc docletpath="${xerces.jar}:${eMarketDoclet.jar}"
         packagenames="com.networksByteDesign.*"
         sourcepath="${source.path}"
         verbose="true">
    <doclet name="com.foo.CustomDoclet" path=".">
        <param name="-file" value="${output.file}"/>
```

```
        </doclet>
      </javadoc>
    </target>
```

The CLASSPATH for the doclet is defined by setting either the docletpath or docletpathref attributes. In this example, the docletpath attribute is set to include all the JAR files needed to run this particular doclet. The attribute docletpathref could be used instead to point to an existing refid of a CLASSPATH. The packages to be documented are specified as a comma-separated list in the packagenames attribute. The sourcepath attribute indicates the root directory of the source code directory tree. Within the starting and ending <javadoc> tags, the nested <doclet> element is used to define the doclet class that is to be used to generate documentation. Within the <doclet> tag, one or more nested <param> tags can be used to pass parameters that might be required to run the doclet. In the sample snippet, the parameter -file outputfilename is passed to the doclet in this manner. When this target is executed, it will use the class com.foo.CustomDoclet to generate Javadoc.

batchtest

Story

Though there are a number of ways to implement a Javadoc target in Ant, the approach of using a fileset to define the code set for Javadoc is the method that the developers decide to use.

As the team accumulates more code and unit tests, it's becoming increasingly cumbersome to add the unit test names to the buildfile each time they're created. Also, there's a risk of forgetting this step and failing to run the unit test. John and Jeff check the Ant documentation and find that the <batchtest> task will allow them to create a rule for defining a set of unit tests to be included in the build. The only requirement is that the team must follow a naming convention in order for this to work. The team agrees to name all of their unit test classes with the convention of *classname*, followed by Test.java. So, the Foo class will have a unit test called FooTest.java. The team also has to rename any other unit test source filenames (and corresponding class name) that don't already follow this convention. John and Jeff make the required changes to the buildfile to handle this.

Rather than individually adding each test, the batchtest tag normally is used instead of the test tag. batchtest enables a set of classes to be selected using a fileset. Naming conventions can keep this process from being cumbersome. A convention such as "All unit tests must end in 'Test' and no other classes can end in 'Test'" allows a simple fileset to select all unit tests without needing to be updated every time a new unit test is written. Here is a buildfile snippet showing the batchtest tag:

```
<batchtest>
<fileset dir="${dirs.source}">
```

```
                    <include name="com/**/*Test.class" />
                </fileset>
            </batchtest>
```

Advanced JUnit Target

Now we can use this additional information about the JUnit task to enhance the
unittest target. The more advanced unittest target is shown in Listing 4.6.

LISTING 4.6   unittest and cleanupUnittest Tasks

```xml
<?xml version="1.0" ?>
<project name="eMarket" default="compile" basedir=".">

    <taskdef name="requiredInput"
             classname="com.networksByteDesign.util.RequiredInput"/>

    <property name="dirs.source" value="/usr/projects/eMarket/src"        />
    <property name="dirs.backup" value="${user.home}/backup"              />
    <property name="dirs.temp"   value="/tmp"                             />
    <property name="dirs.deploy" value="/usr/projects/appServer/eMarket" />
    <property name="dirs.doc"    value="docs"                            />

    <!-- compile target -->
    <target name="compile" description="Compile all of the source code.">
        <javac srcdir="${dirs.source}" />
    </target>

    <!-- unittest target -->
    <target name="unittest"
            description="Run the unit tests for the source code.">
        <junit haltonfailure="no"
               printsummary="yes"
               failureproperty="unittestFailed">
            <batchtest>
                <fileset dir="${dirs.source}">
                    <include name="com/**/*Test.class" />
                </fileset>
            </batchtest>
        </junit>
```

LISTING 4.6   Continued

```
        <antcall target="cleanupUnittest" />
        <fail if="unittestFailed" message="One or more unit tests failed."/>
    </target>

    <!-- cleanupUnittest target -->
    <target name="cleanupUnittest">
        <delete>
            <fileset dir="${dirs.temp}">
                <include name="*${ant.project.name}.test" />
            </fileset>
        </delete>
    </target>
</project>
```

The target begins by creating a directory to store the output files from the tests. The JUnit task is called with `haltonfailure` set to `no`, but with the `failureproperty` set to `unittestFailed`. If a unit test fails, a property with the name `unittestFailed` will be set in the project. `printsummary` is set, so the user will get feedback on both successful and failed tests.

The `batchtest` tag sets the classes to be tested as those ending with `Test` and directs all output to the `${testDir}` directory. After the tests have run, you call the `cleanupUnittest` target, which removes some files from the `temp` directory. This could be used to reset the database, shut down a Web server, or perform any other necessary cleanup tasks.

Finally, if the `unittestFailed` attribute is detected, the build is halted with an appropriate error message. This `unittest` target will be the target used when adding `JUnitReport` later in this chapter.

Story

Some of the classes have been renamed, and in order to get rid of the old class files from the development area, the developers have to manually remove them. On one occasion, Scott intended to do the command `rm *.class`, but inadvertently did a `rm *.*` in the directory where he was working, removing the source code as well as the class files. Like other developers, he frequently committed his changes to CVS, so he was able to retrieve his files from CVS without too much loss.

The team has also just introduced a code generation step. Now, the generated Java files should be deleted and regenerated with each build. The buildfile needs a target to clean up class files and generated Java files. The development team needs to be able to do a clean build to validate that the work they're doing compiles correctly.

Listing 4.7 shows the initial clean target created by the team.

LISTING 4.7   Buildfile with a clean Target Added

```
<!-- clean target -->
<target name="clean" description="Clean all system generated files.">
    <delete>
        <fileset dir="${dirs.source}">
            <include name="**/*.class"/>
            <include name="**/eMarket/inventory/RouterA.java"/>
            <include name="**/eMarket/inventory/RouterB.java"/>
            <include name="**/eMarket/inventory/RouterC.java"/>
            <include name="**/eMarket/inventory/RouterD.java"/>
            <include name="**/eMarket/inventory/SwitchA.java"/>
            <include name="**/eMarket/inventory/SwitchB.java"/>
            <include name="**/eMarket/inventory/SwitchC.java"/>
            <include name="**/eMarket/inventory/FirewallA.java"/>
            <include name="**/eMarket/inventory/FirewallB.java"/>
        </fileset>
    </delete>
</target>
```

Story

After implementing the clean target, Scott realizes it's already getting too complicated. The generated Java files and class files are mixed in with CVS-controlled hand-coded Java files. The decision to mix the files requires that the buildfile be changed every time a new hand-coded or generated file is added. The team decides that they need to use a build directory that will contain all of the generated Java files and class files. The buildfile is modified to handle these changes.

Listing 4.8 shows the revised clean target along with the new build directory structure.

LISTING 4.8   Buildfile of 4.8 with a Separate Build Directory Added and the clean Target Modified to Work with the Build Directory

```
<?xml version="1.0" ?>
<project name="eMarket" default="compile" basedir=".">

    <taskdef name="requiredInput"
            classname="com.networksByteDesign.util.RequiredInput"/>
```

LISTING 4.8   Continued

```
    <property name="dirs.source" value="/usr/projects/eMarket/src"        />
    <property name="dirs.backup" value="${user.home}/backup"              />
    <property name="dirs.temp"   value="/tmp"                             />
    <property name="dirs.deploy" value="/usr/projects/appServer/eMarket"  />
    <property name="dirs.doc"    value="docs"                             />
    <property name="dirs.build"  value="build"                            />


    <!-- compile target -->
    <target name="compile" description="Compile all of the source code.">
        <mkdir dir="${dirs.build}"/>

        <copy todir="${dirs.build}">
            <fileset dir="${dirs.source}" includes="**/*.*"/>
        </copy>

        <javac srcdir="${dirs.build}" />
    </target>


    <!-- clean target -->
    <target name="clean" description="Clean all system generated files.">
        <delete dir="${dirs.build}" />
    </target>
</project>
```

Tagging Source Code with CVS

Story

On Monday morning, in the second iteration (of the second release cycle), Lisa arrived at work and found that her computer wouldn't boot. After a tech looked at the machine, they concluded that the hard drive had failed and would have to be replaced. After losing most of the day to the new hard drive installation, reformatting, and software reinstallation, she's ready to pull code from CVS. Because files are compiled and unit tested frequently, they are also checked in frequently. Fortunately, Lisa committed her files into CVS frequently (after they compile and pass unit tests), and had committed her work Friday afternoon, about two hours before she went home. So the impact was only about two hours of work lost, plus the day spent rebuilding her computer. This experience underscores the importance of committing changes to CVS on a frequent basis. Also, the group is no longer using the cron job that performs a tar backup of files because they switched over to CVS.

The development team needs to start tracking their code versions to a release. To accomplish this, they need to start using CVS tagging. CVS tagging allows a tag or label to be placed on the versions of each source file that went into a particular build. Also, the use of tagging needs to be integrated into the build process, so that means changes to the Ant buildfile.

After you've compiled your code, tested the application, and committed your changes to CVS, it's time to consider tagging the build. Tagging is sometimes known as labeling in other revision-control systems. The purpose of tagging is to apply a common label or identifier to the set of source code versions that went into a particular build. This way, it's possible to later rebuild that version of the project without having to specify the correct version of each source file that went into the build. Some teams have specific rules regarding the tagging of builds, and it's important to set tagging policies at the start of the project. In general, tagging is recommended at any release that you might want to retrieve as a unit at some later point. Certainly, major releases of the software fall into this category. However, many times on a development project, significant changes are made to the software that don't necessarily fall neatly into the release schedule. Have you ever worked on a feature, committed your changes, and then wished you could easily go back to the version before the feature was added? If so, tagging could have solved your dilemma.

Listing 4.9 shows a buildfile target that can be used for tagging a set of code in CVS. With this target, you can easily tag all the files in the current source code with a single label that later can be used to retrieve those specific versions of the files.

LISTING 4.9   cvsTag Target

```
<!-- cvsTag target -->
<target name="cvsTag" depends="cvsInit">
    <requiredInput message="Please enter your CVS tag:"
                   addproperty="cvsTag"
                   errorMessage=" You did not enter a CVS tag."/>
    <cvs command="tag ${cvsTag}" dest="${dirs.source}" />
</target>
```

Because a tag is pointless unless you use it, let's add a target for retrieving a set of source code by tag name. These changes are shown in Listing 4.10.

LISTING 4.10   cvsCheckoutTag Target

```
<!-- cvsCheckoutTag target -->
<target name="cvsCheckoutTag" depends="cvsInit">
    <requiredInput message="Please enter your CVS module:"
                   addproperty="cvsModule"
                   errorMessage=" You did not enter a CVS module."/>

    <requiredInput message="Please enter your CVS tag:"
                   addproperty="cvsTag"
                   errorMessage=" You did not enter a CVS tag."/>
```

LISTING 4.10   Continued

```
        <requiredInput message="Please enter working directory:"
                       addproperty="dirs.working"
                       errorMessage="You didn't enter a working directory."
        />

        <mkdir dir="${dirs.working}"/>

        <cvs package="${cvsModule}" tag="${cvsTag}" dest="${dirs.working}"/>
    </target>
```

This should be pretty familiar by now. By simply requesting the tag label, the specific tagged release can be checked out from CVS. When tagging source code and retrieving by a tag is this easy, it's more likely to be a part of your normal workflow. In fact, this is highly recommended.

NOTE

Always tag or label builds that you might want to be able to rebuild in the future. Software releases to customers always should be labeled. It's also recommended to label any point in the development cycle at which functionality has been added or bugs have been fixed. Labeling doesn't have to be for external releases only.

CleanImports

Story

The eMarket development team has nearly completed the next release. In the process, they've also made their build process more robust and complete. There have been a few setbacks, but Michael feels that the team has good policies and procedures in place to deal with the problems they've encountered. Michael decides to make a change to the build process to begin enforcing some project standards. He notices that different developers have a varied style in their use of imports. He and John pair up to add the use of CleanImports. This will modify the code to clean up all of the import statements and maintain consistency.

CleanImports is an Ant tool that cleans Java import statements. It provides an easy mechanism to enforce standardization across a project with minimal effort on the part of the development team.

INSTALLING CLEANIMPORTS

To install CleanImports, follow these steps:

1. Download CleanImports from the following URL:

   `http://www.euronet.nl/users/tomb/cleanImports/index.html`

2. Add the `cleanimports.jar`, `bcel.jar`, and `regexp.jar` files to your `CLASSPATH` or to the Ant `lib` directory.

Listing 4.11 shows the CleanImports tool hooked into the Ant build file along with the `cleanImports` target.

LISTING 4.11 `cleanImports` Target

```xml
<?xml version="1.0" ?>
<project name="eMarket" default="compile" basedir=".">

    <taskdef name="requiredInput"
            classname="com.networksByteDesign.util.RequiredInput"/>

    <taskdef name="cleanimps"
            classname="com.tombrus.cleanImports.ant.CleanImports"/>

    <property name="dirs.source" value="/usr/projects/eMarket/src"      />
    <property name="dirs.backup" value="${user.home}/backup"            />
    <property name="dirs.temp"   value="/tmp"                           />
    <property name="dirs.deploy" value="/usr/projects/appServer/eMarket" />
    <property name="dirs.doc"    value="docs"                           />
    <property name="dirs.build"  value="build"                          />

    <!-- compile target -->
    <target name="compile" description="Compile all of the source code.">
        <mkdir dir="${dirs.build}"/>

        <copy todir="${dirs.build}">
            <fileset dir="${dirs.source}" includes="**/*.*"/>
        </copy>

        <javac srcdir="${dirs.build}" />
    </target>

    <!-- cleanImports target -->
    <target name="cleanImports" description="Cleans import statements.">
        <cleanimps srcdir="${dirs.source}">
```

LISTING 4.11   Continued

```
        <cleanformat>
            <import    comment="Application Libraries"
                       package="com.networksByteDesign"/>
            <import    comment="Standard Java Libraries"
                       package="java"/>
            <import    comment="Extra Java Libraries"
                       package="javax"/>
            <import    comment="External Libraries" />
        </cleanformat>
      </cleanimps>
    </target>
</project>
```

In order for CleanImports to operate, the source code to be checked must be in a compilable state. The location of the source code is provided through the srcdir attribute.

The <cleanformat> tag is where the power of CleanImports comes through. The <import> tags that <cleanformat> contains provide the grouping of import lines. The comment attribute is used to provide a group comment, whereas the package attribute is used to indicate the Java package that should be included in the group. Alternatively, you can use the regexp attribute to provide a pattern to match a set of source code files. Leaving out the package and regexp attributes acts as the default group, catching all remaining source code files.

Placing a <text> tag in the <cleanformat> tag allows you to add additional comments in the import section. Adding a <collapse> tag allows you to configure the use of the wildcard import construct. For example, the following lines would consolidate the Java imports to import java.*; if the number of imports in the class from the Java package was four or more:

```
<collapse above="3">
<import    comment="Standard Java Libraries" package="java"/>
```

Setting the above attribute in the <collapse> tag to 0 would always consolidate the Java imports to the wildcard construct.

These various tools allow a great deal of flexibility in producing import statements that match your team's established standards. Listing 4.12 shows the output of running the cleanImports target.

LISTING 4.12   Output of `cleanImports` Target

```
% ant cleanImports
Buildfile: build.xml

cleanImports:
[cleanimps] Import cleaning was needed for 2 out of 4 files

BUILD SUCCESSFUL
Total time: 10 seconds
```

Listing 4.13 shows the before image of a class, and Listing 4.14 shows the same class after running the `cleanImports` target.

LISTING 4.13   Image of Class Before Running `cleanImports`

```
package com.networksByteDesign.eMarket.inventory;

import java.io.*;
import javax.xml.transform.*;
import javax.xml.transform.stream.*;
import net.firstpartners.nounit.ui.common.CommandPackage;
import net.firstpartners.nounit.report.process.CallChainer;
import javax.xml.transform.stream.StreamSource;
import net.firstpartners.nounit.report.AbstractReport;
import net.firstpartners.nounit.ui.common.SystemValues;
import net.firstpartners.nounit.utility.FileUtil;
import net.firstpartners.nounit.utility.NoUnitException;

import org.jdom.JDOMException;
```

LISTING 4.14   Image of Class After Running `cleanImports`

```
package com.networksByteDesign.eMarket.inventory;

// Standard Java Libraries
import java.io.FileNotFoundException;
import java.io.FileOutputStream;
import java.io.IOException;

// Extra Java Libraries
import javax.xml.transform.Transformer;
import javax.xml.transform.TransformerConfigurationException;
```

LISTING 4.14   Continued

```
import javax.xml.transform.TransformerException;
import javax.xml.transform.TransformerFactory;
import javax.xml.transform.stream.StreamResult;
import javax.xml.transform.stream.StreamSource;

// External Libraries
import net.firstpartners.nounit.report.AbstractReport;
import net.firstpartners.nounit.report.process.CallChainer;
import net.firstpartners.nounit.ui.common.CommandPackage;
import net.firstpartners.nounit.ui.common.SystemValues;
import net.firstpartners.nounit.utility.FileUtil;
import net.firstpartners.nounit.utility.NoUnitException;
import org.jdom.JDOMException;
```

Summary

In this chapter, the development team has begun working through some of the initial issues and growing pains of a development project. We worked through the process of adding Javadoc generation and settled on the use of filesets as the mechanism for specifying the source code.

The unit tests were enhanced to use a <batchtest>, which significantly reduced the maintenance to the build file. A <clean> target was added and then refactored to use a separate build directory when it became obvious that the initial direction would be too complex.

You learned how to tag a CVS release and how to retrieve that tagged release later. You also added a <cleanImports> target, which automatically standardized the import statements across the entire development team.

5

Creating the Automated Nightly Build

The nightly build is a combination of Ant tasks we have used before. The difference is in the packaging. In order for the build to be run as an unattended process, there can be no human intervention required by the build process. Other than that, the goal should be to keep the interactive and unattended versions of the build as similar as possible. Listing 5.1 shows the nightly build process as hooked into our buildfile.

Story

The eMarket project completed its next release, and things went fairly well considering some of the problems the team had encountered. The customer was generally pleased, but made some additional changes to the stories. A few new stories were added, some existing stories were changed, and two were removed entirely. The team (customer and developers) met the following Monday for their next *release planning* meeting. The customer laid out the priorities for user stories to be implemented in the next release. The release plan for the next release was created.

Because the team is starting to implement other parts of the system, and the code base has grown even more, it's time that an automated, unattended build was set up. Two of the developers, Lisa and John, sign up to work on creating the automated build. The first step they must do is modify the buildfile so that it can perform a checkout and update from CVS prior to compiling code.

The nightly build process begins deleting the build directory with <delete> and then creating the build directory with <mkdir>. This ensures that the directory is clean with no old files in it. Also, if the directory doesn't exist, using <delete> is harmless, and won't cause a problem in the buildfile. As an aside, using <mkdir> on a directory that does exist is also harmless. The next step checks out the eMarket package from CVS into the nightly build directory. Then we use the <antcall> task to invoke another target in the same buildfile. In this case we call the compile target, which will compile our source code.

LISTING 5.1   Buildfile with Nightly Build Added

```xml
<?xml version="1.0" ?>
<project name="eMarket" default="compile" basedir=".">

    <taskdef name="requiredInput"
             classname="com.networksByteDesign.util.RequiredInput"/>

    <taskdef name="cleanimps"
             classname="com.tombrus.cleanImports.ant.CleanImports"/>

    <property name="dirs.source"  value="/usr/projects/eMarket/src"      />
    <property name="dirs.backup"  value="${user.home}/backup"            />
    <property name="dirs.temp"    value="/tmp"                           />
    <property name="dirs.deploy"  value="/usr/projects/appServer/eMarket" />
    <property name="dirs.doc"     value="docs"                           />
    <property name="dirs.build"   value="build"                          />
    <property name="dirs.nightly" value="/usr/projects/eMarket/nightly"  />

    <!-- compile target -->
    <target name="compile" description="Compile all of the source code.">
        <mkdir dir="${dirs.build}"/>

        <copy todir="${dirs.build}">
            <fileset dir="${dirs.source}" includes="**/*.*"/>
        </copy>

        <javac srcdir="${dirs.build}" />
    </target>

    <!-- clean target -->
    <target name="clean" description="Clean all system generated files.">
        <delete dir="${dirs.build}" />
    </target>

    <!-- nightlyBuild target -->
    <target name="nightlyBuild"
            description="Conducts the nightly build process">

        <delete dir="${dirs.nightly}" />
        <mkdir dir="${dirs.nightly}" />


        <cvs package="eMarket" dest="${dirs.nightly}" />
```

LISTING 5.1   Continued

```
        <antcall target="compile" />
    </target>

</project>
```

Loggers and Listeners

Story

Lisa and John completed the first phase of the buildfile. However, Mark would like the team to get notifications to let everyone know when a build has run, and whether it succeeded or failed. Also, if a build fails, he would like the team to get error messages to show why the build failed so they can go fix the problems. After some discussion, he decides that an e-mail notification is a must have. Also, Michael said that if it's not too much work, he would like to have the build process generate an HTML report that can be automatically posted. That way, the developers can have a look each morning to see if they did anything to break the build, and fix it.

Ant loggers and listeners are constructs that enable you to monitor the build process and to define actions to be taken in response to events. A *listener* receives an event when a build is started and when it ends, when a target starts and ends, when a task starts and ends, and when a message is logged. A *logger* extends the listener class and provides some extra capabilities. It's aware of the logging level (quiet, debug, verbose), and it also has a handle to the standard output and standard error print streams. Thus, it's capable of logging information to either a console window or a logfile. Loggers also have some features for use with emacs. Ant 1.5.3 defines six standard or built-in loggers/listeners:

- `DefaultLogger`
- `AnsiColorLogger`
- `NoBannerLogger`
- `XmlLogger`
- `MailLogger`
- `Log4jListener`

It is also possible to develop your own loggers and listeners. Creating custom loggers and listeners is covered in Appendix B.

DefaultLogger

Whenever Ant is run, it uses `DefaultLogger` if no logger is specified. Like any of the loggers and listeners, `DefaultLogger` can be explicitly specified on the command line with the following syntax:

```
ant -logger org.apache.tools.ant.DefaultLogger
```

The full package name of the logger/listener class must be specified. Running the default logger explicitly doesn't do anything special that just running Ant won't accomplish, but serves to illustrate how to specify a logger class.

NoBannerLogger

NoBannerLogger causes Ant to not display a target name that has executed if the target did not generate output. NoBannerLogger is enabled with the following syntax:

```
ant -logger org.apache.tools.ant.NoBannerLogger
```

Using the buildfile that generated the output in Listing 5.2 with the NoBannerLogger would result in the output shown in Listing 5.3. In this case, the targets that did not produce output were completely removed from the output.

LISTING 5.2   Running cvsUpdate Without NoBannerLogger

```
% ant cvsUpdate
Buildfile: build.xml

cvsInit:

cvsLogin:

cvsUpdate:
     [cvs] Using cvs passfile: /Users/lberreta/.cvspass
     [cvs] cvs update: Updating .

BUILD SUCCESSFUL
Total time: 2 seconds
```

Running with the NoBannerLogger removes the tasks that produce no output as shown in Listing 5.3.

LISTING 5.3   Running cvsUpdate with NoBannerLogger

```
% ant cvsUpdate -logger org.apache.tools.ant.NoBannerLogger
Buildfile: build.xml

cvsUpdate:
     [cvs] Using cvs passfile: /Users/lberreta/.cvspass
     [cvs] cvs update: Updating .

BUILD SUCCESSFUL
Total time: 2 seconds
```

MailLogger

The MailLogger enables a user to direct Ant to send e-mail messages upon completion of a build, whether the build succeeded or failed. The MailLogger can be configured to send different e-mails to different users, depending on the outcome of the build. Let's modify the buildfile to send an e-mail after it completes. To accomplish this, you'll need to do two things. First, the required properties for the MailLogger class must be set up. Second, Ant must be run with the MailLogger logger option. Recall that there are several options for setting properties. Properties can be set in the buildfile, read from a properties file, passed in through the command line, or even set in an environment variable in an initialization file. For clarity in this example, the properties will be set in the buildfile. MailLogger requires several properties:

- Address to which the mail is to be sent in the case of success and failure. This can be the same e-mail address.

- Location where the mail is originating.

- The mail server, if the localhost is not to be used.

- The message for build success.

- The message for build failure.

Listing 5.4 shows the necessary properties set for use with the MailLogger class.

LISTING 5.4   Buildfile for Use with MailLogger

```
<property name="MailLogger.from"
          value="eMarketDev@networksByteDesign.com"/>
<property name="MailLogger.success.to"
          value="eMarketDev@networksByteDesign.com"/>
<property name="MailLogger.failure.to"
          value="eMarketDev@networksByteDesign.com"/>
<property name="MailLogger.success.subject"
          value="eMarket Nightly Build Succeeded"/>
<property name="MailLogger.failure.subject"
          value="eMarket Nightly Build Failed"/>
```

The properties have been set outside of any targets so that they will be evaluated before the execution of targets. The originator of the e-mail messages has been defined as eMarketDev@networksByteDesign.com. There are two destinations, one for success and another for build failure. In this buildfile, success or failure results in a message to eMarketDev@networksByteDesign.com. If the build succeeds, the output is sent with the title "eMarket Nightly Build Succeeded." If the build fails, the output also is sent, but with the title "eMarket Nightly Build Failed." Because the property

`MailLogger.mailhost` isn't defined, the localhost is assumed. If the localhost isn't running an SMTP mail server, the `MailLogger.mailhost` should be set to a machine that is running an SMTP server.

Now that the properties have been configured, Ant needs to be run with the `MailLogger` option. This can be done explicitly through the command line, as follows:

```
ant -logger org.apache.tools.ant.listener.MailLogger
```

Also, this option can be set in the `ANT_ARGS` environment variable in an Ant initialization file to avoid having to type it in the command line. For more information about using Ant initialization files, see Chapter 2.

AnsiColorLogger

`AnsiColorLogger` embeds color-coded escape sequences into the output of Ant. This causes the output of the logfile to be rendered in color on terminals that support ANSI color codes. Here's an example of running a buildfile with `AnsiColorLogger`:

```
ant -logger org.apache.tools.ant.listener.AnsiColorLogger –logfile build.log
```

XmlLogger

`XmlLogger` can be used to generate the build output as XML. The output can be sent to the console or to a file with the `–logfile` option. After the output is generated in XML, an XSLT stylesheet can be applied to transform the output into some other format, such as HTML. Here's an example of running the buildfile with `XmlLogger`:

```
ant -logger org.apache.tools.ant.XmlLogger -logfile build.log
```

This generates the XML file shown in Listing 5.5.

LISTING 5.5   Output of the `XmlLogger`

```
<?xml version="1.0" encoding="UTF-8" ?>
<?xml-stylesheet type="text/xsl" href="log.xsl"?>

<build time="3 seconds">
    <target name="compile" time="2 seconds">
        <task location="file:/usr/projects/eMarket/build.xml:20:"
              name="mkdir" time="0 seconds">
            <message priority="info">
```

LISTING 5.5   Continued

```
                    <![CDATA[Created dir: /usr/projects/eMarket/build]]>
                </message>
            </task>
            <task location="file:/usr/projects/eMarket/build.xml:22:"
                  name="copy" time="0 seconds">
                <message priority="info">
                    <![CDATA[Copying 13 files to /usr/projects/eMarket/build]]>
                </message>
            </task>
            <task location="file:/usr/projects/eMarket/build.xml:26:"
                  name="javac" time="1 second">
                <message priority="info">
                    <![CDATA[Compiling 13 source files]]>
                </message>
            </task>
        </target>
</build>
```

We can convert the resulting XML file into HTML. Ant includes an XSLT stylesheet for that very purpose in ANT_HOME/etc, called log.xsl. By default, Ant creates a reference to log.xsl in the current directory. You can override the location and filename of the XSL file by setting the ant.XmlLogger.stylesheet.uri property. If the property is set to an empty string, no reference is added to the XML log file. If you are deploying the output to a development Web site, you can deploy the XML log file and the log.xsl file, or you can transform the log file into HTML before deployment. Because Ant 1.5.3 has an <xslt> task (which runs the same task as <style>), the buildfile can be modified to perform the transformation as part of the build process. Modifying the original buildfile (without the changes for MailLogger) to include the <xslt> task for the transformation results in the code shown in Listing 5.6. The output from the <buildLogFormat> target can be seen in Figure 5.1.

LISTING 5.6   Buildfile Used to Generate the Output of Figure 5.1

```
    <!-- buildLogformat target -->
    <target name="buildLogFormat">
        <xslt in="build.log" out="build.html" style="log.xsl"/>
    </target>
```

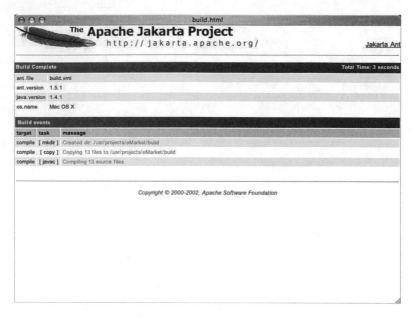

FIGURE 5.1   The build generates this output after running through Ant's log.xsl.

Log4jListener

Log4j, another Apache Jakarta project, is a tool for embedding logging messages into Java code.

INSTALLING LOG4J

To install Log4J, follow these steps:

1. Download Log4J from the following URL:

   `http://jakarta.apache.org/log4j/docs/download.html`

2. Expand the `tar.gz` or zip file.

3. Put the `log4j.jar` file in your system CLASSPATH.

With log4j, each message is set to a particular level:

- fatal
- error
- warn
- info
- debug

The level of the message determines whether it is printed at runtime based on configuration information in a properties file. When a Java program containing log4j messages executes, log4j looks in the Java CLASSPATH for a properties file called log4j.properties (it can also be configured with an XML file). In the property file, a logging level can be set. The level represents a high-water mark, in that all messages at that level or above in severity will print. Fatal-level messages always print. If the level were set to warn, all messages at the warn, error, and fatal levels would print. Listing 5.7 shows a log4j.properties file that can be used with Ant.

LISTING 5.7 A log4j.properties File That Can Be Used with Ant

```
# Set root category priority to DEBUG and its only appender to A1.
log4j.rootCategory=DEBUG, stdout

# stdout
log4j.appender.stdout=org.apache.log4j.ConsoleAppender
log4j.appender.stdout.layout=org.apache.log4j.PatternLayout
log4j.appender.stdout.layout.ConversionPattern= [%t] %-5p %c %x%n        %m%n
```

Assuming that you have a valid log4j.properties or log4j.xml file in your CLASSPATH, running Ant with the following options results in log4j output from the Ant Java classes as shown in Listing 5.8.

LISTING 5.8 Abbreviated Output Resulting from Running Ant with the Log4jListener

```
% ant compile -listener org.apache.tools.ant.listener.Log4jListener
Buildfile: build.xml
[main] INFO  org.apache.tools.ant.Project
       Build started.
[main] DEBUG org.apache.tools.ant.Project
       Detected Java version: 1.4 in:
       /System/Library/Frameworks/JavaVM.framework/Versions/1.4.1/Home
[main] DEBUG org.apache.tools.ant.Project
       Detected OS: Mac OS X
[main] DEBUG org.apache.tools.ant.Project
        +User task: propertyfile
       org.apache.tools.ant.taskdefs.optional.PropertyFile
[main] DEBUG org.apache.tools.ant.Project
       Build sequence for target `compile' is [compile]

compile:
[main] INFO  org.apache.tools.ant.Target
       Target "compile" started.
[main] INFO  org.apache.tools.ant.taskdefs.Mkdir
       Task "mkdir" started.
```

LISTING 5.8   Continued

```
[main] INFO  org.apache.tools.ant.taskdefs.Mkdir
      Task "mkdir" finished.
[main] INFO  org.apache.tools.ant.taskdefs.Copy
      Task "copy" started.
[main] INFO  org.apache.tools.ant.taskdefs.Copy
      Task "copy" finished.
[main] INFO  org.apache.tools.ant.taskdefs.Javac
      Task "javac" started.
[main] INFO  org.apache.tools.ant.taskdefs.Javac
      Task "javac" finished.
[main] INFO  org.apache.tools.ant.Target
      Target "compile" finished.

BUILD SUCCESSFUL
Total time: 3 seconds
[main] INFO  org.apache.tools.ant.Project
      Build finished.
```

Filemappers

A *filemapper* is used to tell Ant what type of target file to create as the result of an operation. Filemappers are used in conjunction with tasks that accept a set of files and output other files. The <copy> task is an example of a task that can make use of a filemapper. This task copies a set of files from one place to another. In the process of copying, you might want to change some aspect of the file, such as its name. A filemapper provides a transformation function to map one set of files into another set of files. The mapping operation is specified with the <mapper> tag. Ant provides six built-in types of mappers:

- identity
- flatten
- merge
- glob
- regexp
- package

The mapper type can be defined in two ways. The first technique is to use the type attribute, along with one of the type names listed. To define a mapper that specifies the flatten operation, use the syntax <mapper type="flatten"/>. The other technique is to specify the full class name of the mapper class to be used. To define a flatten mapper that is the logical equivalent of the previous example with the class name would require the syntax <mapper classname="org.apache.tools.ant. util.FlatFileNameMapper"/>.

When the mapper type is set, you must define the set of files on which to operate. The mapper contains an attribute named to, which is used to set the destination value, and an attribute named from, which is used to set the pattern for the originating files. Suppose that you want to perform a change such that any files that end in .txt will end in .log, using the glob type. You would use this syntax:

```
<mapper type="glob" from="*.txt" to="*.log"/>
```

Mappers do not support the nested <fileset> element, so the to and from attributes are the only means of defining the files on which to perform the mapping operation. Also, you should avoid using / and \ in the to and from attributes of any mapper because Ant will not handle them correctly in this case. For these cases, use ${file.separator} for correct behavior and platform independence.

Identity

Let's look at the predefined mappers. The identity mapper simply passes the source file to the destination unchanged. It's analogous to multiplying a number by 1. The result of the product is the original number.

Flatten

The flatten mapper removes all leading directory information and copies all originating files to the same directory. Flatten ignores the to and from attributes. The flatten mapper would convert the input /usr/projects/logs/test/test1.log into test1.log.

Listing 5.9 shows an example that copies a set of files down a directory tree that end in .jsp to the deployment directory.

LISTING 5.9   Use of the flatten Mapper Option

```
<!-- deploy target -->
<target name="deploy" description="Simple deployment of the app">
    <jar jarfile="${ant.project.name}.jar">
        <fileset dir="${dirs.build}" includes="**/*.class" />
    </jar>
    <copy file="${ant.project.name}.jar" todir="${dirs.deploy}" />
    <copy todir="${dirs.deploy}">
        <mapper type="flatten" />
        <fileset dir="${dirs.build}" includes="**/*.jsp"/>
    </copy>
</target>
```

Merge

The merge mapper's target filename is always the file specified in the to attribute. This mapper ignores the from attribute.

Glob

The next filemapper is the glob mapper. This mapper enables the use of the * in both the to and from attributes. The easiest way to understand the glob mapper is to look at an example. Consider the following mapper syntax:

```
<mapper type="glob" from="*.txt" to="*.log"/>
```

Suppose that this mapper encounters the following files:

- /usr/projects/examples/test1/output.txt

- /usr/projects/examples/test1/subtest/results.txt

- /usr/projects/examples/test2/subtest/output.csv

The mapper first attempts to match the value in the from attribute. The behavior of wildcards in the mapper is different than with normal patterns. For the first file, the asterisk in the from attribute (*.txt) matches the string /usr/projects/examples/test1/output. Normally, you would need the pattern ** to match a set of directories. Next the mapper substitutes the string into the asterisk portion of the pattern in the to attribute. So, the resulting string is /usr/projects/examples/test1/output.log. In this way, the glob mapper has changed output.txt to output.log. In the next line, the same process occurs and /usr/projects/examples/test1/subtest/results.txt is changed to /usr/projects/examples/test1/subtest/results.log. Even though there is another directory in the pathname, it still matches the pattern because txt occurs in the line. In the third line, nothing in the pathname /usr/projects/examples/test2/subtest/output.csv matches the pattern *.log. So, this string is left unchanged.

Regexp

As the name implies, the regexp mapper enables you to use regular expressions in the from and to attributes of the mapper. If the expression in the from attribute matches a filename in the fileset, a new name is constructed based on the regular expression given in the to attribute. An example should make that a bit more clear.

Suppose that you have a set of files that are named according to the following convention. Each file starts with the name of the company from which the data file was received, followed by the word DataFeed, followed by the date they were received, and ending with a suffix of .xml. So, for example, one of the files is called RoutersRUsDataFeed20030215.xml because it's data received from the company RoutersRUs on February 15, 2003. These files must be renamed to follow a different convention, with the date first and then the name of the company from which they were received. The word DataFeed should be removed entirely. The Ant regexp mapper can be used to perform this mapping. The XML snippet shown next demonstrates the syntax required to perform this mapping. This XML copies the files to the new name in the same directory where the original files are located:

```
<copy todir=".">
    <mapper type="regexp"
            from="^(.*)DataFeed([0-9]*)\.xml$$" to="\2_\1.xml"/>
    <fileset dir="."/>
</copy>
```

Several interesting things can be noted about the regexp mapper. First, just like elsewhere in Ant, a dollar sign must be escaped with another dollar sign ($$). Also, by using () in the from attribute, you can refer back to these subexpressions in the to attribute. \1 through \9 are used to refer to each of the subexpressions, and \0 refers to the entire match.

The engine used by the regexp mapper can be controlled through the use of a property (in a manner similar to setting the Java compiler) or by the classes available in the CLASSPATH. The system property ant.regexp.matcherimpl can be set to the name of the class implementing the regexp class that implements the interface org.apache.tools.ant.util.regexp.RegexpMatcher. If this property isn't set, Ant looks for one of three possible regexp engines in the CLASSPATH, in the following order:

1. The JDK 1.4 classes

2. The jakarta-ORO classes

3. The jakarta-regexp classes

If all three of these are in the classpath, Ant selects the JDK 1.4 classes. If you're using JDK 1.3, Ant looks for the jakarta-ORO classes, and so on.

Package

The package mapper acts just like the glob mapper, except that it replaces the directory syntax with the dot notation of a package. For example, it maps the file

```
com/networksByteDesign/example/mappers/Test.java
```

into

```
com.networksByteDesign.example.mappers.Test
```

Filtersets

Ant has a core task called `<filter>`. Its purpose is to perform a string substitution in the contents of a file when performing an operation on that file. This task looks for a token in the file of the form `@tokenname@` and substitutes another string for that token. The task `<filter>` can be used with a directory-based task, such as `<copy>`. Suppose that you have a text file called README that contains the following line:

```
This file was installed by @username@
```

A `filter` attribute can be set up to plug in the actual username when the file is copied:

```
<filter token="username" value="${user.name}"/>

<copy todir="${dirs.destination}" filtering="true">
  <fileset dir="${dirs.source}"/>
</copy>
```

The result of the copy operation is this:

```
This file was installed by Lisa
```

The property username could be configured in each user's initialization file. When the task is run, the username of the person who actually ran the installation procedure is inserted into the file, without having to modify the buildfile. Filters can also load their properties from property files for token replacement definitions.

A `<filterset>` provides a means of defining multiple filters to be used in an operation. It contains multiple `<filters>`. Suppose that your README file said this instead:

```
This file was installed by @username@ on @date@
```

You want to substitute the tokens for username and date with real values in your copy operation. So, you could use a `<filterset>` shown in Listing 5.10.

LISTING 5.10   Example Showing the Use of `<filterset>`

```
<!-- deploy target -->
<target name="deploy" description="Simple deployment of the app">
    <tstamp />

    <jar jarfile="${ant.project.name}.jar">
        <fileset dir="${dirs.build}" includes="**/*.class" />
    </jar>
```

LISTING 5.10 Continued

```
        <copy file="${ant.project.name}.jar" todir="${dirs.deploy}" />

        <copy todir="${dirs.deploy}">
            <mapper type="flatten" />
            <fileset dir="${dirs.build}" includes="**/*.jsp"/>
            <filterset>
                <filter token="username" value="${user.name}"/>
                <filter token="date"     value="${DSTAMP}:${TSTAMP}"/>
            </filterset>
        </copy>
    </target>
```

Assuming that the `username` and `date` attributes are set, when the README file is copied, you would get a resulting file like this:

```
This file was installed by Lisa on February 15, 2003
```

Path-like Structures

Story

Lisa and John choose the MailLogger and set the appropriate properties in the Ant buildfile. Now the development team will receive an e-mail each morning with the results from the nightly build. No matter who shows up first, any problems can be quickly attended to and cause minimal downtime for the team.

After testing the build manually, Lisa and John set the build up to run as a `cron` job on the development server. The next morning, they discovered that much of the code didn't compile due to failed `import` statements. They quickly realize that they need to deal with setting up the Java CLASSPATH for the build so that code will compile and test properly under any user.

A path-like structure is used to define CLASSPATH and PATH in a buildfile, using the constructs `<classpath>` and `<path>`. A pathname can be defined in a path-like structure with either attributes or nested `<pathelement>` tags. Also, when naming or creating a list of pathnames, the separators : or ; can be used. Regardless of the separator used, Ant uses the correct one for the operating system on which it's running.

When specifying a path, you can use an absolute or relative path. If a relative path is used, it's calculated relative to the project's basedir. The parameters to set for path-like structures are `path` and `location`. The Ant documentation states that `path` is intended to be used with predefined paths, where `location` is intended to be used when the user is building up a path. It's still legal to use multiple path elements in a path-like structure. CLASSPATH can be set with the path or location attributes. CLASSPATH can exist only inside a task that requires CLASSPATH, such as <javac> or <javadoc>. Here's an example of two types of syntax for a classpath:

```
<classpath path="${classpath};${more.classpath}" />
```

or

```
<classpath location="/usr/projects/lib/all.jar;/usr/projects/lib/more.jar"/>
```

Here, ${classpath} and ${more.classpath} are properties that have already been set. The path attribute is intended to be used with a predefined path, and the location element is used to specify one or more .jar files or directories. Setting and using properties is covered in detail later in this chapter. CLASSPATH can also be set using a nested <pathelement> construct, as in the following:

```
<classpath>
    <pathelement path="${classpath}"/>
    <pathelement path="${more.classpath}"/>
</classpath>
```

or

```
<classpath>
    <pathelement location="/usr/projects/lib/all.jar"/>
    <pathelement location="/usr/projects/lib/more.jar"/>
</classpath>
```

Within a <classpath>, both path and location pathelements can be used together. Paths can be given a unique reference ID and used elsewhere by their refid, as shown in the following example:

```
<path id="project.classpath">
    <pathelement location="/usr/projects/lib/all.jar"/>
    <pathelement location="/usr/projects/lib/more.jar"/>
</path>
<classpath refid="project.classpath"/>
```

The advantage here is that you can define the path once and use it many times throughout the buildfile.

Nightly Build JUnit Target

Story

With the Java CLASSPATH problems fixed, the build runs that night. Michael quickly realizes that the output from all of the unit tests is too awkward to sort through every day. He needs a way to condense the information into a more easily readable format. Once again, Lisa and John continue modifying the buildfile to handle this. They do some quick research and learn how to set up JUnitReport.

Although the nightly build is an important step, the fact that the code will compile is not an adequate indicator that the build is fully operational. To make sure the application is working correctly, we need to run the unit test suite. As a part of the nightly process, we can set up a nightly unit test target, which has some different requirements from the unittest target. By simply changing some of the attributes, we can produce a different target, better suited to a nightly automated process. Listing 5.11 shows the nightlyUnittest target.

LISTING 5.11   NightlyUnittest Target

```
<!-- nightlyUnittest target -->
<target name="nightlyUnittest"
        description="Run the nightly unit tests for the source code.">
    <junit haltonfailure="no"
           printsummary="yes"
           showoutput="yes"
           failureproperty="unittestFailed">
        <formatter type="plain" usefile="false" />
        <classpath refid="project.classpath"/>
        <batchtest>
            <fileset dir="${dirs.build}">
                <include name="com/**/*Test.class" />
            </fileset>
        </batchtest>
    </junit>

    <antcall target="cleanupUnittest" />
    <fail if="unittestFailed" message="One or more unit tests failed."/>
</target>
```

In this target, showoutput is set to yes, a plain formatter is used, and usefile is set to false, to direct the output to the screen. With these attributes set, the information from the unit-testing process is directed to the nightly log files and makes checking easier with an automated process or the build coordinator. Listing 5.12 shows the output of the nightlyUnittest target.

LISTING 5.12   Output from Run of nightlyUnittest Target

```
% ant nightlyUnittest
Buildfile: build.xml

nightlyUnittest:
    [junit] Running com.networksByteDesign.eMarket.inventory.companyTest
    [junit] Tests run: 2, Failures: 0, Errors: 0, Time elapsed: 0.032 sec
    [junit] Testsuite: com.networksByteDesign.eMarket.inventory.companyTest
    [junit] Tests run: 2, Failures: 0, Errors: 0, Time elapsed: 0.032 sec

    [junit] Testcase: testConstructor took 0.004 sec
    [junit] Testcase: testSetter took 0.001 sec
    [junit] Running com.networksByteDesign.eMarket.inventory.customerTest
    [junit] Tests run: 2, Failures: 1, Errors: 0, Time elapsed: 0.014 sec
    [junit] Testsuite: com.networksByteDesign.eMarket.inventory.customerTest
    [junit] Tests run: 2, Failures: 1, Errors: 0, Time elapsed: 0.014 sec

    [junit] Testcase: testConstructor took 0.003 sec
    [junit]     FAILED
    [junit] Expected exception was not thrown
    [junit] junit.framework.AssertionFailedError:
            Expected exception was not thrown

    [junit] Testcase: testConstructorTestcase: testSetter took 0 sec
    [junit] TEST
            com.networksByteDesign.eMarket.inventory.customerTest FAILED
    [junit] Running com.networksByteDesign.eMarket.inventory.salesItemTest
    [junit] ID = 123
    [junit] Name = Router
    [junit] ID = -123
    [junit] ID = 0
    [junit] Name =
    [junit] Name = null
    [junit] Tests run: 2, Failures: 1, Errors: 0, Time elapsed: 0.187 sec
    [junit] Testsuite:
            com.networksByteDesign.eMarket.inventory.salesItemTest
```

LISTING 5.12   Continued

```
[junit] Tests run: 2, Failures: 1, Errors: 0, Time elapsed: 0.187 sec
[junit] ------------ Standard Output --------------
[junit] ID = 123
[junit] Name = Router
[junit] ID = -123
[junit] ID = 0
[junit] Name =
[junit] Name = null
[junit] ------------ ---------------- --------------

[junit] Testcase: testConstructor took 0.002 sec
[junit]     FAILED
[junit] Expected exception was not thrown
[junit] junit.framework.AssertionFailedError:
        Expected exception was not thrown
[junit] Testcase: testConstructorTestcase: testSetter took 0.014 sec
[junit] TEST
        com.networksByteDesign.eMarket.inventory.salesItemTest FAILED

cleanupUnittest:

BUILD FAILED
file:/usr/projects/eMarket/build.xml:293: One or more unit tests failed.

Total time: 2 seconds
```

JUnitReport

Although the XML formatter provides a lot of valuable information, the output is not the easiest to read. Ant provides a junitreport task to assist in translating the XML output into a more useful format.

INSTALLING JUNITREPORT

To install JUnitReport, follow these steps:

1. Download Xalan from the following URL:

   http://xml.apache.org/xalan-j/

2. Add the xalan.jar file to your CLASSPATH or to the Ant lib directory.

Listing 5.13 shows the junitreport task, which can be added to the bottom of the unittest target.

LISTING 5.13   The JUnitReport Section of the unittest Target

```
<!-- unittestReport target -->
<target name="unittestReport">
    <junitreport todir="${dirs.test}">
        <fileset dir="${dirs.test}">
            <include name="TEST*.xml"/>
        </fileset>
        <report format="frames" todir="${dirs.test}"/>
    </junitreport>
</target>
```

The junitreport task sends its output to the ${dirs.test} directory. The report format is an HTML page that does not use frames. The files used are the TEST*.xml files output by the XML formatter. The XML files are first combined into a single file that contains all the unit test results, for passing to the XSLT. The XML file that contains all the unit test results is then placed in the todir attribute on the junitreport tag. By default, this file is named TEST-TestSuite.xml; this filename can be overridden with the tofile attribute. The HTML file is stored in the todir attribute on the report tag.

Format

When changing the format of the HTML output, you must decide whether to use frames. Depending on the look and usability desired, the frames and noframes approaches call different XSLT files to perform the translation. Figure 5.2 shows the output from the noframes format, and Figure 5.3 shows the output from the frames format.

XSLT Files

If additional formatting changes are needed in the HTML, whether cosmetic or functional, they can be achieved by changing the XSLT files used to transform the XML. The files must be named junit-frames.xsl and junit-noframes.xsl, respectively. The location of the new files can be defined by setting the styledir attribute of the report tag to the directory containing the files.

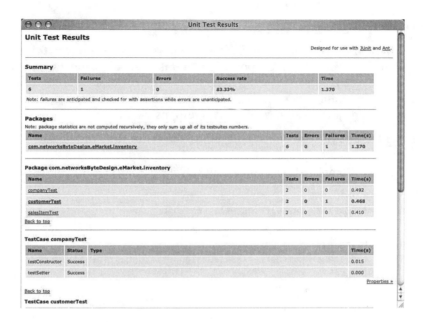

FIGURE 5.2   This JunitReport output is formatted without frames.

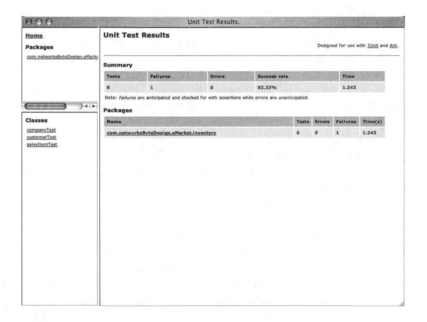

FIGURE 5.3   This JunitReport output is formatted with frames format.

Reports on Sets of Tests

The HTML report shows all of the unit test results. On a large project, this can be overwhelming. If you want the report to show only a small segment of the tests, simply create a JUnitReport target that includes only the desired unit test results. If you have a large team divided into groups that each work on a section of the project, each group then can focus on the tests it is responsible for.

Listing 5.14 shows the completed unit testing targets in the Ant buildfile.

LISTING 5.14   Completed Unit Testing Targets

```xml
<?xml version="1.0" ?>
<project name="eMarket" default="compile" basedir=".">

    <taskdef name="requiredInput"
            classname="com.networksByteDesign.util.RequiredInput"/>

    <taskdef name="cleanimps"
            classname="com.tombrus.cleanImports.ant.CleanImports"/>

    <property name="dirs.source"  value="/usr/projects/eMarket/src"      />
    <property name="dirs.backup"  value="${user.home}/backup"            />
    <property name="dirs.temp"    value="/tmp"                           />
    <property name="dirs.deploy"  value="/usr/projects/appServer/eMarket" />
    <property name="dirs.doc"     value="docs"                           />
    <property name="dirs.build"   value="build"                          />
    <property name="dirs.nightly" value="/usr/projects/eMarket/nightly"  />
    <property name="dirs.lib"     value="/usr/projects/lib"              />
    <property name="dirs.test"    value="test"                           />

    <property name="MailLogger.from"
            value="eMarketDev@networksByteDesign.com"/>
    <property name="MailLogger.success.to"
            value="eMarketDev@networksByteDesign.com"/>
    <property name="MailLogger.failure.to"
            value="eMarketDev@networksByteDesign.com"/>
    <property name="MailLogger.success.subject"
            value="eMarket Nightly Build Succeeded"/>
    <property name="MailLogger.failure.subject"
            value="eMarket Nightly Build Failed"/>

    <path id="project.classpath">
        <pathelement location="${dirs.lib}/all.jar"/>
```

LISTING 5.14   Continued

```
        <pathelement location="${dirs.build}"/>
    </path>

    <!-- compile target -->
    <target name="compile" description="Compile all of the source code.">
        <mkdir dir="${dirs.build}"/>

        <copy todir="${dirs.build}">
            <fileset dir="${dirs.source}" includes="**/*.*"/>
        </copy>

        <javac srcdir="${dirs.build}">
            <classpath refid="project.classpath"/>
        </javac>
    </target>
    <!-- nightlyUnittest target -->
    <target name="nightlyUnittest"
            description="Run the nightly unit tests for the source code.">
        <mkdir dir="${dirs.test}"/>
        <junit haltonfailure="no"
               printsummary="yes"
               showoutput="yes"
               fork="yes"
               failureproperty="unittestFailed">
            <formatter type="xml" usefile="true" />
            <classpath refid="project.classpath"/>
            <batchtest todir="${dirs.test}">
                <fileset dir="${dirs.build}">
                    <include name="com/**/*Test.class" />
                </fileset>
            </batchtest>
        </junit>

        <antcall target="unittestReport" />
        <antcall target="cleanupUnittest" />
        <fail if="unittestFailed" message="One or more unit tests failed."/>
    </target>

    <!-- unittestReport target -->
    <target name="unittestReport">
        <junitreport todir="${dirs.test}">
```

LISTING 5.14   Continued

```
            <fileset dir="${dirs.test}">
                <include name="TEST*.xml"/>
            </fileset>
            <report format="frames" todir="${dirs.test}"/>
        </junitreport>
    </target>
</project>
```

Now with the completed unit test and reporting in place, the development team gets a good indicator each morning as to the status of the build. Any problems can be quickly addressed while the source of the issue is still fresh in the developers' minds.

CruiseControl

Story

Given the rate at which changes are being made, Mark decides that he would like to perform the automated build more often than just nightly. Building and integrating more frequently than just nightly will allow problems to be discovered quickly, and corrective action to be taken before someone goes too far down the wrong path. Also, he would like to get away from the use of cron for initiating automated builds. Mark decides to use CruiseControl to implement a continuous build process, and Lisa and John sign up for this task. CruiseControl will be able to monitor their CVS repository and initiate a build only when code in the repository has changed.

CruiseControl is more than a platform-independent cron job for build processes. The advantage of CruiseControl is that it will monitor a revision control repository, periodically checking to see if anything has changed, and start an Ant build process if changes are detected. The configuration of CruiseControl gives it several pieces of information, including

- The location of the revision control repository

- The location of the Ant buildfile

- The frequency at which to check the repository and possibly perform a build

INSTALLING CRUISECONTROL

To install CruiseControl, follow these steps:

1. Download the CruiseControl distribution from the URL `cruisecontrol.sourceforge.net`.

2. Unzip the downloaded file.

3. Navigate into the `main` directory.

4. Run the build script `build.sh` (for Unix) or `build.bat` (for Windows). This creates a `dist` directory, and puts the `cruisecontrol.jar` file in it.

5. Run CruiseControl with one of the following two methods. (This assumes that the `config.xml` file is in the directory above the `dist` directory, and that we are running our command line from that directory.)

   - Run `cruisecontrol.sh` (for Unix) or `cruisecontrol.bat` (for Windows) with the following syntax:

     ```
     cruisecontrol.sh -projectname eMarket -configfile config.xml
     ```

   - Run CruiseControl from the command line as

     ```
     java -jar dist/cruisecontrol.jar -projectname eMarket
     ➥-configfile config.xml
     ```

Setting up a CruiseControl project requires a configuration file to be created. This file is usually called `config.xml`. Inside the `docs/helloWorld` directory of the CruiseControl distribution, there are baseline configuration files for various revision control systems, including CVS, Clearcase, and Visual SourceSafe. Start with the configuration file for the revision control system you're using and modify it to include the details of your project. Because the eMarket team is using CVS, that baseline config file is their starting point. The config file used for the project can be seen in Listing 5.15.

LISTING 5.15   Sample `config.xml` File for Use with CruiseControl

```xml
<cruisecontrol>
    <project name="eMarket">
        <bootstrappers>
            <currentbuildstatusbootstrapper file="currentbuild.txt" />
        </bootstrappers>
        <modificationset quietperiod="30" dateformat="yyyy-MMM-dd HH:mm:ss">
            <cvs cvsroot="/usr/local/cvsArchive"
                localworkingcopy="/usr/projects/eMarket"/>
        </modificationset>
        <schedule interval="30" intervaltype="relative">
            <ant buildfile="build.xml" target="nightlyBuild" multiple="1" />
        </schedule>
        <log dir="logs" />
        <publishers>
            <currentbuildstatuspublisher file="currentbuild.txt" />
            <email mailhost="mail.networksByteDesign.com"
                    returnaddress="eMarketDev@networksByteDesign.com"
                    buildresultsurl="http://localhost:8080/dev/BuildServlet">
```

LISTING 5.15   Continued

```
                <always address="eMarketDev@networksByteDesign.com" />
                <failure address="eMarketDev@networksByteDesign.com" />
            </email>
        </publishers>
        <plugin name="cvs"
                classname="net.sourceforge.cruisecontrol.sourcecontrols.CVS"
        />
        <plugin name="currentbuildstatusbootstrapper"
                classname="net.sourceforge.cruisecontrol.bootstrappers.Â
                  CurrentBuildStatusBootstrapper"
        />
        <plugin name="ant"
                classname="net.sourceforge.cruisecontrol.builders.AntBuilder"
        />
        <plugin name="email"
                classname="net.sourceforge.cruisecontrol.publishers.Â
                  LinkEmailPublisher"
        />
        <plugin name="currentbuildstatuspublisher"
                classname="net.sourceforge.cruisecontrol.publishers.Â
                  CurrentBuildStatusPublisher"
        />
        <plugin name="labelincrementer"
                classname="net.sourceforge.cruisecontrol.labelincrementers.Â
                  DefaultLabelIncrementer"
        />
    </project>
</cruisecontrol>
```

The first item to be set in the `config.xml` file is the project name. This is the project name given in the Ant buildfile that is to be executed, as shown here:

```
        <project name="eMarket">
```

The <bootstrappers> tag is used to configure bootstrappers, which are run before anything else in CruiseControl, regardless of whether a build actually takes place. The `currentbootstrapper` value is a file used by CruiseControl to tell whether a build is currently taking place. It can be the default value supplied, which is `currentbuild.txt`. Another bootstrapper that can be used is the `CVSBootstrapper`. The problem solved by this bootstrapper is how to extract the Ant buildfile from CVS in an Ant build process. If you rely on the Ant buildfile to perform the CVS update of the code, it will catch all source code changes except any that have occurred in the buildfile itself. The CVSBootstrapper allows you to perform an update of a single file, most likely the buildfile, before launching the Ant build.

The <modificationset> is used to define some information about how to handle changes in the revision control system. The quietperiod is the amount of time in seconds that CruiseControl should wait from the last change before it assumes that it's safe to pull from revision control. The purpose is to avoid pulling a snapshot of code that is in an indeterminate state. Suppose two files have to be updated in CVS. If CruiseControl happened to check after one of the files had been updated, but not the second, the build would most likely fail. Certainly the results would not be what we want. This parameter tells CruiseControl: "If anything changed, wait until everything has been stable for 'n' seconds before starting a build." The dateformat is a pattern describing the date-time format, and the default will usually suffice.

The <cvsroot> parameter must be set to the same value as the CVSROOT environment variable in the developer's environment, which is the location of the CVS ROOT repository.

The schedule interval defines how often CruiseControl will check to see if there are changes in the revision control repository. The default is 30 seconds. You may have to experiment with this value to find out what works best for your development team. Inside the schedule tag, the Ant build processes to be invoked are declared. CruiseControl permits more than one buildfile to be defined here. For the eMarket team, they have only one build process to execute. The parameter called multiple indicates how often the build should be run in the interval. For example, a value of 1 indicates that the build should be run one out of every one intervals, or every time. You might have some build processes or targets that you want to run less often. An example of this might be a clean build. There might be a reason you want to run a "clean" target one out of five times, so the interval would be set to 5. The result would be the XML shown here:

```
<schedule interval="30" intervaltype="relative">
    <ant buildfile="build.xml" target="clean"   multiple="5" />
    <ant buildfile="build.xml" target="eMarket" multiple="1" />
</schedule>
```

The log parameter defines where logging information is collected. The logger will merge generated log files into a single place after the build has run. The most notable example would be the results of unit tests. These would be condensed into a single logfile along with other build information to have a single place to look for build output.

The publishers are run after the build has run. A publisher sends build result information to some destination. The currentbuildstatuspublisher writes information to the file for the benefit of the CruiseControl JSP interface. The e-mail publisher will send a notification of the results of the build to the addresses specified. Different addresses can be configured for a successful build, or one that failed.

Finally, `plugin` names define the classes that CruiseControl needs to do the work. The defaults that are defined in the baseline configuration file will suffice for most projects. The plug-ins used for this example are shown in the configuration file.

Summary

In this chapter, our development team undertakes the task of creating an unattended build process. They begin by creating a nightly build target that checks out the latest version of the source from CVS and compiles it.

We then covered the wide variety of loggers and listeners provided through Ant. The development team finally settled on the MailLogger for producing feedback from the nightly build. We also looked at the different filemappers that Ant provides.

When the nightly build had some `CLASSPATH` issues, we looked at the concept of setting the `CLASSPATH` in the Ant targets. We also added a nightly `unittest` target. This provided the information necessary to hook in JUnitReport to provide HTML pages with the results of the `unittest` run.

Finally, we integrated CruiseControl to provide a continuous build process.

Deployment to a Test Environment

In the preceding chapter, the eMarket team structured their buildfile to be suitable for performing a nightly build. Up to this point, all of the testing has been done on the development server. As they begin to move to deploying to a test server, and eventually to their production environment, the buildfile has to change to accommodate the new requirements.

Story

The eMarket project team is in the middle of another release cycle. The first release to the customer was made available on the development server. Until now, deployment has only involved copying the appropriate files to the directory structure for the Web and app servers. Because the deployment area is in the reloadable classpath of the app server, it hasn't even been necessary to restart the app server after deployment. The team did put some steps into place to tar and untar files to the development server area.

This time around, the team will deploy to a test server, so they need to start getting things in place. The first steps will be to refactor the buildfile to clean it up. In refactoring the buildfile, the team will design it to perform essentially the same process on the development and test servers. The deployment process will now create JAR files, using the Ant <jar> task, and package everything up into a WAR file for deployment with the <war> task. WAR files will now be the means of deployment to the development server, test server, and eventually to the production Web server farm.

John and Lisa begin work on refactoring the buildfile. As they start to make the necessary changes for deploying to development and test, they quickly realize that most of the steps involved are common to deployment to both environments. In the development environment, deployment involves copying the final WAR file to the webapps directory on the same server. For the test environment, they simply need to FTP the WAR file to the webapps directory of the test app server. Lisa and John refactor the buildfile to create JAR files of certain common utilities, and a WAR file for deployment of the entire Web application.

Deployment of an application can be a complex operation. Fortunately, Ant is well suited for deploying many different types of applications. Depending on the nature of the application, different considerations are involved in the design of the deployment process. For example, if the application is written in C++, and is a standalone executable, all that may be required is a simple FTP of the executable file to a server. If the executable happens to be dynamically linked, and requires .so or .dll libraries to be included, deployment may also require additional steps. An entire directory structure may need to be tarred or zipped, and the resulting compressed file would be expanded on a destination server with the inverse operation, such as untar or unzip. A Java application might be simply deployed as a set of class files, or a JAR file that needs to be constructed and transferred to a release area. If the Java application is a Web application, a WAR file may need to be built that includes the appropriate deployment descriptors. An application with Enterprise JavaBeans (EJBs) may also have special requirements for deployment. Regardless of the requirements, just about any deployment process can be automated with Ant. In this chapter, we will examine how to use Ant to solve some of the problems commonly involved in creating a deployment process.

Working with JAR Files

The <jar> task is used to create Java JAR (*Java ARchive*) files for release. This task was briefly introduced in Chapter 3, "The First Iteration." The <jar> task, however, has many more capabilities that have not yet been discussed, which will be covered in this chapter.

The directory structure within a JAR file consists of a META-INF directory that contains the manifest, usually called MANIFEST.MF. The manifest contains meta-information about the contents of the JAR, which we'll examine in a few moments. Also contained within the JAR is a directory structure that matches the package structure of the contained class files. With the Ant <jar> task, it's possible to control various aspects of JAR file construction, such as the contents of the manifest file, or whether directory entries are included in the JAR file.

Let's look at the changes that the eMarket Team will have to make to their buildfile in preparation for creating a JAR file. The buildfile already has a compile target that uses <javac> to compile the Java source code. Currently, the eMarket team has a step that performs code generation, so the Java source code files get copied to a staging area and then compiled. The <javac> task does have an attribute that can be used to compile the class files to a destination directory tree that matches the package structure. This is essentially invoking the javac compiler with the -d option. We'll cover the use of this a bit later. Our reasons for handling the build in this manner are: First, not all of the class files will be included in the JAR file. The unit test classes will not be included because we are not going to deploy the unit tests to the test and production servers. The servlet classes will be in the `classes` directory of the final WAR file and do not need to be in the JAR. Second, there are files that are not class files that need to be included in the final WAR file, such as the `web.xml` file. So, rules will be required in the buildfile to sort through all of these requirements anyway.

The `compile` target shown in the following code creates the destination build directory with the `<mkdir>` task. This directory is where the generated and handwritten Java files will be copied. Next, the target copies the source code to the staging area with the `<copy>` task. Finally, the `<javac>` task is invoked to compile the Java source code:

```
<target name="compile" description="Compile all of the source code.">
    <mkdir dir="${dirs.build}"/>

    <copy todir="${dirs.build}">
        <fileset dir="${dirs.source}" includes="**/*.*"/>
    </copy>

    <javac srcdir="${dirs.build}">
        <classpath refid="project.classpath"/>
    </javac>

</target>
```

The first step is to modify the buildfile to construct the actual JAR file using the `<jar>` task. The `<jar>` task requires at a minimum the name of the JAR to create (the `jarfile` attribute), and the name of the directory at which to begin the jar operation. The starting point for the jar operation can be defined either through the `basedir` attribute, or by using a nested `<fileset>`. We will use the latter. In setting the `jarfile` attribute, we make use of the built-in Ant property `${ant.project.name}`, and append the `.jar` suffix. So, the JAR file will be called `eMarket.jar`. Next, the `basedir` is specified using a `<fileset>`. The directory to start at is specified with the `dir` attribute, and we filter the fileset with the `includes` attribute to include only class files. Here is the XML task definition showing our use of the `<jar>` task.

```
<jar jarfile="${ant.project.name}.jar">
    <fileset dir="${dirs.build}" includes="**/*.class" />
</jar>
```

To recap, this snippet will build a JAR file in the directory determined by the value of the property `${dirs.build}`, with the name `eMarket.jar`. Ant will include all class files found in the directory set by the property ${dirs.build} into the JAR file. Now let's include this target in the buildfile that will set the appropriate properties, compile the class, and construct the basic JAR file. This buildfile is shown in Listing 6.1.

LISTING 6.1   Buildfile That Includes a Target to Build a JAR File Using the Ant <jar> Task

```xml
<?xml version="1.0" ?>
<project name="eMarket" default="compile" basedir=".">

    <taskdef name="requiredInput"
             classname="com.networksByteDesign.util.RequiredInput"/>

    <taskdef name="cleanimps"
             classname="com.tombrus.cleanImports.ant.CleanImports"/>

    <property name="dirs.source"  value="/usr/projects/eMarket/src"       />
    <property name="dirs.backup"  value="${user.home}/backup"             />
    <property name="dirs.temp"    value="/tmp"                            />
    <property name="dirs.deploy"  value="/usr/projects/appServer/eMarket" />
    <property name="dirs.doc"     value="docs"                           />
    <property name="dirs.build"   value="build"                          />
    <property name="dirs.nightly" value="/usr/projects/eMarket/nightly"   />
    <property name="dirs.lib"     value="/usr/projects/lib"              />
    <property name="dirs.test"    value="test"                           />

    <property name="MailLogger.from"
             value="eMarketDev@networksByteDesign.com"/>
    <property name="MailLogger.success.to"
             value="eMarketDev@networksByteDesign.com"/>
    <property name="MailLogger.failure.to"
             value="eMarketDev@networksByteDesign.com"/>
    <property name="MailLogger.success.subject"
             value="eMarket Nightly Build Succeeded"/>
    <property name="MailLogger.failure.subject"
             value="eMarket Nightly Build Failed"/>

    <path id="project.classpath">
        <pathelement location="${dirs.lib}/all.jar"/>
        <pathelement location="${dirs.build}"/>
    </path>
```

LISTING 6.1   Continued

```
<!-- compile target -->
<target name="compile" description="Compile all of the source code.">
    <mkdir dir="${dirs.build}"/>

    <copy todir="${dirs.build}">
        <fileset dir="${dirs.source}" includes="**/*.*"/>
    </copy>

    <javac srcdir="${dirs.build}">
        <classpath refid="project.classpath"/>
    </javac>
</target>

<!-- deploy target -->
<target name="deploy" description="Simple deployment of the app">
    <tstamp />

    <jar jarfile="${ant.project.name}.jar">
        <fileset dir="${dirs.build}" includes="**/*.class" />
    </jar>

    <copy file="${ant.project.name}.jar"
          todir="${dirs.deploy}" />

    <copy todir="${dirs.deploy}">
        <mapper type="flatten" />
        <fileset dir="${dirs.build}" includes="**/*.jsp"/>
        <filterset>
            <filter token="username" value="${user.name}"/>
            <filter token="date"
                    value="${DSTAMP}:${TSTAMP}"/>
        </filterset>
    </copy>
</target>

</project>
```

As an aside, some teams create timestamped versions of their generated objects through the use of the <tstamp> and <dstamp> tasks discussed in Chapter 2, "Creating Initial Spikes." Remember that these tasks set a timestamp on several intrinsic properties of Ant: ${DSTAMP}, {TSTAMP}, and ${TODAY}. These properties can be used later in the buildfile for anything that might need a timestamp in it. For example, the ${DSTAMP} property could be used to copy the JAR file to a file that has the current date in the filename, in the following manner:

```
<copy file="${dist}/${jarfile.name}"
      tofile="${dist}/${jarfile.prefix}-${DSTAMP}.jar"/>
```

This is a simple way of automatically versioning generated objects. The source code is simply one aspect of re-creating a build. Other components such as the version of the compiler, system libraries, and tool versions all play a part in re-creating the same generated objects. This is one reason being able to retrieve the generated object as it was built on a specific date may be useful to a team.

The eMarket team's buildfile now has a target to perform the creation of a JAR file. From the command line, we can perform the command jar -tvf eMarket.jar, which shows the structure of the resulting JAR file. The output of this command can be seen in Listing 6.2.

LISTING 6.2   The Structure of the JAR File Resulting from the Buildfile of Listing 6.1

```
% jar -tvf eMarket.jar
    0 Sat Jan 25 11:17:46 CST 2003 META-INF/
   55 Sat Jan 25 11:17:46 CST 2003 META-INF/MANIFEST.MF
    0 Sat Jan 25 11:17:30 CST 2003 com/
    0 Sat Jan 25 11:17:30 CST 2003 com/networksByteDesign/
    0 Sat Jan 25 11:17:30 CST 2003 com/networksByteDesign/eMarket/
    0 Sat Jan 25 11:17:34 CST 2003 com/networksByteDesign/eMarket/inventory/
  708 Sat Jan 25 11:17:34 CST 2003
               com/networksByteDesign/eMarket/inventory/company.class
 1464 Sat Jan 25 11:17:34 CST 2003
               com/networksByteDesign/eMarket/inventory/companyTest.class
  689 Sat Jan 25 11:17:34 CST 2003
               com/networksByteDesign/eMarket/inventory/customer.class
 1466 Sat Jan 25 11:17:34 CST 2003
               com/networksByteDesign/eMarket/inventory/customerTest.class
 1031 Sat Jan 25 11:17:34 CST 2003
               com/networksByteDesign/eMarket/inventory/salesItem.class
 1468 Sat Jan 25 11:17:34 CST 2003
               com/networksByteDesign/eMarket/inventory/salesItemTest.class
    0 Sat Jan 25 11:17:34 CST 2003 com/networksByteDesign/spike/
  149 Sat Jan 25 11:17:34 CST 2003 com/networksByteDesign/spike/test1.class
  149 Sat Jan 25 11:17:34 CST 2003 com/networksByteDesign/spike/test2.class
```

LISTING 6.2   Continued

```
149 Sat Jan 25 11:17:34 CST 2003 com/networksByteDesign/spike/test3.class
149 Sat Jan 25 11:17:34 CST 2003 com/networksByteDesign/spike/test4.class
149 Sat Jan 25 11:17:34 CST 2003 com/networksByteDesign/spike/test5.class
149 Sat Jan 25 11:17:34 CST 2003 com/networksByteDesign/spike/test6.class
149 Sat Jan 25 11:17:34 CST 2003 com/networksByteDesign/spike/test7.class
```

We see that the directory structure mirrors the package structure of the Java classes. Also included is the META-INF directory with the manifest file.

The filesonly Attribute

If for some reason, you wanted to create a JAR file that doesn't have empty directory entries in it, but only the actual fully qualified files (class and manifest), you could use the filesonly attribute on the <jar> task. In the example shown previously in Listing 6.2, doing a jar -tvf yields the following entries:

```
com/
com/networksByteDesign/
com/networksByteDesign/eMarket/
com/networksByteDesign/eMarket/inventory
com/networksByteDesign/eMarket/inventory/company.class
```

Using the filesonly attribute will result in the removal of entries that don't have a class file associated with them. So, the only entry that would be left is

```
com/networksByteDesign/eMarket/inventory/company.class
```

The directory structure, which matches the package structure, is kept intact, which is required for the JAR file to work correctly. The filesonly attribute only removes entries in the JAR file that don't have a file included as part of the entry, such as com/, and com/networksByteDesign/, and so on. The filesonly attribute is optional, and the default behavior of the <jar> task is to act as if the attribute is set to false. In the following snippet, the definition of <jar> task in our buildfile is changed to illustrate the use of this attribute:

```
<jar jarfile="${ant.project.name}.jar" filesonly="true">
    <fileset dir="${dirs.build}" includes="**/*.class" />
</jar>
```

If we rerun our buildfile, the result is a JAR file with the structure shown in Listing 6.3. Note that the META-INF directory still has a directory entry.

LISTING 6.3   The JAR File Structure That Results from Setting the `filesonly` Attribute to `true`

```
% jar -tvf eMarket.jar
    0 Sat Jan 25 11:26:02 CST 2003 META-INF/
   55 Sat Jan 25 11:26:02 CST 2003 META-INF/MANIFEST.MF
  708 Sat Jan 25 11:17:34 CST 2003
                 com/networksByteDesign/eMarket/inventory/company.class
 1464 Sat Jan 25 11:17:34 CST 2003
                 com/networksByteDesign/eMarket/inventory/companyTest.class
  689 Sat Jan 25 11:17:34 CST 2003
                 com/networksByteDesign/eMarket/inventory/customer.class
 1466 Sat Jan 25 11:17:34 CST 2003
                 com/networksByteDesign/eMarket/inventory/customerTest.class
 1031 Sat Jan 25 11:17:34 CST 2003
                 com/networksByteDesign/eMarket/inventory/salesItem.class
 1468 Sat Jan 25 11:17:34 CST 2003
                 com/networksByteDesign/eMarket/inventory/salesItemTest.class
  149 Sat Jan 25 11:17:34 CST 2003 com/networksByteDesign/spike/test1.class
  149 Sat Jan 25 11:17:34 CST 2003 com/networksByteDesign/spike/test2.class
  149 Sat Jan 25 11:17:34 CST 2003 com/networksByteDesign/spike/test3.class
  149 Sat Jan 25 11:17:34 CST 2003 com/networksByteDesign/spike/test4.class
  149 Sat Jan 25 11:17:34 CST 2003 com/networksByteDesign/spike/test5.class
  149 Sat Jan 25 11:17:34 CST 2003 com/networksByteDesign/spike/test6.class
  149 Sat Jan 25 11:17:34 CST 2003 com/networksByteDesign/spike/test7.class
```

Using Nested Filesets

As previously mentioned, the `<jar>` task can be used with a nested `<fileset>` element, as opposed to the `basedir` attribute. The advantage to using a nested `<fileset>` is the ability to exclude and include certain files. Suppose we have unit test files that we don't want to include in our JAR file. As mentioned earlier, we don't want to include our JUnit tests' class files in a JAR file. Because we followed the naming convention of ending in `Test.java`, we can create a rule for excluding the unit tests. For example, the class `Sort.java` has a unit test called `SortTest.java`. In addition to being useful in specifying the unit tests in a `<batchtest>`, a naming convention also enables us to easily exclude these files from our JAR file. Using the `<fileset>` element, we can exclude the class `SortTest` from our JAR file. The modified `<jar>` task definition is shown in the following XML snippet:

```
<!-- deploy target -->
<target name="deploy" description="Simple deployment of the app">
    <tstamp />
```

```
        <jar jarfile="${ant.project.name}.jar" filesonly="true">
            <fileset dir="${dirs.build}">
                <exclude name="**/*Test.class" />
                <include name="**/*.class" />
            </fileset>
        </jar>

        <copy file="${ant.project.name}.jar" todir="${dirs.deploy}" />
        <copy file="${ant.project.name}.jar"
            tofile="${dirs.backup}/${ant.project.name}-${DSTAMP}.jar" />

        <copy todir="${dirs.deploy}">
            <mapper type="flatten" />
            <fileset dir="${dirs.build}" includes="**/*.jsp"/>
            <filterset>
                <filter token="username" value="${user.name}"/>
                <filter token="date"     value="${DSTAMP}:${TSTAMP}"/>
            </filterset>
        </copy>
    </target>
```

Executing this target will result in a JAR file that contains only the classes we want to deploy, while omitting the unit test classes.

Another factor we can control in JAR file creation is the contents of the manifest file in the META-INF directory. By default, the <jar> task creates a default manifest, which is shown here:

```
Manifest-Version: 1.0
Created-By: Apache Ant 1.5.3
```

The Ant <manifest> task can be used to create a custom manifest file. The <manifest> task has two attributes, and uses nested <attribute> elements. The first attribute, which is required, is file. This nested attribute defines the name of the manifest file to create. The second attribute, which is optional, is mode. The mode attribute indicates whether <manifest> should update or replace the target manifest file. Defining the contents of the manifest file is accomplished with <attribute> elements. Listing 6.4 shows a buildfile that uses the <manifest> task to create a custom manifest file, and include it in the JAR file. This listing also illustrates some of the nested attribute values that are available for the <manifest> task.

LISTING 6.4   Buildfile to Generate a Manifest File Called MANIFEST.MF, Which Is the Standard Name for This File

```
<!-- manifest target -->
<target name="manifest">
    <property name="version" value="1.1" />
    <tstamp />

    <manifest file="${dirs.build}/MANIFEST.MF">
        <attribute name="Built-By" value="eMarket Team"/>
        <section name="common">
            <attribute name="Specification-Title"
                       value="test" />
            <attribute name="Specification-Version"
                       value="${version}" />
            <attribute name="Specification-Vendor"
                       value="Networks Byte Design, Inc." />
            <attribute name="Implementation-Title"
                       value="common" />
            <attribute name="Implementation-Version"
                       value="${version} ${DSTAMP}" />
            <attribute name="Sealed"
                       value="true"/>
            <attribute name="Implementation-Vendor"
                       value="Networks Byte Design, Inc." />
        </section>
    </manifest>
</target>

<!-- deploy target -->
<target name="deploy"
        depends="manifest"
        description="Simple deployment of the app">
    <jar jarfile="${ant.project.name}.jar"
         filesonly="true"
         manifest="${dirs.build}/MANIFEST.MF">
        <fileset dir="${dirs.build}">
            <exclude name="**/*Test.class" />
            <include name="**/*.class" />
        </fileset>
    </jar>
```

LISTING 6.4   Continued

```
            <copy file="${ant.project.name}.jar" todir="${dirs.deploy}" />
            <copy file="${ant.project.name}.jar"
                  tofile="${dirs.backup}/${ant.project.name}-${DSTAMP}.jar" />

            <copy todir="${dirs.deploy}">
                <mapper type="flatten" />
                <fileset dir="${dirs.build}" includes="**/*.jsp"/>
                <filterset>
                    <filter token="username" value="${user.name}"/>
                    <filter token="date"     value="${DSTAMP}:${TSTAMP}"/>
                </filterset>
            </copy>
        </target>
```

Listing 6.5 shows the `MANIFEST.MF` file that was generated by running the `manifest` target.

LISTING 6.5   The `MANIFEST.MF` File Generated by the Buildfile of Listing 6.4

```
Manifest-Version: 1.0
Created-By: Apache Ant 1.5.3
Built-By: eMarket Team

Name: common
Specification-Title: test
Specification-Version: 1.1
Specification-Vendor: Networks Byte Design, Inc.
Implementation-Title: common
Implementation-Version: 1.1 20030125
Sealed: true
Implementation-Vendor: Networks Byte Design, Inc.
```

The `<manifest>` task permits all aspects of the manifest file to be defined. Ant still added the `Created-By` line. Most of the attributes are self-explanatory. An interesting attribute is the value of `Sealed`. Setting the `Sealed` attribute in a JAR file to `true` results in a sealed JAR file. Using a sealed JAR file means that the JVM expects all classes in a package to originate from the same JAR file. This prevents the possibility of accidentally or deliberately overriding a class and including it in the classpath prior to the sealed JAR file. Any attempt to override a class in the JAR file with a class outside the JAR file will result in a "sealing violation" at runtime. Another interesting point is that the `Implementation-Version` attribute has information included from the `<tstamp>` task. If you use the intrinsic Ant attribute `${DSTAMP}` in that attribute in the buildfile, the creation date is automatically embedded in the manifest file.

Packages within a JAR file can be sealed. An optional step, sealing a package, means that all the classes with that package must be contained within this one JAR file. Classes that are part of the package cannot be picked up from anywhere else, or a sealing violation will occur at runtime. There are several reasons why you might want to seal packages in a JAR file. One reason is security considerations, particularly in applets. Sealing will prevent someone from overriding a class file with their own implementation that contains malicious code.

Another reason for sealing packages in a JAR file is simply to prevent an incompatible version of a class from being picked up elsewhere. Suppose that during development, someone removes a class from a package, but inadvertently fails to remove all dependencies to that class. If a user happens to have a copy of the class somewhere in their classpath, it will get picked up at runtime. This could cause a problem that could be hard to track down. However, if the package is sealed within its JAR file, this discrepancy will be immediately detected at runtime because a sealing violation will occur.

JAR files are sealed with an entry in the `manifest.mf` file found in the `META-INF` directory of the JAR file. Here is an example of a manifest entry that will cause the package `com.networksByteDesign.eMarket.util` to be sealed:

```
Name: com/networksByteDesign/eMarket/util/
Sealed: true
```

The first line contains the name of a package within the JAR file, which in this case is `com/networksByteDesign/eMarket/util/`. The next line, `Sealed: true`, indicates that the package right before it is to be sealed. This sealed declaration only applies to the previous package because it occurs immediately after it with no blank lines in between. This is actually true of any header that follows the `Name` value. That is, any header that immediately follows the `Name` header will apply to it. Now at runtime, if the JVM attempts to pick up a class in this package that is not part of this JAR file, the sealing violation makes the problem immediately apparent.

Signed JAR Files

Ant also contains a task for signing JAR files, called `<signjar>`. This task invokes the `jarsigner` process and requires that the user have a set of public keys, which adds some additional complexity.

JAR files can be deployed or can be expanded back into their directory structure. Some teams may elect not to include the JAR file in their classpath, but might deploy their classes by expanding the JAR file to a directory that is included in the classpath. The one thing to be careful of when doing this is to clean up old class files before expanding the JAR file. Otherwise, you run the risk of "garbage" piling up, which consists of old, obsolete class files that might have an impact on the behavior of the application.

Expanding a JAR File with `<unjar>`

Ant provides the `<unjar>` task to expand a single JAR file, or set of JAR files. The attributes associated with `<unjar>` are

- `src` (or a nested `<fileset>`)
- `dest`
- `overwrite`

The example in Listing 6.6 will expand the JAR file we created in Listing 6.4 into the directory defined by the `${dirs.deploy}` property.

LISTING 6.6   Target to Expand a JAR File

```
<!-- expand target -->
<target name="expand" description="Expands the project jar file.">
    <unjar src="${dirs.deploy}/${ant.project.name}.jar"
           dest="${dirs.deploy}" />
</target>
```

The `<unjar>` task will overwrite the target files by default. This behavior can be changed by setting the overwrite attribute to `false`, as shown in Listing 6.7.

LISTING 6.7   Target to Expand a JAR File Without Overwriting Existing Files

```
<!-- expand target -->
<target name="expand" description="Expands the project jar file.">
    <unjar src="${dirs.deploy}/${ant.project.name}.jar"
           overwrite="false"
           dest="${dirs.deploy}" />
</target>
```

Now, if the JAR file has been previously expanded, the files won't be overwritten if the expand target is run again. The only way to re-expand the JAR file is to remove the old files first.

USE OF `overwrite` **ATTRIBUTE OF** `<unjar>` **TASK**

The use of `overwrite` will only prevent existing files from being overwritten. Suppose we have the following scenario. Our src directory has a class called `Simple.java`. We perform the build and deployment, expanding the JAR file. In our deployment directory, we have the directory containing `com/networksByteDesign/eMarket/utils/Simple.class`. Suppose a developer adds a new class called `Simple2.java`, and makes changes to the class `Simple.java` that has dependencies on `Simple2`. The package is rebuilt and redeployed with the `<unjar>` task, with `overwrite="false"`. The result is that the file `Simple.class` is not replaced, but `Simple2.class` is added. However, `Simple.class` is not compatible with `Simple2.class`. The result will be a runtime error.

Deploying Applications as WAR Files

A *Web Component Archive,* or WAR file, can be deployed to an app server by dropping into the webapps directory of the app server, and restarting the server. The WAR file is then expanded. A WAR file is structured in the following way. The top-level directory is called the *document root.* Below the document root is a directory called WEB-INF. This directory is not directly visible in the URL for the Web application. The WEB-INF directory contains a file called web.xml, which is the deployment descriptor for the application contained to be deployed. Class files for the application should be contained beneath the WEB-INF directory. Some application servers do vary on where the app is to be deployed. Most application servers, such as Tomcat, expect the servlet classes to reside beginning in a directory called WEB-INF/classes.

The Ant <war> task invokes the JAR process, but contains some nice shortcuts for creating the proper directory structure for a WAR file. Let's begin by writing the Ant target to construct a WAR file for deployment to some generic application server. Listing 6.8 shows a buildfile target that uses the <war> task to build our WAR file.

LISTING 6.8   Buildfile for Creating a WAR File

```
<!-- deploy target -->
<target name="deploy"
        depends="manifest"
        description="Simple deployment of the app">
    <jar jarfile="${ant.project.name}.jar"
         filesonly="true"
         manifest="${dirs.build}/MANIFEST.MF">
        <fileset dir="${dirs.build}">
            <exclude name="**/*Test.class" />
            <exclude name="**/*Servlet.class" />
            <include name="**/*.class" />
        </fileset>
```

LISTING 6.8   Continued

```
        </jar>

        <copy file="${ant.project.name}.jar" todir="${dirs.deploy}" />
        <copy file="${ant.project.name}.jar"
            tofile="${dirs.backup}/${ant.project.name}-${DSTAMP}.jar" />

        <war destfile="${ant.project.name}.war"
            filesonly="true"
            webxml="${dirs.source}/web.xml"
            manifest="${dirs.build}/MANIFEST.MF">
            <classes dir="${dirs.build}">
                <include name="**/*Servlet.class" />
            </classes>
            <lib dir=".">
                <include name="${ant.project.name}.jar" />
            </lib>
        </war>

        <copy todir="${dirs.deploy}">
            <mapper type="flatten" />
            <fileset dir="${dirs.build}" includes="**/*.jsp"/>
            <filterset>
                <filter token="username" value="${user.name}"/>
                <filter token="date"     value="${DSTAMP}:${TSTAMP}"/>
            </filterset>
        </copy>
    </target>
```

The buildfile of Listing 6.8 will create the WAR file shown in Listing 6.9.

LISTING 6.9   WAR File Created with the <war> Task in the Buildfile of Listing 6.8

```
% jar -tvf eMarket.war
   0 Sat Jan 25 13:41:26 CST 2003 META-INF/
 331 Sat Jan 25 13:41:26 CST 2003 META-INF/MANIFEST.MF
   0 Sat Jan 25 13:41:26 CST 2003 WEB-INF/classes/
1267 Sat Jan 25 13:36:06 CST 2003
WEB-INF/classes/com/networksByteDesign/eMarket/inventory/CompanyServlet.class
5068 Sat Jan 25 13:36:06 CST 2003
WEB-INF/classes/com/networksByteDesign/eMarket/inventory/CustomerServlet.class
4269 Sat Jan 25 13:36:06 CST 2003
```

LISTING 6.9 Continued

```
WEB-INF/classes/com/networksByteDesign/eMarket/inventory/SalesItemServlet.class
3958 Sat Jan 25 13:36:06 CST 2003
WEB-INF/classes/com/networksByteDesign/eMarket/MainMenuServlet.class
   0 Sat Jan 25 13:41:26 CST 2003 WEB-INF/lib/
4692 Sat Jan 25 13:36:08 CST 2003 WEB-INF/lib/eMarket.jar
2909 Sat Jan 25 12:27:32 CST 2003 WEB-INF/web.xml
```

The `<war>` task will take the `web.xml` file named in the `webxml` attribute and place it in the `WEB-INF` directory. The `classes` directory is a subdirectory of the `WEB-INF` directory. This buildfile didn't explicitly create the `WEB-INF` directory; the `<war>` task created it automatically.

Another possibility for our WAR file might be that we want to include some JavaServer Pages (JSP files). In addition to JSP pages, a tag library might also be part of the distribution. For this deployment, we need to place the Java class files, the deployment descriptor, the JSP pages, and the `taglib.tld` file in their correct positions in the WAR file. JSP files can be precompiled, and in fact, this is a good idea for security reasons. JSP precompilation is covered in Chapter 10, "Additional Teams Adopt the XP Process."

NOTE

Numerous security vulnerabilities have occurred in Web application servers that can serve JSP pages where the source code for the JSP pages was exposed. If you precompile the JSP pages, the source code is never deployed to the production servers. This is one technique you can use to help mitigate the risk of exposing source code to an attacker.

In this example, the JSP files are in the `src` directory, along with the Java source code, the `web.xml` deployment descriptor, and the `tablib.tld` tag library descriptor. Later in this chapter, we'll look at ways to dynamically generate several types of deployment descriptors with a tool called XDoclet. This buildfile is shown in Listing 6.10.

LISTING 6.10 Buildfile for Creating WAR File for Deployment on Apache Tomcat, Containing JSPs and Taglibs

```
<!-- deploy target -->
<target name="deploy"
        depends="manifest"
        description="Simple deployment of the app">
    <jar jarfile="${ant.project.name}.jar"
```

LISTING 6.10   Continued

```
                filesonly="true"
                manifest="${dirs.build}/MANIFEST.MF">
            <fileset dir="${dirs.build}">
                <exclude name="**/*Test.class" />
                <exclude name="**/*Servlet.class" />
                <include name="**/*.class" />
            </fileset>
        </jar>

        <copy file="${ant.project.name}.jar"
            tofile="${dirs.backup}/${ant.project.name}-${DSTAMP}.jar" />

        <war destfile="${ant.project.name}.war"
            filesonly="true"
            webxml="${dirs.source}/web.xml"
            manifest="${dirs.build}/MANIFEST.MF">
            <fileset dir="${dirs.build}" includes="taglib.tld" />
            <fileset dir="${dirs.build}" includes="**/*.jsp"   />
            <classes dir="${dirs.build}">
                <include name="**/*Servlet.class" />
            </classes>
            <lib dir=".">
                <include name="${ant.project.name}.jar" />
            </lib>
        </war>

        <copy file="${ant.project.name}.jar" todir="${dirs.deploy}" />

        <copy todir="${dirs.deploy}">
            <mapper type="flatten" />
            <fileset dir="${dirs.build}" includes="**/*.jsp"/>
            <filterset>
                <filter token="username" value="${user.name}"/>
                <filter token="date"     value="${DSTAMP}:${TSTAMP}"/>
            </filterset>
        </copy>
    </target>
```

The resulting WAR file contains the structure as shown in Listing 6.11.

LISTING 6.11   The Structure of the WAR File Containing JSP Pages and Taglibs, Created Through the Buildfile of Listing 6.10

```
% jar -tvf eMarket.war
    0 Sat Jan 25 15:00:18 CST 2003 META-INF/
  331 Sat Jan 25 15:00:18 CST 2003 META-INF/MANIFEST.MF
  665 Sat Jan 25 15:00:14 CST 2003 taglib.tld
  192 Sat Jan 25 15:00:14 CST 2003 FAQ.jsp
 2414 Sat Jan 25 15:00:14 CST 2003 Login.jsp
 2717 Sat Jan 25 15:00:14 CST 2003 Signup.jsp
    0 Sat Jan 25 15:00:18 CST 2003 WEB-INF/classes/
 1267 Sat Jan 25 15:00:16 CST 2003
WEB-INF/classes/com/networksByteDesign/eMarket/inventory/CompanyServlet.class
 5068 Sat Jan 25 15:00:16 CST 2003
WEB-INF/classes/com/networksByteDesign/eMarket/inventory/CustomerServlet.class
 4269 Sat Jan 25 15:00:16 CST 2003
WEB-INF/classes/com/networksByteDesign/eMarket/inventory/SalesItemServlet.class
 3958 Sat Jan 25 15:00:16 CST 2003
WEB-INF/classes/com/networksByteDesign/eMarket/MainMenuServlet.class
    0 Sat Jan 25 15:00:18 CST 2003 WEB-INF/lib/
 4692 Sat Jan 25 15:00:18 CST 2003 WEB-INF/lib/eMarket.jar
 2909 Sat Jan 25 12:27:32 CST 2003 WEB-INF/web.xml
```

Deployment with XDoclet

Story

One afternoon, Michael and John deployed a build on the development server and began running a few tests of the Web interface. They began to encounter a problem with a particular page. While they were attempting to select an item to get more product details, the application would hang. They spent the rest of the afternoon going through logging information, and adding additional log4j statements into the code to try to trace the problem. They double-checked and verified that all of the unit tests had run and that everything had passed.

Eventually they tracked down the problem. A new EJB had been added, but the deployment descriptor hadn't been updated to reflect this change. In fact, this was a general problem in that sometimes it was easy to forget to add or modify entries in the deployment descriptors. This was true for EJBs, for taglibs, and for the web.xml file as well. The problem was compounded by the fact that unit tests do not catch this type of mistake. The problem did slow down the velocity of the iteration.

Several possibilities were considered, which included finding a way to validate deployment descriptors, and dynamically generating the deployment descriptors. After a few quick spike tests, and a discussion with the group, the group agreed that they would start to dynamically generate all deployment descriptors with the tool XDoclet.

XDoclet is a doclet engine that generates several different types of deployment descriptors, and even some Java source code for EJBs. XDoclet is available through SourceForge, and is intended solely for use with Ant. It has numerous features and is itself extensible. In fact, there are so many nuances about XDoclet that a book could probably be written about the subject. We'll limit the scope of the discussion of XDoclet to a few core examples that will meet the needs of the eMarket team, which includes three major capabilities of XDoclet. XDoclet will be used to generate the following:

1. The web.xml deployment descriptor for a WAR file

2. Deployment descriptors and supporting Java classes for Enterprise JavaBeans (EJBs)

3. A tag library descriptor (taglib.tld) for use with JavaServer Pages (JSPs)

INSTALLING XDOCLET

To install XDoclet, follow these steps:

1. Download XDoclet from

   http://sourceforge.net/projects/xdoclet/

2. Unzip the XDoclet zip file.

3. The lib directory contains the xdoclet.jar file. Put this JAR file in your classpath.

Generating a Web Deployment Descriptor with XDoclet

XDoclet has a task called <webdoclet> that is intended for the creation of web.xml WAR file deployment descriptors. In order to use XDoclet, special javadoc tags must be embedded in the source code that will be processed when the doclet runs. For <webdoclet> there is a set of tags that are of the form @web:*tagname*. Listing 6.12 shows a simple servlet class that has XDoclet tags embedded in it. Deployment descriptor values are set as attributes of the tag. Several servlet parameters can be set with the tag @web:servlet. For example, if the servlet name is MainMenuServlet, the display-name is set to Main Menu Servlet, and the load-on-startup value is set to 1. Using another XDoclet tag, the @web:servlet-mapping tag, a URL mapping is set up.

NOTE

The value of a tag in the Java source code can be a property that will exist in the Ant buildfile used to run XDoclet. For example, the servlet name could be set as a property in the buildfile as ${servlet-name}. This property could be used in the tag in the Java code, as shown here:

@web:servlet name="${servlet-name}"

The code for the `MainMenuServlet` is shown in Listing 6.12.

LISTING 6.12   Simple Java Servlet with XDoclet Tags for `<webdoclet>` Embedded in the Source

```java
package com.networksByteDesign.eMarket;

import java.io.*;
import javax.servlet.*;
import javax.servlet.http.*;

/**
 * @web:servlet name="MainMenuServlet"
 *              display-name="Main Menu Servlet"
 *              load-on-startup="1"
 * @web:servlet-mapping url-pattern="/MainMenu"
 */

public class MainMenuServlet extends HttpServlet
{
    public void doGet(HttpServletRequest request,
                      HttpServletResponse response)
        throws IOException, ServletException
    {
        response.setContentType("text/html");

        PrintWriter out   = response.getWriter();
        String      title = "Main Menu";

        out.println("<html>");
        out.println("<head>");
        out.println("<title>" + title + "</title>");
        out.println("</head>");

        out.println("<body bgcolor=\"white\">");
        out.println("<body>");
        out.println("<h1>" + title + "</h1>");
        out.println("</body>");
        out.println("</html>");
    }

    public void doPost(HttpServletRequest request,
                       HttpServletResponse response)
```

LISTING 6.12   Continued

```
     throws IOException, ServletException
  {
     doGet(request, response);
  }
}
```

As previously mentioned, XDoclet is designed to be used exclusively within Ant. Listing 6.13 shows a buildfile for generating the web.xml file for the servlet of Listing 6.12, compiling the Java code, and building a WAR file for deployment.

LISTING 6.13   Buildfile for Generating a web.xml Deployment Descriptor and Creating a WAR File

```
<taskdef name="webdoclet"
         classname="xdoclet.web.WebDocletTask"/>

<!-- xdoclet target -->
<target name="xdoclet">
    <webdoclet sourcepath="${dirs.build}"
               destdir="${dirs.build}"
               mergedir="{dirs.build}"
               force="${xdoclet.force}">

        <fileset dir="${dirs.build}">
            <include name="**/*Servlet.java" />
        </fileset>

        <deploymentdescriptor servletspec="2.3"
                              destdir="${dirs.build}"/>
    </webdoclet>
</target>
```

As with other tasks that are not part of ant.jar or optional.jar, we need to declare the mapping between task name and class with a <taskdef> tag at the top of the buildfile, which also includes a classpath definition for the classes required for XDoclet. The xdoclet target calls the <webdoclet> task of XDoclet. The attributes of <webdoclet> set here are for the source directory of the Java code on which to run Javadoc, the destination directory for the generated web.xml file, the mergedir, which will be discussed in a moment, and the force attribute. The force attribute forces the regeneration of XDoclet files.

It's possible that XDoclet may not be able to generate everything that you might want in a deployment descriptor through the doclet engine. Also, as a developer, you may not want to have to change the source code each time some aspect of the deployment descriptor changes. To handle these possibilities, XDoclet allows parts of the overall deployment descriptor to be maintained in separate component files, and then to be merged into the overall generated `web.xml` file. This is accomplished in part by setting the `mergedir` attribute of `<webdoclet>`. XDoclet then looks for certain files in the `sourcedir` that are called mergepoints. For example, one of the mergepoints is a file called `web-security.xml`. If this file exists, it should contain security settings to be included in the deployment descriptor. If this file exists in the `sourcepath` directory, `<webdoclet>` will include this file in the final `web.xml` file.

The mergepoints for `<webdoclet>` are discussed in the XDoclet javadoc under the `webdoclet` section, and are listed following, using the same convention as the documentation. The symbol `{0}` is used (as in the XDoclet documentation) to indicate the name of the servlet. If we wanted to use the `web-env-entries` mergepoint for our example, we would create a file named `web-env-entries-HelloWorldServlet.xml`. The following are the mergepoints for `<webdoclet>`:

- `web-settings.xml`
- `filter-mappings.xml`
- `servlet-mappings.xml`
- `mime-mappings.xml`
- `error-pages.xml`
- `taglibs.xml`
- `ejb-resourcerefs-{0}.xml`
- `web-security.xml`
- `web-sec-roles.xml`
- `web-env-entries-{0}.xml`
- `web-ejbrefs-{0}.xml`
- `web-ejbrefs-local-{0}.xml`
- `welcomefiles.xml`
- `servlets.xml`
- `filters.xml`

If these files exist, they are merged into the final deployment descriptor.

For this example, we will also create a mergepoint file called web-security.xml, and include some security settings in it. Listing 6.14 shows the web-security.xml file for this example. Note that the mergepoint files are complete XML files. The files only need to contain well-formed XML. The XML does not have to be a valid document with a single root directory, for example, because it's going to be included in the final web.xml file.

LISTING 6.14   A <webdoclet> Mergepoint File Called web-security.xml That Will Become Part of the Final web.xml Deployment Descriptor

```
<security-constraint>
    <web-resource-collection>
        <web-resource-name>Restricted</web-resource-name>
        <description>Declarative security tests</description>
        <url-pattern>/restricted/*</url-pattern>
        <http-method>HEAD</http-method>
        <http-method>GET</http-method>
        <http-method>POST</http-method>
        <http-method>PUT</http-method>
        <http-method>DELETE</http-method>
    </web-resource-collection>
    <auth-constraint>
        <role-name>Echo</role-name>
    </auth-constraint>
    <user-data-constraint>
        <description>no description</description>
        <transport-guarantee>NONE</transport-guarantee>
    </user-data-constraint>
</security-constraint>
```

Execution of the buildfile in Listing 6.13 will result in generation of the deployment descriptor shown in Listing 6.15.

LISTING 6.15   The web.xml Deployment Descriptor Generated Through the Use of the <webdoclet> Task of XDoclet

```
<?xml version="1.0" encoding="UTF-8"?>
<!DOCTYPE web-app PUBLIC
 "-//Sun Microsystems, Inc.//DTD Web Application 2.3//EN"
 "http://java.sun.com/dtd/web-app_2_3.dtd">

<web-app>
```

LISTING 6.15   Continued

```
<!--
  To use non XDoclet filters, create a filters.xml file that
  contains the additional filters (e.g. Sitemesh) and place it in your
  projects merge dir.  Don't include filter-mappings in this file,
  include them in a file called filter-mappings.xml and put that in
  the same directory.
  -->

<!--
  To use non XDoclet servlets, create a servlets.xml file that
  contains the additional servlets (e.g. Struts) and place it in your
  projects merge dir.  Don't include servlet-mappings in this file,
  include them in a file called servlet-mappings.xml and put that in
  the same directory.
  -->

 <servlet>
    <servlet-name>MainMenuServlet</servlet-name>
    <display-name>Main Menu Servlet</display-name>
    <servlet-class>com.networksByteDesign.eMarket.MainMenuServlet
    </servlet-class>

    <load-on-startup>1</load-on-startup>

 </servlet>

<servlet-mapping>
    <servlet-name>CompanyServlet</servlet-name>
    <url-pattern>/Company</url-pattern>
</servlet-mapping>
<servlet-mapping>
    <servlet-name>CustomerServlet</servlet-name>
    <url-pattern>/Customer</url-pattern>
</servlet-mapping>
<servlet-mapping>
    <servlet-name>SalesItemServlet</servlet-name>
    <url-pattern>/SalesItem</url-pattern>
</servlet-mapping>
<servlet-mapping>
    <servlet-name>MainMenuServlet</servlet-name>
    <url-pattern>/MainMenu</url-pattern>
</servlet-mapping>
```

LISTING 6.15 Continued

```
<session-config>
   <session-timeout>0</session-timeout>
</session-config>


<!--
To specify mime mappings, create a file named mime-mappings.xml,
put it in your project's mergedir.
Organize mime-mappings.xml following this DTD slice:

<!ELEMENT mime-mapping (extension, mime-type)>
-->


<!--
To specify error pages, create a file named error-pages.xml,
put it in your project's mergedir.
Organize error-pages.xml following this DTD slice:

<!ELEMENT error-page ((error-code | exception-type), location)>
-->


<!--
To add taglibs by xml, create a file called taglibs.xml and place it
in your merge dir.
-->


<security-constraint>
  <web-resource-collection>
      <web-resource-name>Restricted</web-resource-name>
      <description>Declarative security tests</description>
      <url-pattern>/restricted/*</url-pattern>
      <http-method>HEAD</http-method>
      <http-method>GET</http-method>
      <http-method>POST</http-method>
      <http-method>PUT</http-method>
      <http-method>DELETE</http-method>
  </web-resource-collection>
  <auth-constraint>
      <role-name>Echo</role-name>
  </auth-constraint>
  <user-data-constraint>
      <description>no description</description>
      <transport-guarantee>NONE</transport-guarantee>
```

LISTING 6.15   Continued

```
    </user-data-constraint>
</security-constraint>

</web-app>
```

Generating EJB Deployment Descriptors and Classes with XDoclet

The next capability of XDoclet we will examine is the generation of various deployment descriptors and Java classes for Enterprise JavaBeans (EJBs). XDoclet has the capability of generating Java source code for EJB supporting classes, as well as deployment descriptors. Let's create a simple entity bean for deployment to the JBoss EJB container. This entity bean will use container-managed persistence, and will have its Home and Remote interfaces generated through XDoclet. Also, it will require three deployment descriptor files. First is the generic `ejb-jar.xml` file. Second, for use in JBoss, we also generate the `jboss.xml` and `jaws.xml` deployment descriptors. XDoclet has several subtasks that can be used to accomplish these goals. The task `<ejbdoclet>` will generate the generic `ejb-jar.xml` file. XDoclet also has a set of vendor-specific tasks. As with `<webdoclet>`, there is also a set of tags for use in the javadoc comments of the Java code that will be picked up by the doclet engine by using some of the vendor-specific subtasks.

First, let's set up the Java code for our simple entity bean, and embed the necessary XDoclet tags in the code. Listing 6.16 shows a very simple entity bean. Before the class declaration and before several of the methods are deployment descriptor declarations.

LISTING 6.16   A Simple EJB with `<ejbdoclet>` Tag Information for Generation of Deployment Descriptors

```
package com.networksByteDesign.eMarket.inventory.data;

import java.rmi.RemoteException;
import javax.ejb.*;

/**
 * Company entity bean
 *
 * @ejb:bean name="CompanyBean" type="CMP" jndi-name="Company"
 * @ejb:interface
 * remote-class="com.networksByteDesign.eMarket.inventory.data.Company"
 */
```

LISTING 6.16 Continued

```java
public class CompanyBean implements EntityBean
{
    /**
     * @return name of object
     *
     * @ejb:interface-method view-type="both"
     * @ejb:transaction type="Supports"
     * @ejb:persistent-field
     *
     */
    public String getName() {return name_;}

    /**
     * @param name name of object
     *
     * @ejb:interface-method view-type="both"
     */
    public void setName(String name) {name_ = name;}

    /**
     * @return id of object
     *
     * @ejb:persistent-field
     * @ejb:pk-field
     *
     * @jboss:dbms-column city_id
     */
    public String getId() {return id_;}

    /**
     * @param id id of object
     */
    public void setId(String id) {id_ = id;}

    /**
     * Create object.
     *
     * @ejb:create-method
     * @ejb:permission role-name="Administrator"
     */
```

LISTING 6.16   Continued

```
public String ejbCreate(String id) {
    id_ = id;
    return null;
}

public void ejbPostCreate(String id) {
}

public void ejbActivate() {}
public void ejbPassivate() {}
public void ejbLoad() {}
public void ejbStore() {}
public void ejbRemove()  throws javax.ejb.RemoveException {}

public void setEntityContext(EntityContext ctx) {this.ctx = ctx;}
public void unsetEntityContext() {this.ctx = null;}

transient private EntityContext ctx;
public String name_;
public String id_;
}
```

Tags that have the form @ejb:*name* are used for specifying generic deployment
descriptor parameters. These values will ultimately be generated and placed in the
ejb-jar.xml file. If we wanted to include specific parameters for certain EJB containers such as JBoss, or WebLogic, we would use the tags for those containers, which are
of the form @jboss:*name* and @weblogic:*name*, respectively.

Next, the Ant buildfile required for the generation step of our example needs to be
created. Because we intend to deploy this on JBoss, several subtasks of XDoclet will
be called. The first is <ejbdoclet>, which will generate the generic part, and also the
<jboss> task, which will generate the jboss.xml and jaws.xml files. In addition
to these subtasks, several subtags of <ejbdoclet> will be employed. The
<remoteinterface/> and <homeinterface/> tags will cause XDoclet to generate
Home and Remote interface Java source code for the entity bean. The user doesn't
have to use these subtasks, and can still write their own interfaces. However, for this
example, we will allow <ejbdoclet> to generate the interfaces. The tag <dataobject>
will cause XDoclet to generate data object code for the EJB classes. It has four
optional attributes, and we will just accept the default values here. The <entitypk>
tag will result in the generation of a primary key Java class. Finally the <entitycmp>
task creates Java classes for container-managed persistence entity beans. Listing 6.17
shows the buildfile for our EJB deployment descriptor example.

LISTING 6.17   Buildfile That Uses XDoclet `<ejbdoclet>` to Generate Deployment
Descriptors for EJB Deployment

```xml
<?xml version="1.0" ?>
<project name="eMarket" default="compile" basedir=".">

    <taskdef name="requiredInput"
            classname="com.networksByteDesign.util.RequiredInput"/>

    <taskdef name="cleanimps"
            classname="com.tombrus.cleanImports.ant.CleanImports"/>

    <taskdef name="webdoclet"
            classname="xdoclet.web.WebDocletTask"/>

    <taskdef name="ejbdoclet"
            classname="xdoclet.ejb.EjbDocletTask"/>

    <property name="dirs.source"  value="/usr/projects/eMarket/src"      />
    <property name="dirs.backup"  value="${user.home}/backup"            />
    <property name="dirs.temp"    value="/tmp"                           />
    <property name="dirs.deploy"  value="/usr/projects/appServer/eMarket" />
    <property name="dirs.doc"     value="docs"                           />
    <property name="dirs.build"   value="build"                          />
    <property name="dirs.nightly" value="/usr/projects/eMarket/nightly"  />
    <property name="dirs.lib"     value="/usr/projects/lib"              />
    <property name="dirs.test"    value="test"                           />

    <property name="MailLogger.from"
            value="eMarketDev@networksByteDesign.com"/>
    <property name="MailLogger.success.to"
            value="eMarketDev@networksByteDesign.com"/>
    <property name="MailLogger.failure.to"
            value="eMarketDev@networksByteDesign.com"/>
    <property name="MailLogger.success.subject"
            value="eMarket Nightly Build Succeeded"/>
    <property name="MailLogger.failure.subject"
            value="eMarket Nightly Build Failed"/>

    <path id="project.classpath">
        <pathelement location="${dirs.lib}/all.jar"/>
        <pathelement location="${dirs.build}"/>
    </path>
```

LISTING 6.17   Continued

```
<!-- compile target -->
<target name="compile"
        depends="xdoclet"
        description="Compile all of the source code.">

    <javac srcdir="${dirs.build}">
        <classpath refid="project.classpath"/>
    </javac>
</target>

<!-- xdoclet target -->
<target name="xdoclet">
    <mkdir dir="${dirs.build}"/>

    <copy todir="${dirs.build}">
        <fileset dir="${dirs.source}" includes="**/*.*"/>
    </copy>

    <webdoclet sourcepath="${dirs.build}"
               destdir="${dirs.build}"
               mergedir="${dirs.build}"
               force="${xdoclet.force}">

        <fileset dir="${dirs.build}">
            <include name="**/*Servlet.java" />
        </fileset>

        <deploymentdescriptor servletspec="2.3"
                              destdir="${dirs.build}"/>
    </webdoclet>

    <ejbdoclet sourcepath="${dirs.build}"
               destdir="${dirs.build}"
               ejbspec="2.0"
               force="${xdoclet.force}">

        <fileset dir="${dirs.build}">
            <include name="**/*Bean.java" />
        </fileset>

        <dataobject/>
        <remoteinterface/>
```

LISTING 6.17   Continued

```
            <homeinterface/>
            <entitypk/>
            <entitycmp/>
            <deploymentdescriptor destdir="${dirs.build}"/>

            <jboss xmlencoding="UTF-8" destdir="${dirs.build}"/>
        </ejbdoclet>
    </target>
</project>
```

The destination directory for the output is `${dirs.build}`. This is done because `<ejbdoclet>` is generating Java source code in addition to the deployment descriptors. The goal is to keep generated Java classes separate from handwritten classes, to make a clean build easier to implement, and also to make revision control easier. If generated Java source code were mixed in with the code that is controlled in revision control, this situation could become messy and confusing very quickly. After the xdoclet target executes, the following items will have been generated:

- `ejb-jar.xml`
- `jboss.xml`
- `jaws.xml`
- `CompanyBeanPK.java`
- `CompanyBeanHome.java`
- `CompanyBeanData.java`
- `CompanyBeanCMP.java`
- `Company.java`
- `CustomerBeanPK.java`
- `CustomerBeanHome.java`
- `CustomerBeanData.java`
- `CustomerBeanCMP.java`
- `Customer.java`
- `SalesItemBeanPK.java`
- `SalesItemBeanHome.java`
- `SalesItemBeanData.java`

- `SalesItemBeanCMP.java`

- `SalesItem.java`

After completion of the code and deployment descriptor generation, several familiar steps are performed to compile the Java source code and package everything into an Enterprise Archive (EAR) file. The resulting deployment descriptors and the `CompanyBeanHome.java` class are shown in Listings 6.18, 6.19, 6.20, and 6.21.

LISTING 6.18   The `ejb-jar.xml` Deployment Descriptor Generated by the Buildfile of Listing 6.17

```
<?xml version="1.0" encoding="UTF-8"?>
<!DOCTYPE ejb-jar PUBLIC
 "-//Sun Microsystems, Inc.//DTD Enterprise JavaBeans 2.0//EN"
 "http://java.sun.com/dtd/ejb-jar_2_0.dtd">

<ejb-jar >

   <description>No Description.</description>
   <display-name>Generated by XDoclet</display-name>

   <enterprise-beans>

     <!-- Session Beans -->

     <!--
       To add session beans that you have deployment descriptor info for,
       add a file to your merge directory called session-beans.xml that
       contains the <session></session> markup for those beans.
     -->

     <!-- Entity Beans -->
     <entity >
        <description><![CDATA[Company entity bean]]></description>

        <ejb-name>CompanyBean</ejb-name>

        <home>
        com.networksByteDesign.eMarket.inventory.data.CompanyBeanHome
        </home>
        <remote>
        com.networksByteDesign.eMarket.inventory.data.Company
```

LISTING 6.18   Continued

```
</remote>

<ejb-class>
com.networksByteDesign.eMarket.inventory.data.CompanyBeanCMP
</ejb-class>
<persistence-type>Container</persistence-type>
<prim-key-class>
com.networksByteDesign.eMarket.inventory.data.CompanyBeanPK
</prim-key-class>
<reentrant>False</reentrant>
<cmp-version>2.x</cmp-version>
<abstract-schema-name>CompanyBean</abstract-schema-name>
<cmp-field >
   <description><![CDATA[]]></description>
   <field-name>name</field-name>
</cmp-field>
<cmp-field >
   <description><![CDATA[]]></description>
   <field-name>id</field-name>
</cmp-field>

</entity>

<entity >
   <description><![CDATA[Customer entity bean]]></description>

   <ejb-name>CustomerBean</ejb-name>

   <home>
   com.networksByteDesign.eMarket.inventory.data.CustomerBeanHome
   </home>
   <remote>
   com.networksByteDesign.eMarket.inventory.data.Customer
   </remote>

   <ejb-class>
   com.networksByteDesign.eMarket.inventory.data.CustomerBeanCMP
   </ejb-class>
   <persistence-type>Container</persistence-type>
   <prim-key-class>
   com.networksByteDesign.eMarket.inventory.data.CustomerBeanPK
   </prim-key-class>
```

LISTING 6.18   Continued

```
<reentrant>False</reentrant>
<cmp-version>2.x</cmp-version>
<abstract-schema-name>CustomerBean</abstract-schema-name>
<cmp-field >
   <description><![CDATA[]]></description>
   <field-name>name</field-name>
</cmp-field>
<cmp-field >
   <description><![CDATA[]]></description>
   <field-name>id</field-name>
</cmp-field>

</entity>

<entity >
  <description><![CDATA[SalesItem entity bean]]></description>

  <ejb-name>SalesItemBean</ejb-name>

  <home>
  com.networksByteDesign.eMarket.inventory.data.SalesItemBeanHome
  </home>
  <remote>
  com.networksByteDesign.eMarket.inventory.data.SalesItem
  </remote>

  <ejb-class>
  com.networksByteDesign.eMarket.inventory.data.SalesItemBeanCMP
  </ejb-class>
  <persistence-type>Container</persistence-type>
  <prim-key-class>
  com.networksByteDesign.eMarket.inventory.data.SalesItemBeanPK
  </prim-key-class>
  <reentrant>False</reentrant>
  <cmp-version>2.x</cmp-version>
  <abstract-schema-name>SalesItemBean</abstract-schema-name>
  <cmp-field >
     <description><![CDATA[]]></description>
     <field-name>name</field-name>
  </cmp-field>
  <cmp-field >
     <description><![CDATA[]]></description>
```

LISTING 6.18   Continued

```
            <field-name>id</field-name>
        </cmp-field>

    </entity>

  <!--
    To add entity beans that you have deployment descriptor info for, add
    a file to your merge directory called entity-beans.xml that contains
    the <entity></entity> markup for those beans.
  -->

    <!-- Message Driven Beans -->
  <!--
    To add message driven beans that you have deployment descriptor info
    for, add a file to your merge directory called
    message-driven-beans.xml that contains the
    <message-driven></message-driven> markup for those beans.
  -->

</enterprise-beans>

<!-- Relationships -->

<!-- Assembly Descriptor -->
<assembly-descriptor >
   <security-role>
      <description>
      description not supported yet by ejbdoclet
      </description>
      <role-name>Administrator</role-name>
   </security-role>

<method-permission >
   <description>description not supported yet by ejbdoclet</description>
      <role-name>Administrator</role-name>
   <method >
      <description><![CDATA[Create object.]]></description>
      <ejb-name>CompanyBean</ejb-name>
      <method-intf>Home</method-intf>
      <method-name>create</method-name>
      <method-params>
         <method-param>java.lang.String</method-param>
```

LISTING 6.18   Continued

```
        </method-params>
    </method>
</method-permission>

<!-- finder permissions -->

<method-permission >
    <description>description not supported yet by ejbdoclet</description>
        <role-name>Administrator</role-name>
    <method >
        <description><![CDATA[Create object.]]></description>
        <ejb-name>CustomerBean</ejb-name>
        <method-intf>Home</method-intf>
        <method-name>create</method-name>
        <method-params>
            <method-param>java.lang.String</method-param>
        </method-params>
    </method>
</method-permission>

<!-- finder permissions -->

<method-permission >
    <description>description not supported yet by ejbdoclet</description>
        <role-name>Administrator</role-name>
    <method >
        <description><![CDATA[Create object.]]></description>
        <ejb-name>SalesItemBean</ejb-name>
        <method-intf>Home</method-intf>
        <method-name>create</method-name>
        <method-params>
            <method-param>java.lang.String</method-param>
        </method-params>
    </method>
</method-permission>

<!-- finder permissions -->

<!-- transactions -->
<container-transaction >
    <method >
        <ejb-name>CompanyBean</ejb-name>
```

LISTING 6.18 Continued

```
        <method-intf>Local</method-intf>
        <method-name>getName</method-name>
        <method-params>
        </method-params>
    </method>
    <trans-attribute>Supports</trans-attribute>
</container-transaction>
<container-transaction >
    <method >
        <ejb-name>CompanyBean</ejb-name>
        <method-intf>Remote</method-intf>
        <method-name>getName</method-name>
        <method-params>
        </method-params>
    </method>
    <trans-attribute>Supports</trans-attribute>
</container-transaction>
<container-transaction >
    <method >
        <ejb-name>CustomerBean</ejb-name>
        <method-intf>Local</method-intf>
        <method-name>getName</method-name>
        <method-params>
        </method-params>
    </method>
    <trans-attribute>Supports</trans-attribute>
</container-transaction>
<container-transaction >
    <method >
        <ejb-name>CustomerBean</ejb-name>
        <method-intf>Remote</method-intf>
        <method-name>getName</method-name>
        <method-params>
        </method-params>
    </method>
    <trans-attribute>Supports</trans-attribute>
</container-transaction>
<container-transaction >
    <method >
        <ejb-name>SalesItemBean</ejb-name>
        <method-intf>Local</method-intf>
        <method-name>getName</method-name>
```

LISTING 6.18   Continued

```
            <method-params>
            </method-params>
          </method>
          <trans-attribute>Supports</trans-attribute>
        </container-transaction>
        <container-transaction >
          <method >
            <ejb-name>SalesItemBean</ejb-name>
            <method-intf>Remote</method-intf>
            <method-name>getName</method-name>
            <method-params>
            </method-params>
          </method>
          <trans-attribute>Supports</trans-attribute>
        </container-transaction>

        <!-- finder transactions -->
      </assembly-descriptor>

</ejb-jar>
```

LISTING 6.19   The `jboss.xml` Deployment Descriptor Generated as Part of the
Buildfile of Listing 6.17

```
<?xml version="1.0" encoding="UTF-8"?>
<!DOCTYPE jboss PUBLIC
 "-//JBoss//DTD JBOSS 2.4//EN"
 "http://www.jboss.org/j2ee/dtd/jboss_2_4.dtd">

<jboss>

    <enterprise-beans>

        <entity>
            <ejb-name>CompanyBean</ejb-name>
            <jndi-name>Company</jndi-name>
        </entity>
        <entity>
            <ejb-name>CustomerBean</ejb-name>
            <jndi-name>Customer</jndi-name>
        </entity>
        <entity>
```

LISTING 6.19   Continued

```
            <ejb-name>SalesItemBean</ejb-name>
            <jndi-name>SalesItem</jndi-name>
        </entity>

    </enterprise-beans>

    <resource-managers>
    </resource-managers>

</jboss>
```

LISTING 6.20   The jaws.xml Deployment Descriptor, Also Generated as Part of the Buildfile of Listing 6.17

```
<?xml version="1.0" encoding="UTF-8"?>
<!DOCTYPE jaws PUBLIC
 "-//JBoss//DTD JAWS 2.4//EN"
 "http://www.jboss.org/j2ee/dtd/jaws_2_4.dtd">

<jaws>
    <datasource>java:/DefaultDS</datasource>
    <type-mapping></type-mapping>
    <debug>false</debug>

    <enterprise-beans>

        <entity>
            <ejb-name>CompanyBean</ejb-name>

            <cmp-field>
                <field-name>id</field-name>
                <column-name>id</column-name>

            </cmp-field>
            <cmp-field>
                <field-name>name</field-name>
                <column-name>name</column-name>

            </cmp-field>

        </entity>
```

LISTING 6.20   Continued

```
    <entity>
        <ejb-name>CustomerBean</ejb-name>

        <cmp-field>
            <field-name>id</field-name>
            <column-name>id</column-name>

        </cmp-field>
        <cmp-field>
            <field-name>name</field-name>
            <column-name>name</column-name>

        </cmp-field>

    </entity>

    <entity>
        <ejb-name>SalesItemBean</ejb-name>

        <cmp-field>
            <field-name>id</field-name>
            <column-name>id</column-name>

        </cmp-field>
        <cmp-field>
            <field-name>name</field-name>
            <column-name>name</column-name>

        </cmp-field>

    </entity>

  </enterprise-beans>

</jaws>
```

LISTING 6.21   Example of One of the Generated Java Source Code Classes, the
CompanyBeanHome.java Interface

```
/*
 * Generated file - Do not edit!
 */
package com.networksByteDesign.eMarket.inventory.data;

import java.lang.*;
import javax.ejb.*;
import java.rmi.RemoteException;

/**
 * Home interface for CompanyBean. Lookup using {1}
 * @xdoclet-generated at Jan 25, 2003 4:43:39 PM
 */
public interface CompanyBeanHome
   extends javax.ejb.EJBHome
{
   public static final String COMP_NAME="java:comp/env/ejb/CompanyBean";
   public static final String JNDI_NAME="Company";

   /**
    * Create object.
    */
   public Company create(java.lang.String id)
      throws java.rmi.RemoteException,javax.ejb.CreateException;

   public Company findByPrimaryKey(CompanyBeanPK pk)
      throws java.rmi.RemoteException,javax.ejb.FinderException;
}
```

Taglib Deployment with XDoclet

JavaServer Pages (JSPs) can contain Java code for creating dynamic content. Web
page designers may not have Java development skills, and software developers may
not necessarily be the best Web page designers. A better separation of responsibilities
can be achieved in JSP design with the use of tag libraries. A tag library is a collection
of custom tags. Custom tags define an identifier that a Web developer can reference
to get dynamic content in their Web page without having to know how to write Java
code. Java developers can focus on creating a set of tag libraries to perform certain
functions for generating dynamic content, such as accessing a database.

One of the tasks associated with the use of tag libraries is maintaining a `taglib.tld` deployment descriptor. XDoclet contains the `<jsptaglib>` task, which is a subtask of `<webdoclet>`, specifically for creating and maintaining taglib deployment descriptors. Because the attributes of `<webdoclet>` were covered in a previous example, we won't detail them again here. As before, `<webdoclet>` takes a nested fileset to describe the files to operate on. The `<jsptaglib>` subtask has no required attributes, but several optional attributes are used in this buildfile. As the name indicates, the `taglibversion` attribute is used to define the version number of the tag library. The default value is `1.0`, so it actually doesn't need to be set in this example, because that is the desired value. We set it as an advisable practice, so other developers who may work on this code won't forget to change the value later. The `jspversion` sets the version of the JSP spec that the `<jsptaglib>` subtask will follow for the generation of the taglib descriptor (tld) file. The `displayname` is an optional short name, and `description` contains a short description intended for the users of the tag library. Putting this all together, we have the buildfile of Listing 6.22.

LISTING 6.22   The Buildfile for Generation of the Tag Library Descriptor File `taglib.tld`

```
<!-- xdoclet target -->
<target name="xdoclet">
    <mkdir dir="${dirs.build}"/>

    <copy todir="${dirs.build}">
        <fileset dir="${dirs.source}" includes="**/*.*"/>
    </copy>

    <webdoclet sourcepath="${dirs.build}"
               destdir="${dirs.build}"
               mergedir="${dirs.build}"
               force="${xdoclet.force}">

        <fileset dir="${dirs.build}">
            <include name="**/*Servlet.java" />
        </fileset>

        <deploymentdescriptor servletspec="2.3"
                              destdir="${dirs.build}"/>
    </webdoclet>

    <webdoclet sourcepath="${dirs.build}"
               destdir="${dirs.build}"
               force="${xdoclet.force}">
```

LISTING 6.22   Continued

```
                <fileset dir="${dirs.build}">
                    <include name="**/*.java" />
                </fileset>

                <jsptaglib taglibversion="1.0"
                           jspversion="1.1"
                           displayname="eMarket"
                           description="eMarket tag library"/>
            </webdoclet>

            <ejbdoclet sourcepath="${dirs.build}"
                       destdir="${dirs.build}"
                       ejbspec="2.0"
                       force="${xdoclet.force}">

                <fileset dir="${dirs.build}">
                    <include name="**/*Bean.java" />
                </fileset>

                <dataobject/>
                <remoteinterface/>
                <homeinterface/>
                <entitypk/>
                <entitycmp/>
                <deploymentdescriptor destdir="${dirs.build}"/>

                <jboss xmlencoding="UTF-8" destdir="${dirs.build}"/>
            </ejbdoclet>
        </target>
```

Like the `<webdoclet>` task, `<jsptaglib>` has mergepoints that can be used to include aspects of the deployment descriptor that are not to be kept in the javadoc comments of the tag library source code. There are several mergepoints, which are defined in the XDoclet documentation:

- `taglib-settings.xml`
- `tag-example-{0}.xml`

The first mergepoint, `taglib-settings.xml` file, is used to define global settings for the tag library. The other mergepoint is one or more optional files that are used to provide an informal description of the tag that illustrates its use.

In this example, the <jsptaglib> task will find the Java code for the tag library in
the sourcepath attribute defined in the <webdoclet> task, because <jspdoclet> is a
subtask of <webdoclet>. The source code for the tag library in our example is shown
in Listing 6.23. The tag jsp:tag is an XDoclet tag for defining a tag library class. The
jsp:tag tag has several attributes. The first, name, is used to define the tag name that
a JSP will use to access this class. The body-content attribute defines the body
content field for the tag, which is JSP. Finally, the description attribute is used to
define a short message that explains what the tag lib class does.

LISTING 6.23   The Source Code for the Tag Library in Our Example

```
package com.networksByteDesign.eMarket.util.TagLib;

import javax.servlet.jsp.*;
import javax.servlet.jsp.tagext.*;
import java.util.Hashtable;
import java.io.Writer;
import java.io.IOException;
import java.util.Date;
import java.text.DateFormat;

/**
 * @jsp:tag name="simple" body-content="JSP" description="Returns today's date"
 */

public class SimpleExample
    implements BodyTag
{
    protected BodyContent bodyOut_;
    protected PageContext pageContext_;
    protected Tag parent_;
    private String atts_[] = new String[1];
    int i = 0;

    private final void setAtt(int index, String value) {
        atts_[index] = value;
    }

    public void setAtt1(String value) {
        setAtt(0, value);
    }

    public void setParent(Tag parent) {
```

LISTING 6.23 Continued

```
        parent_ = parent;
    }

    public void setBodyContent(BodyContent bodyOut) {
        bodyOut_ = bodyOut;
    }

    public void setPageContext(PageContext pageContext) {
        pageContext_ = pageContext;
    }

    public Tag getParent() {
        return parent_;
    }

    public int doStartTag() throws JspException {
        return EVAL_BODY_TAG;
    }

    public int doEndTag() throws JspException {
        return SKIP_BODY;
    }

    public void doInitBody() throws JspException {
            pageContext_.setAttribute("date", getDate());
    }

    public int doAfterBody() throws JspException {
      try {
        if (i == 0) {
          bodyOut_.writeOut(bodyOut_.getEnclosingWriter());
          return SKIP_BODY;
        }
        else {
            pageContext_.setAttribute("date", "bar");
        }
        i++;
        return EVAL_BODY_TAG;
      }
      catch (IOException ex) {
        throw new JspTagException(ex.toString());
```

LISTING 6.23   Continued

```
        }
    }

    public void release() {
        bodyOut_ = null;
        pageContext_ = null;
        parent_ = null;
    }

    private String getDate() {
        return DateFormat.getDateInstance().format(new Date());
    }
}
```

The buildfile of Listing 6.22 will generate the `taglib.tld` descriptor file shown in Listing 6.24.

LISTING 6.24   Generated `taglib.tld` File Using XDoclet

```
<?xml version="1.0" encoding="UTF-8"?>
<!DOCTYPE taglib PUBLIC
 "-//Sun Microsystems, Inc.//DTD JSP Tag Library 1.1//EN"
 "http://java.sun.com/j2ee/dtds/web-jsptaglibrary_1_1.dtd">
<taglib>
    <tlibversion>1.0</tlibversion>
    <jspversion>1.1</jspversion>
    <shortname></shortname>
    <tag>
        <name>eMarket</name>
        <tagclass>com.networksByteDesign.eMarket.util.TagLib</tagclass>
        <bodycontent>JSP</bodycontent>
        <description>eMarket Tag Libs</description>
    </tag>
</taglib>
```

Listing 6.25 shows a JSP page that uses the taglib generated in Listing 6.24.

LISTING 6.25   A Simple JSP Using the Taglib Generated in This Example

```
<%@ taglib uri="taglib.tld" prefix="se" %>
<html>
```

LISTING 6.25 Continued

```
<head>
  <title>FAQ</title>
<head>
<body>
FAQ for eMarket:
<se:eMarket>
  <%= date %>
</se:eMarket>

</body>
</html>
```

Creating an EAR File with the <ear> Task

An Enterprise Archive or EAR file is a special type of JAR file that contains Web application components such as servlets and JSPs, Enterprise JavaBeans (EJBs), and an application deployment descriptor called application.xml. Ant contains the <ear> task for creating an enterprise archive file. The <ear> task creates a JAR file, but contains some special shortcuts that apply only to EAR files. The following target illustrates the use of the <ear> task.

```
<ear destfile="${dirs.build}/eMarket.ear"
     appxml="${dirs.source}/application.xml">
  <fileset dir="${dirs.build}" includes="*.jar,*.war"/>
</ear>
```

The <ear> task has several noteworthy attributes. First, the destfile attribute is used to tell Ant the path and name of the EAR file to create, which in this example is eMarket.ear. Next, the appxml attribute is used to name the deployment descriptor file that should be included in the META-INF directory of the EAR file. This file is expected to be named application.xml. The <ear> task also uses a nested <fileset> element to name the types of files to be included. In this example, the EAR contains all of the JAR and WAR files that are found in the directory defined by the property ${dirs.build}.

Running this task will generate an EAR file with the following structure:

```
3188 Sat Mar 15 11:14:37 CDT 2003 emarket-ejb.jar
2133 Sat Mar 15 11:14:37 CDT 2003 eMarket.war
   2 Sat Mar 15 11:14:37 CDT 2003 META-INF/MANIFEST.MF
 428 Sat Mar 15 11:14:37 CDT 2003 META-INF/application.xml
```

Summary

The eMarket team had to address refactoring their buildfile to handle deployment to both a development and test environment. We looked in depth at the use of the Ant tasks <jar> and <war> and their role in the deployment process. The eMarket team also had a problem caused by not keeping their code and deployment descriptors in sync. They overcame this problem by using a tool called XDoclet to dynamically generate their deployment descriptors. XDoclet, from SourceForge, is intended for use with Ant for the generation of various types of deployment descriptors. By using a tool like XDoclet, the deployment descriptor information can be kept near the methods that they are describing. Also, the use of third-party tools to extend the capabilities of Ant makes it possible to automate additional aspects of your XP project. That's going to increase overall velocity by reducing workload and enhancing the repeatability of your processes.

The Team Size Increases

Why Have Coding Standards?

In Extreme Programming, every developer on the project owns the entire code base. This means that anyone on the project can change any piece of code at any time. The advantage of this policy is that developers don't have to wait for someone else to make changes to code. When developers are kept waiting for a needed change, they will often create a workaround in their own code. Over time, this causes the code to become a mess. Having the authority to change any code at any time means that projects avoid the messy workarounds that often creep into code. But for this to work, there has to be some consistency in the code that is written by different developers, or this policy can rapidly lead to chaos.

Story

The eMarket development team has just completed another release cycle. Recently, several additional developers finished their assignments on different projects, and joined the eMarket project. Company management had planned to add these additional developers to eMarket when their projects were complete. These people came from a project that was not using the XP methodology, and so they will require some training.

Since more people have joined the project, one of the challenges has been to prevent the project from deteriorating into chaos. The new team members are all very capable people, and have been trained on project policies and guidelines. However, it has become apparent that more will have to be done to make sure that project standards are being followed. It's not that members are deliberately not following standards, but some of them have to break old habits. This is especially a problem when two new team members pair up. What's especially bad is when code that doesn't completely follow standards accumulates, and is then checked into the repository. When the team realizes this, the developers have to go back and rework the code to adhere to team standards. This wastes time.

Michael and Sandy discuss this problem and steps that can be taken to prevent it. One possibility is to only allow new team members to pair with experienced team members. This idea is dismissed because it will interfere with the XP approach. Another approach that is commonly used in many organizations is to hold code reviews. However, this approach is time-consuming, and prone to error. With the availability of some very powerful tools, another option is possible. This is to put automated processes into the build process to guarantee that coding standards are being followed correctly. This is the direction the eMarket team takes, and changes are made to the build process to enforce coding standards.

For the total code ownership approach to be effective, several things need to be in place. First, you must be able to have confidence that when the code is changed, existing functionality has not been broken. A suite of unit tests will help to guarantee this, by validating the code every time it's built. The second critical piece is that coding standards must be in place for the entire team. Finally, there must be a mechanism for ensuring that the coding standards are followed at all times. This way, the code will look the same to everyone. These policies are part of the XP methodology.

Failing to have coding standards in place means that a project's source code will be a hodgepodge of styles. Style differences can be anything from an annoyance to a serious problem. For example, suppose one developer denotes member variables in a class by ending the name with an underbar, but a second developer prefixes each name with an "m". A third developer makes no distinction between member variables and local variables in terms of naming style. We've all worked on projects like this. The problem with this is that we have to mentally shift gears each time we open a file written by a different developer. Although this may seem like only a nuisance, it does slow the project down. Also, what happens when we work on the code the third developer wrote (the one who doesn't distinguish between local and member variables)? We have to constantly look elsewhere in the code to determine whether a variable is a member or local variable. Also, where do we look for member variables? Do we look at the beginning of the class, or at the end of the class? It just makes sense to have a standard style for the project, and expect everyone to adhere to the style. Also, we can do some things to make sure that consistent styles are being used.

Enforcing Coding Standards

A recommended policy is to incorporate steps into your XP build processes that will enforce coding standards. It isn't that the members of the team aren't trusted. It's just that we all make mistakes. If we didn't make mistakes, we wouldn't need to unit test our code either. By automating the steps to ensure that source code adheres to project standards, we can catch problems and correct them early. Having this process in place is just another aspect of the continuous testing philosophy of XP.

A number of third-party tools are designed to integrate with Ant and enforce coding standards. In this chapter, we will look at a five tools that you can use for this purpose: Jalopy, PMD, Checkstyle, iContract, and JDepend.

Jalopy

Story

One of the problems with adhering to coding standards has been with coding style. The eMarket team adopted a coding style standard, as part of a set of best practices to be followed. Because some of the team members have to change old habits, they sometimes revert to their own style from time to time. After performing a spike test on Jalopy, Michael and John incorporate the use of this tool into the build process to handle cleanup of code that deviates from the coding style standard.

Jalopy is a tool that will reformat source code to conform to a user-defined style. It is basically a Java beautifier and pretty printer. It deals only with the style of code. It doesn't perform checks for bad practices. Jalopy allows a team to enforce standards on source code style characteristics including indentation, style of braces, whitespace settings, line wrapping, and other items. Jalopy can also take care of generating default Javadoc comments where the Javadoc comments are missing. Also, Jalopy is compatible with CleanImports, which was discussed in Chapter 4, "The First Complete Build Process."

INSTALLING JALOPY

To install Jalopy, follow these steps:

1. Download Jalopy from

   `http://jalopy.sourceforge.net/download.html`

   The binary distribution should meet the needs of most users. Also, Jalopy 0.6.1 requires Ant 1.3 or greater.

2. Unzip the zip file that was just downloaded.

3. Jalopy has the following JAR files in its installation:

   ```
   aelfred-1.2.jar
   jalopy-1.0b10.jar
   jalopy-ant-0.6.1.jar
   jaxp-1.2.jar
   jdom-1.0b8.jar
   log4j-1.2.6.jar
   oro-2.0.6.jar
   sax-2.0.1.jar
   ```

There are two options for using the JAR files. The first is to put all of the JAR files into your system CLASSPATH. If this creates a conflict with other versions of any of these JAR files, there is a second option. That is to use the taskdef definition with a <classpath> declaration in your buildfile. The Jalopy documentation provides an example that is shown here:

```
<taskdef name="jalopy"
         classname="de.hunsicker.jalopy.plugin.ant.AntPlugin">
  <classpath>
    <fileset dir="<INST_DIR>/lib">
      <include name="*.jar" />
    </fileset>
  </classpath>
</taskdef>
```

   4. Jalopy is ready to use within Ant.

The Jalopy tool consists of a core engine, a GUI interface, and plug-ins that allow it to integrate with various IDEs, and of course, the Ant framework. Some of the plug-ins available for Jalopy allow it to integrate with

- Ant
- Command-line use
- Eclipse
- JBuilder
- JDeveloper
- Jedit
- NetBeans

In this chapter, we will only cover the use of Jalopy with Ant.

The first step is to create a configuration file that contains the standards to be enforced. The configuration file is created by running the GUI tool that comes with Jalopy. In the GUI, a source code style is set up and then saved. Jalopy will generate an XML configuration file. Figure 7.1 shows the GUI tool for creating a configuration file.

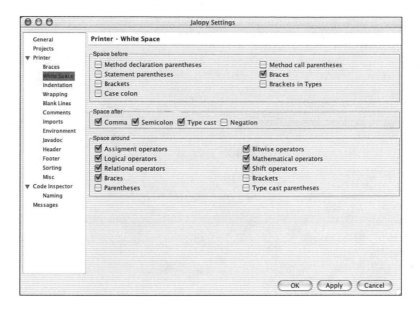

FIGURE 7.1   Jalopy GUI tool for creating a configuration file.

Most people have an opinion on the styles they want in their code, but may not know the name of the style (Sun style braces, and so on). The Jalopy GUI for generating configuration files eliminates the need to know this. The GUI contains two windows. In the left window are options that can be set for various coding standards. In the right window is a sample Java file. As you modify options in the left window, the Java source file in the right window will change to reflect the style that you've selected. When the Java file finally conforms to the standards that you want to enforce, you generate and save the configuration file. A sample configuration file for Jalopy is shown in Listing 7.1. Because the configuration file is generated from a tool, we won't go into the meaning of each of the tags here. It's not necessary to understand them because the XML doesn't need to be directly created or edited by the user. After you save the configuration file, it needs to be placed where it can be accessed by the Ant build process. The Jalopy GUI allows you to select the directory where the configuration file will be saved. After it's created, it should be placed in version control.

LISTING 7.1   Configuration File for Use with Jalopy

```xml
<?xml version="1.0" encoding="UTF-8"?>
<jalopy>
  <general>
    <compliance>
      <version>14</version>
    </compliance>
    <style>
      <description>Sun Java Coding Convention</description>
      <name>Sun</name>
    </style>
  </general>
  <internal>
    <version>6</version>
  </internal>
  <printer>
    <comments>
      <javadoc>
        <check>
          <innerclass>false</innerclass>
          <tags>false</tags>
          <throwsTags>false</throwsTags>
        </check>
        <fieldsShort>true</fieldsShort>
        <generate>
          <class>0</class>
          <constructor>0</constructor>
          <field>0</field>
          <method>0</method>
        </generate>
        <parseComments>false</parseComments>
        <tags>
          <in-line />
          <standard>@web</standard>
        </tags>
        <templates>
          <method>
            <bottom> */</bottom>
            <exception> * @throws $exceptionType$ DOCUMENT ME!</exception>
            <param> * @param $paramType$ DOCUMENT ME!</param>
            <return> * @return DOCUMENT ME!</return>
            <top>/**| * DOCUMENT ME!</top>
```

LISTING 7.1   Continued

```xml
                </method>
            </templates>
        </javadoc>
    </comments>
    <whitespace>
      <after>
        <comma>true</comma>
        <semicolon>true</semicolon>
        <typeCast>true</typeCast>
      </after>
      <before>
        <braces>true</braces>
        <brackets>false</brackets>
        <bracketsTypes>false</bracketsTypes>
        <caseColon>false</caseColon>
        <operator>
          <not>false</not>
        </operator>
        <parentheses>
          <methodCall>false</methodCall>
          <methodDeclaration>false</methodDeclaration>
          <statement>true</statement>
        </parentheses>
      </before>
      <padding>
        <braces>true</braces>
        <brackets>false</brackets>
        <operator>
          <assignment>true</assignment>
          <bitwise>true</bitwise>
          <logical>true</logical>
          <mathematical>true</mathematical>
          <relational>true</relational>
          <shift>true</shift>
        </operator>
        <parenthesis>false</parenthesis>
        <typeCast>false</typeCast>
      </padding>
    </whitespace>
  </printer>
</jalopy>
```

After the configuration file is created, the next step for integration with Ant is to create a buildfile target to run Jalopy against a set of source code. Listing 7.2 shows an Ant target called `format` that does this. This target uses the task `<jalopy>` to execute the Jalopy Ant plug-in. In this target, it is assumed that the `format.xml` file is in the same directory as the buildfile. If it isn't, you need to include the pathname to the file. At the top of the buildfile is the standard `<taskdef>` declaration that maps the taskname `<jalopy>` to a classname. The `<jalopy>` task accepts a nested `<fileset>` element, which is used to define the set of Java source code on which to enforce the project standards. The `<jalopy>` task's convention attribute is used to name the configuration file that was created with the GUI tool. If this attribute is not specified, Jalopy will use its default behavior. The `fileformat` attribute is used to tell Jalopy what file format is intended; the file format controls which end-of-line characters are used for Unix, Mac OS X, or Windows.

LISTING 7.2   Target for Executing Jalopy on Project Source Code

```
<taskdef name="jalopy"
        classname="de.hunsicker.jalopy.plugin.ant.AntPlugin"/>


<!-- format target -->
<target name="format" description="Reformats code to meet team standards">
    <jalopy fileformat="unix"
            convention="format.xml">
        <fileset dir="${dirs.source}" >
            <include name="**/*.java" />
        </fileset>
    </jalopy>
</target>
```

Listing 7.3 shows some sample Java code that doesn't adhere to the style standard that we've defined in the XML configuration file. For example, the braces are at the end of the method declaration line, but our standard style is to have the opening brace on the next line below that. Running Jalopy will actually generate a new version of the file with style problems corrected.

LISTING 7.3   Source Code Example Before Applying a Convention Through Jalopy

```
package com.networksByteDesign.eMarket.inventory.data;

import java.rmi.RemoteException;

import javax.ejb.*;
```

LISTING 7.3   Continued

```java
/**
 * Company entity bean
 *
 * @ejb:bean name="CompanyBean" type="CMP" jndi-name="Company"
 * @ejb:interface
 * remote-class="com.networksByteDesign.eMarket.inventory.data.Company"
 */
public class CompanyBean implements EntityBean {
    transient private EntityContext ctx;
    public String name_;
    public String id_;

    /**
     * @return name of object
     *
     * @ejb:interface-method view-type="both"
     * @ejb:transaction type="Supports"
     * @ejb:persistent-field
     *
     */
    public String getName() {
        return name_;
    }

    /**
     * @param name name of object
     *
     * @ejb:interface-method view-type="both"
     */
    public void setName(String name) {
        name_ = name;
    }

    /**
     * @return id of object
     *
     * @ejb:persistent-field
     * @ejb:pk-field
     *
     * @jboss:dbms-column city_id
     */
```

LISTING 7.3   Continued

```java
public String getId() {
    return id_;
}

/**
 * @param id id of object
 */
public void setId(String id) {
    id_ = id;
}

/**
 * Create object.
 *
 * @ejb:create-method
 * @ejb:permission role-name="Administrator"
 */
public String ejbCreate(String id) {
    id_ = id;

    return null;
}

public void ejbPostCreate(String id) {
}

public void ejbActivate() {
}

public void ejbPassivate() {
}

public void ejbLoad() {
}

public void ejbStore() {
}

public void ejbRemove() throws javax.ejb.RemoveException {
}
```

LISTING 7.3 Continued

```
    public void setEntityContext(EntityContext ctx) {
        this.ctx = ctx;
    }

    public void unsetEntityContext() {
        this.ctx = null;
    }
}
```

Listing 7.4 shows the output that results from executing the `format` target that invokes Jalopy. Jalopy reports how many source files it reformats.

LISTING 7.4   Output That Results from Running the Ant Buildfile for Jalopy

```
% ant format
Buildfile: build.xml

format:
    [jalopy] Jalopy Java Source Code Formatter 1.0b10
    [jalopy] Format 21 source files
    [jalopy] 21 source files formatted

BUILD SUCCESSFUL
Total time: 5 seconds
```

The source code resulting from a pass by Jalopy is shown in Listing 7.5. The code has been modified to clean it up, and it now adheres to the standard defined in the `format.xml` configuration file. After this code has been cleaned up by Jalopy, the next step would be to compile it, run unit tests, and generally validate it. After all of this is complete, the developer should commit the modified code to the source code repository unless you elect to construct your buildfile to perform this step afterward.

LISTING 7.5   Source Code That Has Been Modified by Jalopy to Conform to the Project
             Standard Configuration File

```
package com.networksByteDesign.eMarket.inventory.data;

import java.rmi.RemoteException;
import javax.ejb.*;
```

LISTING 7.5   Continued

```java
/**
 * Company entity bean
 *
 * @ejb:bean name="CompanyBean" type="CMP" jndi-name="Company"
 * @ejb:interface
 *       remote-class="com.networksByteDesign.eMarket.inventory.data.Company"
 */
public class CompanyBean implements EntityBean
{
    transient private EntityContext ctx;
    public String name_;
    public String id_;

    /**
     * DOCUMENT ME!
     *
     * @return name of object
     *
     * @ejb:interface-method view-type="both"
     * @ejb:transaction type="Supports"
     * @ejb:persistent-field
     */
    public String getName()
    {
        return name_;
    }

    /**
     * DOCUMENT ME!
     *
     * @param name name of object
     *
     * @ejb:interface-method view-type="both"
     */
    public void setName(String name)
    {
        name_ = name;
    }

    /**
     * DOCUMENT ME!
```

LISTING 7.5   Continued

```
 *
 * @return id of object
 *
 * @ejb:persistent-field
 * @ejb:pk-field
 * @jboss:dbms-column city_id
 */
public String getId()
{
    return id_;
}


/**
 * DOCUMENT ME!
 *
 * @param id id of object
 */
public void setId(String id)
{
    id_ = id;
}


/**
 * Create object.
 *
 * @param id DOCUMENT ME!
 *
 * @return DOCUMENT ME!
 *
 * @ejb:create-method
 * @ejb:permission role-name="Administrator"
 */
public String ejbCreate(String id)
{
    id_ = id;

    return null;
}


public void ejbPostCreate(String id) {}
```

LISTING 7.5   Continued

```java
    public void ejbActivate() {}

    public void ejbPassivate() {}

    public void ejbLoad() {}

    public void ejbStore() {}

    public void ejbRemove() throws javax.ejb.RemoveException {}

    public void setEntityContext(EntityContext ctx)
    {
        this.ctx = ctx;
    }

    public void unsetEntityContext()
    {
        this.ctx = null;
    }
}
```

The frequency with which the code is run through Jalopy is done is really up to the discretion of the team. It's probably not necessary to run the source code through this process with every build, but once a week may be too infrequent. It really depends on the makeup of the team and how well they are able to follow a certain style. This could be a good process to incorporate in a nightly or weekly build.

PMD

Story

Another problem that has surfaced in the code is some sloppy practices. For example, some developers are using `try-catch` blocks, leaving the `catch` block empty, and doing nothing to handle the exception. Other things need to be cleaned up and are just missed. Some of the other areas that require cleanup include unused variables and failure to follow variable naming conventions. Again, rather than resort to peer code reviews, which will be time-consuming and slow the team down, Michael, the lead developer, looks for additional tools to help automate some of the checking. After searching and spike testing a couple of possibilities, several additional tools emerge that can be integrated into the build process. The first is PMD for catching bad programming practices. The other tools that will be included in the process are Checkstyle, iContract, and JDepend. Michael works with another developer to add these into the build process so that they can be run on a regular basis to catch some of these problems.

PMD is a tool that will scan Java source code and report various problems. Whereas Jalopy deals only with coding style, PMD will detect bad coding practices and report them. If you're familiar with C programming and the use of `lint`, PMD is analogous to the `lint` tool. PMD is available from SourceForge. It can check for a variety of problems such as empty `catch` blocks, unused local variables, empty `if` statements, duplicate `import` statements, unused private methods, classes that could be implemented as singletons, and variable and method name problems. Unlike Jalopy, which generates modified source code, PMD only reports problems, and doesn't actually modify the code. It's worth mentioning that some IDEs have capabilities like this built in, or the facility to support the use of these tools. For example, the Eclipse IDE supports plug-ins for Jalopy, PMD, and Checkstyle, which are tools that will be covered in this chapter. Also, plug-ins are available to allow PMD to integrate with the following IDEs and tools:

- Jedit

- JBuilder

- NetBeans/Forte/Sun ONE

- IntelliJ

- IDEA

- Maven

- Ant

- Eclipse

- Emacs

INSTALLING PMD

To install PMD, follow these steps:

1. Download PMD from

   `http://sourceforge.net/projects/pmd`

2. PMD contains three JAR files in the lib directory:

   - `pmd-1.02.jar`

   - `xercesImpl-2.0.2.jar`

   - `xmlParserAPIs-2.0.2.jar`

Put these JAR files in your system CLASSPATH, or declare them in the `<classpath>` declaration inside the `<taskdef>` declaration as shown here:

```
<taskdef name="pmd"
         classname="net.sourceforge.pmd.ant.PMDTask">
  <classpath>
    <fileset dir="<PMD_INST_DIR>/lib">
      <include name="*.jar" />
    </fileset>
  </classpath>
</taskdef>
```

3. PMD is ready for use in Ant.

Listing 7.6 shows an example of a target that uses PMD. The `<taskdef>` line declares the task, and assigns the class to be executed. Next, we declare a target called `checkCode`. As the description indicates, this target will check for code that has an improper structure. The target invokes the `<pmd>` task. PMD's `verbose` attribute causes very descriptive output to be produced when the task is run.

LISTING 7.6   Ant Buildfile Target for Using PMD to Validate Source Code Structure

```
<taskdef name="pmd"
         classname="net.sourceforge.pmd.ant.PMDTask"/>

<!-- checkCode target -->
<target name="checkCode" description="Checks code for improper structure">
    <pmd verbose="true"
         rulesetfiles="rulesets/basic.xml,rulesets/design.xml"
         shortFilenames="true"
         failonerror="no">
        <formatter type="html" toFile="${dirs.build}/pmd_report.html"/>
        <fileset dir="${dirs.source}">
            <include name="**/*.java"/>
        </fileset>
    </pmd>
</target>
```

The `<pmd>` task has several attributes, as shown in the buildfile of Listing 7.6. The `reportFile` attribute is used to define the output file to which PMD will write its report. The `verbose` attribute turns on verbose output, as the name indicates. The `rulesetfiles` attribute is used to specify a comma-delimited list of XML-based rule files. The default rule sets that are supplied with PMD can be used. PMD comes with the following rulesets included in the distribution:

- Basic—Practices that everyone should follow.

- Naming—Detects names that are too long or too short.

- Unused Code—Identifies variables and methods that are not used.

- Design—Identifies code that has a design that is suspect (that is, everything is static).

- Import Statements—Catches problems with imports, such as duplicate imports, or importing `java.lang`.

- JUnit Tests—Catches common problems with JUnit test classes.

- Strings—Catches problems with String manipulation.

- Braces—Catches bad practices with braces, such as using `if-else` without braces.

- Code Size—Detects problems such as methods or classes that are too long, or methods that have an excessive number of arguments.

It's also possible to generate your own rule files. This is somewhat more complex and is covered in the documentation that comes with PMD. Reports can be in two formats, XML or HTML, and this behavior is set in the `format` attribute. The attribute `failonerror` is set to false so that the build will continue even if an error occurs. It could be set to `true` if you want the build to stop upon detection of a problem. Finally, `<pmd>` will accept a nested `<fileset>`, which is used in this example to define the code to be examined. Running the `checkCode` target of Listing 7.6 produces the output shown in Listing 7.7. It also creates the HTML-based report shown in Figure 7.2.

LISTING 7.7   The Output That Results from Running the `checkCode` Target of Listing 7.6

```
% ant checkCode
Buildfile: build.xml

checkCode:
    [pmd] com/networksByteDesign/eMarket/inventory/company.java
    [pmd] com/networksByteDesign/eMarket/inventory/CompanyServlet.java
    [pmd] com/networksByteDesign/eMarket/inventory/companyTest.java
    [pmd] com/networksByteDesign/eMarket/inventory/customer.java
    [pmd] com/networksByteDesign/eMarket/inventory/CustomerServlet.java
    [pmd] com/networksByteDesign/eMarket/inventory/customerTest.java
    [pmd] com/networksByteDesign/eMarket/inventory/data/CompanyBean.java
    [pmd] com/networksByteDesign/eMarket/inventory/data/CustomerBean.java
    [pmd] com/networksByteDesign/eMarket/inventory/data/SalesItemBean.java
    [pmd] com/networksByteDesign/eMarket/inventory/salesItem.java
    [pmd] com/networksByteDesign/eMarket/inventory/SalesItemServlet.java
```

LISTING 7.7 Continued

```
    [pmd] com/networksByteDesign/eMarket/inventory/salesItemTest.java
    [pmd] com/networksByteDesign/eMarket/MainMenuServlet.java
    [pmd] com/networksByteDesign/eMarket/util/TagLib.java
    [pmd] com/networksByteDesign/spike/test1.java
    [pmd] com/networksByteDesign/spike/test2.java
    [pmd] com/networksByteDesign/spike/test3.java
    [pmd] com/networksByteDesign/spike/test4.java
    [pmd] com/networksByteDesign/spike/test5.java
    [pmd] com/networksByteDesign/spike/test6.java
    [pmd] com/networksByteDesign/spike/test7.java

BUILD SUCCESSFUL
Total time: 5 seconds
```

The report in Figure 7.2 contains a list of problems that PMD found in the source code that it checked, based on the rules files supplied.

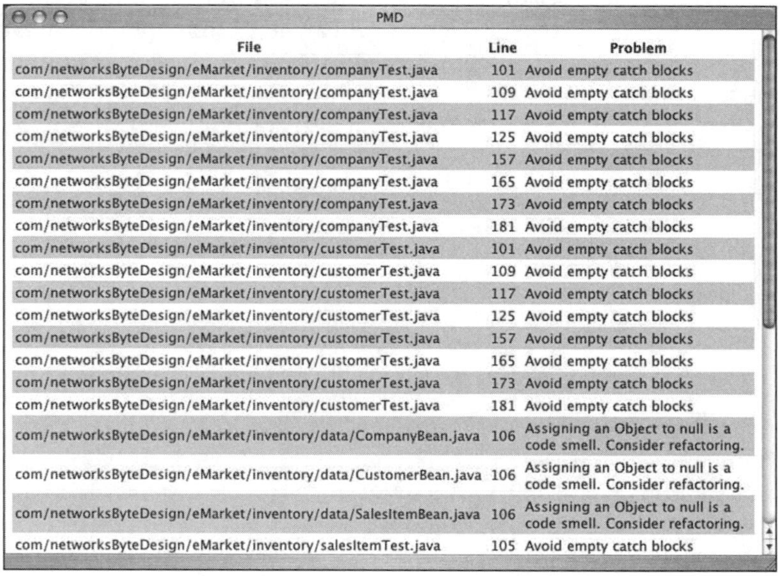

PMD

File	Line	Problem
com/networksByteDesign/eMarket/inventory/companyTest.java	101	Avoid empty catch blocks
com/networksByteDesign/eMarket/inventory/companyTest.java	109	Avoid empty catch blocks
com/networksByteDesign/eMarket/inventory/companyTest.java	117	Avoid empty catch blocks
com/networksByteDesign/eMarket/inventory/companyTest.java	125	Avoid empty catch blocks
com/networksByteDesign/eMarket/inventory/companyTest.java	157	Avoid empty catch blocks
com/networksByteDesign/eMarket/inventory/companyTest.java	165	Avoid empty catch blocks
com/networksByteDesign/eMarket/inventory/companyTest.java	173	Avoid empty catch blocks
com/networksByteDesign/eMarket/inventory/companyTest.java	181	Avoid empty catch blocks
com/networksByteDesign/eMarket/inventory/customerTest.java	101	Avoid empty catch blocks
com/networksByteDesign/eMarket/inventory/customerTest.java	109	Avoid empty catch blocks
com/networksByteDesign/eMarket/inventory/customerTest.java	117	Avoid empty catch blocks
com/networksByteDesign/eMarket/inventory/customerTest.java	125	Avoid empty catch blocks
com/networksByteDesign/eMarket/inventory/customerTest.java	157	Avoid empty catch blocks
com/networksByteDesign/eMarket/inventory/customerTest.java	165	Avoid empty catch blocks
com/networksByteDesign/eMarket/inventory/customerTest.java	173	Avoid empty catch blocks
com/networksByteDesign/eMarket/inventory/customerTest.java	181	Avoid empty catch blocks
com/networksByteDesign/eMarket/inventory/data/CompanyBean.java	106	Assigning an Object to null is a code smell. Consider refactoring.
com/networksByteDesign/eMarket/inventory/data/CustomerBean.java	106	Assigning an Object to null is a code smell. Consider refactoring.
com/networksByteDesign/eMarket/inventory/data/SalesItemBean.java	106	Assigning an Object to null is a code smell. Consider refactoring.
com/networksByteDesign/eMarket/inventory/salesItemTest.java	105	Avoid empty catch blocks

FIGURE 7.2 The HTML-based report generated by PMD.

After the report has been produced, a developer must go back and fix these problems.

Checkstyle

Another source code style checking tool from SourceForge is Checkstyle.

INSTALLING CHECKSTYLE

To install Checkstyle, follow these steps:

1. Download Checkstyle from

   `http://checkstyle.sourceforge.net/#download`

2. Checkstyle has a JAR file in its distribution called

   `checkstyle-all-2.4.jar`

   Put this JAR file in your system `CLASSPATH`, or the `lib` directory of your
   Ant installation.

3. Declare the class in the `<taskdef>` declaration as shown here:

   ```
   <taskdef name="checkstyle"
            classname="com.puppycrawl.tools.checkstyle.CheckStyleTask"/>
   ```

4. Checkstyle is ready to use.

The purpose of Checkstyle is to perform an automated code review of source code to ensure that developers are adhering to coding standards. Checkstyle can be configured to support nearly any coding style, and it includes a configuration file that follows Sun Microsystems Coding Conventions.

Checkstyle can check for common problems with source code including the following areas: naming conventions, `import` statements, Javadoc comments, blocks, modifiers, whitespace, and naming conventions. Checkstyle can also be used with third-party plug-ins for integration with tools like Eclipse/WSAD or IntelliJ. A list of available plug-ins can be found at the Checkstyle home page: `http://checkstyle.sourceforge.net/`.

At first glance, Checkstyle might look as if it's performing the exact same function as PMD. There is some overlap, but there are also some differences. If you compare the capabilities of each, you will see that they each cover some areas that the other does not cover. That's why we elected to use both in the buildfile.

The `<checkstyle>` Ant task, like other tools, uses a `<fileset>` element to define the set of source code on which to perform the style checking. For custom style checking, the user has to supply a set of properties as key/value pairs. For example, one property is `checkstyle.maxlinelen`, which defines the maximum line length. This can be set as `checkstyle.maxlinelen=80`. Properties can be set in one of two ways. They can be explicitly declared in the Ant target as shown in Listing 7.8, or they can be placed in a property file. The Checkstyle Web site provides a sample properties file as a starting point for creating your own configuration.

LISTING 7.8   Ant Target to Execute the Checkstyle Tool Against a Set of Java
Source Code

```
<taskdef name="checkstyle"
         classname="com.puppycrawl.tools.checkstyle.CheckStyleTask"/>
<!-- codeReview target -->
<target name="codeReview" description="Conduct a code review.">
    <checkstyle>
        <fileset dir="${dirs.source}" includes="**/*.java"/>

        <property key="checkstyle.javadoc.scope"
                  value="private"/>
        <property key="checkstyle.require.packagehtml"
                  value="false"/>
        <property key="checkstyle.require.version"
                  value="false"/>
        <property key="checkstyle.allow.noauthor"
                  value="false"/>
        <property key="checkstyle.javadoc.checkUnusedThrows"
                  value="false"/>
        <property key="checkstyle.pattern.member"
                  value="^[a-z][a-zA-Z0-9]*$"/>
        <property key="checkstyle.pattern.publicmember"
                  value="^f[A-Z][a-zA-Z0-9]*$"/>
        <property key="checkstyle.pattern.const"
                  value="^[A-Z](_?[A-Z0-9]+)*$"/>
        <property key="checkstyle.pattern.static"
                  value="^[a-z][a-zA-Z0-9]*$"/>
        <property key="checkstyle.pattern.parameter"
                  value="^[a-z][a-zA-Z0-9]*$"/>
        <property key="checkstyle.pattern.package"
                  value="^[a-z]+(\.[a-zA-Z_][a-zA-Z_0-9]*)*$"/>
        <property key="checkstyle.pattern.type"
                  value="^[A-Z][a-zA-Z0-9]*$"/>
        <property key="checkstyle.pattern.method"
                  value="^[a-z][a-zA-Z0-9]*$"/>
        <property key="checkstyle.pattern.localvar"
                  value="^[a-z][a-zA-Z0-9]*$"/>
        <property key="checkstyle.pattern.localfinalvar"
                  value="^[a-z][a-zA-Z0-9]*$"/>
        <property key="checkstyle.header.file"
                  value=""/>
        <property key="checkstyle.header.ignoreline"
                  value=""/>
```

LISTING 7.8   Continued

```
<property key="checkstyle.header.regexp"
          value="false"/>
<property key="checkstyle.ignore.imports"
          value="false"/>
<property key="checkstyle.illegal.imports"
          value="sun"/>
<property key="checkstyle.maxlinelen"
          value="80"/>
<property key="checkstyle.tab.width"
          value="8"/>
<property key="checkstyle.ignore.importlength"
          value="false"/>
<property key="checkstyle.ignore.maxlinelen"
          value="^$"/>
<property key="checkstyle.maxmethodlen"
          value="150"/>
<property key="checkstyle.maxconstructorlen"
          value="150"/>
<property key="checkstyle.maxfilelen"
          value="2000"/>
<property key="checkstyle.maxparameters"
          value="7"/>
<property key="checkstyle.allow.tabs"
          value="false"/>
<property key="checkstyle.ignore.whitespace"
          value="false"/>
<property key="checkstyle.ignore.whitespace.cast"
          value="false"/>
<property key="checkstyle.paren.pad"
          value="nospace"/>
<property key="checkstyle.wrap.operator"
          value="nl"/>
<property key="checkstyle.ignore.public.in.interface"
          value="false"/>
<property key="checkstyle.allow.protected"
          value="false"/>
<property key="checkstyle.allow.package"
          value="false"/>
<property key="checkstyle.pattern.publicmember"
          value="^f[A-Z][a-zA-Z0-9]*$"/>
<property key="checkstyle.ignore.braces"
          value="true"/>
```

LISTING 7.8 Continued

```
              <property key="checkstyle.block.try"
                        value="stmt"/>
              <property key="checkstyle.block.catch"
                        value="text"/>
              <property key="checkstyle.block.finally"
                        value="stmt"/>
              <property key="checkstyle.lcurly.type"
                        value="eol"/>
              <property key="checkstyle.lcurly.method"
                        value="eol"/>
              <property key="checkstyle.lcurly.other"
                        value="eol"/>
              <property key="checkstyle.rcurly"
                        value="same"/>
              <property key="checkstyle.pattern.todo"
                        value="TODO:"/>
              <property key="checkstyle.ignore.longell"
                        value="false"/>
              <property key="checkstyle.illegal.instantiations"
                        value=""/>
        </checkstyle>
    </target>
```

Running the target in Listing 7.8 against a sample set of source code yields the output shown in Listing 7.9. This output contains a list of problems that Checkstyle found based on the configuration properties we supplied in the target.

LISTING 7.9 Results of Running the Checkstyle Tool in Ant

```
% ant codeReview
Buildfile: build.xml

codeReview:
[checkstyle] com/networksByteDesign/eMarket/util/TagLib.java:4:
             Unused import - java.io.Writer.
[checkstyle] com/networksByteDesign/eMarket/util/TagLib.java:7:
             Unused import - java.util.Hashtable.
[checkstyle] com/networksByteDesign/eMarket/util/TagLib.java:8:
             Avoid using the '.*' form of import.
[checkstyle] com/networksByteDesign/eMarket/util/TagLib.java:9:
             Avoid using the '.*' form of import.
```

LISTING 7.9   Continued

```
[checkstyle] com/networksByteDesign/eMarket/util/TagLib.java:18:
             Type Javadoc comment is missing an @author tag.
[checkstyle] com/networksByteDesign/eMarket/util/TagLib.java:19:1:
             '{' should be on the previous line.
[checkstyle] com/networksByteDesign/eMarket/util/TagLib.java:20:27:
             Missing a Javadoc comment.
[checkstyle] com/networksByteDesign/eMarket/util/TagLib.java:20:27:
             Variable 'bodyOut_' must be private and have accessor methods.
[checkstyle] com/networksByteDesign/eMarket/util/TagLib.java:21:27:
             Missing a Javadoc comment.
[checkstyle] com/networksByteDesign/eMarket/util/TagLib.java:21:27:
             Variable 'pageContext_' must be private & have accessor methods
[checkstyle] com/networksByteDesign/eMarket/util/TagLib.java:22:19:
             Missing a Javadoc comment.
[checkstyle] com/networksByteDesign/eMarket/util/TagLib.java:22:19:
             Variable 'parent_' must be private and have accessor methods.
[checkstyle] com/networksByteDesign/eMarket/util/TagLib.java:23:22:
             Missing a Javadoc comment.
[checkstyle] com/networksByteDesign/eMarket/util/TagLib.java:23:22:
             Name 'atts_' must match pattern '^[a-z][a-zA-Z0-9]*$'.
[checkstyle] com/networksByteDesign/eMarket/util/TagLib.java:24:9:
             Missing a Javadoc comment.
[checkstyle] com/networksByteDesign/eMarket/util/TagLib.java:24:9:
             Variable 'i' must be private and have accessor methods.
[checkstyle] com/networksByteDesign/eMarket/util/TagLib.java:26:5:
             Missing a Javadoc comment.
[checkstyle] com/networksByteDesign/eMarket/util/TagLib.java:27:5:
             '{' should be on the previous line.
[checkstyle] com/networksByteDesign/eMarket/util/TagLib.java:31:5:
             Missing a Javadoc comment.
[checkstyle] com/networksByteDesign/eMarket/util/TagLib.java:32:5:
             '{' should be on the previous line.
[checkstyle] com/networksByteDesign/eMarket/util/TagLib.java:36:5:
             Missing a Javadoc comment.
[checkstyle] com/networksByteDesign/eMarket/util/TagLib.java:37:5:
             '{' should be on the previous line.
[checkstyle] com/networksByteDesign/eMarket/util/TagLib.java:41:5:
             Missing a Javadoc comment.
[checkstyle] com/networksByteDesign/eMarket/util/TagLib.java:42:5:
             '{' should be on the previous line.
[checkstyle] com/networksByteDesign/eMarket/util/TagLib.java:46:5:
             Missing a Javadoc comment.
```

LISTING 7.9   Continued

```
[checkstyle] com/networksByteDesign/eMarket/util/TagLib.java:47:5:
             '{' should be on the previous line.
[checkstyle] com/networksByteDesign/eMarket/util/TagLib.java:51:5:
             Missing a Javadoc comment.
[checkstyle] com/networksByteDesign/eMarket/util/TagLib.java:52:5:
             '{' should be on the previous line.
[checkstyle] com/networksByteDesign/eMarket/util/TagLib.java:56:5:
             Missing a Javadoc comment.
[checkstyle] com/networksByteDesign/eMarket/util/TagLib.java:57:5:
             '{' should be on the previous line.
[checkstyle] com/networksByteDesign/eMarket/util/TagLib.java:61:5:
             Missing a Javadoc comment.
[checkstyle] com/networksByteDesign/eMarket/util/TagLib.java:62:5:
             '{' should be on the previous line.
[checkstyle] com/networksByteDesign/eMarket/util/TagLib.java:66:5:
             Missing a Javadoc comment.
[checkstyle] com/networksByteDesign/eMarket/util/TagLib.java:67:5:
             '{' should be on the previous line.
[checkstyle] com/networksByteDesign/eMarket/util/TagLib.java:71:5:
             Missing a Javadoc comment.
[checkstyle] com/networksByteDesign/eMarket/util/TagLib.java:72:5:
             '{' should be on the previous line.
[checkstyle] com/networksByteDesign/eMarket/util/TagLib.java:74:9:
             '{' should be on the previous line.
[checkstyle] com/networksByteDesign/eMarket/util/TagLib.java:75:15:
             'if' is not followed by whitespace.
[checkstyle] com/networksByteDesign/eMarket/util/TagLib.java:76:13:
             '{' should be on the previous line.
[checkstyle] com/networksByteDesign/eMarket/util/TagLib.java:80:13:
             '}' should be on the same line.
[checkstyle] com/networksByteDesign/eMarket/util/TagLib.java:82:13:
             '{' should be on the previous line.
[checkstyle] com/networksByteDesign/eMarket/util/TagLib.java:89:9:
             '}' should be on the same line.
[checkstyle] com/networksByteDesign/eMarket/util/TagLib.java:90:14:
             'catch' is not followed by whitespace.
[checkstyle] com/networksByteDesign/eMarket/util/TagLib.java:91:9:
             '{' should be on the previous line.
[checkstyle] com/networksByteDesign/eMarket/util/TagLib.java:96:5:
             Missing a Javadoc comment.
[checkstyle] com/networksByteDesign/eMarket/util/TagLib.java:97:5:
             '{' should be on the previous line.
```

LISTING 7.9   Continued

```
[checkstyle] com/networksByteDesign/eMarket/util/TagLib.java:103:5:
             Missing a Javadoc comment.
[checkstyle] com/networksByteDesign/eMarket/util/TagLib.java:104:5:
             '{' should be on the previous line.

BUILD FAILED
file:build.xml:465: Got 577 errors.

Total time: 19 seconds
```

Unlike some of the other tools we've examined, Checkstyle doesn't actually modify your source code, but generates a list of problems that it finds. It basically lets the computer perform a code review for you.

iContract

One technique of software design is to design by contract. In this approach, a contract is established that defines the interface and the semantics of the code. When designing by contract, the interface eventually acts as the contract. This contract includes the method signature and the semantics of the use of the interface. Unless the contract is adhered to, it is worthless. One way to guarantee that the contract is being followed is to use a tool like iContract.

INSTALLING ICONTRACT

Ant contains an optional task for running iContract. However, the tool must be installed to use it:

1. Download iContract from

   `http://www.reliable-systems.com/tools/request-forms/request-icontract.htm`

2. Download the Zip file, which is actually a JAR file.

3. Rename the `.zip` suffix to `.jar`.

4. Put the JAR file in your system CLASSPATH.

5. iContract is ready for use with Ant.

---

iContract allows interface contracts to be specified in the source code with special Javadoc comments. iContract is essentially a preprocessor that processes the special Javadoc comments, and inserts code into the original source that will enforce runtime semantic checking. The error checking ensures that the conditions of the contract (the semantics) are not violated. Also, these special comments will be ignored by the Javadoc processor. In fact, iContract comments are innocuous if you happen to pick up code that has them, but decide not to use them.

Listing 7.10 shows an example of the use of the <icontract> Ant task to instrument code. First, required directories are created with <mkdir>. The <icontract> task has several attributes that need to be set. The srcdir attribute defines the directory to start searching for Java files to instrument. The includes and excludes attributes are used to include or exclude files based on a pattern. In our example, we're excluding the JUnit test files, which follow the naming convention of *Test.java. The instrumentdir is the directory where iContract should place the instrumented source code that it generates. The repositorydir declares the directory to place the repository source files.

The <icontract> task also allows a nested <classpath> element, to define the classpath to be used. Another attribute that we did not use in this example is controlfile, which defines a control file to use. A control file is used to define the instrumentation behavior for certain classes. A control file is not required, and the default behavior is simply not to use one. If you decide to use a control file, you can generate one with the IControl tool available at the iContract Web site.

LISTING 7.10   An Ant Target for Using iContract to Enforce the Design by Contract

```
<path id="project.classpath">
    <pathelement location="${dirs.lib}/all.jar"/>
    <pathelement location="${dirs.build}"/>
    <pathelement location="${dirs.lib}/iContract-jdk1_2.jar"/>
</path>

<!-- instrument target -->
<target name="instrument">
    <mkdir dir="${dirs.build}/instrument"   />
    <mkdir dir="${dirs.build}/repository"    />

    <icontract srcdir="${dirs.source}"
               excludes="**/*Test.java"
               instrumentdir="${dirs.build}/instrument"
               repositorydir="${dirs.build}/repository">
        <classpath refid="project.classpath"/>
    </icontract>
</target>
```

Listing 7.11 shows an example of a Javadoc comment for instrumenting your source code.

LISTING 7.11   Example of a Javadoc Comment for Defining Contract Semantics for a Method

```
/**
    * DOCUMENT ME!
    *
    * @param name name of object
    *
    * @ejb:interface-method view-type="both"
    * @pre name != null
    */
   public void setName(String name)
   {
       name_ = name;
   }
```

In Listing 7.11, notice the use of the @pre tag. This tag tells iContract to verify that the argument name is not null. iContract will generate instrumentation that asserts that name is not null. If it is null, the assertion will fail and it's up to the user of our code to fix their code, because they are violating the contract. The instrument target generates the output shown in Listing 7.12. Note that iContract warns if it has to generate a target file.

LISTING 7.12   Output Resulting from Executing the Target of Listing 7.10

```
% ant instrument
Buildfile: build.xml

instrument:
[icontract] Warning: targets file not specified. generating file: targets
[icontract] You should consider using iControl to create a target file.

BUILD SUCCESSFUL
Total time: 9 seconds
```

An example of the resulting instrumenting code is shown in Listing 7.13. When this code is compiled and run, runtime exceptions will be generated if the semantics of the contract are violated.

LISTING 7.13   Example of the Instrumented Code Generated by iContract

```
/**
      * DOCUMENT ME!
      *
      * @param name name of object
      *
      * @ejb:interface-method view-type="both"
      * @pre name != null
      */
     public void setName(String name)
     {
/*|*/    //#*#------------------------------------------------------------
/*|*/    try {
/*!*/    // true if at least one pre-cond conj. passed.
/*|*/    boolean __pre_passed = false;
/*|*/    //checking com.networksByteDesign.eMarket.inventory.data.CompanyBean
/*!*/    //           ::setName(java.lang.String)
/*|*/    if (! __pre_passed ) {
/*!*/    // succeeded in:
/*!*/    // com.networksByteDesign.eMarket.inventory.data.CompanyBean
/*!*/    // ::setName(java.lang.String)
/*|*/    if((name != null /* do not check prepassed */)) __pre_passed = true;
/*|*/    else
/*!*/    // failed in:
/*!*/    // com.networksByteDesign.eMarket.inventory.data.CompanyBean
/*!*/    // ::setName(java.lang.String)
/*|*/      __pre_passed = false;
/*|*/    }
/*|*/    if (!__pre_passed) {
/*|*/      throw new java.lang.Error(
/*!*/      "com/networksByteDesign/eMarket/inventory/data/CompanyBean.java" +
/*!*/      ":40 : error: precondition violated " +
/*!*/      "(com.networksByteDesign.eMarket.inventory.data.CompanyBean" +
/*!*/      "::setName(java.lang.String)): (/*declared in " +
/*!*/      "com.networksByteDesign.eMarket.inventory.data.CompanyBean" +
/*!*/      "::setName(java.lang.String)*/ (name != null)) "
/*|*/    ); }}
/*|*/    catch ( RuntimeException ex ) {
/*|*/      String txt = "";
/*!*/    if (ex.getClass()==java.lang.Error.class) { txt = ex.toString();; }
/*|*/      else txt =
/*!*/      "com/networksByteDesign/eMarket/inventory/data/CompanyBean.java" +
```

LISTING 7.13   Continued

```
/*!*/      ":40:  exception <<"+ex+">> occured while evaluating" +
/*!*/      " PRE-condition in " +
/*!*/      "com/networksByteDesign/eMarket/inventory/data/CompanyBean.java" +
/*!*/      ":40:  " +
/*!*/      "com.networksByteDesign.eMarket.inventory.data.CompanyBean" +
/*!*/      "::setName(java.lang.String)): (/*declared in " +
/*!*/      "com.networksByteDesign.eMarket.inventory.data.CompanyBean" +
/*!*/      "::setName(java.lang.String)*/ (name != null)) "
/*|*/   ;
/*|*/      throw new java.lang.Error(txt);}
/*|*/
/*|*/   //----------------------------------------------------------#*#
/*|*/
        name_ = name;
```

You might wonder why you would need iContract when you could manually add the code that iContract inserts. There are several advantages to using iContract. First, iContract is performing a code generation step, so it's going to be less error-prone than a manual coding process. Second, you can turn this on and off. You may want to turn on the instrumentation for development and testing, but turn it off in production to increase the execution speed of your code. Finally, iContract adds information that goes into the Javadoc comments, so it is enhancing your documentation.

iContract is an excellent tool for detecting problems caused by violating the intended semantics of an API. iContract's semantic checking goes far beyond the simple type checking performed by the compiler. If your project is having problems caused by improper use of code semantics, consider using iContract at least during the testing phase. This could be turned off prior to release to production.

JDepend

JDepend is a tool for automatically generating quality metrics for a set of Java source code. JDepend allows you to gather metrics about parameters, such as the number of classes and interfaces in a project. It can determine what are termed *afferent couplings* (number of dependencies between classes in a package) and *efferent couplings* (number of dependencies by classes in a package on classes that exist outside the package). JDepend will also report the number of abstract classes in the package, and other ratios based on some of the parameters just mentioned.

Ant contains an optional task called `<jdepend>` that will invoke the JDepend tool. Listing 7.14 shows an example of a target for using JDepend in a build process.

LISTING 7.14   An Ant Target to Run the JDepend Tool

```
<!-- jdepend target -->
<target name="jdepend">
    <jdepend>
        <sourcespath>
            <pathelement location="${dirs.build}" />
        </sourcespath>
        <classpath location="${dirs.build}"/>
    </jdepend>
</target>
```

The `outputfile` is an optional attribute that defines the location where JDepend should write the report of its findings. It is optional and is not being used here. If this attribute isn't set, JDepend will write to STDOUT. The nested `<sourcespath>` element defines the location of the set of source code that should be examined. The report generated by JDepend is shown in Listing 7.15.

LISTING 7.15   Output from the Target of Listing 7.14

```
% ant jdepend
Buildfile: build.xml

jdepend:

    [jdepend] -------------------------------------------------
    [jdepend] - Package: com.networksByteDesign.eMarket
    [jdepend] -------------------------------------------------
```

LISTING 7.15   Continued

```
[jdepend] Stats:
[jdepend]     Total Classes: 2
[jdepend]     Concrete Classes: 2
[jdepend]     Abstract Classes: 0

[jdepend]     Ca: 0
[jdepend]     Ce: 5

[jdepend]     A: 0
[jdepend]     I: 1
[jdepend]     D: 0

[jdepend] Abstract Classes:

[jdepend] Concrete Classes:
[jdepend]     com.networksByteDesign.eMarket.MainMenuServlet
[jdepend]     com.networksByteDesign.eMarket.__REP_MainMenuServlet

[jdepend] Depends Upon:
[jdepend]     java.io
[jdepend]     java.lang
[jdepend]     java.util
[jdepend]     javax.servlet
[jdepend]     javax.servlet.http

[jdepend] Used By:
[jdepend]     Not used by any packages.


[jdepend] -------------------------------------------------
[jdepend] - Package: com.networksByteDesign.eMarket.inventory
[jdepend] -------------------------------------------------

[jdepend] Stats:
[jdepend]     Total Classes: 12
[jdepend]     Concrete Classes: 12
[jdepend]     Abstract Classes: 0

[jdepend]     Ca: 0
[jdepend]     Ce: 3

[jdepend]     A: 0
[jdepend]     I: 1
```

LISTING 7.15   Continued

```
[jdepend]    D: 0

[jdepend] Abstract Classes:

[jdepend] Concrete Classes:
[jdepend]    com.networksByteDesign.eMarket.inventory.CompanyServlet
[jdepend]    com.networksByteDesign.eMarket.inventory.CustomerServlet
[jdepend]    com.networksByteDesign.eMarket.inventory.SalesItemServlet
[jdepend]    com.networksByteDesign.eMarket.inventory.__REP_CompanyServlet
[jdepend]    com.networksByteDesign.eMarket.inventory.__REP_CustomerServlet
[jdepend]    com.networksByteDesign.eMarket.inventory.__REP_SalesItemServlet
[jdepend]    com.networksByteDesign.eMarket.inventory.__REP_company
[jdepend]    com.networksByteDesign.eMarket.inventory.__REP_customer
[jdepend]    com.networksByteDesign.eMarket.inventory.__REP_salesItem
[jdepend]    com.networksByteDesign.eMarket.inventory.company
[jdepend]    com.networksByteDesign.eMarket.inventory.customer
[jdepend]    com.networksByteDesign.eMarket.inventory.salesItem

[jdepend] Depends Upon:
[jdepend]    java.io
[jdepend]    java.lang
[jdepend]    java.util

[jdepend] Used By:
[jdepend]    Not used by any packages.

[jdepend] -------------------------------------------------
[jdepend] - Package: com.networksByteDesign.eMarket.inventory.data
[jdepend] -------------------------------------------------

[jdepend] Stats:
[jdepend]    Total Classes: 6
[jdepend]    Concrete Classes: 6
[jdepend]    Abstract Classes: 0

[jdepend]    Ca: 0
[jdepend]    Ce: 3

[jdepend]    A: 0
[jdepend]    I: 1
[jdepend]    D: 0
```

LISTING 7.15   Continued

```
[jdepend] Abstract Classes:

[jdepend] Concrete Classes:
[jdepend] com.networksByteDesign.eMarket.inventory.data.CompanyBean
[jdepend] com.networksByteDesign.eMarket.inventory.data.CustomerBean
[jdepend] com.networksByteDesign.eMarket.inventory.data.SalesItemBean
[jdepend] com.networksByteDesign.eMarket.inventory.data.__REP_CompanyBean
[jdepend] com.networksByteDesign.eMarket.inventory.data.__REP_CustomerBean

[jdepend] Depends Upon:
[jdepend]     java.lang
[jdepend]     java.util
[jdepend]     javax.ejb

[jdepend] Used By:
[jdepend]     Not used by any packages.

[jdepend] --------------------------------------------------
[jdepend] - Package: com.networksByteDesign.eMarket.util
[jdepend] --------------------------------------------------

[jdepend] Stats:
[jdepend]     Total Classes: 2
[jdepend]     Concrete Classes: 2
[jdepend]     Abstract Classes: 0

[jdepend]     Ca: 0
[jdepend]     Ce: 6

[jdepend]     A: 0
[jdepend]     I: 1
[jdepend]     D: 0

[jdepend] Abstract Classes:

[jdepend] Concrete Classes:
[jdepend]     com.networksByteDesign.eMarket.util.TagLib
[jdepend]     com.networksByteDesign.eMarket.util.__REP_TagLib

[jdepend] Depends Upon:
[jdepend]     java.io
```

LISTING 7.15   Continued

```
[jdepend]       java.lang
[jdepend]       java.text
[jdepend]       java.util
[jdepend]       javax.servlet.jsp
[jdepend]       javax.servlet.jsp.tagext

[jdepend] Used By:
[jdepend]       Not used by any packages.

[jdepend] ------------------------------------------------
[jdepend] - Package: com.networksByteDesign.spike
[jdepend] ------------------------------------------------

[jdepend] Stats:
[jdepend]       Total Classes: 14
[jdepend]       Concrete Classes: 14
[jdepend]       Abstract Classes: 0

[jdepend]       Ca: 0
[jdepend]       Ce: 2

[jdepend]       A: 0
[jdepend]       I: 1
[jdepend]       D: 0

[jdepend] Abstract Classes:

[jdepend] Concrete Classes:
[jdepend]       com.networksByteDesign.spike.__REP_test1
[jdepend]       com.networksByteDesign.spike.__REP_test2
[jdepend]       com.networksByteDesign.spike.__REP_test3
[jdepend]       com.networksByteDesign.spike.__REP_test4
[jdepend]       com.networksByteDesign.spike.__REP_test5
[jdepend]       com.networksByteDesign.spike.__REP_test6
[jdepend]       com.networksByteDesign.spike.__REP_test7
[jdepend]       com.networksByteDesign.spike.test1
[jdepend]       com.networksByteDesign.spike.test2
[jdepend]       com.networksByteDesign.spike.test3
[jdepend]       com.networksByteDesign.spike.test4
[jdepend]       com.networksByteDesign.spike.test5
[jdepend]       com.networksByteDesign.spike.test6
[jdepend]       com.networksByteDesign.spike.test7
```

LISTING 7.15   Continued

```
[jdepend] Depends Upon:
[jdepend]    java.lang
[jdepend]    java.util

[jdepend] Used By:
[jdepend]    Not used by any packages.


[jdepend] -------------------------------------------------
[jdepend] - Package: java.io
[jdepend] -------------------------------------------------
[jdepend] No stats available: package referenced, but not analyzed.


[jdepend] -------------------------------------------------
[jdepend] - Package: java.lang
[jdepend] -------------------------------------------------
[jdepend] No stats available: package referenced, but not analyzed.


[jdepend] -------------------------------------------------
[jdepend] - Package: java.text
[jdepend] -------------------------------------------------
[jdepend] No stats available: package referenced, but not analyzed.


[jdepend] -------------------------------------------------
[jdepend] - Package: java.util
[jdepend] -------------------------------------------------
[jdepend] No stats available: package referenced, but not analyzed.


[jdepend] -------------------------------------------------
[jdepend] - Package: javax.ejb
[jdepend] -------------------------------------------------
[jdepend] No stats available: package referenced, but not analyzed.


[jdepend] -------------------------------------------------
[jdepend] - Package: javax.servlet
[jdepend] -------------------------------------------------
[jdepend] No stats available: package referenced, but not analyzed.


[jdepend] -------------------------------------------------
[jdepend] - Package: javax.servlet.http
[jdepend] -------------------------------------------------
[jdepend] No stats available: package referenced, but not analyzed.
```

LISTING 7.15   Continued

```
[jdepend] -------------------------------------------------
[jdepend] - Package: javax.servlet.jsp
[jdepend] -------------------------------------------------
[jdepend] No stats available: package referenced, but not analyzed.


[jdepend] -------------------------------------------------
[jdepend] - Package: javax.servlet.jsp.tagext
[jdepend] -------------------------------------------------
[jdepend] No stats available: package referenced, but not analyzed.



[jdepend] -------------------------------------------------
[jdepend] - Package Dependency Cycles:
[jdepend] -------------------------------------------------



[jdepend] -------------------------------------------------
[jdepend] - Summary:
[jdepend] -------------------------------------------------

[jdepend] Name, Class Count, Abstract Class Count, Ca, Ce, A, I, D:

[jdepend] com.networksByteDesign.eMarket,2,0,0,5,0,1,0
[jdepend] com.networksByteDesign.eMarket.inventory,12,0,0,3,0,1,0
[jdepend] com.networksByteDesign.eMarket.inventory.data,6,0,0,3,0,1,0
[jdepend] com.networksByteDesign.eMarket.util,2,0,0,6,0,1,0
[jdepend] com.networksByteDesign.spike,14,0,0,2,0,1,0
[jdepend] java.io,0,0,3,0,0,0,1
[jdepend] java.lang,0,0,5,0,0,0,1
[jdepend] java.text,0,0,1,0,0,0,1
[jdepend] java.util,0,0,5,0,0,0,1
[jdepend] javax.ejb,0,0,1,0,0,0,1
[jdepend] javax.servlet,0,0,1,0,0,0,1
[jdepend] javax.servlet.http,0,0,1,0,0,0,1
[jdepend] javax.servlet.jsp,0,0,1,0,0,0,1
[jdepend] javax.servlet.jsp.tagext,0,0,1,0,0,0,1

BUILD SUCCESSFUL
Total time: 3 seconds
```

This report in Listing 7.15 shows the various types of dependencies. The value of a JDepend report is in measuring how clean your package implementations may or may not be. Sometimes a team creates a set of packages that have circular dependencies, where package A depends on package B, and package B depends on package A. This makes it impossible to perform a clean build of the project. This situation can and does arise when developers include old versions of packages in their build CLASSPATH, and don't perform a clean build on a routine basis. JDepend will detect problems like this. Also, JDepend reports all of the packages your code depends on, which is nice to know for packaging and release, especially if some packages have licensing issues.

If the report shown in Listing 7.15 doesn't suit the style you would prefer, or if you would like to automatically generate something that might be suitable to give to management, there is another option. The <jdepend> task can output its report in XML, and then an XSLT stylesheet can be applied to the resulting XML to produce the format of your choice. Listing 7.16 shows an alternative target that specifies the format as XML. Following execution of the <jdepend> task, the <style> task is used to apply a stylesheet and transform the output.

LISTING 7.16   An Alternative Target That Specifies the Output Format as XML

```
<!-- jdepend target -->
<target name="jdepend">
    <jdepend outputfile="${dirs.build}/jdepend-report.xml" format="xml">
        <sourcespath>
            <pathelement location="${dirs.build}" />
        </sourcespath>
        <classpath location="${dirs.build}"/>
    </jdepend>

    <style basedir="${dirs.build}" destdir="${dirs.build}"
           includes="jdepend-report.xml"
           style="${ant.home}/etc/jdepend.xsl" />
</target>
```

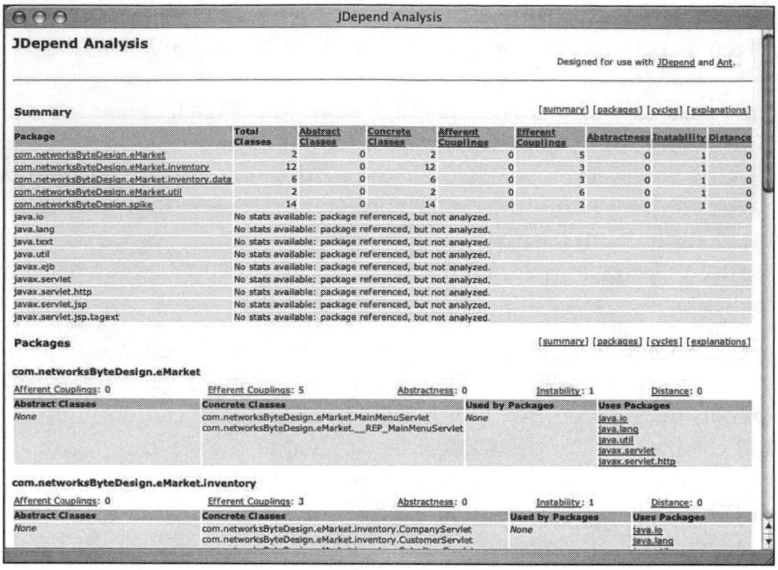

FIGURE 7.3   The HTML-based JDepend Analysis Report.

Summary

In this chapter, we considered the reasons for maintaining code standards on an XP project. Because everyone on the project owns the code, and can modify it at any time, XP says that standards should be set and then followed. Sometimes this is more easily said than done. Although peer code reviews can be performed to check up on code quality, we learned that a number of tools and products for maintaining code quality can be incorporated into an automated build process. Many of these tools, if properly used, can actually take the place of developer code reviews. You must make an initial investment of time to learn to use the tools and incorporate them into a build process. However, some of the time involved is required to define code standards in the first place. This has to be done whether the reviews are manual or automated.

The advantages of incorporating automated tools for maintaining code standards into the build process include

- Less developer time is consumed with the code review process.

- Each developer receives instant feedback on code quality.

- The automated process is more thorough and less error-prone.

- Automated processes will be more consistent than a group of developers.

Deployment to a Production Environment

The nature of XP demands that you continually steer a project toward the intended goal. If you do continuous testing and integrating, problems become immediately apparent. Because of the iterative nature of XP processes, anything that can be effectively automated should be automated. As the eMarket team is discovering, even the normally manual process of tagging code in CVS is a step that can be automated. When implementing XP, think beyond the conventional wisdom of other methodologies. In XP, you want to eliminate mistakes and increase project velocity while staying on track and maintaining high quality. Automating processes wherever possible is the way to achieve this.

Story

The eMarket development team has been performing frequent releases and would like to generate CVS reports about their releases. Developers have not always tagged some of the sources that went into a release. Although nothing catastrophic has happened yet, it's apparent that they need more feedback on this part of the process. They decide to implement an automated CVS reporting capability in their build process.

CVS Reporting

One of the core values of XP is feedback. Getting high-quality feedback in a project will increase your ability to spot problems and take corrective action before it's too late. Automating the generation of feedback whenever possible increases the timeliness and value of the feedback. Information that's difficult to extract, or is out of date, is of little value.

Several tools can be used to generate automated reports about the state of a CVS repository. In the following sections, we'll examine several types of reports that can be automatically generated as part of the build process. These reports can provide insight to a team leader or developers about several aspects of the CVS repository.

CVS Comments Report

Let's begin by generating a report of the files that have been committed to CVS, and the associated comments inserted by each developer when the changes were committed. This target will make use of the Ant <cvschangelog> task. Listing 8.1 shows the cvsComments target, which will generate the report just described.

LISTING 8.1   CVS Comments Target That Will Generate a Report in HTML of Files and Associated Comments That Have Been Committed to CVS

```
<!-- cvsComments target -->
<target name="cvsComments" depends="cvsInit">
    <mkdir dir="${dirs.build}"/>
    <tstamp />

    <cvschangelog dir="${dirs.source}"
                  destfile="${dirs.build}/cvsComments.xml"
                  daysinpast="1" />

    <style in="${dirs.build}/cvsComments.xml"
           out="${dirs.build}/cvsComments_${DSTAMP}.html"
           style="${ant.home}/etc/changelog.xsl">
        <param name="title"
               expression="CVS Comments - ${TODAY}"/>
        <param name="module" expression="${dirs.source}"/>
    </style>
</target>
```

The <cvschangelog> task entry, shown in the following code snippet, will run the cvs log command against the repository, and generate the output in XML:

```
<cvschangelog dir="${dirs.source}"
              destfile="${dirs.build}/cvsComments.xml"
              daysinpast="1" />
```

The dir attribute indicates the directory from which to run the cvs log command. The destfile attribute is the location of the file in which to write the XML output. Because we want this target to produce a daily report of what was checked into CVS, the `daysinpast` attribute is set to 1. We will see later that the `<cvschangelog>` task has other attributes that allow a great deal of customization of the information to be extracted from CVS.

The output of the `<cvschangelog>` task is an XML representation of each file that was committed to CVS, the date and timestamp indicating when it was committed, the developer who committed the file, and the comments added by the developer. This XML file can be utilized to produce a variety of reports that can be useful to the project management and technical leads. We will start by transforming the XML file with the XSLT stylesheet provided by Ant, and generate the standard report:

```
<style in="${dirs.build}/cvsComments.xml"
       out="${dirs.build}/cvsComments_${DSTAMP}.html"
       style="${ant.home}/etc/changelog.xsl">
   <param name="title"
           expression="CVS Comments - ${TODAY}"/>
   <param name="module" expression="${dirs.source}"/>
</style>
```

The `style` task is used to merge XML and XSLT files and provides an easy way to tap into the power of XSLT as a part of the normal build process. The `in` and `style` attributes are used to refer to the XML and XSLT files respectively. The `out` attribute indicates the file that would be created by the calling of the XSLT parser.

NOTE

All of the output files we are creating are being placed in the `buildDir` directory. This is being done intentionally to make it easy to differentiate between files that should be checked into version control and files that are generated or created as part of our build process. This allows us to easily clean up all generated files by simply deleting the `buildDir` directory. Also when we check files into CVS, we don't need to spend the effort to ignore various files that are transient in nature; we can focus only on those files where information is being mastered.

We do understand that some development teams prefer to check generated files into version control. Although we don't suggest that as a best practice, all of the build files described in this book would support that practice by simply using `sourceDir` wherever we use `buildDir`.

The XSLT file provided with Ant for generating a CVS comment report takes three optional parameters. `Title` is the title at the top of the page. `Module` is the name of the CVS module that was checked out from version control. `CVSweb` is a URL that points to the location of the CVS Web product if you have installed that on your machine. This product allows the user to view different versions of CVS-controlled files from a Web interface.

The end result of this target is an HTML report showing each file that was checked into CVS the previous day along with its associated comments. Figure 8.1 shows the HTML report that was generated using this target.

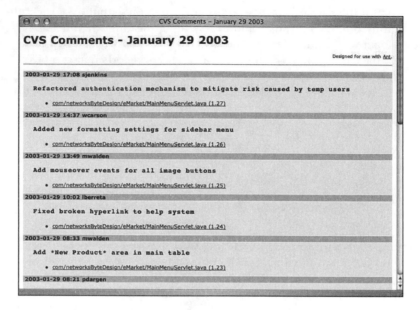

FIGURE 8.1   The HTML-based CVS Comments Report created by applying a stylesheet to the generated XML.

Weekly CVS Report

The CVS Comments Report created in the last section is useful in itself. However, with a few extra steps, we can create custom reports that will allow developers and project leaders to attain a better understanding of other important information. The next target to be added is called the `weeklyCVSReport`, and is shown in Listing 8.2.

LISTING 8.2   Weekly CVS Report Target

```
<!-- weeklyCVSReport target -->
<target name="weeklyCVSReport" depends="cvsInit">
    <mkdir dir="${dirs.build}"/>
    <tstamp />
```

LISTING 8.2   Continued

```
        <cvschangelog dir="${dirs.source}"
                    destfile="${dirs.build}/cvsComments.xml"
                    daysinpast="7"
                    usersfile="userMapping.lst" />

        <style in="${dirs.build}/cvsComments.xml"
            out="${dirs.build}/weeklyCVS_${DSTAMP}.html"
            style="${ant.home}/etc/changelog.xsl">
          <param name="title"
                expression="Weekly CVS Report ending ${TODAY}"/>
          <param name="module" expression="${dirs.source}"/>
        </style>
    </target>
```

In this target, there are several improvements to the CVS Comments report. First, we have created a weekly report, rather than a daily one. We've added an attribute called the `usersfile`. This attribute names a Java properties file that maps login names to a more readable format. An example of a `file` containing the attributes for use with the `usersfile` attribute is shown in Listing 8.3. By using this mapping, the XML file will contain the users' names rather than their login IDs.

LISTING 8.3   Login Name Mapping File

```
mwalden=Michael Walden
lberreta=Lisa Berreta
sjenkins=Scott Jenkins
wcarson=Warren Carson
pdargen=Phil Dargen
```

The page generated by this target is shown in Figure 8.2.

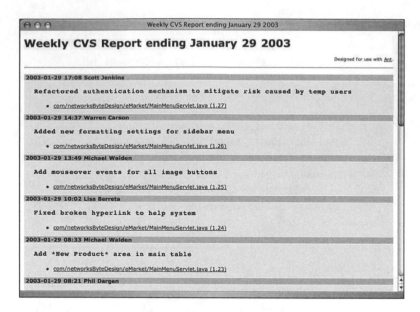

FIGURE 8.2   The Weekly CVS Report generated with buildfile in Listing 8.2.

Release CVS Report

We can also create a target for producing a report of all of the CVS commits and comments over a period of time. This target, called the `releaseCVSReport` target, is shown in Listing 8.4. The `releaseCVSReport` target combines the use of the `<input>` task with the `<cvschangelog>` task. The result is that a user can enter a date range, and the `<cvschangelog>` task will be able to extract information based on the start and end dates, rather than a number of days. This target also allows the user to input the report title and pass it to the `<style>` task as a parameter for report generation.

LISTING 8.4   Release CVS Report Target

```
<!-- releaseCVSReport target -->
<target name="releaseCVSReport" depends="cvsInit">

    <mkdir dir="${dirs.build}"/>
    <tstamp />

    <requiredInput message="Please enter start date:"
                   addproperty="startDate"
                   errorMessage=" You didn't enter a start date."/>
```

LISTING 8.4 Continued

```
        <requiredInput message="Please enter end date:"
                     addproperty="endDate"
                     errorMessage=" You didn't enter an end date."/>

        <requiredInput message="Please enter report title:"
                     addproperty="reportTitle"
                     errorMessage=" You didn't enter a report title."/>

        <cvschangelog dir="${dirs.source}"
                     destfile="${dirs.build}/cvsComments.xml"
                     start="${startDate}"
                     end="${endDate}"
                     usersfile="userMapping.lst" />

        <style in="${dirs.build}/cvsComments.xml"
             out="${dirs.build}/releaseCVS_${DSTAMP}.html"
             style="${ant.home}/etc/changelog.xsl">
           <param name="title"  expression="${reportTitle}"/>
           <param name="module" expression="${dirs.source}"/>
        </style>
    </target>
```

Story

After adding the CVS Report Target to the buildfile, Michael and Lisa realize that the target could be used to generate a technical release notes document. The only prerequisite for this to work is that all of the developers' comments must be of sufficient quality and at the appropriate level of detail. As the lead developer, Michael sends out a set of guidelines to the rest of the development team for writing comments when committing files to CVS. The benefit is that now the release notes will be automatically generated any time they are needed. Because none of the developers especially love to write documentation, this is a welcome addition to the build process.

Creating Technical Release Notes from CVS Comments

If the developers' comments are properly written, the report could be used as a technical release notes document. Following a practice like this is an excellent way of leveraging work for multiple purposes, and is a common practice in software development. Although we consider this concept when we think of code reuse, we often forget that the same pattern applies to other segments of software development. If the CVS comments are intended for use in a report like this, it does help to set guidelines for the developers, to engage in certain best practices. This includes the following:

- Use well-written comments that describe an overview of what was done as opposed to a line-by-line rehash of the code.

- Make small, well-defined changes and check in frequently.

- As always in XP, test changes before checking in code.

- Focus on necessary changes, and not "fluff."

CVS Tag Report

The final CVS report that we will generate involves reporting based on CVS tags. This target is similar to the "Release CVS Report" target developed earlier. However, instead of creating the report based on a date range, the report will be based on a tag range. A user can enter the names of two CVS tags, and this target will generate a report of all of the CVS entries between the versions marked with the specified tags. This target is shown in Listing 8.5.

LISTING 8.5   CVS Tag Report Target

```
<!-- cvsTagReport target -->
<target name="cvsTagReport" depends="cvsInit">

    <requiredInput message="Please enter cvs module:"
                  addproperty="cvsModule"
                  errorMessage="You didn't enter your cvs module."/>

    <requiredInput message="Please enter first tag:"
                  addproperty="firstTag"
                  errorMessage="You didn't enter a CVS tag."/>

    <requiredInput message="Please enter second tag:"
                  addproperty="secondTag"
                  errorMessage="You didn't enter a second CVS tag."/>

    <cvstagdiff destfile="${dirs.build}/tagdiff.xml"
                package="${cvsModule}"
                startTag="${firstTag}"
                endTag="${secondTag}" />

      <style in="${dirs.build}/tagdiff.xml"
            out="${dirs.build}/tagdiff_${firstTag}_${secondTag}.html"
            style="${ant.home}/etc/tagdiff.xsl">
        <param name="title"
```

LISTING 8.5 Continued

```
                expression="Comparison of: ${firstTag} and ${secondTag}"
        />
        <param name="module" expression="${dirs.source}"/>
    </style>
</target>
```

The `<cvstagdiff>` task is very similar to the `<cvschangelog>` task. This task generates an XML-formatted report of the differences between two versions in a set of files. The output file, indicated by the `destfile` attribute, is the file that contains the XML formatted information about the changes that occurred from one tagged release to another. The `startTag` and `endTag` attributes are the names of the two tags to compare.

As with the `<cvschangelog>` task, there is a standard XSLT that ships with Ant that can be used to format the XML file into HTML. Of course you can always write your own XSLT file to transform the XML file into the format of your choice. The report generated by the CVS Tag Report target is shown in Figure 8.3.

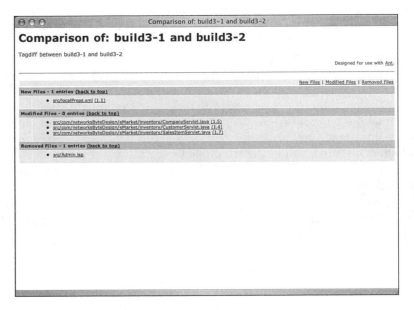

FIGURE 8.3 A report showing the differences between two builds.

The document produced by this target contains valuable information. It can also be very useful to a technical lead when producing the technical release documentation.

Advanced Version Control Techniques for Ant

Story

As the size of the eMarket project code base grows, so does the time required to build. The time required to perform an iterative build has grown enough that everyone in the group is ready to find a way to streamline the build. The step that is taking up a majority of the time is the code generation step. The problem with this step is that the build process is regenerating all of the generated Java code with every iterative build. This is a waste of time because very often the input files haven't been changed at all. The fact is that the generated Java files don't need to be regenerated during most of the builds routinely performed by the development team.

Amy, one of the new team members, works with John to modify the build process to make the code generation step more efficient. What they develop is a modified target called the smartBuild target. This target can actually be used anytime there is a conditional step to be performed. In this case, the smartBuild target will check to see if any of the input files for the code generation step have actually changed, and only perform code generation if really necessary. The result is that a majority of the builds now run much faster, which helps overall project velocity.

Let's create one final CVS-based target before moving on to other topics. The smartBuild target, shown in Listing 8.6, illustrates a technique that can be used to increase the efficiency of a step that may be dependent on a code change. In the example in the story, the eMarket team has a step in their process that performs code generation. The code generation step should only be run if any of the input files to the code generator have actually changed. If none of the inputs have changed, running the code generation step is harmless, but is also a waste of time. With the smartBuild target, the <cvs> tag is used to perform a cvs update, and the output of the command is written to a file defined in the output attribute. If nothing was updated, this file will not be written. We can use this behavior to determine whether any changes occurred, and set an Ant property accordingly. The <loadfile> task is used to set the property filesChanged if the output of the cvs command exists and can be loaded.

LISTING 8.6   SmartBuild Target That Can be Used to Perform a Step Only If Files Actually Changed as a Result of a cvs update

```
<!-- smartBuild target -->
<target name="smartBuild" depends="cvsInit">

    <cvs command="update"
        dest="${dirs.source}"
        output="${dirs.build}/smartBuild.txt" />

    <loadfile property="filesChanged"
            srcFile="${dirs.build}/smartBuild.txt" />
```

LISTING 8.6 Continued

```
    <condition property="mustCodegen">
        <contains string="${filesChanged}" substring=".codegen" />
    </condition>
</target>
```

One reason the team might need this is if some of the manually coded files have changed, but the sources for code generated have not changed. In this situation, the build needs to be run, but we don't actually want to perform the code generation step. In Chapter 10, "Additional Teams Adopt the XP Process," we introduce another technique using selectors to further optimize code generation.

This target illustrates a technique for using existing Ant capabilities to increase the efficiency of an Ant build process. It's possible to do just about anything with Ant, and often with its existing capabilities (as opposed to extending it). Accomplishing things with Ant is a matter of becoming familiar with the tools that are there, and devising creative ways to combine them into something even more useful.

Performing a Distributed Deployment with Remote Ant

Story

Up to this point, the eMarket development team has been executing buildfiles only on the development server. Although they have been deploying a WAR file to the test server, this has only involved an FTP of the file to the test server. The buildfile has still only executed on the development server. However, they now need to execute an Ant deployment process on the test server as part of the overall deployment process. This could be done manually for a single machine, but they would prefer to automate it. Also, they are preparing to put their first release into production, and go live with their Web site. The remote deployment can be run with a SourceForge tool called Remote Ant or Rant.

The production Web server farm is running Apache Tomcat. Lisa and Amy work to install Remote Ant on the production servers. This basically involves deploying the Rant WAR file to the webapps directory. When this is complete, the team is ready to use Rant to perform remote deployments.

All of the deployment operations we have examined so far in this book have involved running an Ant buildfile on a single server. Even if the server performs an operation such as a file transfer (with FTP) to another server, it really still only involves execution of the buildfile on a single server. In this section, we will look at a way to perform a distributed deployment with a tool called Remote Ant, or Rant. Rant is a distributed build (or deployment) system that allows a user to execute Ant buildfiles on another server. With Rant, it's possible to transfer an Ant buildfile to another system (that has Rant installed), and then execute that buildfile remotely.

Rant can be downloaded from sourceforge.net at the following URL:

http://sourceforge.net/projects/remoteant/

Also, a reference to Rant can be found on the Apache Ant Web site at

http://ant.apache.org/projects.html

Rant uses the Apache SOAP implementation, and the SOAP (Simple Object Access Protocol) RPCRouter for its distributed communication infrastructure, so it requires a servlet engine on the target system in order to work. Apache SOAP is an implementation of the W3C SOAP specification. You can learn more about the SOAP specification and the Apache implementation at

http://xml.apache.org/soap/

It's not necessary to understand SOAP in order to use Rant. In fact, the Rant download contains everything you need to run, including Apache SOAP, so it's not even necessary to install SOAP separately. The one aspect of SOAP of interest here is the URL to the RPCRouter.

INSTALLING RANT

To install Rant, follow these steps:

1. Download Rant from:

   ```
   http://sourceforge.net/projects/remoteant/
   ```

For this chapter, we used: rant-0.1.zip. Rant is already configured to work with Apache Tomcat. Getting it to work with other servlet engines requires a good understanding of the deployment descriptors.

2. Unzip the Rant zipfile. It contains a file called rant.war in the directory dist.

3. For Apache Tomcat, all that needs to be done is to copy rant.war to the web-apps directory of your Tomcat installation, and start (or restart) Tomcat.

4. The RPCRouter can be tested with a Web browser. Open a Web browser, and go to the URL of rpcrouter. It will be in the following form:

   ```
   http://hostname:port/rant/servlet/rpcrouter
   ```

If you're running Tomcat on the same machine as your browser, it will probably be something like this:

```
http://localhost:8080/rant/servlet/rpcrouter
```

If Rant configured properly, you should receive the following message:

```
SOAP RPC Router
Sorry, I don't speak via HTTP GET - you have to use HTTP POST to talk to me.
```

If you saw this message on your browser, Rant is ready to be used.

Rant requires two Ant buildfiles; one to execute locally, and the other to execute remotely. Let's begin by setting up a local buildfile. Listing 8.7 shows an example of a local buildfile.

LISTING 8.7   Example of a Local Buildfile for Use with Remote Ant (Rant)

```
<taskdef name="rant"
         classname="com.einnovation.rant.RantTaskDef"/>

<!-- remoteDeploy target -->
<target name="remoteDeploy">
    <rant buildFile="/home/dist/Deploy.xml"

          soapURL="http://localhost:8080/rant/servlet/rpcrouter"➥
          target="deploy"/>
</target>
```

First, a `taskdef` line is used to map the class `com.einnovation.rant.RantTaskDef` to `<rant>` task name. Also within the `taskdef` line, the classpath is defined to include the required JAR files, which are

- `rant.jar`
- `mail.jar`
- `activation.jar`
- `soap.jar`
- `ant.jar`

Next, the local target to be executed, which is `remoteDeploy`, is defined. Within this element is the `<rant>` task element. This requires

- The name of the remote buildfile to execute
- The URL to the RPCRouter, which is the URL used to test via a Web browser as described in the sidebar on installation
- The name of the remote target to execute.

In reality, everything required to perform a remote build is probably not going to be on the destination server. Most likely, the remote buildfile will change with each release, and also the package to be deployed will definitely have changed. In order to handle this, an additional target is added to the local buildfile that will FTP the remote buildfile and the tarball of the latest software release to the destination server. Afterward, it will execute the remote buildfile that was just transferred. The modified buildfile is shown in Listing 8.8.

LISTING 8.8   Modified Local Buildfile for Rant

```
<!-- remoteDeploy target -->
<target name="remoteDeploy" depends="remoteTransfer">
    <rant buildFile="/home/dist/Deploy.xml"
          soapURL="http://localhost:8080/rant/servlet/rpcrouter"
          target="deploy"/>
</target>


<!-- remoteTransfer target -->
<target name="remoteTransfer" depends="deploy">
    <tar tarfile="${ant.project.name}.tar.gz"
         basedir="."
         includes="${ant.project.name}.war"
         compression="gzip" />

    <requiredInput message="Please enter cronus ftp password:"
                   addproperty="ftpPassword"
                   errorMessage="You didn't enter the ftp password."/>

    <ftp server="127.0.0.1" remotedir="/home/dist" action="put"
        userid="cronus" password="${ftpPassword}">
        <fileset dir=".">
            <include name="deploy.xml"/>
            <include name="${ant.project.name}.tar.gz"/>
        </fileset>
    </ftp>
</target>
```

Now we need to define the remote buildfile, which is called `deploy.xml`. This is the buildfile that defines the build or deployment process to be performed on the remote server. For our purposes here, let's assume that the only step required on the remote server is to untar the file to the directory to which `deploy.xml` and `release-1.0.tar` were deposited with FTP. Listing 8.9 shows `deploy.xml`.

LISTING 8.9   The `deploy.xml` Buildfile to be Executed Remotely by Rant

```xml
<?xml version="1.0"?>

<project name="remote-deployment" basedir="." default="deploy">

<target name="deploy">
    <gunzip src="eMarket.tar.gz" />
    <untar src="eMarket.tar" dest="/dist" />
</target>

</project>
```

Story

One problem the team has is that after performing the remote install through Rant, Tomcat needs to be restarted. Tomcat is not configured to use reloadable classpaths in production because it's too slow. In order to pick up new WAR files that have been deployed, they need to reboot Tomcat. The problem is that Rant requires Tomcat to be running the RPCRouter in order to work. But if Tomcat is shut down, there's no way to send a command through Rant to restart it.

Because the production servers are running a variety of forms of Unix, there is a platform-specific solution that they can use. Lisa and Amy use the Ant <exec> task to shell out of Ant to run a Unix at command. The at command in Unix can be used to tell Unix to run a command at some point in the future, say a few minutes from now. What they do is execute an at command from the remote buildfile that will run a script to shut down and restart Tomcat in 5 minutes.

Although this will break platform independence for the remote buildfile, this really isn't an issue because the production servers are all Unix boxes and aren't likely to change any time soon. Sometimes, breaking platform independence is a tradeoff that has to be made to solve a problem with no other solution.

One thing that can't be done directly with Rant is to restart the server that is running Rant and the SOAP RPCRouter. If we send a command to the Ant buildfile to stop the server, the server won't be able to respond to the start command. One solution to this problem, which can be done on Unix- and NT-based systems, is to use the at command. The at command can be used to tell the operating system to execute a command at some point in the future. It's kind of like a one-shot cron. After the command executes, it's removed from the directory containing at jobs. Using this command will break platform independence because the arguments for the at command are certainly different between Unix and NT, and may vary slightly between different varieties of Unix-based platforms.

The technique, shown in Listing 8.10, is to use the <exec> task to run an at command. The at command will run a script that stops the server, and then restarts it.

LISTING 8.10   A Remote Buildfile for Rant That Uses the Operating System's at
                 Command to Restart the Tomcat Server That Rant Is Running On

```xml
<?xml version="1.0"?>

<project name="remote-deployment" basedir="." default="deploy">

<target name="deploy">
    <gunzip src="eMarket.tar.gz" />
    <untar src="eMarket.tar" dest="/dist" />

    <exec executable="at">
        <arg value="-f"/>
        <arg value="restart.sh"/>
        <arg value="now+1minutes"/>
    </exec>
</target>
</project>
```

What was done in the case of Tomcat was to create a two-line script; the first line stops Tomcat and the second line starts Tomcat. The reason for this is so that we can tie the stop and start commands together to allow us to issue a single at command. It is also to guarantee that the stop script finishes running before the start script executes. This script follows this paragraph. When creating the at command, we tell at to run this script 1 minute from now (now+1minutes). The reason for the 1 minute delay is to give the Ant buildfile running on Rant time to complete before Tomcat is rebooted:

```
/usr/software/jakarta-tomcat-4.1.18/bin/shutdown.sh
/usr/software/jakarta-tomcat-4.1.18/bin/startup.sh
```

Restarting the remote application server might require a creative solution. The problem, as mentioned in the story, is that the servlet engine needs to be running the RPCRouter for Rant to work. The only problem with this approach is that if the script were to fail, the only way to recover is to log in to the machine. If you want to accomplish this entirely through Rant, there would not be a way to recover if the servlet engine failed to restart.

Deploying Information to Databases

A software deployment process often involves loading information into a database. Another operation frequently performed on databases during a software upgrade might involve running SQL scripts to modify the database schema. The application may require certain information in the database to be preloaded, such as product information.

Using the Ant SQL Task

Modifying a database schema usually involves running some prepackaged SQL script. Ant has the <sql> task for running SQL commands against a database. The SQL statements can be data definition language (DDL) for modifying the schema, or data modification language (DML) for performing selects, inserts, updates, and deletes.

The required attributes associated with the <sql> task are

- driver
- url
- userid
- password
- src (file containing SQL; required unless SQL is embedded in the tags)

The driver tells Ant which JDBC driver to load and use for connecting to the database. The url attribute specifies to which database Ant is to connect. The userid and password must be a valid user ID/password combination for the database instance. This is the same information you would pass to a DriverManager call in Java. The <sql> task needs to know what SQL statements to execute. This is accomplished in one of two ways. The first is to embed the SQL statement between the <sql> and </sql> tags. The second method is to give the <sql> task the name of a file that contains SQL statements to be executed. Listing 8.11 shows a sample buildfile that could be used to connect to a database and execute a simple SELECT statement. The strings for driver, url, and so on have been deliberately hard-coded in this example to make the example easier to follow.

LISTING 8.11 Buildfile That Uses the Ant <sql> Task to Execute a Simple SELECT Statement

```
<!-- selectSql target -->
<target name="selectSql">
    <sql driver="oracle.jdbc.driver.OracleDriver"
         url="jdbc:oracle:thin:@test.networksByteDesign.com:1521:test"
         userid="installer"
         password="b@ggin$"
         print="true"
         onerror="continue"
```

LISTING 8.11   Continued

```
        output="output.txt">
    select TO_CHAR(SYSDATE) from dual;
    </sql>
</target>
```

This buildfile will select the system time and convert it to a VARCHAR string. As you may recall, dual is a special table in Oracle that can be used when the SQL syntax requires a table, but the table is not really needed. The SYSDATE is one example. Selecting a value from an Oracle sequence is another example. In this example, we also make use of the output attribute of the <sql> task. This attribute is the name of a file that the <sql> results of the SQL statement(s) should be written to. This might be done simply to capture the results of the SQL statement. Another reason to use this attribute might be to pass the results of a set of SQL statements to another task. The print attribute tells Ant to print the results of the statement. The onerror attribute indicates the action that Ant should take if a statement fails. The possible actions are continue, stop, or abort. The output attribute provides a way of passing information to other tasks by writing it to the filesystem.

The src attribute is a means of passing a set of SQL statements into the <sql> task. This is the most likely way of using the <sql> task to perform a large set of SQL statements or even DDL to alter the schema. The <sql> task of Listing 8.11 could be simply modified to a file instead of embedding the SQL, as shown in Listing 8.12.

LISTING 8.12   Example of a Target That Runs SQL Commands Stored in a File

```
    <!--- selectSql target -->
    <target name="selectSql">
        <sql driver="oracle.jdbc.driver.OracleDriver"
            url="jdbc:oracle:thin:@test.networksByteDesign.com:1521:test"
            userid="installer"
            password="b@ggin$"
            print="true"
            onerror="continue"
            output="output.txt"
            src="mycommands.sql"/>
    </target>
```

Again, the output is directed to a file called outfile.txt. This time the commands are read from a file called mycommands.sql. The onerror attribute is set to continue to indicate that the <sql> task should continue operation if it encounters an error.

The most obvious way of loading information into a database would be to have a file containing a series of INSERT statements that add data to a particular table. This is fine for lightweight use. If your process requires a large amount of data (the term "large" here is somewhat arbitrary), the process might run more slowly than you like. This is not because of the Ant <sql> task, but because of the nature of loading data through a series of SQL statements. Some databases, such as Oracle, provide an alternative. Let's examine how that might be used in a build process.

Integrating Oracle SQL*Loader with Ant

Story

During the deployment to the test environment, the eMarket development team used the <sql> task in their deployment process. As part of the build process, a file containing SQL INSERT statements was generated that could be run to load information into the database. The <sql> task in the deployment process then used the src attribute to read the generated file, and executed it during the deployment. This worked fine for the modest amount of data they were loading in the test server.

After they completed the first deployment to the production environment, they discovered a problem. The process worked as it did on the test servers with one exception. Because they were loading a lot more data into the production database than the test database, the data loading into the Oracle database is taking a lot longer than other people in the company would like. One of the DBAs tells Michael that their process is slow because they're using a series of generated SQL statements to insert data into the database, and they need to consider using SQL*Loader.

In order to deal with this problem, they realize two things. First, they need to start doing everything in the test environment that will need to be done in production. This includes not only all of the same steps, but use of the same data. If they had not relied on loading a smaller subset of data in the test environment, they would have realized the scalability problem sooner.

The second thing they need to do is devise a way to execute SQL*Loader in their deployment process. There is no Ant task for using SQL*Loader and they don't want to have to run this step manually. In order to integrate this into their deployment process, they need to write a custom Ant task to integrate Oracle SQL*Loader into their deployment process.

After performing a few spike tests to familiarize themselves with the use of SQL*Loader, Michael and John work on creating the custom task. In order to follow the XP methodology, they only implement the mutators for the command-line options that they actually need. After implementing this custom task, they test by loading the entire production data set into the test database to verify performance and correctness.

Oracle provides a utility for loading information into tables called SQL*Loader. The SQL*Loader utility requires a control file and data file. There are several advantages to using SQL*Loader. The first is speed. SQL*Loader is faster than running a series of INSERT statements. The second advantage is that data can be loaded without having to first convert it to a series of INSERT statements. Ant doesn't have a task for invoking SQL*Loader. However, there are several ways we can attack the problem. One way is to use existing Ant tasks to construct a target that will handle the problem. This could be accomplished by using the <exec> task. Another approach would be to write a custom task to invoke SQL*Loader, which is the approach that will be taken here.

The actual process name for SQL*Loader is `sqlldr` on both Unix- and Windows-based systems. This custom task can be designed to parallel the command-line options available in SQL*Loader. The following are some of the possible command-line options available:

-userid	-discardmax	-silent
-control	-skip	-direct
-log	-load	-parfile
-bad	-errors	-parallel
-data	-rows	-file
-discard	-bindsize	

We will only implement those options in our Custom Ant task, which are currently needed by the eMarket team. Most of the options require an additional argument, which is the value to be passed in. For example, `-userid` expects a string that contains the userid/password. Other arguments, such as -silent, are just flags used to turn certain behavior on or off. Recall that a custom task has a bean interface for attributes, which is a mutator (or setter) method for each attribute. Each of those mutator methods accepts a string for the value of the attribute. Most of the options need to accept an additional argument. For those arguments, we'll accept the string value passed in the attribute, and store it for use when launching the command. For the other arguments that act as flags, we'll provide the option to set the attribute to `true` or `false`. When processing those attributes, the setter method will test to determine if the value is `true`. If the String value is `true`, the setter method sets a Boolean value to `true`.

Finally, we should provide an option to cause the task to stop if a failure occurs, or `haltonfailure` flag. Listing 8.13 contains the Java code for a custom task to invoke the Oracle SQL*Loader. This task accepts a collection of files as a <fileset> and creates output and logfiles for each individual input file. The advantage to using a custom task over constructing a target from some Ant tasks such as <exec> will be seen in a moment.

LISTING 8.13 Custom Ant Task for Invoking Oracle SQL*Loader

```
package com.networksByteDesign.util;

import org.apache.tools.ant.*;
import org.apache.tools.ant.taskdefs.*;
import org.apache.tools.ant.types.*;
import java.io.File;
import java.io.FileReader;
import java.io.FileWriter;
import java.io.FileNotFoundException;
import java.io.BufferedReader;
import java.io.IOException;
import java.util.Vector;
import java.util.Enumeration;

public class LoadTask extends MatchingTask
{

    public void execute() throws BuildException
    {
        Vector controlList = new Vector();
        if (fileset_ != null)
        {
            DirectoryScanner ds = fileset_.getDirectoryScanner(project);

            String[] includedFiles = ds.getIncludedFiles();
            String cmd = null;

            for (int j=0; j<includedFiles.length; j++)
            {
                control_ = includedFiles[j];
                String baseControl = control_.substring(0, control_.length() - 4);
                log_  = baseControl + ".log";
                bad_  = baseControl + ".bad";
                data_ = baseControl + ".dat";
                cmd = buildCmd();
                controlList.add(cmd);
            }
        }
        else if (control_ != null)
        {
            String cmd = buildCmd();
```

LISTING 8.13   Continued

```
                    controlList.add(cmd);
                }
                else
                {
                    throw new BuildException("no control files were specified");
                }
                // Get a handle on the JVM Runtime Object
                Runtime rt = Runtime.getRuntime();

                Enumeration enm = controlList.elements();
                while (enm.hasMoreElements())
                {
                    String cmd = (String)enm.nextElement();
                    // Execute the tool
                    try
                    {
                        Process proc = rt.exec(cmd);
                        int code = proc.waitFor();
                        if ((haltonfailure_) && (code != 0))
                        {
                            throw new
                                BuildException("sql loader failed with error code: "
                                                    + code);
                        }
                    }
                    catch (IOException e)
                    {
                        System.out.println("Caught Exception: " +e.toString());
                    }
                    catch (InterruptedException ie)
                    {
                        System.out.println("Caught Exception: " +ie.toString());
                    }
                }
            }

    public void addFileset(FileSet set)
    {
        fileset_ = set;
    }
```

LISTING 8.13 Continued

```java
public void setUserid( String userid)
{
    userid_ = userid;
}

public void setHaltonfailure(String haltonfailure)
{
    if (haltonfailure.equals("true")) {
        haltonfailure_ = true;
    }
}

private String buildCmd()
{
    StringBuffer command = new StringBuffer();
    command.append("sqlldr");
    if (userid_ != null)
    {
        command.append(" -userid " + userid_);
    }

    if (control_ != null)
    {
        command.append(" -control " + control_);
        command.append(" -log " + log_);
        command.append(" -bad " + bad_);
        command.append(" -data " + data_);
    }

    return command.toString();
}


private FileSet fileset_;
private String  userid_;
private String  control_;
private String  log_;
private String  bad_;
private String  data_;
private boolean haltonfailure_ = false;
}
```

If we had just built the custom task to accept each of the SQL*Loader tasks, we would then have a task that could load a single control/datafile pair. Although this is useful, the same effect could have been achieved in other ways with existing Ant tasks. This custom task is more seamlessly integrated into the build process because it provides clean syntax for accepted options and a collection of files, and then running SQL*Loader. To accomplish this, the method `addFileset` was added, to accept a nested `<fileset>` element. The `<fileset>` element can then be used to describe an entire set of control files to run with SQL*Loader. This will make for a much more flexible build process if we can run this task on a fileset, rather than having to specify each individual file in XML in the buildfile. Also, Ant does a great job of taking care of the operating system dependencies in providing the list of files that match the criteria.

Let's look at how the custom task works. The `execute` method needs to build the command to launch SQL*Loader, and then run it. What we've done is to design the task to check for the presence of a fileset, and if it doesn't exist, the task will then check for an individual control filename being passed via that attribute. Within the `execute` method, a vector is created to handle the list of commands that will be executed, which may be one or more. If the fileset member is null, meaning no fileset was passed in, then the `execute` method checks for a control filename to operate on. If this too is null, it throws an exception, because it can't proceed. If the fileset isn't null, the task proceeds to operate on that, and will ignore the `controlfile` attribute, even if it's set. Next, the fileset's `getDirectoryScanner` method is called, passing in the implicit `project` member, to get an instance of a `DirectoryScanner` object. The `getIncludedFiles` method of the `DirectoryScanner` is called to return a list of filenames. For each control filename in the String array, the private method `buildCmd` is called. This method constructs a string with all of the correct arguments. Note that just before calling the `buildCmd` method, we set the name of the logfile and "bad" file to be the name of the control file with `.log` and `.bad` appended respectively. This is to provide output for each invocation of the `sqlldr` process. Otherwise, each execution of the loader would overwrite the previous file.

The command string returned by this method is placed in a vector of commands to execute. Finally, when the list is complete, the `execute` method obtains a reference to the `Runtime` object, and performs an exec of the command string. The exec task returns a `Process` object, for which we call the `waitFor` method. This causes the task to block while the command is executed, and allows us to get the return code of the process. This is where we implement the `haltonfailure` option. If the `haltonfailure` boolean member is set to `true`, and the exec'ed process returns a return code other than 0, we know an error occurred, and the process throws a `BuildException`.

The next step is to see how to use this task in a buildfile. Listing 8.14 shows a sample buildfile that runs SQL*Loader on a set of control files that end in the `.ctl` suffix.

LISTING 8.14   Buildfile to Use the Custom SQL*Loader Ant Task Developed in
                This Section

```
<!-- loadData target -->
<target name="loadData" >
    <loadTask userid="installer@ test.networksByteDesign.com /b@ggin$"
              haltonfailure="false">
        <fileset dir=".">
            <include name="**/*.ctl"/>
        </fileset>
    </loadTask>
</target>
```

In this example, the control, log, and bad attributes are not set, because a fileset is
used to define the set of control files. The task will automatically create log and bad
filenames for each of the control files. Listing 8.15 shows a sample control file used
with this example.

LISTING 8.15   Sample Control File Used in the SQL*Loader Example

```
LOAD DATA
  APPEND INTO TABLE TestUserTable
  (
  fname CHAR TERMINATED BY "," ENCLOSED BY '"',
  lname CHAR TERMINATED BY "," ENCLOSED BY '"',
  email CHAR TERMINATED BY "," ENCLOSED BY '"'
  )
```

One of the advantages of SQL*Loader is that the data to be loaded doesn't have to be
converted into INSERT statements. It can be put into a CSV (Comma Separated
Variable) form that might have even been generated in a spreadsheet. Listing 8.16
shows an example of a data file that will be loaded into the eMarket database with
the <sqlloader> custom task that we created.

LISTING 8.16   Example of a Data File for Use with SQL*Loader

```
"Test 1","User","test1@networksByteDesign.com"
"Test 2","User","test2@networksByteDesign.com"
"Test 3","User","test3@networksByteDesign.com"
"Test 4","User","test4@networksByteDesign.com"
"Test 5","User","test5@networksByteDesign.com"
"Test 6","User","test6@networksByteDesign.com"
"Test 7","User","test7@networksByteDesign.com"
"Test 8","User","test8@networksByteDesign.com"
```

LISTING 8.16   Continued

```
"Test 9","User","test9@networksByteDesign.com"
"Test 10","User","test10@networksByteDesign.com"
"Test 11","User","test11@networksByteDesign.com"
"Test 12","User","test12@networksByteDesign.com"
"Test 13","User","test13@networksByteDesign.com"
"Test 14","User","test14@networksByteDesign.com"
"Test 15","User","test15@networksByteDesign.com"
"Test 16","User","test16@networksByteDesign.com"
"Test 17","User","test17@networksByteDesign.com"
"Test 18","User","test18@networksByteDesign.com"
"Test 19","User","test19@networksByteDesign.com"
"Test 20","User","test20@networksByteDesign.com"
```

When the <sqlloader> task is run, it generates output files that provide information as to how the load worked. Listing 8.17 shows an output file resulting from a run of SQL*Loader with the custom <sqlloader> task.

LISTING 8.17   Example of Output from a Run of SQL*Loader

```
SQL*Loader: Release 9.0.1.0.0 - Production on Fri Jan 31 08:28:54 2003

(c) Copyright 2001 Oracle Corporation.  All rights reserved.

Control File:   src/testUsers.ctl
Data File:      src/testUsers.dat
  Bad File:     src/testUsers.bad
  Discard File: none specified

 (Allow all discards)

Number to load: ALL
Number to skip: 0
Errors allowed: 50
Bind array:     64 rows, maximum of 256000 bytes
Continuation:    none specified
Path used:      Conventional

Table TESTUSERTABLE, loaded from every logical record.
Insert option in effect for this table: APPEND
```

LISTING 8.13 Continued

Column Name	Position	Len	Term	Encl	Datatype
FNAME	FIRST	*	,	"	CHARACTER
LNAME	NEXT	*	,	"	CHARACTER
EMAIL	NEXT	*	,	"	CHARACTER

Table TESTUSERTABLE:
  20 Rows successfully loaded.
  0 Rows not loaded due to data errors.
  0 Rows not loaded because all WHEN clauses were failed.
  0 Rows not loaded because all fields were null.

Space allocated for bind array: 49536 bytes(64 rows)
Read   buffer bytes: 1048576

Total logical records skipped: 0
Total logical records read: 20
Total logical records rejected: 0
Total logical records discarded: 0

Run began on Fri Jan 31 08:28:54 2003
Run ended on Fri Jan 31 08:28:54 2003

Elapsed time was: 00:00:00.05
CPU time was: 00:00:00.02

To recap, using SQL*Loader will provide a speed increase over a series of INSERT statements, and does not require the data to be converted to a series of SQL statements. This task could have been invoked using the Ant <exec> task and passing in the arguments. However, by creating a custom Ant task, we demonstrated the use of this technique, and created a task that can accept <filesets> for passing in a group of files to be run by SQL*Loader. This technique can be easily applied to other third-party tools that you may want to integrate into Ant.

Summary

In this chapter, we looked at techniques and tools to handle some advanced deployment issues. We added additional targets to handle some of the CVS tagging operations. The advantage of doing this is that it removes some of the mundane work for the developers, and ensures that these operations will be done in a consistent fashion.

The tool Remote Ant, or Rant, can be used to execute an Ant build file on another server. Rant does require a Web server and servlet engine running a SOAP RPCRouter in order to work. It does open up possibilities for remote deployment.

We also looked at ways to load information into a database. One technique is to use the <sql> task directly, with SQL embedded in the XML. Another technique is to dynamically generate SQL in another process, and write it to a file. The <sql> task can then be used to execute the generated file. Finally, we developed a custom task to use Oracle SQL*Loader. The approach used in this custom task can also be used to integrate other third-party tools into Ant.

9

Company Reorganized—Working with a New Subteam

Story

The eMarket development team arrived at work one morning and learned that NetworksByteDesign Inc. is about to have a major reorganization. The eMarket project will still be completed as planned, but the corporation has decided to rearrange some areas of responsibility. The impact on the eMarket development team is that they will now have to work closely with another group who will be providing some of the code for the business objects. This also means that they will have to work together closely and agree upon some process standards.

After the reorganization, the two groups attempt to agree upon some standards for the project. Each group likes the processes and tools that it is familiar with. Almost immediately, some conflict arises over these differences. The other team uses the NetBeans IDE to develop and build code, whereas eMarket uses Ant with Emacs for their development, build, and deployment processes. Neither side wants to give up their practices and tries to convince the other to see it their way.

Management has learned about the conflict over differences, and has put pressure on the lead developers to sort it out quickly. Michael, the lead developer on eMarket, meets with the other lead developer to discuss options. The other team concedes that they have experienced some difficulties with build environments. Because each developer sets up their own development environment with the IDE, problems sometimes arise that are caused by the differences between developers' build environments. Also, they always have to write custom scripts for deployment, which is done in Perl. It would be nice to standardize.

On the eMarket side, some of the newer developers don't care for Emacs and would prefer to use an IDE. However, the team never dealt with making that an option. Because many IDEs including NetBeans will work with Ant, the teams are able to at least agree on integrating the Ant build environment with NetBeans, and allowing any developer who wants to use it to have that option. Also, it is possible to execute Perl scripts in Ant using the <exec> task, but most of the deployment processes developed so far in Ant will easily accommodate the new code that will have to be written.

NetBeans IDE and Ant

NetBeans is an Integrated Development Environment (IDE) written in Java. This IDE can be used to develop code in Java, HTML, XML, JSP, C/C++, and other languages.

Also, the NetBeans IDE (not the Platform version) is free for personal and commercial use. NetBeans is available at http://www.netbeans.org/.

NetBeans specifically supports integration with Ant as a build tool. NetBeans also provides support for other features such a debugger, integration with a version control system, and easy integration with various compilers and build tools. Most of NetBeans' capabilities are contained in separate pluggable modules. By taking this approach, a specific implementation is not tied to the IDE. For example, a debugger is tied to a specific JVM. By separating this function into pluggable modules, the user can choose from a variety of JVMs and debuggers. The same is true of other features such as support for CORBA, Apache Tomcat integration, and InstallShield. A list of the pluggable modules available for NetBeans can be found at

http://www.netbeans.org/devhome/modules/by-module.html

At the time this book was written, the latest version of NetBeans was version 3.4. Version 3.4 contains a module for integration of Ant 1.4.1. In order to use Ant 1.5.3, an update must be downloaded from the NetBeans Update Center, which can be found under the main menu, in Tools->Update Center. The 3.4.1 release will support Ant 1.5.3, and the NetBeans 4.0 development releases also currently support Ant 1.5.3.

The NetBeans IDE has some very nice integration with Ant. NetBeans itself is built with Ant. NetBeans recognizes Ant buildfiles and provides a special icon for them. Figure 9.1 shows the NetBeans IDE interface for Ant configuration settings.

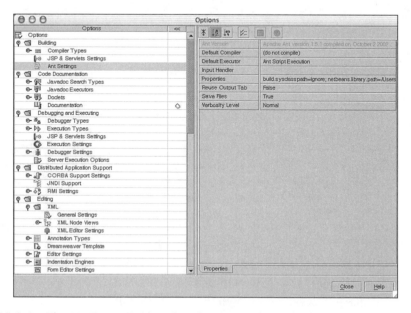

FIGURE 9.1   The NetBeans IDE interface for Ant configuration settings.

NetBeans provides a template for creating new buildfiles. It also provides syntax-sensitive coloring of the XML file, in the text editor. You can edit your buildfiles in the text editor. The buildfile can then be opened in Explorer, and any target can be run by clicking on it. Compilation errors appear in a buffer that is hyperlinked to the source code, so you can jump to the source code by clicking on the error. Figure 9.2 shows an example of selecting a target to run in Ant through the NetBeans GUI interface, and the output after running an Ant buildfile.

Overall, if you like using an IDE, Ant does integrate very well with several IDEs. As you have seen in this section, the NetBeans IDE is a good development environment that provides excellent integration with Ant.

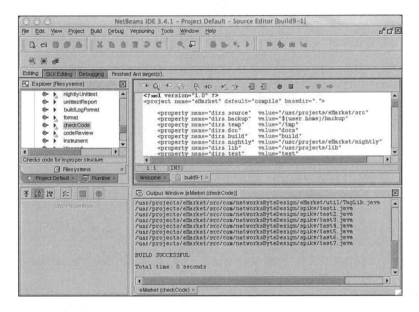

FIGURE 9.2   Result of running an Ant target in the NetBeans GUI interface.

Styler

Story

The group has refactored some of their code generation XSLT. They originally had a single XSLT transformation for each type set of code they want to generate. This has led to replication of certain commonly used operations on their XSLT stylesheets. So, Amy and Michael paired up to refactor these stylesheets. What they did was to break out common functions into their own transformation, so each one can form a stage in a pipelined set of transformations.

The buildfile could be configured to use the <style> or <xslt> task (they actually invoke the same code). Using these tasks would be acceptable for this purpose, but it would mean a lot of intermediate files. The real downside in this situation is that the buildfile would be harder to maintain. Before the developers refactored, they planned to use a task for this purpose called <styler>. By using <styler> in this instance, the buildfile will be more maintainable. Also, they've gained the advantage of having XSLT modules that can be put together to form a variety of more complex operations.

Styler is a tool that enables you to easily perform advanced transformation operations on a set of files. The advantage of Styler is from an execution standpoint. Sometimes transformations need to be performed that would be awkward to accomplish in Ant using the <xslt> or <style> task. Styler can perform a single transformation as the <style> task does. Styler allows you to perform multiple transformations in a parallel or a pipelined fashion. It can handle transformations that may split or merge files. Styler can also process non-XML files (such as HTML) and apply a transformation other than XSLT. Finally, it can also apply a custom XMLReader or XMLFilter class to handle new formats.

INSTALLING STYLER

To install Styler, follow these steps:

1. Download `styler.jar`, the manual, and the javadoc at

   `http://www.langdale.com.au/styler/`

2. Put `styler.jar` either in the `lib` directory of your Ant installation or into your system CLASSPATH.

3. Make sure that the JAR files for Xalan 2 are either in the system CLASSPATH or the `lib` directory of Ant.

4. If you're processing HTML files, make sure the JAR file for JTidy is in the CLASSPATH or the Ant `lib` directory. JTidy is available at

   `http://sourceforge.net/projects/jtidy`

5. If you're writing custom XMLReader or XMLFilter classes, you'll need version 0.11 of the `fragmentedXML.jar` file in your CLASSPATH or Ant `lib` directory. This is available at

   `http://simonstl.com/projects/fragment/`

6. Add the following <taskdef> declaration to your buildfile:

   `<taskdef classname="au.com.Langdale.styler.StylerTask" name="styler"/>`

7. Styler is ready for use in Ant.

Let's look at a simple example that illustrates the benefits of using Styler in certain situations. Listing 9.1 shows an example of an Ant target that uses the <style> task supplied with Ant. In this target, called `pipeline`, a series of XSL transformations are being applied to a set of XML files. The files are first transformed with the stylesheet called `style1.xsl`. The resulting output of this transform will then be processed through another transformation called `style2.xsl`. In this way, a series of steps are performed in a pipelined process. One of the problems with the `<style>` task is that there's no mechanism for performing a series of transformations directly. Each step has to be performed and written to a temporary file, and then read in for the next stage of the pipeline. Also, from a buildfile standpoint, it's just awkward to have to repeat the `<style>` over and over. It also increases the volume of statements in the buildfile and makes it more difficult to read and understand.

LISTING 9.1   A Target That Consists of A Pipelined Set of XSLT Transformations

```
<!-- pipeline target -->
<target name="pipeline">
    <style style="${dirs.source}/sample1.xsl"
           includes="${dirs.source}/samples/*.sample"
           destdir="${dirs.build}"
           extension=".sample1" />

    <style style="${dirs.source}/sample2.xsl"
           includes="${dirs.build}/*.sample1"
           destdir="${dirs.build}"
           extension=".sample2" />

    <style style="${dirs.source}/sample3.xsl"
           includes="${dirs.build}/*.sample2"
           destdir="${dirs.build}"
           extension=".sample3" />

    <style style="${dirs.source}/sample4.xsl"
           includes="${dirs.build}/*.sample3"
           destdir="${dirs.build}"
           extension=".sample4" />

    <style style="${dirs.source}/sample5.xsl"
           includes="${dirs.build}/*.sample4"
           destdir="${dirs.build}"
           extension=".sample" />
</target>
```

Listing 9.1 shows a target that performs a pipelined set of transformations on a set of XML files using the Ant task `<style>`. This is awkward because there's no direct way to apply a pipelined set of transforms to files with the `<style>` or `<xslt>` task.

Now let's contrast the way in which this was done in `<style>` with the way the same process could be accomplished in `<styler>`. Listing 9.2 shows a target that accomplishes the same purpose as the target in Listing 9.1. The `<styler>` task has a very nice interface for handling the pipelined process. First, the set of XML files to be transformed is defined with a nested `<fileset>` element. Next, the pipeline of transforms is defined with a series of `<transform>` elements. The order in which these elements are listed is the order in which the transformations will be applied. The end result of both versions of the `pipeline` target is identical. The difference is that the version that uses `<styler>` is more efficient and the Ant target is much more concise.

The real advantage of Styler in this situation has more to do with software maintenance. Suppose the order of the transformations performed in this task needs to change. With the first approach, the targets need to be modified rather significantly, and with a good probability of error. With the Styler approach, it's just a matter of moving a single line, which is much less likely to pose a problem. If a mistake were made, how likely is it that the error would be detected? If the transform changed the structure of the XML, it's possible that the whole process might break, and would be quickly detected. The more serious possibility is if the transform only changed content, and the process didn't break. It's possible that the final file might have been created, but with incorrect information in it. If the user is unaware that the report is incorrect, this is a dangerous situation.

Because most of the cost of software is in the maintenance phase, it makes sense to use techniques that are more easily maintained. Styler enables you to develop build processes that must perform more complex transformations that are easier to maintain.

LISTING 9.2   The Use of Styler

```
<taskdef name="styler"
        classname="au.com.Langdale.styler.StylerTask"
        classpathref="project.classpath"/>

<!-- pipeline target -->
<target name="pipeline">
    <styler>
        <fileset dir="${dirs.source}/samples">
            <include name="*.sample"/>
        </fileset>

        <transform file="${dirs.source}/sample1.xsl" />
        <transform file="${dirs.source}/sample2.xsl" />
        <transform file="${dirs.source}/sample3.xsl" />
        <transform file="${dirs.source}/sample4.xsl" />
        <transform file="${dirs.source}/sample5.xsl" />

        <output dir="${dirs.build}"/>
```

LISTING 9.2   Continued

```
        </styler>
    </target>
```

Styler is capable of other operations that were described in the beginning of this section. We won't illustrate all of the capabilities in this chapter, but you can get more information in the manual available when you download Styler.

Using the `<tempfile>` and `<purge>` Tasks

One of the things you can do is to use the `<tempfile>` task to create temporary filenames. This task will supply you with filenames that are guaranteed to be unique. It doesn't actually create the file, but guarantees that the filename it gives you did not exist when the task executed. This is useful when doing anything that requires a large number of temporary files. One example of this might be when running a performance test. Listing 9.3 shows a possible use of the `<tempfile>` task in a performance-testing target. The details of the performance test are not shown here, because the focus is on `<tempfile>`. This task can be used to specify a prefix, suffix, and destination directory.

LISTING 9.3   A Conceptual Target for Performance Testing That Could Use the `<Tempfile>` Task to Create Unique Temporary Files

```
<!-- perfTest target -->
<target name="perfTest">
    <tempfile property="files.temp"
              prefix="perfTest"
              suffix=".xml"
              destdir="${dirs.temp}" />

    ...

</target>
```

When the target of Listing 9.3 is run, it generates a series of temporary files as shown in Listing 9.4. What this task does is generate unique numbers to include in the filename, and it checks to make sure that the file doesn't already exist before creating it.

LISTING 9.4 The Temporary Files Created by Running the `perfTest` Target of
Listing 9.3

```
/tmp/perfTest-1304546298.xml
/tmp/perfTest-1492056930.xml
/tmp/perfTest-1981872928.xml
/tmp/perfTest-694887857.xml
/tmp/perfTest-906069031.xml
/tmp/perfTest1492040215.xml
/tmp/perfTest1639429692.xml
/tmp/perfTest2098804555.xml
/tmp/perfTest32687637.xml
/tmp/perfTest616382367.xml
```

Story

One of the problems that the eMarket team ran into after creating the performance test target is
that the temporary files started piling up. This is because they want to keep the results of the last
few tests around, so they can't just remove the directory. They discover a handy task called <purge>
that will delete all but the most recent temporary files, and it's easy to hook into a buildfile. The
<purge> task is downloaded and added to the build process by two of the developers.

The <purge> task, as mentioned in the story, is useful for deleting all but the most
recent set of files in a fileset.

INSTALLING PURGE

Follow these steps to install Purge:

1. Download `purge.jar` from
   http://www.dallaway.com/ant/
2. Put `purge.jar` in the `lib` directory of your Ant installation.
3. Purge is ready to use in Ant.

Listing 9.5 shows a target that makes use of the <purge> task. The <taskdef>
declaration shows an alternative means of getting a task's class into the CLASSPATH.
If you elect not to put the `purge.jar` file in the `lib` directory, you can declare the
CLASSPATH as shown in this example. Next, the purgeFiles target is set up. This calls
<purge> with the keep attribute set to 5. This will cause purge to keep the last five
files in the <fileset>. Next, a nested fileset is added to describe the files to purge.
For the eMarket team example, they will match the `perfTest*.xml` pattern.

LISTING 9.5   Ant Target That Uses the <purge> Target to Remove All But the Last
Five Temporary Files

```
<taskdef name="purge"
        classname="com.dallaway.ant.Purge"
        classpathref="project.classpath"/>


<!-- purgeFiles target -->
<target name="purgeFiles">
    <purge keep="5">
        <fileset dir="${dirs.temp}">
            <include name="**/perfTest*.xml" />
        </fileset>
    </purge>
</target>
```

The resulting output from executing the purgeTest target is shown in Listing 9.6. It
lists the files that are deleted by the target. When it's complete, five of the temporary
files will be left in the directory. The <purge> task will recursively move down the
directory to perform deletions. Also, the <purge> task has a test attribute that, if set to
true, will show what is going to be deleted without actually performing any deletion.

LISTING 9.6   Output of the purge Task

```
% ant purgeFiles
Buildfile: build.xml

purgeFiles:
    [purge] Purging /tmp
    [purge] Deleting /tmp/perfTest1492040215.xml
    [purge] Deleting /tmp/perfTest1639429692.xml
    [purge] Deleting /tmp/perfTest2098804555.xml
    [purge] Deleting /tmp/perfTest32687637.xml
    [purge] Deleting /tmp/perfTest616382367.xml


BUILD SUCCESSFUL
Total time: 3 seconds
```

AntEater

An important aspect of testing in an XP process is *functional testing*. A functional test
focuses solely on testing the inputs and outputs of a component or system, while
ignoring its internal implementation. In functional testing, the component or

system under test is treated as a black box. To effectively include functional testing into your overall XP process, it would be nice to automate it. A good tool for this is called AntEater.

Story

Some of the functional testing of the Web applications is time-consuming and tiring when it has to be done on a routine, iterative basis. Some of the workload could be eliminated if at least part of the functional testing could be automated. The unit testing is already automated with JUnit.

The group decides to adopt the use of AntEater into their build and testing process. This will perform some automated functional testing of Web applications, and reduce the manual workload. Also, having a suite of functional tests that can be run automatically will make acceptance testing a bit easier.

AntEater is a functional testing framework that is based on Ant. It supports functional testing of Web applications and XML Web Services. AntEater has a built-in Web server, which allows you to write various tests of HTTP/HTTPS requests and responses. Your test can send an HTTP/HTTPS request to a Web server and test the response for certain criteria. The HTTP headers and response codes can be easily checked. The response body can be validated using Regular Expressions, Xpath, Relax NG, contentEquals, and even some binary formats. It's also possible to listen to incoming HTTP/HTTPS requests at a particular URL on a machine, and check the incoming message parameters for accuracy. AntEater is a good tool for testing tools that use SOAP, such as ebXML.

INSTALLING ANTEATER

Follow these steps to install Anteater:

1. Download Anteater from

   http://aft.sourceforge.net/download.html

2. Expand the gzipped tarball or zip file that you downloaded.

3. Add Anteater's `bin` directory to your system PATH.

4. Anteater can be run from the command line with the following syntax:

   `anteater -f <test-file> [<target-name>]`

In this syntax, `<test-file>` is the name of the functional test "buildfile" that you want to run. The `<target-name>` is optional, if you don't want to run the default target.

AntEater is of particular interest because of its design. In reality, AntEater is a specific implementation of Ant, and was built using Ant as a framework. This is a very different approach from creating custom tasks to hook into Ant, but is an interesting concept to evaluate.

Because of AntEater's common origin with Ant, it is used much like Ant. Functional tests are created that have the same format as Ant buildfiles.

An example of a test file is shown in Listing 9.7.

LISTING 9.7   Functional Test File for Sending an HTTP Request and Validating the Response That Was Returned

```xml
<?xml version="1.0"?>

<project name="anteater-test" default="check-website">
    <taskdef resource="META-INF/Anteater.tasks"/>
    <typedef resource="META-INF/Anteater.types"/>

    <property name="url"
              value="http://test.networksByteDesign.com/login.html"/>

    <target name="check-website">
        <echo>Now downloading and testing ${url}</echo>
        <httpRequest href="${url}">
            <match>
                <regexp>Welcome</regexp>
            </match>
        </httpRequest>
    </target>
</project>
```

Let's look at the elements of an AntEater functional test file. Again, it uses the same syntax as an Ant buildfile because it was derived from Ant. The `<taskdef>` lines are used to include the AntEater types and classes. A property called `url` is set to the value of the URL that we want to test. The target `check-website` does the actual testing, using the `<httpRequest>` task. The `<httprequest>` task is an example of what are known as Action Tasks in Anteater. Action Tasks are used to make an HTTP request to a server, or to wait for incoming HTTP requests on a particular URL. The `<httprequest>` task hits the page just as a browser would, and then checks the response that returns with a regular expression checker. Also, the `<httpRequest>` task supports the use of Basic Authentication. If the `user` and `password` attributes are set, Anteater will use basic authentication; otherwise, no authentication is used. There is no support for other types of authentication such as MD5. In this simple example, we expect the word "Welcome" to appear in the Web page that would come back. Using a regular expression, AntEater checks the result of the `HttpResponse` that is returned from the Web site. If the response contains the regular expression in the `<regexp>` tags, which in this case is "Welcome," the functional test will pass. Otherwise it will fail.

AntEater can be run from the command line with the syntax:

anteater -f test.xml

where `test.xml` is the name of the functional test `buildfile`. Listing 9.8 shows the results of running this functional test.

LISTING 9.8   Results of Running the Functional Test Shown in Listing 9.7

```
% anteater -f test.xml
Anteater 0.9.15


Buildfile: test.xml


check-website:
    [echo] Now downloading and testing
            http://test.networksByteDesign.com/login.html
[httpRequest] test.xml:12:
              Starting http://test.networksByteDesign.com/login.html
test.xml:14: Running test [Regexp: Welcome ][1;31m
              Failure: Expected to match pattern: Welcome
Got: 'Date: Fri, 31 Jan 2003 23:02:07 GMT
Server: Apache/1.3.27 (Darwin)
Last-Modified: Fri, 31 Jan 2003 22:59:47 GMT
ETag: "12077f-553-3e3affe3"
Accept-Ranges: bytes
Content-Length: 1363
Connection: close
Content-Type: text/html


<!DOCTYPE HTML PUBLIC "-//W3C//DTD HTML 4.0 Transitional//EN">
<HTML>
<HEAD>
  <TITLE>Login</TITLE>
</HEAD>
<TABLE height="100%" cellSpacing="0" cellPadding="0" width="100%">
  <FORM action="j_security_check" method="post">
  <TR>
    <TD valign="center" align="middle">
      <TABLE cellSpacing="1" cellPadding="2" width="210" bgColor="#a9a9a9">
        <TR>
          <TD STYLE="FONT-SIZE: 12pt; COLOR: #ffffff; TEXT-ALIGN: center">
               <B>LOGIN</B> 
```

LISTING 9.8   Continued

```
                </TD>
            </TR>
            <TR>
                <TD bgColor="#e0e0e0">
            <TABLE class="default" cellSpacing="1" cellPadding="1">
                <TR>
                    <TD align="right">
                      <B>Username :</B> </TD>
                    <TD> <INPUT size="16" name="j_username"></TD>
                </TR>
                <TR>
                    <TD align="right">
                      <B>Password :</B> </TD>
                    <TD><INPUT size="16" name="j_password" type="password"></TD>
                </TR>
                <TR>
                    <TD align="middle" colSpan="2">
                         
                    <INPUT type="submit" value="Login" name="j_security_check"/>
                    </TD>
                </TR>
            </table>
            </TD>
        </TR>
    </TABLE>
    </TD>
  </TR>
  </FORM>
</TABLE>
</body>
</html>

    ... done (120ms)

BUILD FAILED
file:test.xml:12: Task at file:test.xml:12:  failed

Total time: 2 seconds
```

In this example, the test failed. As Listing 9.8 shows in the results of running the AntEater test:

```
Failure: Expected to match pattern: Welcome
```

We were expecting to have the word "Welcome" in the response, and it wasn't found. Notice the power of a test like this. We're not checking the entire HTML structure that is returned just for a key expression in the returned values. This is important because one of the problems with checking Web sites is that often tests try to match the entire value that comes back. That means that even a simple change in the appearance of the page will cause the test to fail. But the failure is artificial because the page is functionally correct. By using regular expressions, you can avoid some of these types of problems.

Another slight variation of the test is shown in Listing 9.9. This time, the regular expression checker is searching for the word "LOGIN" in the response. Because the response in this test does contain the expression "LOGIN," the test passes.

LISTING 9.9   A Variation on the Original Functional Test That Looks for the Expression "LOGIN" in the Response

```xml
<?xml version="1.0"?>

<project name="anteater-test" default="check-website">
    <taskdef resource="META-INF/Anteater.tasks"/>
    <typedef resource="META-INF/Anteater.types"/>

    <property name="url"
            value="http://test.networksByteDesign.com/login.html"/>

    <target name="check-website">
        <echo>Now downloading and testing ${url}</echo>
        <httpRequest href="${url}">
            <match>
                <regexp>LOGIN</regexp>
            </match>
        </httpRequest>
    </target>
</project>
```

The result of the successful execution of the functional test is shown in Listing 9.10.

LISTING 9.10 Output from the Successful Execution of the Functional Test in Listing 9.9

```
% anteater -f test.xml
Anteater 0.9.15


Buildfile: test.xml


check-website:
    [echo] Now downloading and testing
            http://test.networksByteDesign.com/login.html
[httpRequest] test.xml:12:
              Starting http://test.networksByteDesign.com/login.html
test.xml:14: Running test [Regexp: LOGIN ]    ... done (57ms)
test.xml:12: Finished http://test.networksByteDesign.com/login.html (175ms)


BUILD SUCCESSFUL
Total time: 1 second
```

Groups

Groups in Anteater are containers for definitions that can be given a name and reused later in the script. Here's an example of the <group> container:

```
<group id="emarket.test">
    <session/>
    <logger type="xml"/>
    <property name="host" value="test.networksByteDesign.com"/>
    <property name="port" value="8080"/>
    <property name="url" value="http://www.networksByteDesign.com/eMarket/"/>
</group>
```

The group container called eMarket.test has now been created. This group can be used with Action Tasks that will inherit the objects in that group. For example, the group just created can be used with <httpRequest> as shown here:

```
<httpRequest group="eMarket.test" href="${url}"/>
```

In this example, this instance of <httpRequest> will inherit the group eMarket.test's session object, its logger, and any properties that were set in the group container. Groups can also contain other groups as objects, and the same inheritance rules apply.

Session

The session tag is used to create a `<session>` object. Because the default group creates a session object, this isn't normally required. If you have some reason for creating a separate named session, the `<session>` tag can be used for this purpose. The Javadoc for AntEater indicates that the session object contains cookies, and provides methods for accessing them. Also, a session can be shared between tasks in two ways. First, it can be given an id, and then referred to with the `refid` attribute. Second, it can be put in a group container, and then the group can be referenced in Action Tasks as described in the section on Groups.

Creating Conditional Logic

Anteater supports conditional logic with `<if>`, `<then>`, and `<else>` tags. Also, properties can be conditionally set with the `<match>` tag, and used with `<if>`, `<then>`, and `<else>`.

The `<match>` tag is used to contain a set of conditions that are logically ANDed together. If each condition is true, then the `<match>` is true, and a property can be set with the `assign` attribute. For example:

```
<match assign="succeeded">
  <method value="GET"/>
  <parameter name="region" value="123"/>
</match>
```

In this case, if the method used to send form data in a test was GET, and the value of the parameter region was 123, then the `<match>` condition is true, and the property succeeded is set.

The tag `<if>` can be used to test on the existence of a property with `<isset>`, as shown in the following example.

```
<if>
  <isset property="succeeded"/>
  <then>
    <echo>The Test Succeeded</echo>
  </then>
  <else>
    <echo>The Test Failed</echo>
  </else>
</if>
```

In this example, if the property succeeded was set, the message "The Test Succeeded" will be printed out. Otherwise, the message "The Test Failed" will be echoed,

Multiple <match> tags can be used in Anteater Action Tasks to create more complex Boolean logic. All conditions within a match tag have a logical AND performed between them, and groups of <match> sets are logically ORed together. Consider this example:

```
<listener path="http://www.networksByteDesign.com/eMarket/">
    <match>
        <method value="GET"/>
        <parameter name="region" value="123"/>
        <sendResponse href="${getHref}"/>
    </match>
    <match>
        <method value="POST"/>
        <parameter name="region" value="789"/>
        <sendResponse href="${postHref}"/>
    </match>
</listener>
```

The <listener> element is set to listen for an incoming request on the URL defined with the path attribute. Within the listener element are several <match> conditions, and the following logic will result: The listener will respond if either the method is GET AND the cookie named region has a value of 123, OR the method is POST AND the value of region is 789. If either set of logically ANDed conditions evaluates to true, the script will take the appropriate action.

These examples illustrate some of the capabilities of the AntEater tool as a functional testing framework for Web-based applications. AntEater has some other features that we didn't elaborate on here, such as the ability to generate XML and HTML reports of tests, and to group test scripts by functionality. AntEater is an excellent tool for unattended, noninteractive testing of Web applications and Web services.

Custom Task for Detection of Missing Unit Tests

Story

During functional testing of one of the Web apps, Lisa and John experience some problems that are initially puzzling. One of the apps is returning incorrect results under certain conditions. They retrace their work and rerun their own unit tests, but can't seem to find the problem. As they investigate further, they discover that one of the classes they are using, which was developed by the other group, doesn't have a unit test. As they check a bit further, they find that there are actually a number of classes scattered around that don't have unit tests.

They discuss this with their lead developer, Michael, and the project leader, Sandy. What Michael decides to do is to generate a report of classes that are missing unit tests to provide to Sandy. She will take this and work with the project leader of the other team to make sure these areas get covered.

Michael works with Amy, another developer, to develop a custom task that will identify classes that don't have a corresponding unit test class, and report them. This custom task is then hooked into their build process, and is run every morning to catch new code that might have been committed to CVS that is lacking a unit test. This information is provided to Sandy.

In this section, we'll create a custom task for Ant that will be used to identify source code that does not have a unit test class associated with it. This is somewhat different from the use of NoUnit, which will be covered in the next chapter. If the unit tests are named according to a naming convention, they can be easily identified. All of our unit tests have been named with the word "Test" appended to the filename, before the .java extension. For example, the class Parser.java would be expected to have an associated unit test called ParserTest.java. If it doesn't have a test, we want to identify that and include it in a report. Listing 9.11 shows the custom task that will be used to accomplish this.

LISTING 9.11   Custom Ant Task for Finding a Set of Classes That Do Not Have a Corresponding Test Class

```
package com.networksByteDesign.util;

import org.apache.tools.ant.*;
import org.apache.tools.ant.taskdefs.*;
import org.apache.tools.ant.types.*;
import java.util.Iterator;
import java.util.HashSet;
import org.apache.tools.ant.util.FileNameMapper;

public class MissingTestsTask extends MatchingTask
{
    public void execute()
    {
        // Get a handle on the DirectoryScanner for each fileset
        DirectoryScanner dsFiles =
            filesetFiles_.getDirectoryScanner(project);
        DirectoryScanner dsTests =
            filesetTests_.getDirectoryScanner(project);
```

LISTING 9.11   Continued

```
// Get a list of the included files for each fileset
String[] fileList = dsFiles.getIncludedFiles();
String[] testList = dsTests.getIncludedFiles();

// Create the HashSets
HashSet testSet = new HashSet();
HashSet fileSet = new HashSet();

// Get a FileNameMapper from the mapperElement that
// was passed in from the buildfile
FileNameMapper mapper = null;
if (mapperElement_ != null)
{
    mapper = mapperElement_.getImplementation();
}

try
{
    // Perform the file name mapping on the list of Test
    // filenames and load them into a HashSet
    for (int i = 0; i < testList.length; i++)
    {
        String[] results = mapper.mapFileName(testList[i]);
        testSet.add(results[0]);
    }

    // Load the names of the files from the
    // FilesFileset into a HashSet
    for (int k=0; k<fileList.length; k++)
    {
        fileSet.add(fileList[k]);
    }

    // Remove all of the mapped names in the Test
    // Names HashSet from the File Names HashSet
    fileSet.removeAll(testSet);

    // The remaining files are those that don't have
    // a corresponding test.  Use an interator to get the
    // names, and then print the list.
    Iterator testIter = fileSet.iterator();
```

LISTING 9.11   Continued

```
            System.out.println("The following classes do not have tests:");
            while (testIter.hasNext())
            {
                System.out.println(testIter.next());
            }
        }
        catch (Exception e)
        {
            System.err.println(e);
        }
    }

    public void addTestsFileset(FileSet set)
    {
        filesetTests_ = set;
    }

    public void addFilesFileset(FileSet set)
    {
        filesetFiles_ = set;
    }

    public Mapper createMapper() throws BuildException
    {
        if (mapperElement_ != null)
        {
            throw new BuildException("Cannot define more than one mapper",
                                 location);
        }
        mapperElement_ = new Mapper(project);
        return mapperElement_;
    }

    private Mapper    mapperElement_;
    private FileSet   filesetTests_;
    private FileSet   filesetFiles_;
}
```

This custom task accepts two filesets. One of the filesets will be used to identify the files that are to be checked for the existence of unit tests. The second fileset will identify the set of unit tests that exist. We could write this task to accept multiple

<fileset> elements. The problem with this approach is that inside the custom task class, the two filesets are indistinguishable. We need to have a way of distinguishing the two filesets. Fortunately, Ant uses Java reflection to identify the method to call when parsing the XML, and we can take advantage of this. To distinguish between these two filesets in the buildfile, we will give them different names. The fileset associated with the files we want to check will be called <Filesfileset>, and the other one, which is associated with the set of unit tests, will be called <Testsfileset>. When Ant calls the setter methods in the class, it will look for methods called addTestsfileset(Fileset set) and addFilesfileset(Fileset set). There is nothing special about these names. But the names in the buildfile need to correlate to the setter methods in the custom task. If we wanted to just use the <fileset> construct instead, our method name would have been addFileset(Fileset set).

Now, let's look at how this task will identify classes with missing unit tests. We will take the set of filenames to be tested, and put those filenames into a HashSet. Next, we will take the set of test filenames and add them to a second HashSet with some modification. Each of the test filenames will apply a rule to remove the "Test" identifier from their name before being placed in the HashSet. Suppose for example, the file Parser.java is to be tested to determine whether it has a test class. The filename Parser.java will be placed in the first HashSet containing filenames. Next, the test filename, ParserTest.java, will be placed in the second HashSet, but with the "Test" part of the name removed. So the second HashSet will now have simple Parser.java in it. The reason for modifying the test filenames before adding to the second HashSet is so that those names will exactly match the names of the classes that they test. When we're all done filling the two HashSets, we can compare them to determine which files don't have unit tests.

To apply the rule for removing the "Test" name from the unit test files, we will make use of the Ant <mapper>. We will use a <mapper> to pass in a regular expression that defines the rule we used in naming our unit test files. We must also add a setter method to our task to accept the <mapper>. This method is called createMapper(), which actually is used to obtain a mapperElement from the project member, which is part of the ProjectComponent class that is an ancestor of the Task class. The project member is used to create both the DirectoryScanners in the execute() method, and the mapperElement in the createMapper() method. The createMapper() method simply creates an instance of the Mapper class, and stores it for use in the execute method.

Let's recap what we've covered so far. We have three setter methods in our task. Two of the methods are used to accept filesets. They are named so that the files and tests filesets can be distinguished in the task. The third setter is used to accept a <mapper> element. Now let's look at what happens inside the execute() method. First, each fileset has its getDirectoryScanner method called, passing in project to get a handle on the DirectoryScanner. The DirectoryScanner applies the rules for inclusion and exclusion in the <fileset> elements. From each DirectoryScanner, we call the getIncludedFiles() method to get an array of Strings containing the names that met the criteria in the <fileset>. Then we create a pair of HashSets to store values.

The next step is interesting. We use the Mapper that was stored previously to get a FileNameMapper with the getImplementation() method. This takes care of creating the correct type of mapper (that is, regexp mapper in this case). We can now use this FileNameMapper to apply the regular expression in the buildfile to each of the file-names on the String array of unit test names. We loop through the unit test file-names, and call the FileNameMapper's mapFileName(String name) method, passing in the name of the unit test. It returns the modified name. So in this case, if we pass in ParserTest.java, it will return Parser.java. After the name mapping is performed, the modified name is added to the HashSet for unit test names. Then we loop through the list of filenames to be tested and simply add those to the correct HashSet, with no modification.

We now have a pair of HashSets to compare. Next, we will use the HashSet's removeAll(HashSet) method. We will call this method on the filenames HashSet, passing in the unit test names HashSet. This will have the effect of removing all names from the filenames HashSet that have a corresponding unit test. When we're done, the filenames HashSet will contain only the names of files that don't have a unit test. All that's left to do is use an Iterator to walk across the set, and print the name of each file that is lacking a unit test.

Now, let's create a buildfile to use the custom task we just created. Listing 9.12 shows a buildfile. The <taskdef> element is added at the top to identify the Java class that is our custom task. Next we create a target called missingTests. This target contains the custom task element. We'll discuss the <mapper> in a moment. Inside the missingTests element, we have two filesets that are used to describe the files to be tested and the set of unit tests that exist. Because our tests all end in Test.java, we want to include those in the list of unit tests, but exclude them from the list of files to be tested. This is done with the <include> and <exclude> elements in the fileset. The mapper is used to pass in the regular expression we discussed, which is used to strip out the identifier for the test class. In our case, the naming convention for naming a test is to use the class name being tested, appended with Test.java. So our regexp mapper will perform a mapping to remove this naming convention. Again, the reason for this was detailed earlier in the discussion of the custom task.

LISTING 9.12   Buildfile Showing the Use of the Custom Ant Task for Finding Classes That Do Not Have a Corresponding Test Class

```
<taskdef name="missingteststask"
        classname="com.networksByteDesign.util.MissingTestsTask"
        classpathref="project.classpath"/>
```

LISTING 9.12   Continued

```
<!-- missingTests target -->
<target name="missingTests">
    <missingteststask>
        <mapper type="regexp" from="^(.*)Test\.java$$" to="\1.java"/>
        <testsfileset dir="${dirs.source}">
            <include name="**/*Test.java"/>
        </testsfileset>
        <filesfileset dir="${dirs.source}">
            <include name="**/*.java"/>
            <exclude name="**/*Test.java"/>
        </filesfileset>
    </missingteststask>
</target>
```

Listing 9.13 shows the results of running this custom task on some of the code from the eMarket project. Because some of the classes do not have a corresponding unit test class, they show up in the generated report.

LISTING 9.13   Output That Results from Using the Custom Task to Identify Classes That Do Not Have Unit Tests

```
% ant missingTests
Buildfile: build.xml

missingTests:
[missingteststask] The following classes do not have tests:
[missingteststask]
          com/networksByteDesign/spike/test7.java
[missingteststask]
          com/networksByteDesign/spike/test6.java
[missingteststask]
          com/networksByteDesign/spike/test1.java
[missingteststask]
          com/networksByteDesign/eMarket/inventory/data/CompanyBean.java
[missingteststask]
          com/networksByteDesign/eMarket/inventory/CustomerServlet.java
[missingteststask]
          com/networksByteDesign/spike/test3.java
[missingteststask]
          com/networksByteDesign/eMarket/MainMenuServlet.java
[missingteststask]
          com/networksByteDesign/eMarket/inventory/data/SalesItemBean.java
```

LISTING 9.13   Continued

```
[missingteststask]
          com/networksByteDesign/eMarket/inventory/CompanyServlet.java
[missingteststask]
          com/networksByteDesign/eMarket/inventory/SalesItemServlet.java
[missingteststask]
          com/networksByteDesign/spike/test2.java
[missingteststask]
          com/networksByteDesign/eMarket/util/TagLib.java
[missingteststask]
          com/networksByteDesign/eMarket/inventory/data/CustomerBean.java
[missingteststask]
          com/networksByteDesign/spike/test5.java
[missingteststask]
          com/networksByteDesign/spike/test4.java


BUILD SUCCESSFUL
Total time: 3 seconds
```

Code Coverage Tools for Use with JUnit

In addition to checking for missing unit tests, a development team may want to obtain some code coverage metrics on their testing. Code coverage lets you know just how much of your code you are actually exercising when performing a test. If your unit tests always pass, but are only testing a small percentage of your actual code, then it's likely that your code base may still have problems when it's released. Knowing how much of the code is being tested will help to assign a degree of confidence to the value of your testing, and help you to determine whether this area needs to be improved.

Several code coverage tools are available for use with JUnit. One such tool is called Quilt, and is available from SourceForge at:
http://quilt.sourceforge.net/overview.html. Quilt covers the following aspects of code: statements, branches, and path. It will report the total percentage of each of these flows within a set of source code that were actually traversed during the test. Another code coverage tool for use with JUnit is Clover. This is available at:
http://www.thecortex.net/clover/tutorial/index.html. Clover produces a nice HTML-based report that shows source code with line numbers, and a metric showing the number of times each line was executed.

Ant's Bean Scripting Framework Capability

Ant, as you have seen, is extensible by permitting users to write custom tasks and plug those tasks into their build processes. But Ant is also extensible in another way, through another feature of Ant that may not be as well known. Ant supports the Bean Scripting Framework (BSF), which is a framework that allows scripting languages to be called within Java objects. Supported scripting languages include

- JavaScript
- Python
- Tcl
- NetRexx
- Rexx

INSTALLING BSF

To install BSF, follow these steps:

1. Download `bsf.jar` from

   oss.software.ibm.com/developerworks/projects/bsf

2. Put `bsf.jar` in your system CLASSPATH or in the `lib` directory of your Ant installation.

INSTALLING RHINO (JAVASCRIPT)

1. Download `js.jar` from

   www.mozilla.org/rhino

2. Put `js.jar` in your system CLASSPATH or in the `lib` directory of your Ant installation.

BSF was originally developed at IBM's T.J. Watson Research Center. It later moved to the IBM AlphaWorks Web site, and has since "graduated" (as the AlphaWorks site states) from there. It has been incorporated into IBM WebSphere. The Apache Software Foundation has adopted BSF as a subproject of Jakarta.

Within Ant, BSF will allow you to embed the scripting language of your choice to do things that require a procedural programming capability. Using BSF, it's possible to do just about anything that could be done in Java. Also, BSF scripts have access to the runtime environment. Some of the disadvantages to using BSF are that your buildfiles now will have a dependency on one or more scripting languages.

As of Ant 1.5, the BSF engine in Ant supports Beanshell. Beanshell is a free, light-weight Java source code interpreter that will execute standard Java statements and expressions. Using Beanshell within the BSF capability of Ant is another option for executing Java code from within a buildfile without having to write a custom task. This can be useful if you want to do something simple that really doesn't warrant the creation of a custom task.

One reason why you might want to use BSF scripting is that it's an alternative to writing a custom task. If you're using Ant but you're not a Java developer, writing BSF scripts is a viable alternative to writing custom tasks. Also, BSF provides a way to work in existing scripts when migrating to Ant.

Story

The team needs to put together a quick stress test to run against the database. Because they have all the pieces in place in an Ant buildfile, they would like to use this as the basis of the stress test, and just have the target called in a looping fashion. Ant is not a scripting language, but it does have the capability to allow other scripting languages to be embedded in a buildfile. Two of the developers copy and paste some of the XML for database access into a test buildfile. They then modify the file to use the <script> task, and add in JavaScript code that will call their target multiple times in a loop. The whole point is to run the test until they are able to see a particular failure that happens intermittently.

The stress test is set up in the lab and run. They quickly get tired of watching it run, so they add a few extra features. The <mail> target is set up to send an e-mail when failure occurs, and the <sound> target is also used to play a sound upon test failure. This way, they can sit in the lab and work on other things while the test runs, but are alerted as soon as it fails so they can look into it.

Scripting in a buildfile is done with the optional <script> task. Listing 9.14 shows an example of the use of the scripting capability in Ant. In this example, there is a target that will perform a stress test called stressor. The stressor target will invoke JUnit tests with the name StressTest in them. The goal of this buildfile is to repetitively execute the stress test target with the goal of stressing the system. One way we might call this task multiple times would be to simply repeat the target over and over in the buildfile. This is akin to repeating a statement over and over in a Java program rather than using a loop mechanism. It would be nice to perform a procedural programming operation like looping in an Ant buildfile.

Using BSF, it is possible to perform such an operation in a buildfile. Look at the target in Listing 9.14 called stressTestLoop. In this target, the <script> task is used to execute JavaScript. The JavaScript creates a loop and inside the loop it invokes the stressor target by calling the stressor.execute() method. We can then obtain the property stressFailed using the method eMarket.getProperty("stressFailed") where eMarket is the name of the project. By testing on this property, we can use it to break out of the loop when the test fails, just as we would in any other procedural program.

LISTING 9.14   Target That Uses BSF to Execute JavaScript for Performing a Stress
Test Within an Ant Buildfile

```
<!-- stressor target -->
<target name="stressor">
    <mkdir dir="${dirs.test}"/>
    <junit haltonfailure="no"
           printsummary="yes"
           failureproperty="stressFailed">
        <classpath refid="project.classpath"/>
        <batchtest todir="${dirs.test}">
            <fileset dir="${dirs.build}">
                <include name="com/**/*StressTest.class" />
            </fileset>
        </batchtest>
    </junit>
</target>


<!-- stressTestLoop target -->
<target name="stressTestLoop">
    <script language="javascript"> <![CDATA[
        for (i=1; i<=10; i++)
        {
            stressor.execute();
            if(eMarket.getProperty("stressFailed"))
            {
                break;
            }
        }
    ]]> </script>
</target>


<!-- stressTest target -->
<target name="stressTest" depends="stressTestLoop" if="stressFailed">
    <sound>
        <success source="drama.wav" />
        <fail    source="drama.wav" />
    </sound>

    <mail from="build@networksByteDesign.com"
          tolist="devTeam@networksByteDesign.com"
          subject="Stress test Failed"
          mailhost="mail.networksByteDesign.com"
          encoding="plain"/>
</target>
```

Assuming we invoked the stressTest target, which depends on the stressTestLoop target, stressTest will execute when the loop completes. This target tests the property stressFailed to determine whether the test failed. Recall that the if attribute of a target will cause conditional execution of the target. In this case, the target will only execute if the property stressTest is set. If the test did fail, this target performs some interesting steps.

The stressFailed target uses the <sound> task. The <sound> task can be used to alert you when a build finished and whether the build succeeded or failed. It accepts the nested elements <success> and <fail> to define the sound to be played when the event occurs. The attribute source is used to point to the WAV file that is to be played. The loops attribute specifies the number of times to play the sound, and the duration attribute is the length of time in milliseconds to play the sound. In this case, the buildfile is set up to only play a sound if the test failed. We couldn't use the <success> or <fail> elements because they are events that have to do with the success or failure of the build. In this case, the stress test could fail, but the actual build process used to invoke the stress test will have succeeded in the sense that it ran without any Ant errors.

Mail Task

The next task used within the stressFailed target is the <mail> task. This task is used to send an SMTP mail message in a buildfile. The <mail> task can be used to mail a file or set of files defined with a nested <fileset> element. In this case, we're just sending a message with a subject, and an empty body that indicates that the stress test failed. The attributes of the <mail> task are fairly self-explanatory. The from attribute defines who the e-mail is from, which is build@networksByteDesign, and the tolist attribute can be used to create a comma-separated list of recipients. The subject line is where we indicate that the stress test failed. The mailhost attribute is used to tell the <mail> task which SMTP mail server to use. The encoding attribute, which allows you to set the encoding method, has allowed values of plain, mime, uu (for UUEncoding), or auto.

INSTALLATION FOR MAIL TASK

The <mail> task is a core task of Ant. However, it does have some additional JAR files that need to be installed.

1. Download mail.jar, which can be found at

   http://java.sun.com/products/javamail/

2. Download activation.jar, which can be found at

   http://java.sun.com/products/javabeans/glasgow/jaf.html

3. These JAR files need to either be put into the lib directory of the Ant installation, or put into your system CLASSPATH.

4. The <mail> is ready for use.

Summary

In this chapter, we looked at some of the ways in which different needs can be accommodated in an XP process using Ant. Ant does integrate with a number of IDEs on the market, and we looked at the use of NetBeans. We looked at the `<styler>` task, which provides an efficient way to perform more complex transformation tasks than can be accomplished with just `<style>`/`<xslt>`. We examined the use of the `<tempfile>` and `<purge>` tasks for managing large volumes of temporary files that might be created during a testing process.

The AntEater functional testing tool was examined. AntEater is based on Ant, contains a Web server, and is great for testing Web applications and Web services. We also created a custom Ant task for detecting classes that are missing unit tests. In creating this custom task, we had a chance to see how to use the Regular Expression mapper available in Ant, and how to deal with multiple `<filesets>` that need to be uniquely identified.

Ant's support of the Bean Scripting Framework (BSF) was discussed. We developed an example using this capability to run JavaScript inside a buildfile. In the same buildfile, we demonstrated the use of two other tasks, `<mail>` and `<sound>`, to generate alerts about build events.

10

Additional Teams Adopt the XP Process

The buildfile needs to be refactored for use by multiple teams. The first step is to make sure there are no project-specific values hard-coded into the buildfile. Next, we need to ensure that the proper hooks are placed in the build process to allow teams to add their specific needs. Given the current state of our buildfile, some changes need to be made to meet these new requirements.

Story

The iNet team is another software product team in NetworksByteDesign Inc. This group actually develops commercial software that is sold to customers. They have heard good things about the eMarket team and their success in developing the eMarket Web site, and they decided to see about adopting some of eMarket's practices. The iNet team is already using XP, but has implemented many of their processes with custom scripts. They're interested in using Ant, and after speaking to the eMarket team, adopt some of the eMarket team's build processes.

Because iNet does release software to customers, they have some unique requirements that eMarket didn't have. First, they do a lot more code generation than eMarket and need to make this more efficient. Also, they need to prevent a competitor from reverse-engineering their proprietary source code.

They find that by adopting eMarket's build process, they will be able to make a few changes to meet their requirements. Also, eMarket is willing to help out with technical questions that the iNet team might have. With this, the iNet team goes forward with adopting the Ant processes into their project.

Some of the tasks that need to be performed on the buildfile include

- Remove XML indicator from the top of the buildfile.

- Remove project tags.

- Modify `dirs.source` and `dirs.nightly` to replace hard-coded "eMarket" with `ant.project.name`.

- `MailLogger` mail address needs to use a property that will be set at the project level.

- Modify `MailLogger` subjects to replace hard-coded "eMarket" with `ant.project.name`.

- Modify `JSPTagLib` to replace hard-coded "eMarket" with `ant.project.name`.

- Modify `Manifest-built` by to replace hard-coded "eMarket" with `ant.project.name`.

- Modify `NightlyBuild-cvs` package to replace hard-coded "eMarket" with `ant.project.name`.

- Modify `StressTestLoop` to replace "eMarket" with `project`.

- The `stressTest` target needs the e-mail set to the project `email` property.

- The `compile` target needs to be project dependent because iNet does not use XDoclet.

Creating a Project-Level Buildfile

Now that the buildfile has been cleaned up to be usable by multiple projects, a project-level buildfile needs to be created. One approach could be to use the `<ant>` task to have one buildfile call another. The `<ant>` task can be configured to address such issues as whether the environment from one buildfile should be passed to the next file. Here's an example showing the use of the `<ant>` task to invoke another buildfile:

```
<ant inheritAll="false" antfile="foo.xml"/>
```

In this example, the `<ant>` task will execute the buildfile `foo.xml`. Because the attribute `inheritAll` is set to `false`, the environment in the current build process will not be passed to the new process. If we had not specified this attribute, the default is true, and the environment would be passed. Also, the `antfile` attribute is not set, the default behavior is to look for a buildfile called `build.xml`.

The approach the eMarket and iNet teams are taking is a little different. Because Ant buildfiles are simply XML files, standard XML techniques can be used to set up a basic include file. The project buildfile will be set up to simply include the common buildfile and will not require one of the files to call the other. The reason for this approach is that we want the environment in `common.xml` to be contained within all of the buildfiles that include it. Invoking `<ant>` on a common buildfile would pass our environment to it, not the other way around. Listing 10.1 shows the new eMarket buildfile, which includes a file called `common.xml`, which contains the targets that are common to both projects.

LISTING 10.1   The eMarket Project Buildfile

```
<?xml version="1.0" ?>

<!DOCTYPE project [<!ENTITY common SYSTEM "file:common.xml">]>

<project name="eMarket" default="compile" basedir=".">

    <property name="project.email"
              value="eMarketDev@networksByteDesign.com" />

    <!-- appCompile target -->
    <target name="appCompile"
            depends="xdoclet"
            description="Compile all of the source code.">
    </target>

    &common;

</project>
```

The project buildfile is configured to include the common.xml file, which is inserted at the &common; point in the file. Listing 10.2 shows some code snippets from the stripped-down common.xml file. Notice the cleanup changes that have been made to the common.xml file.

LISTING 10.2   Snippets of the common.xml File

```
<property name="dirs.backup"  value="${user.home}/backup" />
<property name="dirs.temp"    value="/tmp"                 />
<property name="dirs.doc"     value="docs"                 />
<property name="dirs.build"   value="build"                />
<property name="dirs.lib"     value="/usr/projects/lib"    />
<property name="dirs.test"    value="test"                 />
<property name="dirs.source"
          value="/usr/projects/${ant.project.name}/src" />
<property name="dirs.nightly"
          value="/usr/projects/${ant.project.name}/nightly" />


...
<!-- compile target -->
<target name="compile"
        depends="appCompile"
        description="Compile all of the source code.">
```

LISTING 10.2   Continued

```
        <javac srcdir="${dirs.build}">
            <classpath refid="project.classpath"/>
        </javac>
    </target>


    ...
```

Now that the eMarket team has removed their project information from the common build process, the iNet team can set up their own project buildfile. After creating the buildfile and removing the compile dependency on XDoclet, the iNet team is able to get the build process up and running with very little effort. Listing 10.3 shows the iNet project buildfile.

LISTING 10.3   iNet Project Buildfile

```
<?xml version="1.0" ?>

<!DOCTYPE project [<!ENTITY common SYSTEM "file:common.xml">]>

<project name="iNet" default="compile" basedir=".">

    <property name="project.email"
              value="iNetDevTeam@networksByteDesign.com" />

    <!-- appCompile target -->
    <target name="appCompile"
            description="Compile all of the source code.">
        <mkdir dir="${dirs.build}"/>

        <copy todir="${dirs.build}">
            <fileset dir="${dirs.source}" includes="**/*.*"/>
        </copy>
    </target>

    &common;

</project>
```

By introducing the project-specific hook in the appCompile target, each project can handle particular build issues without complicating the common.xml file. Listing 10.4 shows the output of calling the compile target on the eMarket project. Note the xdoclet target being executed on this build.

LISTING 10.4   Output from the `compile` Target on the eMarket Project

```
% ant compile
Buildfile: build.xml

xdoclet:
    [mkdir] Created dir: build
     [copy] Copying 295 files to build
[webdoclet] Generating Javadoc
[webdoclet] Javadoc execution
[webdoclet] Loading source file
    build/com/networksByteDesign/eMarket/inventory/CompanyServlet.java...
[webdoclet] Loading source file
    build/com/networksByteDesign/eMarket/inventory/CustomerServlet.java...
[webdoclet] Loading source file
    build/com/networksByteDesign/eMarket/inventory/SalesItemServlet.java...
[webdoclet] Loading source file
    build/com/networksByteDesign/eMarket/MainMenuServlet.java...

...

[ejbdoclet] Generating Javadoc
[ejbdoclet] Javadoc execution
[ejbdoclet] Loading source file
   build/com/networksByteDesign/eMarket/inventory/data/CompanyBean.java...
[ejbdoclet] Loading source file
   build/com/networksByteDesign/eMarket/inventory/data/CustomerBean.java...
[ejbdoclet] Loading source file
   build/com/networksByteDesign/eMarket/inventory/data/SalesItemBean.java...
[ejbdoclet] Constructing Javadoc information...

appCompile:

compile:
    [javac] Compiling 21 source files

BUILD SUCCESSFUL
Total time: 33 seconds
```

Listing 10.5 shows the output of calling the `compile` target on the iNet project. The iNet team is not required to complicate or slow down their build process with unnecessary XDoclet calls, but is able to configure the build process to meet their specific needs.

LISTING 10.5   Output from the compile Target on the iNet Project

```
% ant compile
Buildfile: build.xml

appCompile:
    [mkdir] Created dir: build
     [copy] Copying 318 files to build

compile:
    [javac] Compiling 68 source files

BUILD SUCCESSFUL
Total time: 6 seconds
```

Using Jikes for Dependency Checking

Story

One of the first things the iNet team wants to add to the buildfile is the use of the Jikes compiler. Jikes, by IBM, is an order of magnitude faster than Javac, and is a stringent compiler. Changing the build process to use this compiler will speed up their compilations considerably, because they have a lot of Java code to compile. Two of their developers modify the buildfile to use Jikes.

Jikes is an open source, high-performance Java compiler. On large Java compiles, a significant performance gain can be seen over the standard Javac compiler. Jikes also can be configured to produce code warnings that are stricter than those provided by the basic compiler. Jikes is a powerful compiler that should certainly be considered by Java developers.

INSTALLING JIKES

To install Jikes, follow these steps:

1. Download from

    `http://www-124.ibm.com/developerworks/projects/jikes/`

2. Uncompress the file and add Jikes to your PATH.

Jikes is hooked into the buildfile through the use of build properties. Although this is not a technique that is the long-term direction for Ant, this is the approach supported prior to Ant 2. The `build.compiler` property can be set to `jikes` to use Jikes rather than Javac for Java compile tasks.

The `build.compiler.fulldepend` property sets up Jikes to conduct dependency checking, which is another selling point for Jikes. The `build.compiler.pedantic` property turns on the very tight checking that Jikes provides. Listing 10.6 shows the iNet project buildfile after being configured to use Jikes.

LISTING 10.6   iNet Buildfile Configured for Use with Jikes

```
<?xml version="1.0" ?>

<!DOCTYPE project [<!ENTITY common SYSTEM "file:common.xml">]>

<project name="iNet" default="compile" basedir=".">

    <property name="project.email"
              value="iNetDevTeam@networksByteDesign.com" />
    <property name="build.compiler"            value="jikes"/>
    <property name="build.compiler.fulldepend" value="true" />
    <property name="build.compiler.pedantic"   value="true" />

    <!-- appCompile target -->
    <target name="appCompile"
            description="Compile all of the source code.">
        <mkdir dir="${dirs.build}"/>

        <copy todir="${dirs.build}">
            <fileset dir="${dirs.source}" includes="**/*.*"/>
        </copy>
    </target>

    &common;

</project>
```

Running the Jikes compiler against the iNet source code shows a style warning from some generated EJB classes. This style information is not caught by the Javac compiler. Listing 10.7 shows the output from the compile using the Jikes compiler.

LISTING 10.7   Output from the iNet Buildfile Using Jikes

```
% ant compile
Buildfile: build.xml

appCompile:
    [mkdir] Created dir: build
     [copy] Copying 295 files to build

compile:
    [javac] Compiling 21 source files

    [javac] Issued 1 semantic warning compiling
    "build/com/networksByteDesign/iNet/RouterA.java"

    [javac]     16.      transient private EntityContext ctx;
    [javac]                        ^-----^
    [javac] *** Warning: While it is legal to list modifiers in any order,
                it is recommended as a matter of style to list "private"
                before "transient".

    [javac] Issued 1 semantic warning compiling
    "build/com/networksByteDesign/iNet/RouterB.java"

    [javac]     16.      transient private EntityContext ctx;
    [javac]                        ^-----^
    [javac] *** Warning: While it is legal to list modifiers in any order,
                it is recommended as a matter of style to list "private"
                before "transient".

    [javac] Issued 1 semantic warning compiling
    "build/com/networksByteDesign/iNet/RouterC.java"

    [javac]     16.      transient private EntityContext ctx;
    [javac]                        ^-----^
    [javac] *** Warning: While it is legal to list modifiers in any order,
                it is recommended as a matter of style to list "private"
                before "transient".

BUILD SUCCESSFUL
Total time: 5 seconds
```

For those developers using Emacs as their editor, there is an additional property called
build.compiler.emacs. Setting this property to "true" generates error messages in a
format that Emacs uses to allow the developer to jump directly to the error line.
Listing 10.8 shows the difference in output when the Emacs property is set.

LISTING 10.8   Output Resulting from Running the Compile Target

```
% ant compile
Buildfile: build.xml

appCompile:
    [mkdir] Created dir: build
     [copy] Copying 295 files to build

compile:
    [javac] Compiling 21 source files
    [javac]
    build/com/networksByteDesign/iNet/RouterA.java
    :16:15:16:21: Warning: While it is legal to list modifiers in any order,
    it is recommended as a matter of style to list "private" before
    "transient".
    [javac]
    build/com/networksByteDesign/iNet/RouterB.java
    :16:15:16:21: Warning: While it is legal to list modifiers in any order,
    it is recommended as a matter of style to list "private" before
    "transient".
    [javac]
    build/com/networksByteDesign/iNet/RouterC.java
    :16:15:16:21: Warning: While it is legal to list modifiers in any order,
    it is recommended as a matter of style to list "private" before
    "transient".

BUILD SUCCESSFUL
Total time: 5 seconds
```

Writing a Custom Task for NoUnit

Story

The iNet team likes the custom task developed by the eMarket team for finding classes that don't
have a unit test. However, they've been using a tool called NoUnit. This tool actually finds some
things that the custom task doesn't, such as methods within a class that have not been properly
tested. They currently execute this tool from the command line, but decide to write a custom task
to smoothly integrate it into the overall build process.

Even if every class has a corresponding unit test, the tests that have been created still might be incomplete and might not fully exercise the code. This is like a doctor conducting a physical and pronouncing you healthy, but after only listening to your heart. It's great that your heart is doing fine, but additional tests must be run to determine whether you are "healthy." The same goes for your code. You want your unit tests to pass, but the focus should be on this question: Is your code "healthy?"

This is where code-coverage tools come into play. These tools look at the code being executed and determine where additional tests should be added to fully test all the code. The tool we look at here is NoUnit, which can be found at `http://nounit.sourceforge.net/`. This small tool produces an HTML file to give a visual representation of where unit tests are lacking. This report provides team leadership with a better picture of the true state of the unit tests.

INSTALLING NOUNIT

To install NoUnit, follow these steps:

1. Download from

   `http://nounit.sourceforge.net/`

2. Download the required supporting `.jar` files from

   `http://sourceforge.net/project/showfiles.php?group_id=40522`

3. Place the `nounit.jar` file and the required supporting `.jar` files in the `CLASSPATH` or in the Ant `lib` directory.

When you download NoUnit, one of the directories is an output directory. This directory contains some GIF images that are used by the HTML page produced by the tool. If you want to clean up the HTML, copy these files into the same directory where the HTML file is written.

Now that you have NoUnit installed, the next item on the agenda is to hook it into Ant. Because NoUnit is a Java application, you could use the Java task and call NoUnit using that mechanism. Because it has a command-line interface, you could use the <exec> task and execute NoUnit as you would any command-line tool. Although both of those techniques would work, here we are going to create a custom task to enable the use of NoUnit from within Ant.

Listing 10.9 shows the code for the NoUnit custom task.

LISTING 10.9   The NoUnit Custom Task

```
package com.networksByteDesign.util;

import net.firstpartners.nounit.ui.common.CommandPackage;
import net.firstpartners.nounit.ui.common.Processor;
```

LISTING 10.9 Continued

```
import net.firstpartners.nounit.utility.NoUnitException;
import org.apache.tools.ant.BuildException;
import org.apache.tools.ant.Task;

public class NoUnitTask extends Task
{
    public void execute()
    {
        if(startDir_ == null || startDir_.trim().length() == 0)
        {
            throw new BuildException
                ("Required attribute startDir not set in noUnit",
                 location);
        }

        if(outputDir_ == null || outputDir_.trim().length() == 0)
        {
            throw new BuildException
                ("Required attribute outputDir not set in noUnit",
                 location);
        }

        if(reportName_ == null || reportName_.trim().length() == 0)
        {
            throw new BuildException
                ("Required attribute reportName not set in noUnit",
                 location);
        }

        if(outputFile_ == null || outputFile_.trim().length() == 0)
        {
            throw new BuildException
                ("Required attribute outputFile not set in noUnit",
                 location);
        }

        String args[] = new String[10];

        args[0] = "start_dir";
        args[1] = startDir_;
        args[2] = "output_dir";
```

LISTING 10.9   Continued

```
        args[3] = outputDir_;
        args[4] = "report_class";
        args[5] = "com.networksByteDesign.util.NoUnitReport";
        args[6] = "report_name";
        args[7] = reportName_;
        args[8] = "output_file";
        args[9] = outputFile_;

        try
        {
            CommandPackage userArgs = new CommandPackage(args);
            Processor mainProcessor = new Processor();
            CommandPackage results = mainProcessor.transform(userArgs);
        }
        catch(NoUnitException e)
        {
            throw new BuildException(e);
        }
    }

    public void setStartDir(String startDir)
    {
        startDir_ = startDir;
    }

    public void setOutputDir(String outputDir)
    {
        outputDir_ = outputDir;
    }

    public void setReportName(String reportName)
    {
        reportName_ = reportName;
    }

    public void setOutputFile(String outputFile)
    {
        outputFile_ = outputFile;
    }

    private String startDir_   = null;
    private String outputDir_  = null;
```

LISTING 10.9   Continued

```
    private String reportName_ = null;
    private String outputFile_ = null;
}
```

The custom task has four attributes:

- The starting directory

- The output directory

- The report name

- The output file

Setters are established for each of these attributes. The execute() method ensures that all attributes have been supplied. The rest of the class sets up the arguments to supply to NoUnit and calls the Processor to generate the HTML file. Listing 10.10 shows the source code for the NoUnit report created for use by the NoUnit task.

LISTING 10.10   NoUnit Task Custom Report

```
package com.networksByteDesign.util;

import java.io.FileNotFoundException;
import java.io.FileOutputStream;
import java.io.IOException;

import javax.xml.transform.Transformer;
import javax.xml.transform.TransformerConfigurationException;
import javax.xml.transform.TransformerException;
import javax.xml.transform.TransformerFactory;
import javax.xml.transform.stream.StreamResult;
import javax.xml.transform.stream.StreamSource;

import net.firstpartners.nounit.report.AbstractReport;
import net.firstpartners.nounit.report.process.CallChainer;
import net.firstpartners.nounit.ui.common.CommandPackage;
import net.firstpartners.nounit.ui.common.SystemValues;
import net.firstpartners.nounit.utility.FileUtil;
import net.firstpartners.nounit.utility.NoUnitException;

import org.jdom.JDOMException;
```

LISTING 10.10   Continued

```java
public class NoUnitReport extends AbstractReport
{
    public static final String XSLT_REPORT    = "report_name";
    public static final String OUTPUT_FILE    = "output_file";
    public static final String classMustExtend = "junit.framework.TestCase";

    public void makeReport(CommandPackage inPackage)
        throws TransformerException,
                TransformerConfigurationException,
                IOException,
                FileNotFoundException ,
                NoUnitException
    {
        String outFile = FileUtil.combineFileAndDirectory
                        (inPackage.getString(this.OUTPUT_FILE),
                         inPackage.getString(CommandPackage.OUTPUT_DIR));
        String xmlFile = FileUtil.combineFileAndDirectory
                        (SystemValues.XML_OUTPUT_NAME,
                         inPackage.getString(CommandPackage.OUTPUT_DIR));
        String xslFile    = inPackage.getString(this.XSLT_REPORT);
        String xmlInOutFile = FileUtil.combineFileAndDirectory
                            (SystemValues.XML_OUTPUT_NAME,
                             inPackage.getString
                             (CommandPackage.OUTPUT_DIR));

        System.out.println("Generating Report:");
        System.out.println("XML in:    " + xmlFile);
        System.out.println("XSLT file:  " + xslFile);
        System.out.println("Output file: " + outFile);
        System.out.println("");

        try
        {
            CallChainer myProcessor = new CallChainer();
            myProcessor.addCallChainInformation(xmlInOutFile,
                                                xmlInOutFile,
                                                classMustExtend);
        }
        catch (JDOMException jde)
        {
            throw new NoUnitException(jde,"XML-JDOM Exception");
        }
```

LISTING 10.10   Continued

```
        TransformerFactory tFactory    = TransformerFactory.newInstance();
        Transformer        transformer = tFactory.newTransformer
                                            (new StreamSource(xslFile));

        transformer.transform(new StreamSource(xmlFile),
                              new StreamResult
                              (new FileOutputStream(outFile)));
    }
}
```

The `NoUnitReport.java` file has no Ant-specific logic, but it deals with calling the appropriate classes to parse the XML file created by NoUnit and to build the HTML page. These classes must be compiled and included in the `CLASSPATH` or in the `ant/lib` directory.

Now that you have a custom NoUnit task, you can create a target in your buildfile to automate the process of calling NoUnit. Listing 10.11 shows the `noUnitCheck` target.

LISTING 10.11   noUnitCheck Target in Ant Buildfile

```
<?xml version="1.0" ?>

<!DOCTYPE project [<!ENTITY common SYSTEM "file:common.xml">]>

<project name="iNet" default="compile" basedir=".">

    <property name="project.email"
              value="iNetDevTeam@networksByteDesign.com" />

    <property name="build.compiler"            value="jikes"/>
    <property name="build.compiler.emacs"      value="true"/>
    <property name="build.compiler.fulldepend" value="true" />
    <property name="build.compiler.pedantic"   value="true" />

    <property name="dirs.nounit" value="/usr/software/nounit" />

    <taskdef name="noUnit"
             classname="com.networksByteDesign.util.NoUnitTask"
             classpathref="project.classpath"/>

    <!-- appCompile target -->
    <target name="appCompile"
```

LISTING 10.11   Continued

```
                description="Compile all of the source code.">
        <mkdir dir="${dirs.build}"/>

        <copy todir="${dirs.build}">
            <fileset dir="${dirs.source}" includes="**/*.*"/>
        </copy>
    </target>

    <!-- noUnitCheck target -->
    <target name="noUnitCheck"
            description="Check for missing or incomplete unit tests.">
        <mkdir dir="${dirs.build}" />

        <copy todir="${dirs.build}" overwrite="yes">
            <fileset dir="${dirs.nounit}/output" />
        </copy>

        <noUnit startDir="${dirs.build}"
                outputDir="${dirs.build}"
                reportName="${dirs.nounit}/xslt/no-unit.xsl"
                outputFile="nounit.html" />
    </target>

    &common;

</project>
```

We simply set the appropriate attributes in our new custom task, and our integration to NoUnit is complete. The output from the Ant build process can be seen in Listing 10.12.

LISTING 10.12   Output Resulting from Executing the `noUnitCheck` Target

```
% ant noUnitCheck
Buildfile: build.xml

noUnitCheck:
    [copy] Copying 8 files to build
  [noUnit] Generating Report:
```

LISTING 10.12   Continued

```
[noUnit] XML in:      build/project.xml
[noUnit] XSLT file:   /usr/software/nounit/xslt/no-unit.xsl
[noUnit] Output file: build/nounit.html


BUILD SUCCESSFUL
Total time: 6 seconds
```

Rather than viewing the information in raw XML format, the no-unit.xsl file generates a nicely formatted HTML page that makes missing unit tests stand out. This type of report really helps a project lead in determining where unit tests may be lacking and helps produce a higher quality test suite. This target creates the ${dirs.build} directory and copies the GIF images before calling the <noUnit> task. This causes the HTML to include the proper graphics rather than show broken image links. The HTML report can be seen in Figure 10.1.

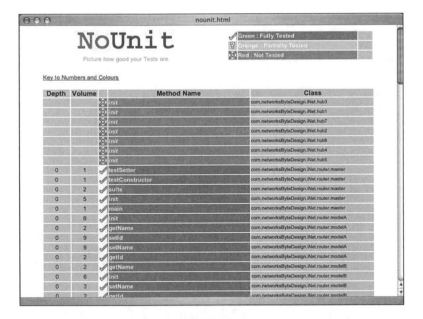

FIGURE 10.1   HTML report showing the results of the NoUnit tool.

Increasing the Efficiency of Code Generation

Story

The iNet Team has a large base of generated code. One of the problems is that there is so much code to generate that the process is extremely slow. Much of the code generation that happens every build iteration is really a waste of time. This is because most of the time only a few source files have actually changed but all of the files get generated. They decide to work on making this more efficient.

Although code-generation techniques can be a powerful way of producing an application, in this case there is a performance drag, which is causing a lengthy build process. A few extra minutes may not seem like a significant issue, but when you factor in the number of builds a developer performs in a day, a few minutes can quickly add up to an hour or more of lost productivity. The build target shown in Listing 10.13 simply copies the files to the build directory and then runs five different code generators in sequential order.

LISTING 10.13   codegen Target Before Optimizations

```
<!-- codegen target -->
<target name="codegen">
    <mkdir dir="${dirs.build}"/>

    <copy todir="${dirs.build}">
        <fileset dir="${dirs.source}" includes="**/*.*"/>
    </copy>

    <style style="${dirs.build}/codegen/dp1.xsl"
           includes="${dirs.build}/*.dp1"
           extension=".dp1_java"
           destdir="${dirs.build}"/>

    <style style="${dirs.build}/codegen/nb.xsl"
           includes="${dirs.build}/*.nb"
           extension=".nb_java"
           destdir="${dirs.build}"/>

    <style style="${dirs.build}/codegen/cl.xsl"
           includes="${dirs.build}/*.cl"
           extension=".cl_java"
           destdir="${dirs.build}"/>

    <style style="${dirs.build}/codegen/q1z.xsl"
           includes="${dirs.build}/*.q1z"
```

LISTING 10.13   Continued

```
                extension=".q1z_java"
                destdir="${dirs.build}"/>


        <style style="${dirs.build}/codegen/gbk.xsl"
                includes="${dirs.build}/*.gbk"
                extension=".gbk_java"
                destdir="${dirs.build}"/>
    </target>
```

Listing 10.14 shows the output of the codegen target. Pay special attention to the time necessary to conduct the build. Optimizing this process could significantly reduce the amount of time to produce the code-generated build.

LISTING 10.14   Output from the codegen Target Prior to Optimizations

```
% ant codegen
Buildfile: build.xml

codegen:
    [mkdir] Created dir: build
     [copy] Copying 295 files to build
    [style] Transforming into build
    [style] Processing build/t1.dp1 to build/t1.dp1_java
    [style] Loading stylesheet build/codegen/dp1.xsl
    [style] Processing build/t10.dp1 to build/t10.dp1_java
    [style] Processing build/t11.dp1 to build/t11.dp1_java


    ...


    [style] Transforming into build
    [style] Processing build/v_10_ar.nb to build/v_10_ar.nb_java
    [style] Loading stylesheet build/codegen/nb.xsl
    [style] Processing build/v_11_ar.nb to build/v_11_ar.nb_java
    [style] Processing build/v_12_ar.nb to build/v_12_ar.nb_java


    ...


    [style] Transforming into build
    [style] Processing build/v1.cl to build/v1.cl_java
    [style] Loading stylesheet build/codegen/cl.xsl
    [style] Processing build/v10.cl to build/v10.cl_java
    [style] Processing build/v11.cl to build/v11.cl_java
```

LISTING 10.13   Continued

```
...

[style] Transforming into build
[style] Processing build/mn10sa.q1z to build/mn10sa.q1z_java
[style] Loading stylesheet build/codegen/q1z.xsl
[style] Processing build/mn11sa.q1z to build/mn11sa.q1z_java
[style] Processing build/mn12sa.q1z to build/mn12sa.q1z_java


...

[style] Transforming into build
[style] Processing build/u1.gbk to build/u1.gbk_java
[style] Loading stylesheet build/codegen/gbk.xsl
[style] Processing build/u10.gbk to build/u10.gbk_java
[style] Processing build/u11.gbk to build/u11.gbk_java


...


BUILD SUCCESSFUL
Total time: 4 minutes 20 seconds
```

Developing the smartCopy Target

Story

Two of the developers on the iNet team come up with an idea after seeing the smartBuild target that was developed by the eMarket team. They implement a smartCopy target that will only copy the source files to the build area. This way, the code generator will only codeGen the sources that have actually changed. To further increase the speed of the build, they make use of the Ant `<parallel>` task. This will allow the code generation pieces to be executed in parallel. The smartCopy target helps increase efficiency when only a few source files have changed. The use of `<parallel>` increases efficiency when many or all of the source files have to be run through code generation.

In this section, we'll use another feature of Ant, called selectors, to optimize our code generation step. Let's take a brief look at the types of selectors available within Ant.

Selectors

Selectors are used in conjunction with the `<fileset>` element. A selector allows you to discriminate which files will be included in a fileset by other means than just the filename. Ant includes a set of core selectors, and also selector containers, which can contain other selectors.

Ant has seven core selectors:

- `<contains>`
- `<date>`
- `<depend>`
- `<depth>`
- `<filename>`
- `<present>`
- `<size>`

The `<depend>` and `<present>` selectors support the use of a nested `<mapper>` element. The `<contains>` selector will include files that have a certain text string. Here's an example:

```
<fileset dir="." includes="**/*.java">
    <contains text="extends" casesensitive="yes"/>
</fileset>
```

This `<fileset>` and `<selector>` combination will select files that contain the word extends, allowing Java files that are derived from base classes to be identified and used in a task.

The `<date>` selector permits you to select files based on their timestamp. In the following example, the date selector will pick files that have a timestamp prior to January 1, 2003. The `<copy>` task, which supports the nested `<fileset>` will then copy files based on their timestamp.

```
<copy todir="${gen.dir}">
  <fileset dir="${src}" includes="**/*.java">
    <date datetime=""01/01/2003 12:01 AM" when="after"/>
  </fileset>
</copy>
```

The `<depend>` selector can be used with a nested `<mapper>` to create dependencies between types of files. This selector will be discussed in the next section, "Creating the smartCopy Target with `<depend>`."

The `<depth>` selector allows you to define filesets that will only go to a certain number of levels in a directory tree. In the following example, the `<depth>` selector is used with a `<tarfileset>`, which is a type of `<fileset>`, to cause a tarfile to be created that only follows partially down a directory tree. The value of max starts with 0. So, a value of 0 will cause the zero level (or a single level) to be copied. A value of 1 will copy two levels, and so on.

```
<target name="test">
  <tar destfile="foo.tar">
    <tarfileset dir="foobar" includes="**/*">
      <depth max="1"/>
    </tarfileset>
  </tar>
</target>
```

The `<filename>` selector gives you the default behavior that is available in `<filesets>` with the `<include>` and `<exclude>` nested elements, so we won't create an example here.

The `<present>` element can also be used to create a dependency between files, and uses a nested mapper. The following example shows the use of `<present>`. In this example, the `<tarfileset>` will only pick up the files in directory foo1 ending in .java if a corresponding file ending in .xml exists in directory foo2.

```
<target name="test.present">
  <tar destfile="foo.tar">
    <tarfileset dir="./foo1" includes="**/*">
      <present targetdir="./foo2">
        <mapper type="glob" from="*.java" to="*.xml"/>
      </present>
    </tarfileset>
  </tar>
</target>
```

Creating the `smartCopy` Target with `<depend>`

Let's now use a selector to optimize our code generation. Suppose we have a process that generates Java code from XML, and consists of the following steps. First, the XML files are copied to the gen directory. Next, the code generator is run on the XML files to produce Java source code. Then the Java files are compiled to produce class files. If a large number of files are involved, or the code generation is time-consuming, we would prefer to only perform this step for XML files that have actually changed.

The way to achieve this optimization goal is to use the `<depend>` selector to form a dependency between the source XML file and the class file that will result from it. We tie the dependency to the class file rather than the generated Java file because the generated Java files will be removed each time we perform the build.

Listing 10.15 shows the smartCopy task, which can be used to optimize a code generation step. This target makes use of the `<depend>` selector and the glob file mapper to create a dependency between the source and the generated files. This target can be

used to cause only source files that have changed to actually be code generated. The
<delete> task is first used to remove the source files from the generation directory.
Next, the <copy> task is used to copy the XML files that have changed to the code
generation directory. This is where the <depend> selector is able to optimize the copy,
allowing us to only copy the files that are more recent than the class files that
depend on them. Inside the <fileset> is a nested <depend> selector. This <depend>
selector in turn contains a global <mapper>, which is used to create a mapping
between source files and the files they will generate, such as files with the .dp1 suffix
and the generated .dp1_java suffix. By using this <mapper>, the <depend> selector
now identifies a dependency between the two.

LISTING 10.15 Codegen Using smartCopy Target

```
<!-- codegen target -->
<target name="codegen">
    <mkdir dir="${dirs.build}"/>

    <copy todir="${dirs.build}">
        <fileset dir="${dirs.source}" includes="**/*.xsl"/>
    </copy>

    <antcall target="smartCopy" />

    <style style="${dirs.build}/codegen/dp1.xsl"
           includes="${dirs.build}/*.dp1"
           extension=".dp1_java"
           destdir=""/>

    <style style="${dirs.build}/codegen/nb.xsl"
           includes="${dirs.build}/*.nb"
           extension=".nb_java"
           destdir=""/>

    <style style="${dirs.build}/codegen/cl.xsl"
           includes="${dirs.build}/*.cl"
           extension=".cl_java"
           destdir=""/>
```

LISTING 10.15   Continued

```
        <style style="${dirs.build}/codegen/q1z.xsl"
               includes="${dirs.build}/*.q1z"
               extension=".q1z_java"
               destdir=""/>

        <style style="${dirs.build}/codegen/gbk.xsl"
               includes="${dirs.build}/*.gbk"
               extension=".gbk_java"
               destdir=""/>
</target>

<property name="LAST_BUILD"
          value="${dirs.build}/LAST_BUILD.properties"/>
<property file="${LAST_BUILD}"/>

<!-- smartCopy -->
<target name="smartCopy">
    <delete>
        <fileset dir="${dirs.build}">
            <include name="*.dp1"/>
            <include name="*.cl"/>
            <include name="*.gbk"/>
            <include name="*.nb"/>
            <include name="*.q1z"/>
        </fileset>
    </delete>

    <copy todir="${dirs.build}">
        <fileset dir="${dirs.source}" includes="**/*.dp1">
            <depend targetdir="${dirs.build}">
                <mapper type="glob" from="*.dp1" to="*.dp1_java"/>
            </depend>
        </fileset>
        <fileset dir="${dirs.source}" includes="**/*.cl">
            <depend targetdir="${dirs.build}">
                <mapper type="glob" from="*.cl" to="*.cl_java"/>
            </depend>
        </fileset>
        <fileset dir="${dirs.source}" includes="**/*.gbk">
            <depend targetdir="${dirs.build}">
                <mapper type="glob" from="*.gbk" to="*.gbk_java"/>
```

LISTING 10.15   Continued

```
            </depend>
        </fileset>
        <fileset dir="${dirs.source}" includes="**/*.nb">
            <depend targetdir="${dirs.build}">
                <mapper type="glob" from="*.nbk" to="*.nb_java"/>
            </depend>
        </fileset>
        <fileset dir="${dirs.source}" includes="**/*.q1z">
            <depend targetdir="${dirs.build}">
                <mapper type="glob" from="*.q1z" to="*.q1z_java"/>
            </depend>
        </fileset>
    </copy>
</target>
```

Listing 10.16 shows the output from our new smartCopy enhanced code generator.

LISTING 10.16   Output from the smartCopy Version of codegen

```
% ant codegen
Buildfile: build.xml

codegen:

smartCopy:
[propertyfile] Updating property file: build/LAST_BUILD.properties
     [copy] Copying 11 files to build
    [style] Transforming into build
    [style] Processing build/t1.dp1 to build/t1.dp1_java
    [style] Loading stylesheet build/codegen/dp1.xsl
    [style] Transforming into build
    [style] Processing build/v_20_ar.nb to build/v_20_ar.nb_java
    [style] Loading stylesheet build/codegen/nb.xsl
    [style] Transforming into build
    [style] Processing build/v31.cl to build/v31.cl_java
    [style] Loading stylesheet build/codegen/cl.xsl
    [style] Processing build/v32.cl to build/v32.cl_java
    [style] Processing build/v33.cl to build/v33.cl_java
    [style] Processing build/v34.cl to build/v34.cl_java
    [style] Transforming into build
    [style] Processing build/mn12sa.q1z to build/mn12sa.q1z_java
```

LISTING 10.16   Continued

```
[style] Loading stylesheet build/codegen/q1z.xsl
[style] Processing build/mn37sa.q1z to build/mn37sa.q1z_java
[style] Processing build/mn50sa.q1z to build/mn50sa.q1z_java
[style] Transforming into build
[style] Processing build/u47.gbk to build/u47.gbk_java
[style] Loading stylesheet build/codegen/gbk.xsl
[style] Processing build/u9.gbk to build/u9.gbk_java


BUILD SUCCESSFUL
Total time: 19 seconds
```

Although the `smartCopy` target offers huge performance gains when only a few files are modified, the team still looks for a way to improve performance when large-scale changes are made. Because all of the code generators run independently of each other, the team looks at using the `<parallel>` tasks to run the `<style>` tasks simultaneously. The `<parallel>` task is used to create separate threads of execution for sets of tasks within a build. This task has no attributes. When using the `<parallel>` task, you must be careful not to initiate threads that will interact with each other. An example of a potential problem would be separate threads that attempt to write the same file. Also, if any of the threads throws an unhandled exception, the rest of the threads will continue to execute to completion, but the overall build will fail. Listing 10.17 shows the changes to the `codegen` target to wrap the code generators in the `<parallel>` task.

LISTING 10.17   The codegen Target with `<parallel>` Task

```
<!-- codegen target -->
<target name="codegen">
    <mkdir dir="${dirs.build}"/>

    <copy todir="${dirs.build}">
        <fileset dir="${dirs.source}" includes="**/*.xsl"/>
    </copy>

    <antcall target="smartCopy" />

    <parallel>

    <style style="${dirs.build}/codegen/dp1.xsl"
            includes="${dirs.build}/*.dp1"
            extension=".dp1_java"
            destdir=""/>
```

LISTING 10.17   Continued

```
        <style style="${dirs.build}/codegen/nb.xsl"
               includes="${dirs.build}/*.nb"
               extension=".nb_java"
               destdir=""/>

        <style style="${dirs.build}/codegen/cl.xsl"
               includes="${dirs.build}/*.cl"
               extension=".cl_java"
               destdir=""/>

        <style style="${dirs.build}/codegen/q1z.xsl"
               includes="${dirs.build}/*.q1z"
               extension=".q1z_java"
               destdir=""/>

        <style style="${dirs.build}/codegen/gbk.xsl"
               includes="${dirs.build}/*.gbk"
               extension=".gbk_java"
               destdir=""/>

    </parallel>
  </target>
```

Care needs to be taken to ensure that there are no dependencies between the targets or in contention for resources. When the tasks are truly independent, this simple task can provide tangible results with little effort. Listing 10.18 shows the output of the <parallel> enhanced codegen when all files have been modified.

LISTING 10.18   Output from the <parallel> Enhanced codegen Target

```
% ant codegen
Buildfile: build.xml

codegen:

smartCopy:
   [delete] Deleting 250 files from build
[propertyfile] Updating property file: build/LAST_BUILD.properties
     [copy] Copying 250 files to build
    [style] Transforming into build
    [style] Processing build/u1.gbk to build/u1.gbk_java
```

LISTING 10.18   Continued

```
[style] Loading stylesheet build/codegen/gbk.xsl
[style] Transforming into build
[style] Transforming into build
[style] Processing build/v_10_ar.nb to build/v_10_ar.nb_java
[style] Processing build/t1.dp1 to build/t1.dp1_java
[style] Transforming into build
[style] Loading stylesheet build/codegen/nb.xsl
[style] Processing build/v1.cl to build/v1.cl_java
[style] Loading stylesheet build/codegen/cl.xsl
[style] Loading stylesheet build/codegen/dp1.xsl
[style] Transforming into build
[style] Processing build/mn10sa.q1z to build/mn10sa.q1z_java
[style] Loading stylesheet build/codegen/q1z.xsl
[style] Processing build/t10.dp1 to build/t10.dp1_java
[style] Processing build/v10.cl to build/v10.cl_java
[style] Processing build/mn11sa.q1z to build/mn11sa.q1z_java
[style] Processing build/t11.dp1 to build/t11.dp1_java
[style] Processing build/v11.cl to build/v11.cl_java

...


[style] Processing build/mn5sa.q1z to build/mn5sa.q1z_java
[style] Processing build/u9.gbk to build/u9.gbk_java
[style] Processing build/mn6sa.q1z to build/mn6sa.q1z_java
[style] Processing build/t6.dp1 to build/t6.dp1_java
[style] Processing build/t7.dp1 to build/t7.dp1_java
[style] Processing build/mn7sa.q1z to build/mn7sa.q1z_java
[style] Processing build/t8.dp1 to build/t8.dp1_java
[style] Processing build/mn8sa.q1z to build/mn8sa.q1z_java
[style] Processing build/mn9sa.q1z to build/mn9sa.q1z_java
[style] Processing build/t9.dp1 to build/t9.dp1_java


BUILD SUCCESSFUL
Total time: 59 seconds
```

Creating Unique Build Numbers

Story

The iNet Team likes to tag every build that gets installed into testing with a version number for tracking purposes. To remove the manual aspect of this, and to make the process less error-prone, they decide to make use of the `buildnumber` task, which automatically creates a unique build number in sequence. This number is then used in a target to automatically tag the source code in CVS that went into the build.

The `buildnumber` target is a simple target that increments a number from a text file and sets a build property with the next value. This process should only be used in those environments where there are not multiple copies of the `build.number` file. For example, the nightly build process could use this approach, but multiple developers running in different workspaces would all generate the same `build.numbers`. For those distributed scenarios, a more sophisticated mechanism would need to be developed.

If you have a target that is only intended to run on a single machine, you might want to take some steps to ensure that the target only runs on the intended machine. Here's one way to accomplish this. Note that this approach is only to prevent the accidental running of a target on a machine on an unintended platform. It is by no means a security measure. The `<available>` task can be used to determine whether a system resource exists and to set a property if the resource does exist. Consider the following example:

```
<target name="init">
    <available file="/usr/eMarket/theBuildMachine" type="dir"
               property="isBuildMachine"/>
</target>

<target name="build" depends="init" if="isBuildMachine">
    <echo>executed target</echo>
</target>
```

The target `build` is the target that we only want to execute on a specific machine. On the build machine, we would manually create a directory one time called `/usr/eMarket/theBuildMachine`. This directory is left there. Any other machine that is not intended to run the `build` target cannot have this directory in its filesystem. When the `build` target executes, it first runs the `init` target, because of the dependency. The `init` target executes the `<available>` task, which checks for the existence of the directory `/usr/eMarket/theBuildMachine`. If this directory exists, presumably the build is running on the intended machine, and the property `isBuildMachine` is set. Then the target `build` checks its `if` condition. It will only run if `isBuildProperty` is set. If the property is set, the `build` target will execute. If the property is not set, the `build` target will do nothing else.

Again, this is not a security mechanism. It's obvious from the buildfile what conditions are checked, and it would be easy for anyone to defeat this mechanism. The goal here is simply to prevent the unintended running of a target by accident.

Listing 10.19 shows an `incrementBuild` target, which simply gets the next build number and tags the current workspace with the build number.

LISTING 10.19   `incrementBuild` Target for Tagging a CVS Release

```
<!-- incrementBuild target -->
<target name="incrementBuild">
    <buildnumber/>
    <property name="tag" value="iNet-${build.number}" />
    <cvs command="tag ${tag}" dest="${dirs.source}"/>
    <echo message="Release tagged with following build number: ${tag}"/>
</target>
```

It's worth noting that the `<buildnumber>` task has a `file` attribute. This attribute can be used to point to a specific file for storing the build number. If the file attribute is not set, `<buildnumber>` defaults to using a file called `build.number`. Listing 10.20 shows the output from running the `incrementBuild` task. This approach can help a team quickly determine what files were part of a particular build and can often significantly reduce debugging and support time.

LISTING 10.20   Output from the `incrementBuild` Target

```
% ant incrementBuild
Buildfile: build.xml

incrementBuild:
    [cvs] Using cvs passfile: /Users/gkillian/.cvspass
    [cvs] cvs server: Tagging .
    [cvs] cvs server: Tagging com
    [cvs] cvs server: Tagging com/networksByteDesign
    [cvs] cvs server: Tagging com/networksByteDesign/iNet

    ...

    [cvs] T mn11sa.q1z
    [cvs] T mn12sa.q1z
    [cvs] T mn13sa.q1z
    [cvs] T mn14sa.q1z
    [cvs] T mn15sa.q1z
```

LISTING 10.20   Continued

```
    [cvs] T mn16sa.q1z
    [echo] Release tagged with following build number: iNet-3


BUILD SUCCESSFUL
Total time: 4 seconds
```

The build.number file is simply a property file with the build.number as the key. The work in reading and writing the property file as well as incrementing the value is encapsulated in the buildnumber task:

```
#Build Number for ANT. Do not edit!
#Sun Feb 02 15:07:45 CST 2003
build.number=4
```

Obfuscating JAR Files

Story

As part of their commercial release, the iNet team has to perform a few steps to ensure the confidentiality of their code. One step they take is to compile all JSP pages, so that the source code isn't shipped with the product. The other step they take is to obfuscate all JAR files prior to shipping. This is to prevent reverse-engineering of their code. Because this is a critical part of the release process, the iNet development team takes steps to incorporate this into their build process. They use the <jspc> task to invoke the JSP compiler, and also integrate the yGuard tool for code obfuscation into their Ant build processes.

To provide an additional layer of security or for performance gains, JSP pages can be converted into their servlet equivalents and compiled at build time rather than at runtime. After running the JSP pages through the JSP compiler, the resulting servlets can be compiled as normal Java code and the resulting class files deployed to the application server.

INSTALLING JSP COMPILER

To install the JSP compiler, follow these steps:

1. Download Tomcat from

    `http://jakarta.apache.org/tomcat/`

2. Place the jasper-compiler.jar and jasper-runtime.jar files in the CLASSPATH or in the Ant lib directory.

3. Place servlet.jar in the system CLASSPATH, or the lib directory of your Tomcat installation.

Listing 10.21 shows the `jspCompile` target, which calls the `<jspc>` task passing the JSP pages that are to be compiled.

LISTING 10.21   `jspCompile` Target for Compiling JSP Pages

```
<!-- jspCompile target -->
<target name="jspCompile">
    <mkdir dir="${dirs.build}"/>

    <copy todir="${dirs.build}">
        <fileset dir="${dirs.source}" includes="**/RegisterStep*.jsp"/>
    </copy>

    <jspc destdir="."
          srcdir="${dirs.build}"
          uriroot=".">
        <include name="**/RegisterStep*.jsp"/>
    </jspc>
</target>
```

A very simple JSP page is shown in Listing 10.22. This page will be used to demonstrate what the JSP compiler does when supplied with a valid JSP page. The example should be saved as `RegisterStep1.jsp`.

LISTING 10.22   Simple JSP Page for Demonstrating Use of JSPC

```
<html>
<head>
  <title>Register Step 1</title>
<head>
<body>
<h1>Register Steps 1</h1>
<hr width="50%"/>
</body>
</html>
```

Listing 10.23 shows the same JSP page after being converted by the `<jspc>` task into a servlet. The resulting output is the same, but this file can be compiled and the class files deployed, rather than distributing the JSP page itself.

LISTING 10.23   JSP Page That Has Been Converted into a Servlet

```java
package org.apache.jsp;

import javax.servlet.*;
import javax.servlet.http.*;
import javax.servlet.jsp.*;
import org.apache.jasper.runtime.*;

public class RegisterStep1_jsp extends HttpJspBase {


  private static java.util.Vector _jspx_includes;

  public java.util.List getIncludes() {
    return _jspx_includes;
  }

  public void _jspService(HttpServletRequest request,
                          HttpServletResponse response)
        throws java.io.IOException, ServletException {

    JspFactory _jspxFactory = null;
    javax.servlet.jsp.PageContext pageContext = null;
    HttpSession session = null;
    ServletContext application = null;
    ServletConfig config = null;
    JspWriter out = null;
    Object page = this;
    JspWriter _jspx_out = null;


    try {
      _jspxFactory = JspFactory.getDefaultFactory();
      response.setContentType("text/html;charset=ISO-8859-1");
      pageContext = _jspxFactory.getPageContext(this, request, response,
                  null, true, 8192, true);
      application = pageContext.getServletContext();
      config = pageContext.getServletConfig();
      session = pageContext.getSession();
      out = pageContext.getOut();
      _jspx_out = out;
```

LISTING 10.23   Continued

```
        out.write("<html>\n");
        out.write("<head>\n  ");
        out.write("<title>Register Step 1");
        out.write("</title>\n");
        out.write("<head>\n");
        out.write("<body>\n");
        out.write("<h1>Register Steps 1");
        out.write("</h1>\n");
        out.write("<hr width=\"50%\"/>\n");
        out.write("</body>\n");
        out.write("</html>\n");
      } catch (Throwable t) {
      out = _jspx_out;
      if (out != null && out.getBufferSize() != 0) out.clearBuffer();
      if (pageContext != null) pageContext.handlePageException(t);
      } finally {
      if (_jspxFactory != null)
          _jspxFactory.releasePageContext(pageContext);
      }
    }
}
```

Precompiling your JSP files means that they are now servlets. You would now have to either refer to them as servlets or put in a mapping to the JSP name in your deployment descriptor. Now that the JSP pages have been converted into servlets, the remaining task is to obfuscate the class files. *Obfuscating* is the process of making the decompiling of the class files difficult or impossible to perform. To understand why this is an issue, let's look at an example from the iNet project. Listing 10.24 is a simple servlet from the iNet application.

LISTING 10.24   Servlet from the iNet Application

```
package com.networksByteDesign.iNet;

import java.io.*;
import javax.servlet.*;
import javax.servlet.http.*;


/**
 * DOCUMENT ME!
 *
```

LISTING 10.24   Continued

```
 * @web:servlet name="MainMenuServlet" display-name="Main Menu
 *        Servlet" load-on-startup="1"
 * @web:servlet-mapping url-pattern="/MainMenu"
 */
public class MainMenuServlet extends HttpServlet
{
    public void doGet(HttpServletRequest request,
        HttpServletResponse response)
        throws IOException, ServletException
    {
        response.setContentType("text/html");

        PrintWriter out = response.getWriter();
        String title = "Main Menu";

        out.println("<html>");
        out.println("<head>");
        out.println("<title>" + title + "</title>");
        out.println("</head>");

        out.println("<body bgcolor=\"white\">");
        out.println("<body>");
        out.println("<h1>" + title + "</h1>");
        out.println("<hr>");
        out.println("</body>");
        out.println("</html>");
    }

    public void doPost(HttpServletRequest request,
        HttpServletResponse response)
        throws IOException, ServletException
    {
        doGet(request, response);
    }
}
```

When the servlet is compiled into bytecodes, many people believe this is difficult or impossible to reconstruct. However, many decompilers exist that can easily reconstruct the source code. For example, the bytecodes for the servlet in Listing 10.24 were run through a popular decompiler called Mocha. Listing 10.25 shows the output from the Mocha program when supplied with only the bytecodes for the servlet.

LISTING 10.25   Mocha Decompiled Version of the Servlet

```java
/* Decompiled by Mocha from MainMenuServlet.class */
/* Originally compiled from MainMenuServlet.java */

package com.networksByteDesign.iNet;

import javax.servlet.http.*;
import java.io.IOException;
import java.io.PrintWriter;
import javax.servlet.ServletException;

public synchronized class MainMenuServlet extends HttpServlet
{
    public void doGet(HttpServletRequest httpServletRequest,
                      HttpServletResponse httpServletResponse)
        throws IOException, ServletException
    {
        httpServletResponse.setContentType("text/html");
        PrintWriter printWriter = httpServletResponse.getWriter();
        String string = "Main Menu";
        printWriter.println("<html>");
        printWriter.println("<head>");
        printWriter.println(string + "</title>");
        printWriter.println("</head>");
        printWriter.println("<body bgcolor=\"white\">");
        printWriter.println("<body>");
        printWriter.println(string + "</h1>");
        printWriter.println("<hr>");
        printWriter.println("</body>");
        printWriter.println("</html>");
    }

    public void doPost(HttpServletRequest httpServletRequest,
                       HttpServletResponse httpServletResponse)
        throws IOException, ServletException
    {
        doGet(httpServletRequest, httpServletResponse);
    }

    public MainMenuServlet()
    {
    }
}
```

If this class file had contained sensitive or proprietary information, this technique could have been used to easily extract the information from the class files. For commercial applications, this is typically not a valid alternative. Using an obfuscator scrambles the information in the class file. The class file will still execute, but after the file has been obfuscated, it is extremely difficult to reconstruct the source.

The iNet team is using a bytecode obfuscator called yGuard. yGuard is a free tool that comes with an Ant task for hooking into the build process. yGuard provides a powerful tool in the buildfile for those applications that need this extra protection.

INSTALLING YGUARD

To install yGuard, follow these steps:

1. Download from

   `http://www.yworks.com/en/products_yguard_about.htm`

2. Uncompress the file and place the yguard.jar file in the CLASSPATH or in the Ant lib directory.

The obfuscate target in Listing 10.26 shows how simply the bytecode obfuscator can be introduced into the build process. yGuard provides numerous options in the Ant task to control the level of obfuscation as well as choosing specifically which files will be obfuscated and which ones will be left untouched. The various options should allow any usage of the class files to be set up with the highest level of protection possible while allowing access to the information that is required. Listing 10.26 shows a very restrictive obfuscation target.

LISTING 10.26   obfuscate Target for the iNet Team

```
<taskdef name="obfuscate"
         classname="com.yworks.yguard.ObfuscatorTask"
         classpathref="project.classpath"/>


<!-- obfuscate target -->
<target name="obfuscate">
    <obfuscate logfile="${dirs.build}/log.xml"
               replaceclassnamestrings="true">
        <inoutpair in="${ant.project.name}.jar"
                   out="${ant.project.name}_obf.jar"/>
        <property name="language-conformity" value="illegal"/>
        <property name="naming-scheme" value="mix"/>
    </obfuscate>
</target>
```

The `logfile` attribute on the `<obfuscate>` task sets the name of the log file for the obfuscation process. The `replaceclassnamestrings` attribute is set to `true` to tell yGuard to replace hard-coded strings that contain a class name.

At least one `<inoutpair>` element must be set to use the `<obfuscate>` task. The `in` attribute is the original JAR file, and the `out` attribute defines the name of the obfuscated JAR file.

`property` elements are used to give hints to the obfuscation engine. The property `language-conformity` when set to `illegal` will produce class files that will crash some tools that attempt to decompile the class. The property `naming-scheme` when set to `mix` is a compromise between `small`, which produces very short names and results in a small JAR file, and `best`, which produces long names that are difficult to break, but may double the size of the JAR file.

yGuard works by taking a normal JAR file and producing an obfuscated JAR. Listing 10.27 shows the output of the `obfuscate` target, which creates the obfuscated JAR file.

LISTING 10.27   Output of the obfuscate Target

```
% ant obfuscate
Buildfile: build.xml

obfuscate:
[obfuscate] YGuard Obfuscator - http://www.yworks.com/products/yguard
[obfuscate] Using NameMakerFactory: yGuardNameFactory
            [naming-scheme: mix; language-conformity: illegal]
Parsing jar iNet.jar
Obfuscating Jar iNet.jar to iNet_obf.jar

BUILD SUCCESSFUL
Total time: 4 seconds
```

To get an idea of what yGuard is doing, let's look at a normal JAR file. Listing 10.28 shows the output of looking inside a normal JAR file. Notice that readable filenames and directories exist.

LISTING 10.28   A Normal JAR File

```
% jar -tvf iNet.jar
      0 Sun Feb 02 15:49:52 CST 2003 META-INF/
    328 Sun Feb 02 15:49:52 CST 2003 META-INF/MANIFEST.MF

   ...
```

LISTING 10.28 Continued

```
1930 Sun Feb 02 15:19:36 CST 2003 RegisterStep1_jsp.class
1930 Sun Feb 02 15:19:36 CST 2003 RegisterStep2_jsp.class
1930 Sun Feb 02 15:19:36 CST 2003 RegisterStep3_jsp.class
1930 Sun Feb 02 15:19:36 CST 2003 RegisterStep4_jsp.class
```

On the other hand, the obfuscated JAR file shows very different results. Listing 10.29 shows the output of the obfuscated file, which now has extra directories and files, and does not seem to follow any rhyme or reason.

LISTING 10.29 An Obfuscated JAR File

```
% jar -tvf iNet_obf.jar
 6679 Sun Feb 02 15:50:16 CST 2003 META-INF/MANIFEST.MF
  921 Sun Feb 02 15:50:16 CST 2003 O/A/new/A/o000.class
  902 Sun Feb 02 15:50:16 CST 2003 O/A/new/A/super.class
 1240 Sun Feb 02 15:50:16 CST 2003 O/A/new/A/A/Object.class
 1239 Sun Feb 02 15:50:16 CST 2003 O/A/new/A/A/super.class
 1237 Sun Feb 02 15:50:16 CST 2003 O/A/new/A/A/new.class
 1239 Sun Feb 02 15:50:16 CST 2003 O/A/new/A/A.class
 2215 Sun Feb 02 15:50:16 CST 2003 O/A/new/o000/A.class
  383 Sun Feb 02 15:50:16 CST 2003 O/A/super/new.class
  381 Sun Feb 02 15:50:16 CST 2003 O/A/super/C.class
  381 Sun Feb 02 15:50:16 CST 2003 O/A/super/B.class
  385 Sun Feb 02 15:50:16 CST 2003 O/A/super/super.class
  636 Sun Feb 02 15:50:16 CST 2003 O/A/super/oO.class
  381 Sun Feb 02 15:50:16 CST 2003 O/A/super/A.class
  381 Sun Feb 02 15:50:16 CST 2003 O/A/super/D.class
 1911 Sun Feb 02 15:50:16 CST 2003 o000/super/super/C.class
 1911 Sun Feb 02 15:50:16 CST 2003 o000/super/super/B.class
 1910 Sun Feb 02 15:50:16 CST 2003 o000/super/super/A.class
 1915 Sun Feb 02 15:50:16 CST 2003 o000/super/super/super.class
```

In fact, the obfuscation process can make it difficult to even unjar the files. For example, the iNet JAR file could not be opened using the normal Java tools. Listing 10.30 shows the output from an attempt to unjar the obfuscated file. The settings in our `obfuscate` target cause many tools to break when trying to read the filenames, including unjar and most decompilers.

LISTING 10.30   Attempt to Unjar an Obfuscated JAR File

```
% jar -xvf iNet_obf.jar
extracted: META-INF/MANIFEST.MF
java.io.IOException: o00000000000000000/A/new/A : could not create directory
    at sun.tools.jar.Main.extractFile(Main.java:709)
    at sun.tools.jar.Main.extract(Main.java:678)
    at sun.tools.jar.Main.run(Main.java:190)
    at sun.tools.jar.Main.main(Main.java:904)
```

Story

The iNet team found the process developed by the eMarket team to be very useful. They did have their own unique requirements because of the fact that they are releasing commercial software, rather than deploying their software to an eCommerce Web site, as eMarket does. Still, it formed an excellent starting point for their build process. By making a few changes, they were able to increase the efficiency of their builds through the use of the Jikes compiler, the `smartCopy` target, and the `<parallel>` task. They also integrated their other tools for JSP compilation and code obfuscation to protect the company's source code when shipping the product.

Summary

In this chapter, we looked at how our build process can be refactored to meet the needs of multiple projects. We went through a series of steps to allow use of the common build targets by project teams.

After the project build process was completed, we began adding new tools into the project buildfile. We began by changing one of the projects to use Jikes for compiling of Java code. We then created a custom task for calling NoUnit, a program for determining untested methods within a suite of unit tests.

We addressed the performance issues of a time-consuming code generation target. We created the `smartCopy` target for helping the code generator focus on only the files that have changed. We also looked at the `parallel` task for performing multiple build tasks at the same time. We also added a target to tag a release with a system-generated build number.

Finally, we dealt with a couple of security issues. We started by using a JSP compiler to convert our JSP pages to servlets. We then added the yGuard code to obfuscate our bytecodes and make the process more difficult to decompile.

With minor changes, our buildfile is now ready for use by a different project, and although the second team's needs are very different from those of the original team, the build process is already proving to be a productive tool.

11

Creating an Enterprise-wide Solution

To achieve the extra layers in the build process, the architecture group decides to expand on the current structure and make minimal changes to the process. To add the department layer, a few small modifications need to be made to the project and common buildfiles. The project buildfiles need to be modified to point to the department buildfile. The common buildfile will need to add a dependency on the department buildfiles.

Story

The eMarket and iNet teams have both been successful at delivering software of high quality and in a timely fashion. The upper management of NetworksByteDesign Inc. have recently done an evaluation of all of their projects, and looked at the quality and performance of each group. Based on their findings, they have decided to make a commitment to using the XP methodology company-wide. Although they won't require every project to immediately adopt XP, they will begin migrating new projects over to the XP methodology. They have also developed a transition plan for ongoing projects that are not on XP to begin adopting this methodology.

One of the first steps is to restructure the build, testing, and deployment processes to support some company standards, but still allow departments and projects to use different tools that may be more suitable for their particular needs. Adopting XP and an Ant process doesn't mean that every group has to have identical tools. The architecture group at NetworksByteDesign is assigned to take the build processes that INet and eMarket have, and refactor them to be used across the enterprise.

Listing 11.1 shows the eMarket project buildfile after being modified to include the sales.xml file. Sales.xml is the department buildfile for the eMarket project.

LISTING 11.1   eMarket Project Buildfile with Department Hook

```xml
<?xml version="1.0" ?>

<!DOCTYPE project [<!ENTITY sales SYSTEM "file:sales.xml">
                   <!ENTITY common SYSTEM "file:common.xml">]>

<project name="eMarket" default="compile" basedir=".">

    <property name="project.email"
              value="eMarketDev@networksByteDesign.com" />

    <!-- appCompile target -->
    <target name="appCompile"
            depends="xdoclet"
            description="Compile all of the source code.">
    </target>

    &common;
    &sales;

</project>
```

The department buildfile currently only contains an unused hook in the `compile` target. As this file is included in the project buildfile, it does not have the project tags that a buildfile would normally have. The `deptCompile` target is dependent on the `appCompile` target, which allows compile modifications to take place at multiple layers. Listing 11.2 shows the department buildfile for the Sales department.

LISTING 11.2   Sales Department Buildfile

```xml
    <!-- deptCompile target -->
    <target name="deptCompile"
            depends="appCompile"
            description="Compile all of the source code.">
    </target>
```

The only change necessary in the common buildfile is to make the `compile` target dependent on the `deptCompile` target rather than directly on the `appCompile` target. Listing 11.3 shows the `compile` target from the common buildfile with the necessary changes.

LISTING 11.3   Compile Target from the Common Buildfile with the Department Modifications

```
<!-- compile target -->
<target name="compile"
        depends="deptCompile"
        description="Compile all of the source code.">

    <javac srcdir="${dirs.build}">
        <classpath refid="project.classpath"/>
    </javac>
</target>
```

Encrypting the Output of a Build

Story

Some of the groups use teams or individual developers that are not always on site. Because the corporation does not have a VPN, but often needs to send documents over the Internet, they have a requirement that documents are encrypted with public-key encryption.

One of the problems with the build process is that they can't use the MailLogger to send information about the build because it's not encrypted. The risk is that if someone were eavesdropping, they might be able to glean a user id or password, or just some insight into the code from the output.

The architecture team creates a custom logger to solve this problem. Called the EncryptedMailLogger, this logger will perform public-key encryption of the output of a build prior to inserting it into an email. By incorporating this logger, teams can meet the corporate security requirement of encrypting information that is to be sent over the Internet.

The MailLogger provides an effective mechanism for communicating the results of a build to a specific user or list of users. By simply setting a few properties in the buildfile and calling Ant with the -logger option, the MailLogger will send the results of the build to the appropriate individuals. The eMarket team had previously used the MailLogger to accomplish these tasks.

To accomplish the encryption requirement, the team first needed to choose an appropriate encryption algorithm. They decided on GnuPG, which is a free replacement for PGP. The fact that GnuPG is free, available on multiple platforms, and widely used contributed to their decision.

INSTALLING GNUPG

GnuPG can be obtained from the GnuPG Web site at

http://www.gnupg.org/

1. Download and uncompress the GnuPG package.

2. Place gpg in your system PATH.

3. Run

   gpg --gen-key

   This will create your encryption keys.

   If you are running Cygwin on Windows, this command must be run from the DOS shell.

   The first question is to select what kind of key you want. Select the DSA and ElGamal(default) option. The others are for signing only.

4. The next question is what size key do you want? Selecting a key size is a tradeoff between encryption speed and degree of security. The shorter the key, the quicker and the less secure it is. We used the default value of 1024 as a key size. If security is the most important consideration, select GPG's maximum size, which is currently 2048.

5. The next question is how long should the key remain valid? The expiration determines how long the key will remain valid. This is entirely a user decision. After entering the value, you will have to type y to confirm the expiration date.

6. You will then be asked to enter your real name, comment, and e-mail address. Ignore the comment that says to enter it in a single line. Enter only your name. Press Enter, and then enter the e-mail address. Press Enter again and enter the comment. GPG will ask you to confirm your entries after all three values have been entered.

7. Enter a passphrase. The passphrase will be needed to decrypt messages, so remember this value.

8. When the key generation completes, it creates a directory called /gnupg that contains the key values.

The EncryptedMailLogger extends the MailLogger and simply intercepts the log before it is e-mailed. It then calls the gpg program to encrypt the log before sending the now-encrypted message to the user selected in the buildfile. Listing 11.4 shows the EncryptedMailLogger class.

LISTING 11.4   EncryptedMailLogger Class

```java
package com.networksByteDesign.util;

import java.io.BufferedInputStream;
import java.io.BufferedWriter;
import java.io.IOException;
import java.io.OutputStreamWriter;
import org.apache.tools.ant.BuildEvent;
```

LISTING 11.4   Continued

```java
import org.apache.tools.ant.BuildException;
import org.apache.tools.ant.listener.MailLogger;
import org.apache.tools.ant.util.StringUtils;

public class EncryptedMailLogger extends MailLogger
{
    public void buildFinished(BuildEvent event)
    {
        String encryptedBuffer = encrypt(buffer_.toString());
        super.log(encryptedBuffer);
        super.buildFinished(event);
    }

    /**
     *  Receives and buffers log messages.
     *
     * @param message the message being logged
     */
    protected void log(String message)
    {
        buffer_.append(message).append(StringUtils.LINE_SEP);
    }

    private String encrypt(String message)
    {
        StringBuffer result  = new StringBuffer(100);
        int          buflen  = 128;
        int          numRead = 0;
        byte[]       buf     = new byte[buflen];
        String       cmd     = "gpg -e -a -r cronus";
        Runtime      rt      = Runtime.getRuntime();
        try
        {
            Process proc = rt.exec(cmd);
            StringBuffer sBuffer = new StringBuffer();

            BufferedWriter out =
                new BufferedWriter
                (new OutputStreamWriter(proc.getOutputStream()));
```

LISTING 11.4   Continued

```
            out.write(message, 0, message.length());
            out.close();

            BufferedInputStream bstrm =
                new BufferedInputStream(proc.getInputStream());
            while ((numRead = bstrm.read(buf, 0, buflen)) != -1)
            {
                String line = new String(buf, 0, numRead);
                result.append(line);
            }
        }
        catch (IOException e)
        {
            System.err.println(e.getMessage());
        }

        return result.toString();
    }

    /** Buffer in which the message is constructed prior to sending */
    private StringBuffer buffer_ = new StringBuffer();
}
```

In the preceding example, you need to either create a GPG user called "cronus," or substitute the name of a valid user for "cronus." To use the EncryptedMailLogger, use the -logger option for Ant, but supply the EncryptedMailLogger class. The EncryptedMailLogger class must be on the CLASSPATH to be found by Ant. Listing 11.5 shows the running of a compile target using the EncryptedMailLogger.

LISTING 11.5   Calling a compile Target Using the EncryptedMailLogger

```
% ant compile -logger com.networksByteDesign.util.EncryptedMailLogger
Buildfile: build.xml

appCompile:
    [mkdir] Created dir: build
     [copy] Copying 628 files to build

deptCompile:
```

LISTING 11.5   Continued

```
compile:
    [javac] Compiling 451 source files

BUILD SUCCESSFUL
Total time: 9 seconds
```

Rather than the normal mail logger where the build results are sent as the body of the e-mail, the `EncryptedMailLogger` sends the body as an encrypted message. Listing 11.6 shows the body of the e-mail sent by the `compile` target run in Listing 11.5.

LISTING 11.6   E-mail Sent by the `EncryptedMailLogger`

```
-----BEGIN PGP MESSAGE-----
Version: GnuPG v1.2.1 (Darwin)

hQEOAxwCjF0wl6ePEAP/S77HWzDMW8jRfI5MFAVDR/7iqKojvDXP96EJwrwJ4Bn5
+/+C6eiY8rOeE/B4Mj0WdgU0dZstvxYCKjGk5Jq1Fs6ehsRChcrvmEEvEwMZAv+3
du+OJotXDQfdQKIonzZjYgKb8JLtkETyE3O558pP16bGDERoY0K4kDXJDP4hYk0D
/RhsFSJvofqRnQhT2o3922jNxU+f6cJWd6nfco4B6jBhKhctCkmqujmlUyX0MZ3Q
QsAigg5FtTXRZuFOlF2wX285/mfWqV0sAR+queLYRaY/wxn+EzuM75lZZ1AMQpU5
lyrUqYw/waLcY7g6nu0itlTk/B6MGdycFR77+qcs8+Y90sATAQKrzdUmamo6AXcr
i6w9O8hgNUft8XR35b7oukV1zT4wWKE2L3iYR3Tw/tprBPFhqGZeKJG54heJDSp6
oQvnrsBbz+j2oGO/L/3vZHAe6MDwxfPiL3BJmY855CQpoG2pBKUHRHnB6IpO1Lw1
KCkBYknmxRFdNWJLTmMLUmCHHuMTAeZBm9OOjeNhjWVR3ewLyA+JCt0Pg7dqdmTz
QLElB2b+J/LVoiyTeVWSZdGPG/lIDg3vTRyuCBaW+faydQ0Vah/xNzQ1boVgV6JW
gqCUgliLoQ==
=rQLv
-----END PGP MESSAGE-----
```

Saving the mail message and passing it to the gpg command enables us to view the decrypted message. The `-r` parameter allows us to set the user for whom the e-mail was encrypted. The `-d` parameter tells gpg to decrypt the file. Listing 11.7 shows the output of decrypting the e-mail message.

LISTING 11.7   Decrypting the E-mail Message

```
% gpg -r cronus -d email.txt

You need a passphrase to unlock the secret key for
user: "cronus (cronus) <cronus@networksByteDesign.com>"
1024-bit ELG-E key, ID 3097A78F, created 2003-01-25 (main key ID 299612EA)
```

LISTING 11.7   Continued

```
Enter passphrase: **********
    gpg: encrypted with 1024-bit ELG-E key, ID 3097A78F, created 2003-01-25
    "cronus (cronus) <cronus@networksByteDesign.com>"

appCompile:
    [mkdir] Created dir: build
     [copy] Copying 628 files to build

deptCompile:

compile:
    [javac] Compiling 451 source files
```

Incorporating JUnit into the Build Process

Story

Some groups in the company use the Apache testing tool called Cactus. This tool provides a servlet engine, and facilitates testing of servlets, even before they are entirely complete. Another job of the architecture team is to incorporate the ability to run Cactus into the build process. Because Cactus uses JUnit, it makes sense to include this in the suite of testing tools available to the organization.

Cactus is a unit testing tool from Apache that can be used to test server-side code. This includes servlets, EJBs, JSPs, and tag libraries. Cactus has a nice integration with Ant, and permits the automation of server-side code testing as part of the build and testing process. One of the problems with unit testing with straight JUnit is that it doesn't directly support testing of code like this. Some things can be done to mitigate the problem. For example, in a servlet, you can put all business logic in business objects that are used within the servlet. The servlet would only extract information from the incoming `HttpRequest` object and write HTML output to the `HttpResponse` object. By separating the business logic from the display logic, the business objects can be more easily tested. Using a tool like Cactus will permit testing of the final hookup of the business object to the servlet, EJB, or tag library. For example, fake servlet request objects can be configured in the test, and then passed to the servlet as if they received it from an app server.

INSTALLING CACTUS

Cactus can be obtained from the Apache Web site at

`http://jakarta.apache.org/cactus/getting_started.html`

The Web site has detailed instructions for installing and getting started.

Listing 11.8 shows the `runCactusTests` target. This target invokes the `<runservertests>` task, which has been defined in a `<taskdef>` statement to use the class `org.apache.cactus.ant.RunServerTestsTask`. The attribute `testURL` is the URL that the Cactus unit tests are to use to test the request and response. The attributes `startTarget` and `stopTarget` provide the names of Ant targets in the buildfile that the task is to use, in this case, to start and stop the Tomcat server. Finally, the `testTarget` attribute is the name of an Ant target in the buildfile that performs the actual test, which is the `cactusTest` target. The Cactus tests are actually JUnit tests, and the target can therefore use the `<junit>` task to set parameters about the test.

When the `runCactusTests` target is executed, the `<runservertests>` task will use the `startTarget` attribute to start the Tomcat server. The `<runservertests>` task then waits until Tomcat is started before proceeding with the actual unit test. After the unit test is completed, the `<runservertests>` task calls `stopTarget` , and waits until the server has stopped before the rest of the build process proceeds.

LISTING 11.8   Department Buildfile with Cactus Targets

```
<!-- deptCompile target -->
<target name="deptCompile"
        depends="appCompile"
        description="Compile all of the source code.">
</target>


<taskdef name="runservertests"
        classname="org.apache.cactus.ant.RunServerTestsTask"
        classpathref="project.classpath"/>


<!-- runCactusTests target -->
<target name="runCactusTests" description="Run Cactus tests">
    <property name="tomcat.home" value="/usr/software/tomcat" />

    <runservertests
     testURL=
   "http://localhost:8080/test/ServletRedirector?Cactus_Service=RUN_TEST"
     startTarget="startTomcat"
     stopTarget="stopTomcat"
```

LISTING 11.8   Continued

```
        testTarget="cactusTests"/>
</target>


<!-- startTomcat target -->
<target name="startTomcat">
    <java classname="org.apache.catalina.startup.Bootstrap" fork="yes">
        <jvmarg value="-Dcatalina.home=${tomcat.home}"/>
        <jvmarg value="-Dcatalina.base=${tomcat.home}"/>
        <arg value="start"/>
        <classpath>
            <fileset dir="${tomcat.home}">
                <include name="bin/bootstrap.jar"/>
            </fileset>
        </classpath>
    </java>
</target>


<!-- stopTomcat target -->
<target name="stopTomcat">
    <java classname="org.apache.catalina.startup.Bootstrap" fork="yes">
        <jvmarg value="-Dcatalina.home=${tomcat.home}"/>
        <jvmarg value="-Dcatalina.base=${tomcat.home}"/>
        <arg value="stop"/>
        <classpath>
            <fileset dir="${tomcat.home}">
                <include name="bin/bootstrap.jar"/>
            </fileset>
        </classpath>
    </java>
</target>


<!-- cactusTests target -->
<target name="cactusTests">
    <junit printsummary="yes"
            haltonfailure="yes"
            haltonerror="yes"
            fork="yes">
```

LISTING 11.8 Continued

```
        <classpath>
            <pathelement
                location="${tomcat.home}/webapps/test/WEB-INF/classes"/>
            <pathelement location="${tomcat.home}/webapps/test/conf"/>
            <fileset dir="${tomcat.home}/common/lib">
                <include name="**/*.jar"/>
            </fileset>
        </classpath>

        <formatter type="plain" usefile="false"/>
        <test name="TestSampleServlet"/>
    </junit>
</target>
```

Listing 11.9 shows the output that results from running the Cactus tests. Cactus first started the Tomcat server, then ran the tests, and finally shut down Tomcat. Notice that the output reports the number of failures and also the time that each unit test took to run. Because it's based on JUnit, the output of the test is in the same format.

LISTING 11.9 Output from the runCactusTests Target

```
% ant runCactusTests
Buildfile: build.xml

runCactusTests:

startTomcat:
    [java] Starting service Tomcat-Standalone
    [java] Apache Tomcat/4.1.18

cactusTests:
    [junit] Running TestSampleServlet
    [junit] Tests run: 1, Failures: 0, Errors: 0, Time elapsed: 0.684 sec
    [junit] Testsuite: TestSampleServlet
    [junit] Tests run: 1, Failures: 0, Errors: 0, Time elapsed: 0.684 sec

    [junit] Testcase: testSaveToSessionOK took 0.68 sec
```

LISTING 11.9   Continued

```
stopTomcat:
    [java] Stopping service Tomcat-Standalone
[runservertests] Server stopped !

BUILD SUCCESSFUL
Total time: 23 seconds
```

Adding Targets to Control a WebLogic Server

Story

A few of the teams in the corporation use BEA WebLogic. Ant has a few optional tasks for working with the WebLogic server, listed under EJBC tasks, including tasks for starting and stopping the WebLogic server. At the request of several of these groups, the architecture team adds targets to the basic buildfiles for controlling a WebLogic server.

WebLogic is a popular and powerful application server capable of hosting the various aspects of a J2EE application. One of the many advantages of Ant is the ability to provide a seamless build process that works equally well with various open source tools as with large commercial applications. Being able to provide the necessary tools through the Ant buildfile rather than relying directly on proprietary tools allows a team to focus on the important tasks as well as provide flexibility in moving from one tool to another.

Listing 11.10 shows targets to start and stop the WebLogic server. The wlrun and wlstop tasks are provided as an optional task for Ant and can be found in the Ant documentation under EJBTasks. Although the WebLogic tasks are shown here, other application server tasks are documented on the Ant Web site as well.

LISTING 11.10   Targets to Start and Stop the WebLogic Server

```
<property name="dirs.weblogic" value="c:/bea/weblogic700" />

<!-- startWeblogic -->
<target name="startWeblogic">
  <wlrun taskname="networksByteDesign"
         classpath="${dirs.weblogic}/server/lib/weblogic.jar"
         name="networksByteDesignServer"
         domain="networksByteDesign"
         home="${dirs.weblogic}/samples/server/"
         policy="${dirs.weblogic}/server/lib/weblogic.policy"
```

LISTING 11.10   Continued

```
            username="weblogic"
            password="weblogic"
            beahome="${dirs.weblogic}/samples/server/"/>
    </target>

    <!-- stopWeblogic -->
    <target name="stopWeblogic">
        <wlstop classpath="${dirs.weblogic}/server/lib/weblogic.jar"
                url="t3://localhost:7001"
                user="weblogic"
                password="weblogic"
                beahome="${dirs.weblogic}/samples/server/"/>
    </target>
```

Listing 11.11 shows portions of the output from the startWeblogic task. Instead of trying to remember the details of starting the WebLogic server, you can hide the complexities behind an Ant target that is well documented.

LISTING 11.11   Output from the startWeblogic Task

```
% ant startWeblogic
Buildfile: build.xml

restartWeblogic:

startWeblogic:
 [networksByteDesign] Starting WebLogic Server...
 [networksByteDesign] <Feb 2, 2003 11:20:37 AM CST> <Info> <Management>
                      <141089><Bootstrapping Server based on WebLogic
                      Server 6.X configuration directory structure.>
 [networksByteDesign] <Feb 2, 2003 11:20:40 AM CST> <Notice> <Management>
                      <140005> <Loading configuration
                      C:\bea\weblogic700\samples\server\.\config\
                      networksByteDesign\config.xml>
 [networksByteDesign] <Feb 2, 2003 11:20:45 AM CST> <Warning> <Management>
                      <141087> <Unrecognized property: system.home>

 ...

 [networksByteDesign] <Feb 2, 2003 11:21:43 AM CST> <Notice>
                      <WebLogicServer> <000354> <Thread
                      "ListenThread.Default" listening on port 7001>
```

LISTING 11.11   Continued

```
[networksByteDesign] <Feb 2, 2003 11:21:43 AM CST> <Notice> <Management>
                     <141030> <Starting discovery of Managed Server...
                     This feature is on by default, you may turn this off
                     by passing -Dweblogic.management.discover=false>
[networksByteDesign] <Feb 2, 2003 11:21:43 AM CST> <Notice>
                     <WebLogicServer> <000331> <Started WebLogic Admin
                     Server "networksByteDesignServer" for domain
                     "networksByteDesign" running in Development Mode>
[networksByteDesign] <Feb 2, 2003 11:21:44 AM CST> <Notice>
                     <WebLogicServer> <000365> <Server state changed to
                     RUNNING>
[networksByteDesign] <Feb 2, 2003 11:21:44 AM CST> <Notice>
                     <WebLogicServer> <000360> <Server started in RUNNING
                     mode>
```

Internationalization

Story

Some of the teams, including the iNet team, build software that is sold in foreign countries. Because of this, they need to support multiple languages. This is another capability that the Architecture Team adds to the enterprise-wide build process, so that it will be standardized for teams that need to support this.

Internationalization (I18N) is an area that Java was designed to handle gracefully from its beginnings. Well-designed applications do not hard-code labels and error messages and do not make assumptions about items such as sort order and date and currency formats. Java applications often deal with taking the locale of the user, including language and possible country information, and determining at runtime the values the application needs to be used in another language. Although this works fine for runtime usage, static content such as HTML must be prepared ahead of time.

Language codes are two-letter lowercase codes such as "en" for English and "fr" for French. Before creating our internationalization target, it would be nice if Ant could ensure that the format of our language code is proper. To accomplish this, we will create a custom task to provide regular expression checks of user input. Listing 11.12 shows the source code for this custom task.

LISTING 11.12   RegexpInput Custom Task

```
package com.networksByteDesign.util;

import org.apache.tools.ant.BuildException;
import org.apache.tools.ant.util.regexp.RegexpMatcher;
import org.apache.tools.ant.util.regexp.RegexpMatcherFactory;

public class RegexpInput extends RequiredInput
{
    /**
     * Sets the pattern to match the user's input during the build run.
     * @param pattern The pattern to match.
     */
    public void setPattern(String pattern)
    {
        pattern_     = pattern;
        havePattern_ = true;
    }


    /**
     * Actual test method executed by ant.
     * @exception BuildException
     */
    public void execute () throws BuildException
    {
        if (!havePattern_)
        {
            throw new
                BuildException
                ("Required attribute pattern not set in regexpInput",
                 location);
        }

        super.execute();

        RegexpMatcherFactory factory = new RegexpMatcherFactory();
        RegexpMatcher        regexp  = factory.newRegexpMatcher();

        regexp.setPattern(pattern_);

        if(! regexp.matches(getProject().getProperty(getProperty())))
        {
```

LISTING 11.12   Continued

```
            throw new BuildException(getErrormessage(), location);
        }
    }

    private String  pattern_     = "";
    private boolean havePattern_  = false;
}
```

The `RegexpInput` task is a simple extension of the `RequiredInput` task we created earlier. The key item to note is that rather than creating a regular expression parser, the task obtains a regular expression matcher from the factory maintained by Ant. This allows the custom task to take advantage of whatever regular expression tool the user of the build process has configure Ant to use.

To actually make the language changes in our HTML, we rely on the <translate> task. The <translate> task uses the standard Java resource bundle approach. That is, if the bundle is called `labels.properties` and the locale requested is French-Canadian, the application will look first for a `labels_fr_CA.properties` file. If the requested key is not in the file, the `labels_fr.properties` file will be checked. If the key is not there, it will fall back to the `labels.properties` file.

The <translate> task allows tokens to be placed in the files, which it will replace with the values for the locale specified. The `todir` attribute is the destination directory for the output files. The `starttoken` and `endtoken` attributes define the beginning and end delimiters of a key. The `bundle` attribute is the name of the resource bundle where the key/value pairs are stored. The `bundlelanguage` attribute is the locale-specific language for the resource bundle. The `forceoverwrite` attribute forces the output files to be created even if the output files are newer than the source files. To see this in action, see the completed target in Listing 11.13.

LISTING 11.13   i18n Target

```
<taskdef name="regexpInput"
        classname="com.networksByteDesign.util.RegexpInput"
        classpathref="project.classpath"/>

<!-- i18n target -->
<target name="i18n">
    <mkdir dir="${dirs.build}"/>

    <copy todir="${dirs.build}">
        <fileset dir="${dirs.source}" includes="**/labels*.properties"/>
    </copy>
```

LISTING 11.13   Continued

```
            <regexpInput message="Please enter language:"
                     addproperty="language"
                     errorMessage="You didn't enter a proper language code."
                     pattern="[a-z][a-z]"/>


        <mkdir dir="${dirs.build}/html/${language}"/>


        <translate toDir="${dirs.build}/html/${language}"
                   starttoken="#"
                   endtoken="#"
                   bundle="${dirs.build}/labels"
                   bundlelanguage="${language}"
                   forceoverwrite="yes">
            <fileset dir="${dirs.source}">
                <include name="**/*.html"/>
            </fileset>
        </translate>
    </target>
```

The RegexpInput task ensures that the language code is in the proper format. The target then creates a language-specific directory for the translated HTML. It then processes the HTML files with the language specified by the user.

The properties file is set up as key/value pairs. The labels.properties file is as follows:

```
login=Login
username=User Name
password=Password
```

A French version of the labels resource bundle is as follows. Note that the keys remain the same, and only the values are translated:

```
login=Ouverture
username=Nom D'Utilisateur
password=Mot de passe
```

To see how the process works, let's run our i18n target on a sample HTML file, such as the login.html page shown in Listing 11.14.

LISTING 11.14   The `login.html` Page with Appropriate Tokens

```html
<!DOCTYPE HTML PUBLIC "-//W3C//DTD HTML 4.0 Transitional//EN">
<HTML>
<HEAD>
  <TITLE>#login#</TITLE>
</HEAD>
<TABLE height="100%" cellSpacing="0" cellPadding="0" width="100%">
  <FORM action="j_security_check" method="post">
  <TR>
    <TD valign="center" align="middle">
      <TABLE cellSpacing="1" cellPadding="2" width="310" bgColor="#a9a9a9">
        <TR>
          <TD STYLE="FONT-SIZE: 12pt; COLOR: #ffffff; TEXT-ALIGN: center">
               <B>#login#</B> 
          </TD>
        </TR>
        <TR>
          <TD bgColor="#e0e0e0">
          <TABLE class="default" cellSpacing="1" cellPadding="1">
              <TR>
                <TD align="right">
                  <B>#username# :</B> </TD>
                <TD> <INPUT size="16" name="j_username"></TD>
              </TR>
              <TR>
                <TD align="right">
                  <B>#password# :</B> </TD>
                <TD><INPUT size="16" name="j_password" type="password"></TD>
              </TR>
              <TR>
                <TD align="middle" colSpan="2">
                     
                  <INPUT type="submit" value="#login#"
                          name="j_security_check"/>
                </TD>
              </TR>
            </table>
          </TD>
        </TR>
      </TABLE>
    </TD>
  </TR>
```

LISTING 11.14   Continued

```
  </FORM>
</TABLE>
</body>
</html>
```

We begin by testing our `RegexpInput` task. Instead of entering a two-letter lowercase code, we enter a two-letter uppercase code. Listing 11.15 shows how the `RegexpInput` task catches the discrepancy and reacts accordingly.

LISTING 11.15   Invalid Use of the `RegexpInput` task

```
% ant i18n
Buildfile: build.xml

i18n:
[regexpInput] Please enter language:
FR

BUILD FAILED
file:build.xml:41: You didn't enter a proper language code.
Total time: 7 seconds
```

Listing 11.16 shows how the `RegexpInput` task reacts when we pass the expected information. This time the input is accepted and the i18n target completes its processing.

LISTING 11.16   Valid Use of the `RegexpInput` Task

```
% ant i18n
Buildfile: build.xml

i18n:
[regexpInput] Please enter language:
fr
    [mkdir] Created dir: build/html/fr

BUILD SUCCESSFUL
Total time: 4 seconds
```

The end result can be seen in Figures 11.1 and 11.2. From the same HTML file, the two localized versions are produced. Figure 11.1 shows the English version, and Figure 11.2 shows the French version of the same page.

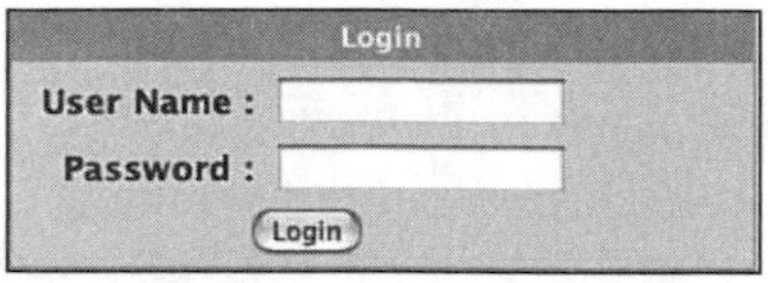

FIGURE 11.1   English version of the login page.

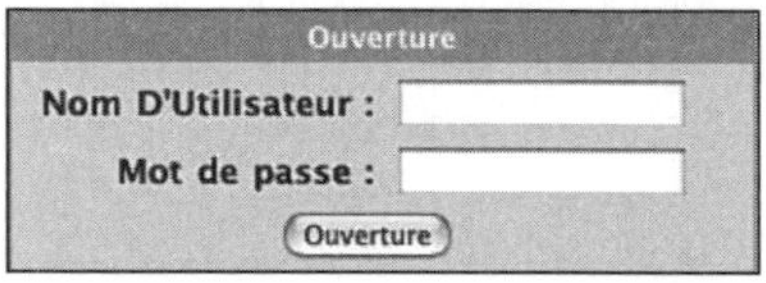

FIGURE 11.2   French version of the login page.

Generating UML Diagrams

Story

Several groups in the company like to work with UML. They would like to be able to use a tool that generates UML diagrams of existing code for documentation purposes. One group uses a tool from SourceForge called ESS-Model that automatically generates UML for Java code, and does it very fast. It only runs on Windows platforms. The architecture team creates a custom task for integrating this tool into the enterprise build process, and makes it available for teams that would like to use it.

UML class diagrams are a useful way to get an overview of the class structure of a package. Many XP developers don't care to use UML, but this is often because of attempting to design the system and all of the classes up front in UML prior to actual coding. The other problem is that UML diagrams are frequently out of date. But a UML diagram that is current, and is an accurate reflection of the system as it stands, can be very useful, even in an XP process. This can be accomplished when the UML diagrams are automatically generated as part of the build process. UML generation is a good candidate for automation for this reason.

Several possible tools were examined for UML generation. Many tools available didn't have a Java API. Our goal is to provide a mechanism for generating documentation as part of a build process that doesn't require the user to manually intervene on the UML generation step. We also gave preference to free and open source tools, because they are readily available to anyone reading this book. Initially, the IBM XMIToolkit was examined. This is a free toolkit that was available at the IBM AlphaWorks site, consisting of a Java API that generates a model file for use in Rational Rose. It appears that this tool has been deprecated. The tool selected for UML generation is called ESS-Model, and is available at either `sourceforge.net`, or at the `essmodel.com` Web site. See the sidebar on installing ESS-Model. The ESS-Model tool is written in Delphi 6, and therefore only runs on Windows platforms. It does, however, generate high-quality UML documentation in HTML, and does it very rapidly.

INSTALLING ESS-MODEL

1. Download ESS-Model from either

   `http://www.essmodel.com/download.html`

   or

   `http://sourceforge.net/projects/essmodel`

2. Unzip the downloaded files.

3. Put the `EssModel.exe` in your system PATH.

For our purpose, it would be nice if there were a way to generate the HTML documentation without having the GUI start up. When we run the Ant buildfile that will be created in this section, the GUI does start up for the UML generation step, but then closes when it's complete. This really isn't a problem; it just would be nice to be able to turn that off.

The only limitation with this tool is that it could give more information when encountering an error condition. It seems to require a fair amount of memory to run properly on larger packages. It does generate such nice documentation that it was worth introducing here. The primary purpose here is to suggest ways to use Ant in your documentation process, and to demonstrate how to integrate tools like this into your build process. If you find a tool you like better, integrating it should be a fairly simple matter. Also in this section, we'll create a custom Ant task that uses `<filesets>` to permit the easy inclusion and exclusion of files within a build process.

First, let's look at an example of the documentation generated by this tool. As an example for this book, we ran the ESS-Model tool against some of the eMarket source code. Figure 11.3 shows an example of output from one of the packages.

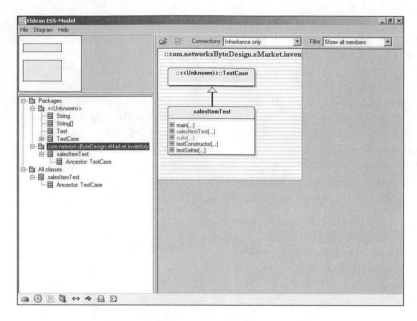

FIGURE 11.3   ESS-Model tool rendering eMarket source code.

The ess_model documentation suggests that when running this tool from a command prompt (again, it only runs on Windows-based platforms), a batch file should be created. The batch file will list all of the Java files down a source directory tree, and put this list into a temporary file. Next, ess_model is invoked against this temporary file. The ess_model tool will generate UML diagrams and bring up the GUI tool so that they can be viewed, and the user can scroll around and jump to views of different packages. By giving the ess_model tool a command-line option, it will perform an additional step of converting this information to HTML documents for release with the software package. The following code shows the batch file that we copied from the ess_model documentation, with a modification, for running the tool from the command line.

```
rem Open essmodel with all java-files from current path and downwards.
dir *.java /S /B > files.tmp
essmodel.exe -dC:\uml @files.tmp
```

Running this command will result in the tool starting up, generating HTML documentation to the target directory, and exiting, and finally opening the documents in the default Web browser.

As a first pass at integrating this into a buildfile, we will take an extremely simple approach that does not require us to extend Ant, and invoke this batch file with the <exec> command, as shown here:

```
<?xml version="1.0" ?>

<project name="documentation" default="  umldoc_1" basedir=".">

    <target name="umldoc_1">

        <exec dir="src" executable="ess.bat"/>

    </target>

</project>
```

The target umldoc_1 uses the Ant <exec> task to define the target directory in which to invoke the ess.bat file, and then runs the batch file. This results in the generation of UML documentation in the form of HTML files.

It's likely that there may be certain packages or even specific files that we want to include or exclude in the generation of our javadoc. For example, we should have unit tests for each of the packages. Although those files are part of the project, they are for internal use by the development team. We really don't want to include those files in our UML diagrams when we release our documentation to another team. Let's enhance our buildfile to permit us to include or exclude files and packages as needed. Also, to be consistent with the behavior of other Ant tasks, let's design a task that uses filesets to do this. To accomplish this, we'll write a class that extends Ant.

Ant has several classes that are intended to serve as base classes for custom tasks. For our purpose here, we'll extend the MatchingTask class because we want to create a task that uses <filesets>.

For this class, we need to create a method called addFileset(FileSet set). This method is invoked when the <fileset> construct is parsed, and the fileset is passed into the private member variable fileset. The fileset will be used in the execute method. There is also a method to receive the destdir attribute as a String. This is the directory we will run the ess_model command in. When attributes are parsed in the XML file, Ant calls these methods, and passes these values into the class. Remember that attributes require a public set method for each attribute so that Ant can pass in the value. The destdir attribute is the only attribute that this task accepts, so there is only a single set method. The setter method simply stores the value for use in the execute method. Listing 11.17 shows the Java code for this custom task.

LISTING 11.17   Custom Task for Calling the ESS-Model Tool

```java
package com.networksByteDesign.util;

import org.apache.tools.ant.*;
import org.apache.tools.ant.taskdefs.*;
import org.apache.tools.ant.types.*;
import java.io.File;
import java.io.FileReader;
import java.io.FileWriter;
import java.io.FileNotFoundException;
import java.io.BufferedReader;
import java.io.IOException;
import java.util.Vector;
import java.util.Enumeration;

public class EssTask extends MatchingTask
{
    public void execute()
    {
        // Get a handle on the Directory Scanner
        log("Enter execute()", Project.MSG_INFO);
        DirectoryScanner ds = fileset_.getDirectoryScanner(project);
        String fileSeparator = System.getProperty("file.separator");
        String absPath = (fileset_.getDir(project)).toString() + fileSeparator;
        log("fileset_.getDir = " + fileset_.getDir(project), Project.MSG_DEBUG);

        // Get the list of files and write them to the temp file
        String listFileName = absPath + tempfile_;

        FileWriter fw = null;
        try
        {
            fw = new FileWriter(new File(listFileName));
            String[] includedFiles = ds.getIncludedFiles();
            for (int j=0; j<includedFiles.length; j++)
            {
             fw.write(absPath + includedFiles[j] + "\n");
             log("add file: " + absPath + includedFiles[j], Project.MSG_DEBUG);
            }
        }
        catch (Exception e)
        {
```

LISTING 11.17   Continued

```java
            log(e.getMessage(), Project.MSG_ERR);
        }
        finally
        {
            try
            {
                fw.close();
            }
            catch (IOException e) {}
        }

        // Get a handle on the JVM Runtime Object
        Runtime rt = Runtime.getRuntime();

        // Set up arguments
        log("listFileName = " + listFileName, Project.MSG_DEBUG);
        String newListFile = listFileName.replace('/', '\\');
        String cmd = "essmodel.exe @" + newListFile + " -d" + destdir_;

        // Execute the tool
        try
        {
            rt.exec(cmd);
        }
        catch (IOException e)
        {
            log(e.getMessage(), Project.MSG_ERR);
        }
        log("Exit execute()", Project.MSG_INFO);
    }

    public void addFileset(FileSet set)
    {
        log("Enter addFileset(FileSet set)", Project.MSG_DEBUG);
        fileset_ = set;
        log("fileset_ = " + fileset_, Project.MSG_DEBUG);
        log("Exit addFileset(FileSet set)", Project.MSG_DEBUG);
    }

    public void setDestdir(String destdir)
    {
```

LISTING 11.17   Continued

```
        log("Enter setDestdir(String destdir)", Project.MSG_DEBUG);
        destdir_ = destdir.replace('/', '\\');
        log("destdir = " + destdir, Project.MSG_DEBUG);
        log("Exit setDestdir(String destdir)", Project.MSG_DEBUG);
    }

    private FileSet fileset_;
    private String  destdir_ = null;
    private String  tempfile_ = "tempFile";
}
```

After the custom task is created and put in the CLASSPATH, the next step is to modify the buildfile to invoke it. Listing 11.18 shows the modified buildfile. At the top is the usual <taskdef> declaration, which tells Ant what class to invoke when encountering the <esstask> tag later in the buildfile. Further down the file is the generateUML target that invokes our custom task. Our custom task requires an attribute, destdir, to define the destination directory. We're then able to use the nested <fileset> element to define the files we want to include. Our <fileset> element can also use the excludes attribute to leave specific files out of the set. All of this is handled inside the custom task by the DirectoryScanner class.

LISTING 11.18   generateUML Target for Calling ESS-Model from Ant

```
<taskdef name="esstask"
         classname="com.networksByteDesign.util.EssTask"
         classpathref="project.classpath"/>

<!-- generateUML target -->
<target name="generateUML">
    <esstask destdir="${dirs.doc}">
        <fileset dir="${dirs.source}"
                 includes="**/*.java"
                 excludes="**/*Test.java" />
    </esstask>
</target>
```

Inside the execute method, we use the FileSet object that was passed in to get a handle on a DirectoryScanner object. The DirectoryScanner class scans a directory tree starting at the path given to it. It will create an array of Strings that contains anything that matches the pattern given in the `includes` attribute. The `DirectoryScanner` will specifically eliminate anything from the list that matches the pattern given in the `excludes` attribute (if one is given). This class will set its operating directory to the value given in the attribute `basedir`. The class is designed so that if that attribute is not set, it will use the user's current working directory. Because of this, after the `basedir` value is set, we then invoke the `DirectoryScanner`'s `scan()` method on the `basedir` directory. This operation causes the list to be created.

After the `scan()` method has been called, we next call the method `getIncludedFiles()`, which returns a String array. In this case, we're going to write the list to a temporary file to pass to the `ess_model` tool, because this is the only way to pass multiple filenames to this tool.

Finally, we're going to invoke the `ess_model` tool from inside the `EssTask` class. We could use the `<exec>` task in our buildfile to invoke the tool, but this will make the task self-contained. Also, because the `ess_model` tool only runs on Windows platforms, making an operating-system-specific call shouldn't matter in terms of platform independence. Invoking the `ess_model` tool is done by using the `Runtime` object. Every Java application has access to a single instance of the `Runtime` object. `Runtime` has a static method called `getRuntime()` that returns the `Runtime` object associated with the application. When we have a handle to the `Runtime` object, we can invoke its `exec()` method to launch a separate process. The `exec()` does return a `Process` object in case you need to get information about the process just invoked. However, we're simply launching the `ess_model` tool and letting it run to completion, so there is no need do anything with the `Process` object.

Throughout the class, there is logging information generated with the `log()` method. The log method accepts two arguments. The first is the message to print to the log, and the second is the level at which to log the message. See Appendix B, "Extending Ant," under the section "Using the Logging System" for a detailed explanation of logging in custom tasks.

Figures 11.4, 11.5, and 11.6 show the documentation that is generated by ESS-Model. What it does is generate Javadoc-type HTML, with links to the actual UML diagrams. Figure 11.4 shows the package overview with links. In Figure 11.5, we see some of the UML diagram generated for the `com.networksByteDesign.emarket.inventory` package. Figure 11.6 shows the `com.networksByteDesign.emarket.inventory.data` package. This illustrates some of the capabilities of this tool.

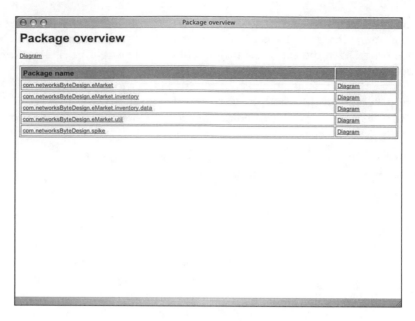

FIGURE 11.4   Output from ESS-Model showing the package overview with links.

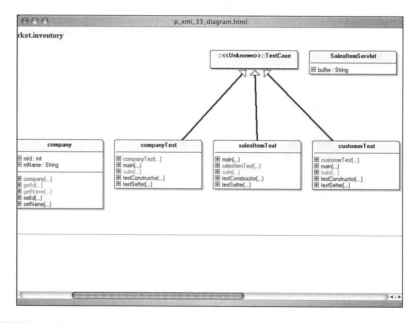

FIGURE 11.5   Output from ESS-Model showing the `com.networksByteDesign.` `emarket.inventory` package.

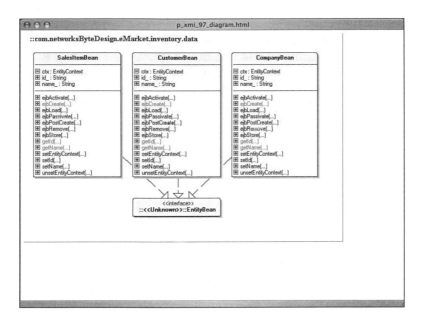

FIGURE 11.6 Output from ESS-Model Showing `com.networksByteDesign.emarket.`
`inventory.data` package.

Summary

In this chapter, we looked at how our build process can be refactored to meet the needs of an enterprise with various levels of responsibilities. We went through a series of steps to allow use of the common build targets by both department and project teams.

When the enterprise build process was in place, we began adding new tools into the project, department, and common buildfiles. We began by creating an EncryptedMailLogger that can send the gpg-encrypted output of a build process via e-mail.

We hooked in two popular tools, one from the open source community and the other a major commercial application. Cactus was hooked into the build process to take advantage of the testing capabilities provided. WebLogic was hooked in to provide minimal control from the Ant build process.

We created a `RegexpInput` task and used it with the `<translate>` task to provide internationalized HTML files. Finally we created a custom task to call ESS-Model, a UML modeling tool. We generated class diagrams from our codebase through our automated build process.

Although the teams will continuously be hooking new requirements and tools into their Ant build process, the structure is in place and the teams have learned how to approach most of the issues they will be faced with. As new developers come onto the projects, they find themselves spending less time focusing on build and deployment issues and more time on the specific issues revolving around their application. For a build and deployment process, that is the ultimate compliment.

A

Installing Ant

Installing Ant can be a very straightforward process. The Ant Web site offers several options to meet the needs of a variety of users. This appendix discusses the decisions that you must make to obtain, build, and install Ant properly. The Ant home page is http://ant.apache.org/index.html. For an overview of obtaining, installing, and building Ant, see http://ant.apache.org/manual/install.html.

Choosing the Correct Edition of Ant

The first decision in obtaining and installing Ant is whether the binary or source edition is appropriate. This decision will be determined by your plans for using Ant after you have it installed. For most users who plan to use Ant to develop a build and deployment process, the binary edition is a good choice. The source edition is needed if you plan to make modifications to Ant itself or are just curious about how Ant is put together. Ant 1.5.3 will be the last version of Ant that will be compatible with Java 1.1.

If you choose the binary edition, remember that Ant is a Java application, and therefore the class files are the same regardless of the platform it will be used on. However, each operating system has its own archival tools and scripting syntax. You will see multiple choices for the binary edition. The class files are constant for each of the download options; it's the wrapper scripts that are different. Ant is available for many platforms including Windows, Solaris, Linux, and Mac OS X.

If you have selected the binary edition, the next choice is whether to choose the release build or a nightly build. The release build is a tested released version and should be the choice most of the time. A nightly build should be used only when you want to get the latest and greatest version.

You might use a nightly build to obtain a particular bug fix, or to get a new feature that has just been introduced. However, these nightly builds are not guaranteed to be tested and ready for public use.

Your other option is to download the source code to Ant and build it yourself. Again, as with the binary edition, there are multiple choices for which source edition to pull. The release and nightly builds are still available and are simply the source versions of their binary counterparts.

On the source side, you also have the option of retrieving the very latest code directly from the CVS repository. This level of access can be used to view the up-to-the-minute revisions to the codebase or to pull a release for possible later submission to the Ant team. You might also choose the CVS source if you are making changes to Ant and want to merge updates to Ant into your changes using CVS. Access to the CVS repository is read-only through the anonymous login. To actually make revisions in the CVS repository, you need Committer access. Instructions for how to gain Committer access or to submit changes to the Ant team are included in the Project Guidelines at the following URL:

```
http://jakarta.apache.org/site/guidelines.html
```

Choosing the version of Ant best suited to your needs will help make the transition to Ant as simple and painless as possible. Most users will select the binary release build, but having the other options available meets the specific needs that arise on development teams from time to time. Table A.1 lists the build that you should choose based on your system requirements.

TABLE A.1   Summary of Ant Edition Choices

Requirements	Choose
Use Ant for creating a build/deployment process	Binary release build
Use a bleeding-edge version of Ant	Binary nightly build
Make modifications to a tested release of Ant	Source release build
Make modifications to a bleeding-edge version of Ant	Source nightly build
Make modifications to Ant with the absolute latest code, possibly for submittal to the Ant team	Source CVS repository
Extend Ant to add new capabilities	Binary or source builds

Obtaining Ant

After you have decided which edition is best for your development team, the next step is to obtain the product from the Ant Web site.

Binary

The latest binary release build can be found at

`http://ant.apache.org/bindownload.cgi`

A listing of the binary nightly builds can be found at

`http://cvs.apache.org/builds/ant/nightly/`

The files with `-bin` are the binary versions.

Source

The latest source release build can be found at

`http://ant.apache.org/srcdownload.cgi`

A listing of the source nightly builds can be found at

`http://cvs.apache.org/builds/ant/nightly/`

The files with `-src` are the source-code versions.

CVS

The URL `http://jakarta.apache.org/site/cvsindex.html` directs you to the most recent instructions on obtaining a CVS workspace for the latest source code. To access the CVS repository, you first must have a CVS client installed on your machine. This is usually included, but not necessarily installed, with installations of Linux, Mac OS X, and Cygwin for Windows.

You can obtain a CVS client at: `www.cvshome.org`. To pull the source code using CVS, run the following commands:

```
cvs -d :pserver:anoncvs@cvs.apache.org:/home/cvspublic login
password: anoncvs
cvs -d :pserver:anoncvs@cvs.apache.org:/home/cvspublic checkout ant
```

You can also view the online CVS repository at

`http://cvs.apache.org/viewcvs/ant/`

Building Ant

The binary distribution should be adequate for the needs of most teams. If you elect to download the source distribution, or obtain the source code directly from CVS, you must go through the process to build Ant.

Full Build

Building Ant is a straightforward process that is documented at

```
http://ant.apache.org/manual/install.html#buildingant
```

The first step is to set the JAVA_HOME environment variable to the directory on your machine where the JDK is installed. If you are currently using the machine to compile Java code, this has probably already been done.

If you are planning on using optional tasks, some library dependencies will have to be resolved before Ant is built. The CLASSPATH considerations when building Ant are actually a separate issue from the CLASSPATH used when running Ant. Optional tasks have two components. First is the actual tool itself, such as JUnit. The tool must be made available in the PATH or CLASSPATH for Ant to use it at run time. If this tool is in a jar file, as is JUnit, that jar file must be in the CLASSPATH to be used. The second component is the Task code, which serves as the interface between the tool, and Ant. These classes are found in optional.jar. So for the case of an optional task like JUnit, two jar files are required in order to use it: junit.jar for the tool, and optional.jar for the task to invoke JUnit.

When building Ant, the optional.jar file will only be built to contain the tasks that the bootstrap version of Ant could find in its CLASSPATH. So in the case of JUnit, the jar file junit.jar must be in the CLASSPATH when Ant is built. If it is not, optional.jar will not contain the <junit> task in optional.jar. If you were to add junit.jar to your installation, and try to use it, Ant will generate an error that it doesn't know what the <junit> task is. Information on library dependencies for optional tasks can be found at http://ant.apache.org/manual/install.html#librarydependencies.

To build Ant, simply enter the appropriate command for your platform.

For Windows:

```
build.bat -Ddist.dir=<directory to place the Ant build> dist
```

For UNIX:

```
build.sh -Ddist.dir=<directory to place the Ant build> dist
```

If necessary, the build process will create a bootstrap version of Ant and use that minimal Ant build to perform the rest of the build. If you have previously created a bootstrap version and the new build file uses features that are not in the bootstrap you created, you might need to rebuild the bootstrap version. This is accomplished by running either bootstrap.bat or bootstrap.sh, depending on your platform. If you want to install the new Ant release into the current ANT_HOME directory, enter the appropriate command for your platform.

For Windows:

```
build install
```

For UNIX:

```
build.sh install
```

Lightweight Build

You can also install a version without producing the Javadoc documentation, which can greatly speed up the process. To create a version without the Javadoc, enter the following command.

For Windows:

```
build install-lite
```

For UNIX:

```
build.sh install-lite
```

Installing Ant

When installing Ant, remember that it is a Java application. So, installing the software revolves primarily around making sure that the environment variables Ant uses are set correctly and that the CLASSPATH contains the classes needed to run Ant. Instructions for installing Ant can be found at

```
http://ant.apache.org/manual/install.html#installing
```

If you are using optional tasks, there are some library considerations. This again requires either adding the .jar files to the system CLASSPATH or copying the .jar files into Ant's lib directory. As discussed in the section on Building Ant, there are two components to an optional task, the tool and the task class used to invoke the tool. First, the tool must be available to Ant. For example, the optional task <junit> invokes the tool JUnit. This tool is contained in junit.jar, so junit.jar must either be in the lib directory of the Ant installation, or in the CLASSPATH. Next, the task class, which serves as the interface between the tool and Ant, must be in optional.jar. Also, optional.jar must be in the lib directory of the Ant installation. If you're building Ant, be sure to read the section about Building Ant for some important considerations about optional tasks. Information on library dependencies can be found at

```
http://ant.apache.org/manual/install.html#librarydependencies
```

The following environment variables must be set for Ant to run properly:

- JAVA_HOME—Should be set to the location where the JDK is installed
- ANT_HOME—Should be set to the location where Ant is installed
- PATH—Should include $ANT_HOME/bin

Invoking Ant runs a wrapper script for a specific operating system, which starts a Java Virtual Machine that runs the Ant Java code. Ant's behavior can be altered by setting environment variables that are passed from the wrapper script to the JVM. Environment variables can also be set in platform-dependent files, which are called by the Ant wrapper scripts. When running Ant on a Unix-based platform, such as Linux, Solaris, Mac OS X and Cygwin, the Unix wrapper script for Ant will look for the file ~/.antrc before invoking Ant in the JVM. The wrapper script for Windows platforms looks for %HOME%/antrc_pre.bat before invoking Ant in the JVM, and %HOME%/antrc_post.bat after running Ant.

Let's look at the environment variables that can be set in a configuration file to alter the behavior of Ant. The environment variable JAVACMD can be set to the full path name of a Java Virtual Machine of your choice. If this isn't specified, the default value is JAVA_HOME/bin/java(.exe), which is probably fine for most users. The purpose of the environment variable ANT_OPTS is really to contain options to pass to the JVM. So any argument that is valid for the JVM that you are using can be set in the ANT_OPTS environment variable. You can run the java -help command to determine the valid arguments for this option. Multiple arguments can be passed to the JVM by enclosing them in single quotes. For example, if you wanted to print the version of the JVM you're using, and set the maximum heap size to 500 Mbytes, you could set the following in your Ant initialization file, as shown here:

```
ANT_OPTS='-showversion -mx500m'
```

When the CLASSPATH is set correctly and the environment variables have been initialized, you are ready to begin using Ant to create your build and deployment process.

Debugging Your Installation

The Ant installation can be tested without a buildfile by running the command:

```
ant -version
```

If Ant is working correctly, it will print its version number.

If your installation fails to work correctly, check the following items:

- Check that all of the required environment variables are set correctly. This includes: JAVA_HOME, ANT_HOME, and that PATH contains ANT_HOME/bin.

- Verify that the ANT_HOME/lib directory contains the jar files: ant.jar and optional.jar.

- Make sure that you don't have incompatible versions of .jar files in the Ant CLASSPATH or in the ANT_HOME/lib directory.

B

Extending Ant

In this appendix, we examine the general principles and characteristics of writing custom components that extend Ant. A number of custom components are developed throughout this book that illustrate many of the techniques of writing custom components. This includes topics such as using nested filesets or writing a custom logger. This appendix provides a basic understanding of the requirements of writing a custom component, how to integrate a custom component into Ant, and the lifecycle of the components during execution of a buildfile.

Custom Tasks

Suppose you want to create a custom task called foo that will have two attributes, and is to be used in a buildfile in the following manner:

```
<foo bar1="xyz" bar2="abc"/>
```

Again, the task is called foo, and its two attributes in this example are called bar1 and bar2. These two attributes are used to pass in meaningful values as strings to the custom task Java class. These attributes need to be stored in class attributes or member variables within the custom task. So, the custom task class needs to have two member variables:

```
private String bar1 = null;
private String bar2 = null;
```

The member variables can be named anything, but it's advisable to use the attribute names to avoid confusion. A custom task can have any number of attributes. The requirement in Ant is that the class implementing the custom task must have a bean interface. That is, it must have a public set*Xxx*() method for each attribute, where

Xxx is the attribute name that will be exposed in the buildfile. Note that the attribute name is all lowercase in the buildfile, but must have the first letter of the name uppercased in the set method. So for the foo task, our custom task's Java class needs to have two set methods that look like this example:

```
public void setBar1(String value)
{
    bar1 = value;
}

public void setBar2(String value)
{
    bar2 = value;
}
```

The class must also define a public default constructor and a public void execute() method, which does the useful work.

Creating a custom task that accepts nested elements requires two things:

- A class that implements the nested element
- A method within the custom task to accept or create an instance of the nested element class

First, you need to have a class that is used with the nested element. For example, Ant has many tasks that support the use of the nested <fileset> element, such as <copy>. Ant has a Java class called Fileset that represents the object contained within the nested <fileset> element. For your nested element, you will also need a class that represents your nested element. For example, let's have a nested element called <myelement>. We need a class called Myelement.

Next, within the custom task that is going to accept this nested element, we need to add methods to accept this class. In general, three possible methods can be implemented: createXxx(), addXxx() and addConfiguredXxx(), where Xxx is the name of the XML tag that will be used in the buildfile. In our example, it is called <myelement>. For this specific example, the possible methods in our custom task are

- public Myelement createMyelement()
- public void addMyelement(Myelement elem)
- public void addConfiguredMyelement(Myelement elem)

There is a difference between these methods. The method createMyelement() requires the task to instantiate the Myelement class and return it to Ant. Using the methods `addMyelement(Myelement)` or `addConfiguredMyelement(Myelement)` will cause Ant to first instantiate the class, and then pass it to the task. The difference between these two methods is the state of the object that will be passed to the custom task. The method `addMyelement(Myelement)` will be called after the no-argument constructor is called on `Myelement`, but before the attribute setters are called. So, the attribute values will not be valid when this method is called. The method `addConfiguredMyelement(Myelement)` is called after the constructor and attribute setters are called on `Myelement`, so the attributes are valid at this time.

As for the class name, it can be anything you want, because the class name must be mapped to the task name with a `<taskdef>` declaration in the buildfile. The class extends `org.apache.tools.ant.Task`, which provides the hooks into the Ant framework. `Task` represents a generic Ant task without any special behavior. Putting this all together, we have a custom task class as shown in Listing B.1.

LISTING B.1   Generic Example of a Simple Custom Task

```
package com.networksByteDesign.util;

// Ant libraries
import org.apache.tools.ant.BuildException;
import org.apache.tools.ant.Task;

public class FooTask extends Task
{
    public void setBar1(String value)
    {
        bar1 = value;
    }

    public void setBar2(String value)
    {
        bar2 = value;
    }

    public void execute() throws BuildException
    {
        boolean errorOccurred = false;

        // do useful work in this method

        // if things go wrong, throw a BuildException.
        // do NOT call System.exit()
        // as it will stop Ant altogether
```

LISTING B.1   Continued

```
    if(errorOccurred)
    {
        throw new BuildException("error message");
    }
}

private String bar1 = null;
private String bar2 = null;
}
```

The `execute()` Method

The `execute()` method is where the actual work of any task gets done. You should remember a couple of things when writing the `execute()` method. If an error occurs, the `execute()` method should throw a `BuildException` with a meaningful error message. The `execute()` method should never call `System.exit()`, because this will cause the JVM that is running Ant to exit. The result is that the entire build process will stop, with little information as to why.

Using the Logging System

Ant has a logging system built in, and it's best to use it for logging information about the execution of the task. This way, these messages will be properly integrated with the use of Ant loggers and listeners. Avoid writing to `System.out` and `System.err` anywhere in the custom task.

Ant allows you to write messages to one of five levels, which are, in order of severity starting with the worst:

- Error
- Warning
- Info
- Verbose
- Debug

These levels are defined as constants in the `org.apache.tools.ant.Project` class. There is a message-level parameter that can be called to set the message logging level. For example, at the Error level, only messages logged at the Error level will be displayed. At the Info level, anything at the Info level and above (Info, Warning,

Error) will get logged. So at the Debug level, everything will get logged. The behavior of the logging system is like that of Log4J or the Java 1.4 logging API.

The way to print a log message is to use one of two overloaded log methods (there is actually a third version that should not be used in custom tasks). These methods send a message to the default log listener of the build.

The methods available for use in a custom task are

```
log(message)
log(message, level)
```

Don't use the method log(message, level, task) as it's not intended for use in custom tasks. For example, you might add the following line of code just prior to throwing a BuildException:

```
log("cannot access resource xyz", Project.MSG_ERROR);
```

Configuring a Task for Use in a Buildfile

After the class is compiled, we have to configure the custom task to make it available for use inside a buildfile. First, the custom task class must be in the CLASSPATH that will be used by Ant. In addition, a mapping must be declared between the task name (foo) and the Java class name (FooTask).

There are two ways to make a class available for use in a buildfile. The first technique is to simply put the class somewhere in the Ant CLASSPATH, and then provide a taskdef definition at the top of the buildfile that declares the mapping. An example of this declaration is shown in Listing B.2.

LISTING B.2   Example of the taskdef Declaration in a Buildfile

```
<?xml version="1.0" ?>
<project name="eMarket" default="default" basedir=".">
<taskdef name="foo" classname="com.networksByteDesign.util.FooTask"/>

<!-- rest of the buildfile -->
</project>
```

After this is done, the task is available for use throughout the buildfile.

A second, more "permanent" method is to add the task definition to the defaults.properties file in the taskdef subdirectory of the org.apache.tool.ant.taskdefs package. Add an entry to the property file like the one shown here:

```
foo=com.networksByteDesign.util.FooTask
```

Then rebuild the ant.jar file, including the custom task class (FooTask.class). This will make the custom task available in all buildfiles that use this Ant installation.

Classes for Extension

Any Ant task class is a candidate to be extended as a custom task. In fact, making use of the built-in functionality is highly encouraged. This is a good way to start with the basic functionality and override the behavior to perform some specific need that you may have. Beyond that, there are six abstract base classes specifically intended for use in custom tasks:

- Task—Base class for all task classes

- MatchingTask—Task that needs to use filesets, and to include or exclude files in the fileset

- AbstractCvsTask—Tasks that will perform CVS operations

- JDBCTask—Tasks that will access databases via JDBC

- Pack—Abstract Base class for tasks that pack

- Unpack—Abstract Base class for tasks that unpack

Each of these abstract base classes has methods defined for specifics to the task that it is intended for. Again, examples of many of these are provided in this book.

Lifecycle of a Task

Ant begins execution in the class org.apache.tools.ant.Main. This class instantiates a class called ProjectHelperImpl, which creates and configures an instance of the Project class. The Project class actually contains references to Target classes, Property classes, and Filter classes that are stored in HashTables within Project. This Project object is available to all tasks, including any custom task that you might develop. It's actually contained in a class called ProjectComponent, which the Task class extends. The inherited Project object contains useful information that can be used by custom tasks, as shown in some of the examples in this book.

After parsing the buildfile and configuring the Project object, Ant instantiates all of the tasks in the buildfile. Tasks are instantiated even if they're only declared in a target but never actually used. Ant calls the no-argument constructor for the task. At this time, attributes and the inherited Project object are not yet available, which is why the constructor can't use them.

After the tasks are instantiated, Ant sets the inherited reference to the Project object in the task. It then calls the init() method on each task. Each instance of a task is initialized only once. When the init() method is called, the class attributes are not yet set. After the init() method is called, any nested elements are parsed, and Ant sets the references to the nested elements by calling the corresponding addXxx() methods on the custom task. However, the set methods for attributes in the custom task class or in the nested elements are not set until runtime, so they are not available at init time.

During execution of the target that uses the custom task, Ant sets all of the attributes for the custom task and any nested elements, using the setXxx() methods that are defined for each class. Afterward, the execute() method is called on the custom task class. This is where the work gets done, and is entirely defined by your implementation. Upon completion of buildfile execution, the Ant JVM exits and the objects are destroyed.

If your custom task is used in more than one target, multiple instances of the custom task class will be instantiated. The order of events will be the same. The init phase will instantiate instances of the custom task, and then the addXxx() methods will be called for nested elements. During the execution phase, the setXxx() methods will be called as each target executes.

For tasks that use a nested fileset, the set of files included in the fileset is determined at the time of target execution. Consider the task example shown in Listing B.3.

LISTING B.3   Nested <fileset> Custom Task

```
package com.networksByteDesign.util;

// Ant libraries
import org.apache.tools.ant.DirectoryScanner;
import org.apache.tools.ant.Project;
import org.apache.tools.ant.taskdefs.MatchingTask;
import org.apache.tools.ant.types.FileSet;

public class FooNestedFilesetTask extends MatchingTask
{
    public void execute()
    {
        DirectoryScanner dsFiles  = files.getDirectoryScanner(project);
        String[]         fileList = dsFiles.getIncludedFiles();

        for(int i=0; i<fileList.length; i++)
        {
            log(fileList[i], Project.MSG_INFO);
        }
    }
```

LISTING B.3   Continued

```
    public void addFileset(FileSet set)
    {
        files = set;
    }

    private FileSet files = null;
}
```

This custom task is used in a buildfile as shown in Listing B.4.

LISTING B.4   Buildfile to Execute the Nested `<fileset>` Custom Task of Listing B.3

```xml
<?xml version="1.0" ?>
<project name="appendixB" default="testFooNestedFilesetTask" basedir=".">

    <taskdef name="fooNestedFilesetTask"
             classname="com.networksByteDesign.util.FooNestedFilesetTask"
             classpath="${ant.home}/lib/custom.jar" />

    <!-- testFooNestedFilesetTask target -->
    <target name="testFooNestedFilesetTask">
        <touch file="example.class"/>
        <fooNestedFilesetTask>
            <fileset dir=".">
                <include name="**/*.class"/>
            </fileset>
        </fooNestedFilesetTask>
    </target>

</project>
```

In this example, the custom task will be handed a fileset of all files in the directory that end in ".class," and will print those files out. The method `addFileset(FileSet set)` will be called at initialization, and a `FileSet` will be passed in. The `execute()` method is not called until target execution. Suppose that the file `example.class` did not exist at the time the script was run. What `FileSet` will the execute method see? It turns out that the file `example.class`, which was created in the target, after the `FileSet` object was passed in, will be seen by the custom task. The `DirectoryScanner` object does pick up files that were just created prior to the invocation of the task's `execute()` method.

It's not mandatory to understand the lifecycle of a task in order to develop custom tasks. However, it is useful to have an understanding of the order of events if you're trying to debug a problem.

Custom Listeners

A custom listener implements the org.apache.tools.ant.listener. BuildListener Interface. This interface provides several callback methods that Ant will invoke when certain build events have occurred. The callback methods receive the BuildEvent object from Ant and can perform special processing. Several events can be received with callbacks:

- buildStarted

- buildFinished

- targetStarted

- targetFinished

- taskStarted

- taskFinished

- messageLogged

Listing B.5 shows a simple custom listener that plays a sound when each task in the buildfile finishes.

LISTING B.5   Audio Feedback Custom Listener

```
package com.networksByteDesign.util;

// Ant libraries
import org.apache.tools.ant.BuildEvent;
import org.apache.tools.ant.BuildListener;
import org.apache.tools.ant.taskdefs.optional.sound.AntSoundPlayer;

// Java libraries
import java.io.File;

public class FooListener implements BuildListener
{
    public FooListener()
    {
        player.addBuildSuccessfulSound(new File("ok.wav"),
```

LISTING B.5   Continued

```
                                            1,
                                            new Long(400));

        player.addBuildFailedSound(new File("drama.wav"),
                                    1,
                                    new Long(400));
    }

    public void messageLogged(BuildEvent event) {}

    public void buildStarted(BuildEvent event) {}

    public void buildFinished(BuildEvent event) {}

    public void targetStarted(BuildEvent event) {}

    public void targetFinished(BuildEvent event) {}

    public void taskStarted(BuildEvent event) {}

    public void taskFinished(BuildEvent event)
    {
        player.buildFinished(event);
    }

    private AntSoundPlayer player = new AntSoundPlayer();
}
```

The `ok.wav` and `drama.wav` files will need to be in the current working directory for them to be found by the `FooListener`, or the listener can be modified to set the directory where the WAV files are located. To run `FooListener` (assuming it's in the `CLASSPATH` and that there is a `build.xml` file in the current directory), run the following command:

```
ant -listener com.networksByteDesign.util.FooListener
```

As each task finishes, the sound file is played. For long-running targets with many tasks, this could be used to provide audio feedback that everything is still running. The listener provides the appropriate hooks to get feedback on the build at various stages and be able to take the appropriate action.

Custom Loggers

A custom logger is really a specialized form of a listener that implements the
BuildLogger interface. The BuildLogger interface extends the BuildListener interface. Ant provides a class called DefaultLogger that implements BuildLogger, and
provides some default implementations for the event callback methods. It gets all the
callbacks that BuildListener receives, plus the following methods:

```
public void setMessageOutputLevel(int)
public void setOutputPrintStream(java.io.PrintStream)
public void setErrorPrintStream(java.io.PrintStream)
public void setEmacsMode(boolean)
```

Rather than relying on System.out or System.err, all custom components should
use Ant's built-in logging to allow the user to control the amount of logging and the
mechanism by which it is delivered. You can also cause some unwelcome behavior
by calling System.out.println() in the messageLogged() event. If you write to standard out in the messageLogged() event, it will cause a recursive loop and crash the
JVM, as shown in this method example:

```
public void messageLogged(BuildEvent event)
{
    // DON'T DO THIS!!!
    System.out.println("This println will cause an infinite loop");
}
```

Listing B.6 shows a custom logger that extends the DefaultLogger and overrides the
taskStarted() method. This custom logger simply adds the name of the task being
executed into the log.

LISTING B.6   Simple Custom Logger That Logs TaskStarted Events

```
package com.networksByteDesign.util;

// Ant libraries
import org.apache.tools.ant.BuildEvent;
import org.apache.tools.ant.DefaultLogger;
import org.apache.tools.ant.Project;
import org.apache.tools.ant.util.StringUtils;

public class FooLogger extends DefaultLogger
{
    public void taskStarted(BuildEvent event)
    {
```

LISTING B.6   Continued

```
        if(Project.MSG_INFO <= msgOutputLevel)
        {
            String msg = StringUtils.LINE_SEP + "<" +
                event.getTask().getTaskName() + ">:";
            printMessage(msg, out, event.getPriority());
            log(msg);
        }
    }
}
```

To run `FooLogger` (assuming it's in the `CLASSPATH` and that there is a `build.xml` file in the current directory), run the command:

```
ant -logger com.networksByteDesign.util.FooLogger
```

With both loggers and listeners, the `Event` object that is passed into the callback method can be used to get a handle on the `Project` object, with the following call:

```
        Project project = event.getProject();
```

Check the Javadoc included with the Ant distribution for more information on the methods available to classes `Event` and `Project`. Look under the "Table of Contents" for the link to "Ant API."

Some Principles for Developing Custom Tasks, Loggers, and Listeners

Here are a few things to keep in mind when writing custom tasks, loggers, and listeners. A custom task, logger, or listener should never call `System.exit()` because this will cause the entire Ant build process to exit. Also, don't instantiate your own regular expression handlers, because you can request a regular expression handler from Ant's regular expression factory. Custom tasks, loggers, and listeners shouldn't write to `STDOUT` or `STDERR`, but should use Ant's logging system. However, don't attempt to use the log method in a constructor because all of the required objects are not yet constructed. There is also a danger in using `System.out.println()` in a custom logger or listener. Using `System.out.println()` in the `messageLogged()` method causes a recursive loop until the JVM crashes.

Input Handlers

Input handlers can be written to allow users to input unique information such as passwords. An example of this is the use of the <input> task. Ant cannot simply read from STDIN because this would preclude the possibility of hooking Ant into an IDE.

Input handlers must implement the interface org.apache.tools.ant.input.InputHandler, which has one method:

```
void handleInput(InputRequest request)
    throws org.apache.tools.ant.BuildException;
```

There are two input handlers supplied with Ant that implement this interface. They are the DefaultInputHandler class, which is what Ant uses when you don't specify an input handler. The other is the org.apache.tools.ant.input.PropertyFileInputHandler class. This input handler will read all input from a properties file. A Java system property called ant.input.properties must be defined to name the property file. The input prompt is used as the key in the property file. If the key cannot be found, the input is considered to be invalid and an exception is thrown.

Listing B.7 shows a custom input logger that extends the DefaultInputHandler. The FooInputHandler relies on the base class to handle the actual input and simply changes the input to all caps after it has been received. By using this input handler in place of the DefaultInputHandler, all users of the <input> task would now receive their input in all caps without modifying the build file.

LISTING B.7   A Custom Input Handler That Capitalizes All Input

```
package com.networksByteDesign.util;

// Ant libraries
import org.apache.tools.ant.BuildException;
import org.apache.tools.ant.input.DefaultInputHandler;
import org.apache.tools.ant.input.InputRequest;

public class FooInputHandler extends DefaultInputHandler
{
    public void handleInput(InputRequest request) throws BuildException
    {
        super.handleInput(request);

        String upperInput = request.getInput().toUpperCase();
        request.setInput(upperInput);
    }
}
```

To invoke Ant with our custom input handler, use the option as shown in this example:

```
ant -inputhandler com.networksByteDesign.util.FooInputHandler
```

If a user entered "foobar" in response to the following <input> task, the value "FOOBAR" would be echoed to the screen.

```
<input message="Please enter class name:"
        addproperty="project.classname"/>
<echo>Your class name is ${project.classname}</echo>
```

Selectors

Selectors are constructs that are used in conjunction with a <fileset>. They provide a way to discriminate a set of files within a <fileset> based on different criteria than the simple filename matching available with the <include> and <exclude> elements. There are two types of selectors built into Ant, "core selectors" and "selector containers." The core selectors are listed and described in Table B.1.

TABLE B.1   Ant's Core Selectors

Core Selector	Function
<contains>	Allows files to be selected based on the text they contain.
<date>	Permits files to be selected based on their timestamp.
<depend>	Files may be selected based on their timestamp relative to a file they depend on.
<depth>	Selection of files to a certain number of levels in a directory tree.
<filename>	Equivalent to the <include> and <excludes> tags.
<present>	Select files that have an equivalent file elsewhere.
<size>	Selection of files based on their size.

Selector containers are selectors that can contain other selectors. These selectors are essentially logical operators for file selection. The set of selector containers is listed and described in Table B.2.

TABLE B.2   Ant's Container Selectors Used to Perform Logical Operations on Groups of Core Selectors

Selector Container	Function
<and>	Logical AND of all of the selectors contained within. All must select for file to be included.
<majority>	A file is selected if the majority of the selectors select it.
<none>	A file is selected if none of the selectors contained within select it.

TABLE B.2   Continued

Selector Container	Function
`<not>`	Logical NOT; selects everything that is not included by the single selector it contains.
`<or>`	Logical OR; a file is selected if any contained selector includes it.
`<selector>`	Used to define a reference, or a named selector that can be referred to in another section of the buildfile.

Here is an example of using a container selector along with core selectors. The container qualifies the core selectors that are contained within it. In this case only files that are 8192 bytes or larger that contain the text "foobar" will be selected.

```
<fileset dir="${dist}" includes="**/*.txt">
   <and>
      <size value="8" units="Ki" when="more"/>
      <contains text="foobar" casesensitive="yes" />
   </and>
</fileset>
```

Besides the core and container selectors available, Ant also provides the capability to create custom selectors. A custom selector class must implement the interface org.apache.tools.ant.types.selectors.FileSelector, or some derivative of it, such as ExtendFileSelector. The FileSelector interface has one method to implement:

```
public boolean isSelected(File baseDir, String fileName, File file)
        throws BuildException
```

This method returns a Boolean to indicate whether or not a file is selected. The baseDir argument is a java.io.File that points to the directory from which to operate. The filename argument is the name of the file, and the final java.io.File is the File object for the file. Using this information, your implementation can select or reject a file based on your own criteria, and return the boolean value to indicate the decision.

Extending the interface org.apache.tools.ant.types.selectors.ExtendFileSelector will allow variables to be set in a custom selector with nested <param> elements. To do this, override the method:

```
public void setParameters(Parameter[] parameters)
```

and then process the parameters in your specific way.

The abstract classes org.apache.tools.ant.types.selectors.BaseExtendSelector or org.apache.tools.ant.types.selectors.BaseSelector will perform validation before calling the isSelected() method. If you want to check state prior to the execution of the isSelected() method, implement the following method:

```
public void verifySettings()
```

Then you need to call the validate() method in your implementation of isSelected() prior to doing anything else, as shown here:

```
public boolean isSelected(File baseDir, String fileName, File file)
    throws BuildException
{
    validate();
    // rest of the implementation here
}
```

The call to validate() will call your verifySettings() implementation. If you don't need to perform validation, or to pass values into your selector with nested <param> elements, extending the FileSelector interface will probably be sufficient for most needs.

Listing B.8 is an example of an implementation of a custom selector. This selector will select a single file from each directory.

LISTING B.8   A Basic Custom Selector Implementation

```
package com.networksByteDesign.util;

// Ant libraries
import org.apache.tools.ant.BuildException;
import org.apache.tools.ant.types.selectors.BaseExtendSelector;

// Java libraries
import java.io.File;
import java.util.HashSet;

public class FooSelector extends BaseExtendSelector
{
    public boolean isSelected(File baseDir, String fileName, File file)
        throws BuildException
    {
        if(fileName.length() == 0)
            return false;

        String path = fileName.substring
            (0, fileName.lastIndexOf(file.getName()));
```

LISTING B.8   Continued

```
        return dirList.add(path);
    }

    private HashSet dirList = new HashSet();
}
```

Listing B.9 shows the buildfile section that hooks in our custom selector. In this example, we use the id attribute of the `<selector>` to refer to the proper selector in our target.

LISTING B.9   Buildfile Section Hooking in a Custom Selector

```
<selector id="fooSelector">
    <custom classname="com.networksByteDesign.util.FooSelector"
            classpath="${ant.home}/lib/custom.jar" />
</selector>

<target name="testSelector">
    <copy todir="to">
        <fileset dir="from">
            <selector refid="fooSelector"/>
        </fileset>
    </copy>
</target>
```

The `<testSelector>` target will copy a single file from each directory from the from directory to the to directory.

Filters

A custom filter can be created simply as a `FilterReader` or as a chainable filter. All custom filters need to extend the class `BaseFilterReader` or some derivative of it. Chainable filters must also implement the `ChainableReader` interface. A set of chainable filters can be assembled together in a manner that is analogous to the chaining of Unix commands with the pipe operator. By doing this, it's possible to assemble a more complex set of operations from smaller filters, just as some very complex operations are possible in Unix by piping the output of one command into the next. The `ChainableReader` interface provides one method that must be implemented:

```
public Reader chain(Reader rdr);
```

This method accepts a `Reader`, which is a Java class for reading character streams, and returns another `Reader`. When the operation is complete, the return value of this method is a new `Reader` that has the same configuration as the one passed in. The returned `Reader` can then be passed to another `ChainableReader`.

The example in Listing B.10 shows a simple custom filter called `FooFilter`. `FooFilter` numbers each of the lines in the files that are passed through it. `FooFilter` extends the class `BaseParamFilterReader`. The `BaseParamFilterReader` class extends the `BaseFilterReader`, and is intended for parameterized readers. `BaseParamFilterReader` provides additional methods for passing in an array of `Parameter` values, if the nested <param> element is to be used.

LISTING B.10   A Basic Custom Filter Implementation

```
package com.networksByteDesign.util;

// Ant libraries
import org.apache.tools.ant.types.Parameter;
import org.apache.tools.ant.filters.BaseParamFilterReader;
import org.apache.tools.ant.filters.ChainableReader;

// Java libraries
import java.io.IOException;
import java.io.Reader;

public final class FooFilter extends BaseParamFilterReader
    implements ChainableReader
{
    private long lineNumber = 0;

    private String queuedData = null;

    public FooFilter()
    {
        super();
    }

    public FooFilter(final Reader in)
    {
        super(in);
    }

    public final Reader chain(final Reader rdr)
    {
```

LISTING B.10   Continued

```
        FooFilter newFilter = new FooFilter(rdr);
        newFilter.setInitialized(true);
        return newFilter;
    }

    public final int read() throws IOException
    {
        if(!getInitialized())
        {
            setInitialized(true);
        }

        int ch = -1;

        if(queuedData != null && queuedData.length() == 0)
        {
            queuedData = null;
        }

        if(queuedData != null)
        {
            ch = queuedData.charAt(0);
            queuedData = queuedData.substring(1);
            if(queuedData.length() == 0)
            {
                queuedData = null;
            }
        }
        else
        {
            queuedData = readLine();
            lineNumber++;
            if(queuedData == null)
            {
                ch = -1;
            }
            else
            {
                queuedData = lineNumber + ". " + queuedData;
                return read();
            }
```

LISTING B.10   Continued

```
        }
        return ch;
    }
}
```

The following method in `BaseFilterReader` invokes the `read()` method that is implemented in the custom filter class:

```
public final int read(final char cbuf[], final int off, final int len)
throws IOException
```

FooFilter also implements the `ChainableReader` interface, and so it must provide an implementation of the method:

```
Public Reader chain(Reader)
```

The implementation of chain creates a new instance of `FooFilter` with the `Reader` that is passed in. It then calls the `setInitialized(boolean)` method to set the initialized value in the base class. Finally, it returns the filter. The initialized flag must be set for the methods in the base class to know that the filter has been properly initialized.

The `read()` method illustrates how to get a line of data from the buffer when implementing a custom filter. This is done by calling the `readLine()` method that is implemented in the `BaseFilterReader` class. The resulting String contains the next line of buffered data. The custom filter's `read()` method can then perform whatever manipulation of the data is necessary. This method returns the number of characters read, or −1 if the end of stream has been reached.

The following snippet shows how to hook our `FooFilter` into a `<filterchain>`.

```
<target name="testFilter">
    <copy todir="to">
        <fileset dir="from" includes="**/*.html"/>
        <filterchain>
            <filterreader
                classname="com.networksByteDesign.util.FooFilter"
                classpath="${ant.home}/lib/custom.jar"/>
        </filterchain>
    </copy>
</target>
```

Mappers

A custom mapper can be developed by extending any of the mapper classes available in Ant. The basis for Ant's built-in mappers and for custom mappers is the interface `org.apache.tools.ant.util.FileNameMapper`. The `FileNameMapper` interface has three methods to be implemented:

```
void setFrom(String from);
void setTo(String to);
String[] mapFileName(String sourceFileName);
```

The `setFrom(String)` method sets the `from` part of the transformation, and the `setTo(String)` method sets the `to` part of the transformation. The method `mapFileName()` accepts a `String`, which defines the name of a source file relative to the base directory. The `mapFileName()` method returns an array of filenames that the source file maps to.

An easier way to implement a custom mapper is to start with one of the mappers already defined in Ant. Listing B.11 shows an example mapper called `FooMapper`. This example extends the `GlobPatternMapper` class, which already implements the required methods of the `FileNameMapper` interface. The `GlobPatternMapper`, which is discussed in Chapter 5, "Creating the Automated Nightly Build," is used to create a mapping between two different file types. We're using the `GlobalPatternMapper` as our base class because we want our class to have nearly the same behavior as the `GlobalPatternMapper`. What this custom mapper does is to override the `extractVariablePart(String fileName)` method from the `GlobPatternMapper` class. This method is called in the `mapFileName()` method from `GlobPatternMapper`. In this case, the custom mapper is creating new filenames that have a random number appended to the name. The result is to map input files to random output filenames.

LISTING B.11 An Example of a Custom Mapper

```java
package com.networksByteDesign.util;

// Ant libraries
import org.apache.tools.ant.BuildException;
import org.apache.tools.ant.util.GlobPatternMapper;

// Java libraries
import java.io.File;
import java.util.Random;

public class FooMapper extends GlobPatternMapper
{
```

LISTING B.11   Continued

```
    protected String extractVariablePart(String fileName)
    {
        File file = new File(fileName);

        String path = fileName.substring
            (0, fileName.lastIndexOf(file.getName()));

        return(path + random.nextLong());
    }

    private Random random = new Random(System.currentTimeMillis());
}
```

Calling the custom mapper is shown in this target example.

```
    <target name="testMapper">
        <mkdir dir="to"/>

        <copy todir="to">
            <fileset dir="from"/>
            <mapper classname="com.networksByteDesign.util.FooMapper"
                    classpath="${ant.home}/lib/custom.jar"
                    from="*.html" to="*.html"/>
        </copy>
    </target>
```

Data Types

Custom data types in Ant should extend the abstract base class
`org.apache.tools.ant.types.DataType`. One of the reasons you might want to create a
custom data type is to handle parameters that may be too complex to deal with by
using existing data types. `DataType` is an abstract base class that extends the class
`ProjectComponent`. `ProjectComponent` is the base class for both `Task` and `DataType`.
`ProjectComponent` also contains a Project object. A custom data type should extend
the class `DataType`. By extending `DataType`, you also get access to the `Project` object in
`ProjectComponent`. The Project class is the primary data model for an Ant project. It
has extensive information about the build process. This includes items like the
default target, hashtables of user and inherited properties, targets, filters, input
handlers, and so on.

For a custom data type to be useful, it really needs to be used in a custom task. Because no existing Ant tasks will know about the custom data type, it can't be used directly with them. Even if you were to extend an existing type as a custom data type, it can't be used with tasks that understand the base class type. For example, suppose you're using a task that accepts a `FileSet`, and you create a custom type called `FooFileSet`. From a Java perspective, a `FooFileSet` is a `FileSet`. So you might wonder if you can pass the `FooFileSet` into the task that accepts a `FileSet`? The answer turns out to be "no." If the attributes are different, there are problems with parsing the XML. If the attributes are identical, but simply provide a different implementation, Ant still constructs the type of object expected in the add or create method associated with the nested type. Attempting to modify the class that the `<filelist>` element uses to actually point to the custom FooFileList type with a `<taskdef>` declaration will also fail. As of version 1.5.3, Ant generates a warning if you attempt to redefine an existing data type such as `<filelist>`, and ignores the typedef declaration.

Here's an interesting distinction in the use of nested elements in custom tasks. If you want Ant to create the object associated with the nested element using the default no-argument constructor, implement an `add` method, as shown here:

```
public void addXXX(YourType)
```

Ant will create the object and pass it in via the `add` method. The class `simple` needs to store the reference to the object being passed in. However, if you want to have more control over the construction of the object, or need to perform some intermediate steps, use a `create` method, for example:

```
public YourType createXXX()
```

This method allows the user to create the object in the method, and then return the reference to the newly created object.

In order to pass a custom data type into a custom task, the custom task must have an add or create method that uses the custom data type. If an add method is used, the argument must be the custom type. If a create method is used, it must return a reference to an object of the custom type. Because the Java code for the custom data task knows about the custom data type, it's not necessary to use the `<typedef>` declaration in the buildfile. Ant will utilize the new data type without a `<typedef>` declaration.

Listing B.12 shows an example of a custom data type that extends the Ant class `FileList`. This custom type will accept a list of package names, and replace the '.' in the package name with the file separator for the platform it's running on. In effect, it transforms the package name into a full path name to the package. The point is to provide an example of the creation of a custom data type.

LISTING B.12 An Example of a Custom Data Type

```
package com.networksByteDesign.util;

// Ant libraries
import org.apache.tools.ant.BuildException;
import org.apache.tools.ant.Project;
import org.apache.tools.ant.types.FileList;

// Java libraries
import java.io.File;
import java.util.StringTokenizer;
import java.util.Stack;
import java.util.Vector;

public class FooDataType extends FileList
{
    public void setPackages(String packages)
    {
        if(packages != null && packages.length() > 0)
        {
            String fileNames = packages.replace('.', File.separatorChar);

            super.setFiles(fileNames);
        }
    }
}
```

The custom data type is used in a custom task called FooDataTypeTask, which is shown in Listing B.13.

LISTING B.13 Custom Task for Use with the Custom Data Type from Listing B.12

```
package com.networksByteDesign.util;

// Application libraries
import com.networksByteDesign.util.FooDataType;

// Ant libraries
import org.apache.tools.ant.BuildException;
import org.apache.tools.ant.Task;
```

LISTING B.13   Continued

```
public class FooDataTypeTask extends Task
{
    public void execute() throws BuildException
    {
        boolean errorOccurred = false;

        // Use the FooDataType class here
        String[] files = packageList.getFiles(project);

        for(int i = 0; i < files.length; i++)
        {
            log("Package[" + i + "] = " + files[i], project.MSG_INFO);
        }

        if(errorOccurred)
        {
            throw new BuildException("error message");
        }
    }

    public FooDataType createPackageList()
    {
        packageList = new FooDataType();

        return packageList;
    }

    private FooDataType packageList = null;
}
```

This custom task's method createPackageList() will be called by Ant when the task
is invoked in the buildfile shown in Listing B.14. Again, the name that follows
create in the method name must match the name used in the nested element of the
buildfile. In the buildfile example, <fooDataTypeTask> accepts a nested
<packageList>. So, the method to create the packageList must be called
createPackageList(). If we had called the nested element <bar>, the create method
would be called createBar().

LISTING B.14   Buildfile Illustrating a Custom Task That Uses a Custom Data Type

```xml
<?xml version="1.0" ?>
<project name="appendixB" default="testDataType" basedir=".">

    <taskdef name="fooDataTypeTask"
            classname="com.networksByteDesign.util.FooDataTypeTask"
            classpath="${ant.home}/lib/custom.jar" />

    <target name="testDataType">
        <fooDataTypeTask>
            <packageList id="classPackages"
                        dir="from"
                        packages="com.networksByteDesign.eMarket
                                    com.networksByteDesign.eMarket.util"/>
        </fooDataTypeTask>
    </target>

</project>
```

Running the buildfile of Listing B.14 will result in the instantiation of the task
FooDataTypeTask. Ant will call the createPackageList() method in the custom task.
This method creates an instance of FooDataType, and returns it. The newly created
custom data type is then available for use in the execute() method of the custom
task. The FooDataTypeTask logs the package names after they have been converted
into directory names.

Summary

The following points are important to remember when writing custom components:

- Tasks must provide a bean interface: a public set*Xxx*() method for each
  attribute where *Xxx* is the attribute name with the first letter uppercased.

- A custom task must provide a default public constructor. The attributes of the
  class are not valid when the constructor is called.

- A custom task must implement the execute() method. This is where the work
  gets done.

- Tasks must be configured to provide a mapping between the task name in the buildfile and the class name that implements the task. This can be accomplished in either of two ways:

  - Define the mapping with a `<taskdef>` in the buildfile, and put the class in the Ant CLASSPATH.

  - Define the mapping in the `default.properties` file in the `<taskdef>` subdirectory of the Ant `org.apache.tool.ant.taskdefs` package. Include the class and rebuild the `ant.jar` file.

- Any task class is a candidate for extension into a custom task, and this practice is encouraged. There are six abstract base classes provided specifically for the development of custom tasks. Each has special characteristics for a particular function.

- If an error occurs in the `execute` method, a `BuildException` should be thrown with a meaningful error message.

- `System.exit()` should never be called in a custom component, because it may cause the entire build process to exit.

- Custom tasks should use Ant's logging facility, and should avoid writing to `System.out` or `System.err`. However, don't use the `log()` method in a custom task's constructor because this will cause a `NullPointerException` at runtime.

- Use Ant's regular expression factory when needed, rather than instantiating your own regular expression handler.

C

Ant 2

Reasons for the Change

The Ant project has outlined their plans for Ant 2 on the Web site. Information about Ant 2 can be found at

```
http://ant.apache.org/ant2/features.html
```

There will be significant architectural changes in Ant 2. Many of these changes are still up in the air and are subject to change. The new architecture will have a separation of the functions into more of a model-view-controller architecture. Ant will include multiple front-end views, including a command line similar to Ant 1 and a GUI front end with Antidote. The model of the buildfile will be clearly separated from the controller, which executes the build process. This separation of functions will allow custom tasks to deal less with Ant internals and more with the custom behavior that is being added.

The goal with Ant 2 is to promote consistency in the syntax, design, and operation of Ant. The purpose of Ant 2 will remain the same as that of Ant 1, which is to serve as a build and deployment tool. However, it will be an opportunity to fix some inconsistencies that exist in Ant 1. Currently, there is inconsistency among tasks in areas like behavior, attribute names, and implementation. For example, the tasks <ear>, <jar>, <war>, and <zip> all perform a similar function. However, each one has a unique attribute used to describe its destination file, which are earfile, jarfile, warfile, and zipfile respectively. In Ant 2, these four tasks will each have an attribute called destfile, which defines the destination file. These types of inconsistencies will be cleaned up in Ant 2. Some of the tools and techniques described in this book may be rolled into Ant itself and no longer require custom programming or third-party tools to accomplish.

Also, some of the Java code will be cleaned up and refactored. Different implementations for common functions will have a façade in front of them.

Differences Between Ant 1 and Ant 2

There are some significant differences between the plans for Ant 2 and the current implementation of Ant. Here are a few of the expected changes:

- Ant 2 will accept buildfiles written in XML. The plan is to allow input in other forms. Ant 2 will use an object model of Project/Target/Task that is expected to be independent of the external representation of the buildfile. More details were not available at the time this book was written.

- In Ant 2, tasks and attributes that are currently deprecated will be removed entirely. So any buildfile that is currently using a deprecated task, such as <deltree> or <copydir>, will not work with Ant 2.

- Ant 2 will allow a user to attach an "aspect handler" to a project—which will define behavior for common behavior throughout the build, such as whether to fail the build on error, or the setting of classpath.

- Similar tasks will be combined into a single task with attributes. For example, the tasks <jar>, <unjar>, <zip>, and <unzip>, which all operate on files with zip file format, will be combined into a single task called <archive>.

- Properties will no longer be immutable. Currently, after a property is set, it cannot be changed later in the build. It will be possible to use properties like variables, which is not possible now.

- Another change will be the removal of built-in "magic" properties such as build.compiler.

- Ant 2 will have a well-defined system for control of user preferences. Currently, there are capabilities available through the use of undocumented features with the ANT_OPTS arguments.

- Ant 2 will add an include capability so that it won't be necessary to use XML operators to include XML fragments.

- Ant 2 will include a GUI front end, and a servlet front end.

- Ant 2 will provide internationalization messages, and will provide utility classes that will allow custom task writers to do this also.

- More build events will also be added for BuildListeners. Also, it will be possible to attach and detach listeners from within the buildfile.

- The behavior of target dependencies will also change. Currently, Ant will attempt to execute a list of target dependencies (in a target depends attribute) from left to right, unless there is another dependency that prevents it. Ant 2 doesn't guarantee this behavior. It will allow build file writers to specify the order explicitly.

- Ant 2 will add the capability to multithread tasks within targets.

- All tasks will be documented in XML. There will be a Document Type Definition (DTD) for Ant XML documentation. Also, libraries of tasks will contain their own documentation to provide an overall view of the library.

- Also, Ant 2 will require JDK version 1.2 or beyond, and JAXP version 1.1 or higher.

As mentioned at the beginning of this appendix, the purpose of Ant will not change. One section on the Ant 2 Web site says that Ant will not become a scripting language. The reasons given are that there are enough scripting languages, and it would make the core of Ant too complex. So, Ant won't have constructs to support its own scripting language. However, Ant 1 currently supports BSF scripting, which permits users to use scripting languages such as JavaScript or Perl in a buildfile. This is done with the <script> task, and is documented in this book. It appears that this capability will still exist in Ant 2.

Transitioning to Ant 2

Tasks designed for the current version of Ant will probably break in Ant 2. If they don't cease to function, they will probably exhibit different behavior. This is because Ant's core API and the names of utility classes are going to change. The Ant development team has plans to ease the transition from Ant 1 to Ant 2. There will probably be tools and utilities to assist in the transition, such as a tool for translation of buildfiles. Also, there will probably be adaptors and utility classes to allow existing custom tasks to be used with minimal change.

Here are a few things to consider when writing Ant 1 tasks to prepare yourself for Ant 2:

- First, get rid of deprecated tasks in your buildfiles, because these are guaranteed to disappear in Ant 2.

- Make sure you're currently using at least Java 1.2.

- Make sure you're currently using JAXP 1.1 or higher.

- Perform spike tests with beta versions of Ant 2 when they become available. Even if you stay with Ant 1 for a while, doing this will provide additional insight into what to do in your Ant 1 buildfiles to minimize the impact of transitioning to Ant 2.

If you keep current with Java and JAXP upgrades, the transition to Ant 2 will be easier. You won't be simultaneously faced with the Java and JAXP upgrade issues, along with Ant 2 upgrade issues.

Perhaps the most important point to remember with writing Ant tasks is to focus on the concepts rather than the syntax. A developer who gains a solid grasp of object-oriented design techniques will find it easy to transition between C++ and Java. In a similar fashion, a developer who has a grasp of the design of build and deployment processes, especially in an XP methodology, will be able to easily transition to the new version of Ant.

D

Complete Buildfile Listings

This appendix lists the final buildfiles developed for NetworksByteDesign. These files are also available on the Sams Web site.

eMarket Team Buildfile

```xml
<?xml version="1.0" ?>

<!DOCTYPE project [<!ENTITY sales SYSTEM
                    "file:sales.xml">
                   <!ENTITY common SYSTEM
                    "file:common.xml">]>

<project name="eMarket" default="compile" basedir=".">

    <property name="project.email"
            value="eMarketDev@networksByteDesign.com"
    />

    <!-- appCompile target -->
    <target name="appCompile"
            depends="xdoclet"
            description="Compile all of the source
                        code.">
    </target>

    &common;
    &sales;

</project>
```

iNet Team Buildfile

```xml
<?xml version="1.0" ?>

<!DOCTYPE project [<!ENTITY network SYSTEM "file:network.xml">
                   <!ENTITY common SYSTEM "file:common.xml">]>

<project name="iNet" default="compile" basedir=".">

    <property name="project.email"
              value="iNetDevTeam@networksByteDesign.com" />

    <property name="build.compiler.emacs"     value="true"/>
    <property name="build.compiler.fulldepend" value="true" />
    <property name="build.compiler.pedantic"   value="true" />

    <property name="dirs.nounit" value="/usr/software/nounit" />

    <!-- appCompile target -->
    <target name="appCompile"
            description="Compile all of the source code.">
        <mkdir dir="${dirs.build}"/>

        <copy todir="${dirs.build}">
            <fileset dir="${dirs.source}" includes="**/*.*"/>
        </copy>
    </target>

    &common;
    &network;

    <taskdef name="noUnit"
             classname="com.networksByteDesign.util.NoUnitTask"
             classpathref="project.classpath"/>

    <taskdef name="obfuscate"
             classname="com.yworks.yguard.ObfuscatorTask"
             classpathref="project.classpath"/>

    <!-- noUnitCheck target -->
    <target name="noUnitCheck"
            description="Check for missing or incomplete unit tests.">
        <mkdir dir="${dirs.build}" />
```

```
    <copy todir="${dirs.build}" overwrite="yes">
        <fileset dir="${dirs.nounit}/output" />
    </copy>

    <noUnit startDir="${dirs.build}"
            outputDir="${dirs.build}"
            reportName="${dirs.nounit}/xslt/no-unit.xsl"
            outputFile="nounit.html" />
</target>

<!-- codegen target -->
<target name="codegen">
    <mkdir dir="${dirs.build}"/>

    <copy todir="${dirs.build}">
        <fileset dir="${dirs.source}" includes="**/*.xsl"/>
    </copy>

    <antcall target="smartCopy" />

    <parallel>

    <style style="${dirs.build}/codegen/dp1.xsl"
           includes="${dirs.build}/*.dp1"
           extension=".dp1_java"
           destdir=""/>

    <style style="${dirs.build}/codegen/nb.xsl"
           includes="${dirs.build}/*.nb"
           extension=".nb_java"
           destdir=""/>

    <style style="${dirs.build}/codegen/cl.xsl"
           includes="${dirs.build}/*.cl"
           extension=".cl_java"
           destdir=""/>

    <style style="${dirs.build}/codegen/q1z.xsl"
           includes="${dirs.build}/*.q1z"
           extension=".q1z_java"
           destdir=""/>
```

```
        <style style="${dirs.build}/codegen/gbk.xsl"
               includes="${dirs.build}/*.gbk"
               extension=".gbk_java"
               destdir=""/>

    </parallel>
</target>

<property name="LAST_BUILD"
          value="${dirs.build}/LAST_BUILD.properties"/>
<property file="${LAST_BUILD}"/>

<!-- smartCopy -->
<target name="smartcopy">
    <delete>
        <fileset dir="${dirs.build}">
            <include name="*.dp1"/>
            <include name="*.cl"/>
            <include name="*.gbk"/>
            <include name="*.nb"/>
            <include name="*.q1z"/>
        </fileset>
    </delete>

    <copy todir="${dirs.build}">
        <fileset dir="${dirs.source}" includes="**/*.dp1">
            <depend targetdir="${dirs.build}">
                <mapper type="glob" from="*.dp1" to="*.dp1_java"/>
            </depend>
        </fileset>
        <fileset dir="${dirs.source}" includes="**/*.cl">
            <depend targetdir="${dirs.build}">
                <mapper type="glob" from="*.cl" to="*.cl_java"/>
            </depend>
        </fileset>
        <fileset dir="${dirs.source}" includes="**/*.gbk">
            <depend targetdir="${dirs.build}">
                <mapper type="glob" from="*.gbk" to="*.gbk_java"/>
            </depend>
        </fileset>
        <fileset dir="${dirs.source}" includes="**/*.nb">
            <depend targetdir="${dirs.build}">
```

```
                        <mapper type="glob" from="*.nbk" to="*.nb_java"/>
                    </depend>
            </fileset>
            <fileset dir="${dirs.source}" includes="**/*.q1z">
                <depend targetdir="${dirs.build}">
                        <mapper type="glob" from="*.q1z" to="*.q1z_java"/>
                    </depend>
            </fileset>
        </copy>
</target>


<!-- incrementBuild target -->
<target name="incrementBuild">
    <buildnumber/>
    <property name="tag" value="iNet-${build.number}" />
    <cvs command="tag ${tag}" dest="${dirs.source}"/>
    <echo message="Release tagged with following build number: ${tag}"/>
</target>


<!-- jspCompile target -->
<target name="jspCompile">
    <mkdir dir="${dirs.build}"/>

    <copy todir="${dirs.build}">
        <fileset dir="${dirs.source}" includes="**/RegisterStep*.jsp"/>
    </copy>

    <jspc destdir="."
          srcdir="${dirs.build}"
          uriroot=".">
        <include name="**/RegisterStep*.jsp"/>
    </jspc>
</target>


<!-- obfuscate target -->
<target name="obfuscate">
    <obfuscate logfile="${dirs.build}/log.xml"
               replaceclassnamestrings="true">
        <inoutpair in="${ant.project.name}.jar"
                   out="${ant.project.name}_obf.jar"/>
        <property name="language-conformity" value="illegal"/>
        <property name="naming-scheme" value="mix"/>
```

```
        </obfuscate>
    </target>

</project>
```

eSupplier Team Buildfile

```xml
<?xml version="1.0" ?>

<!DOCTYPE project [<!ENTITY sales SYSTEM "file:sales.xml">
                   <!ENTITY common SYSTEM "file:common.xml">]>

<project name="eSupplier" default="compile" basedir=".">

    <property name="MailLogger.mailhost"
              value="mail.networksByteDesign.com"/>
    <property name="project.email"
              value="eSupplier@ByteDesign.com" />

    <!-- appCompile target -->
    <target name="appCompile"
            description="Compile all of the source code.">
        <mkdir dir="${dirs.build}"/>

        <copy todir="${dirs.build}">
            <fileset dir="${dirs.source}" includes="**/*.*"/>
        </copy>
    </target>

    &common;
    &sales;

    <taskdef name="regexpInput"
             classname="com.networksByteDesign.util.RegexpInput"
             classpathref="project.classpath"/>

    <!-- i18n target -->
    <target name="i18n">
        <mkdir dir="${dirs.build}"/>

        <copy todir="${dirs.build}">
            <fileset dir="${dirs.source}" includes="**/labels*.properties"/>
        </copy>
```

```
        <regexpInput message="Please enter language:"
                    addproperty="language"
                    errorMessage="You didn't enter a proper language code."
                    pattern="[a-z][a-z]"/>

        <mkdir dir="${dirs.build}/html/${language}"/>

        <translate toDir="${dirs.build}/html/${language}"
                    starttoken="#"
                    endtoken="#"
                    bundle="${dirs.build}/labels"
                    bundlelanguage="${language}"
                    forceoverwrite="yes">
            <fileset dir="${dirs.source}">
                <include name="**/*.html"/>
            </fileset>
        </translate>
    </target>

    <taskdef name="esstask"
            classname="com.networksByteDesign.util.EssTask"
            classpathref="project.classpath"/>

    <!-- generateUML target -->
    <target name="generateUML">
        <esstask destdir="${dirs.doc}">
            <fileset dir="${dirs.source}"
                    includes="**/*.java"
                    excludes="**/*Test.java" />
        </esstask>
    </target>

</project>
```

Sales Department Buildfile

```
    <!-- deptCompile target -->
    <target name="deptCompile"
            depends="appCompile"
            description="Compile all of the source code.">
    </target>
```

```
<taskdef name="runservertests"
         classname="org.apache.cactus.ant.RunServerTestsTask"
         classpathref="project.classpath"/>

<!-- runCactusTests target -->
<target name="runCactusTests" description="Run Cactus tests">
    <property name="tomcat.home" value="/usr/software/tomcat" />

    <runservertests
     testURL=
  "http://localhost:8080/test/ServletRedirector?Cactus_Service=RUN_TEST"
     startTarget="startTomcat"
     stopTarget="stopTomcat"
     testTarget="cactusTests"/>
</target>


<!-- startTomcat target -->
<target name="startTomcat">
    <java classname="org.apache.catalina.startup.Bootstrap" fork="yes">
        <jvmarg value="-Dcatalina.home=${tomcat.home}"/>
        <jvmarg value="-Dcatalina.base=${tomcat.home}"/>
        <arg value="start"/>
        <classpath>
            <fileset dir="${tomcat.home}">
                <include name="bin/bootstrap.jar"/>
            </fileset>
        </classpath>
    </java>
</target>


<!-- stopTomcat target -->
<target name="stopTomcat">
    <java classname="org.apache.catalina.startup.Bootstrap" fork="yes">
        <jvmarg value="-Dcatalina.home=${tomcat.home}"/>
        <jvmarg value="-Dcatalina.base=${tomcat.home}"/>
        <arg value="stop"/>
        <classpath>
            <fileset dir="${tomcat.home}">
                <include name="bin/bootstrap.jar"/>
            </fileset>
```

```
            </classpath>
        </java>
</target>



<!-- cactusTests target -->
<target name="cactusTests">
    <junit printsummary="yes"
           haltonfailure="yes"
           haltonerror="yes"
           fork="yes">

        <classpath>
            <pathelement
                location="${tomcat.home}/webapps/test/WEB-INF/classes"/>
            <pathelement location="${tomcat.home}/webapps/test/conf"/>
            <fileset dir="${tomcat.home}/common/lib">
                <include name="**/*.jar"/>
            </fileset>
        </classpath>

        <formatter type="plain" usefile="false"/>
        <test name="TestSampleServlet"/>
    </junit>
</target>


<property name="dirs.weblogic" value="c:/bea/weblogic700" />


<!-- startWeblogic -->
<target name="startWeblogic">
    <wlrun taskname="networksByteDesign"
           classpath="${dirs.weblogic}/server/lib/weblogic.jar"
           name="networksByteDesignServer"
           domain="networksByteDesign"
           home="${dirs.weblogic}/samples/server/"
           policy="${dirs.weblogic}/server/lib/weblogic.policy"
           username="weblogic"
           password="weblogic"
           beahome="${dirs.weblogic}/samples/server/"/>
</target>


<!-- stopWeblogic -->
<target name="stopWeblogic">
```

```
        <wlstop classpath="${dirs.weblogic}/server/lib/weblogic.jar"
                url="t3://localhost:7001"
                user="weblogic"
                password="weblogic"
                beahome="${dirs.weblogic}/samples/server/"/>
    </target>
```

Network Department Buildfile

```
    <!-- deptCompile target -->
    <target name="deptCompile"
            depends="appCompile"
            description="Compile all of the source code.">
    </target>
```

NetworksByteDesign Common Buildfile

```
    <property name="dirs.backup"  value="${user.home}/backup" />
    <property name="dirs.temp"    value="/tmp"                 />
    <property name="dirs.doc"     value="docs"                 />
    <property name="dirs.build"   value="build"                />
    <property name="dirs.lib"     value="/usr/projects/lib"    />
    <property name="dirs.test"    value="test"                 />
    <property name="dirs.source"
              value="/usr/projects/${ant.project.name}/src" />
    <property name="dirs.nightly"
              value="/usr/projects/${ant.project.name}/nightly" />

    <path id="project.classpath">
        <pathelement location="${dirs.build}"/>
        <fileset dir="/usr/software/ant/lib">
            <include name="**/*.jar"/>
        </fileset>
    </path>

    <taskdef name="requiredInput"
             classname="com.networksByteDesign.util.RequiredInput"
             classpathref="project.classpath"/>

    <taskdef name="cleanimps"
             classname="com.tombrus.cleanImports.ant.CleanImports"
             classpathref="project.classpath"/>
```

```
<taskdef name="webdoclet"
        classname="xdoclet.web.WebDocletTask"
        classpathref="project.classpath"/>

<taskdef name="ejbdoclet"
        classname="xdoclet.ejb.EjbDocletTask"
        classpathref="project.classpath"/>

<taskdef name="jalopy"
        classname="de.hunsicker.jalopy.plugin.ant.AntPlugin"
        classpathref="project.classpath"/>

<taskdef name="pmd"
        classname="net.sourceforge.pmd.ant.PMDTask"
        classpathref="project.classpath"/>

<taskdef name="checkstyle"
        classname="com.puppycrawl.tools.checkstyle.CheckStyleTask"
        classpathref="project.classpath"/>

<taskdef name="rant"
        classname="com.einnovation.rant.RantTaskDef"
        classpathref="project.classpath"/>

<taskdef name="loadTask"
        classname="com.networksByteDesign.util.LoadTask"
        classpathref="project.classpath"/>

<taskdef name="styler"
        classname="au.com.Langdale.styler.StylerTask"
        classpathref="project.classpath"/>

<taskdef name="purge"
        classname="com.dallaway.ant.Purge"
        classpathref="project.classpath"/>

<taskdef name="missingteststask"
        classname="com.networksByteDesign.util.MissingTestsTask"
        classpathref="project.classpath"/>

<property name="MailLogger.from"
         value="${project.email}"/>
```

```
<property name="MailLogger.success.to"
          value="${project.email}"/>
<property name="MailLogger.failure.to"
          value="${project.email}"/>
<property name="MailLogger.success.subject"
          value="${ant.project.name} Nightly Build Succeeded"/>
<property name="MailLogger.failure.subject"
          value="${ant.project.name} Nightly Build Failed"/>

<!-- compile target -->
<target name="compile"
        depends="deptCompile"
        description="Compile all of the source code.">

    <javac srcdir="${dirs.build}">
        <classpath refid="project.classpath"/>
    </javac>
</target>

<!-- xdoclet target -->
<target name="xdoclet">
    <mkdir dir="${dirs.build}"/>

    <copy todir="${dirs.build}">
        <fileset dir="${dirs.source}" includes="**/*.*"/>
    </copy>

    <webdoclet sourcepath="${dirs.build}"
               destdir="${dirs.build}"
               mergedir="${dirs.build}"
               force="${xdoclet.force}">

        <classpath refid="project.classpath"/>
        <fileset dir="${dirs.build}">
            <include name="**/*Servlet.java" />
        </fileset>

        <deploymentdescriptor servletspec="2.3"
                              destdir="${dirs.build}"/>
    </webdoclet>
```

```
            <webdoclet sourcepath="${dirs.build}"
                     destdir="${dirs.build}"
                     force="${xdoclet.force}">

                <classpath refid="project.classpath"/>
                <fileset dir="${dirs.build}">
                    <include name="**/*.java" />
                </fileset>

                <jsptaglib taglibversion="1.0"
                          jspversion="1.1"
                          displayname="${ant.project.name}"
                          description="${ant.project.name} tag library"/>
            </webdoclet>

            <ejbdoclet sourcepath="${dirs.build}"
                     destdir="${dirs.build}"
                     ejbspec="2.0"
                     force="${xdoclet.force}">

                <classpath refid="project.classpath"/>
                <fileset dir="${dirs.build}">
                    <include name="**/*Bean.java" />
                </fileset>

                <dataobject/>
                <remoteinterface/>
                <homeinterface/>
                <entitypk/>
                <entitycmp/>
                <deploymentdescriptor destdir="${dirs.build}"/>

                <jboss xmlencoding="UTF-8" destdir="${dirs.build}"/>
            </ejbdoclet>
        </target>

<!-- manifest target -->
<target name="manifest">
    <property name="version" value="1.1" />
    <tstamp />
```

```
        <manifest file="${dirs.build}/MANIFEST.MF">
            <attribute name="Built-By" value="${ant.project.name} Team"/>
            <section name="common">
                <attribute name="Specification-Title"
                            value="test" />
                <attribute name="Specification-Version"
                            value="${version}" />
                <attribute name="Specification-Vendor"
                            value="Networks Byte Design, Inc." />
                <attribute name="Implementation-Title"
                            value="common" />
                <attribute name="Implementation-Version"
                            value="${version} ${DSTAMP}" />
                <attribute name="Sealed"
                            value="true"/>
                <attribute name="Implementation-Vendor"
                            value="Networks Byte Design, Inc." />
            </section>
        </manifest>
    </target>

    <!-- deploy target -->
    <target name="deploy"
            depends="manifest"
            description="Simple deployment of the app">
        <jar jarfile="${ant.project.name}.jar"
            filesonly="true"
            manifest="${dirs.build}/MANIFEST.MF">
            <fileset dir="${dirs.build}">
                <exclude name="**/*Test.class" />
                <exclude name="**/*Servlet.class" />
                <include name="**/*.class" />
            </fileset>
        </jar>

        <copy file="${ant.project.name}.jar"
            tofile="${dirs.backup}/${ant.project.name}-${DSTAMP}.jar" />

        <war destfile="${ant.project.name}.war"
            filesonly="true"
            webxml="${dirs.build}/web.xml"
            manifest="${dirs.build}/MANIFEST.MF">
```

```
            <fileset dir="${dirs.build}" includes="taglib.tld" />
            <fileset dir="${dirs.build}" includes="**/*.jsp"    />
            <classes dir="${dirs.build}">
                <include name="**/*Servlet.class" />
            </classes>
            <lib dir=".">
                <include name="${ant.project.name}.jar" />
            </lib>
        </war>
</target>


<!-- cleanImports target -->
<target name="cleanImports" description="Cleans import statements.">
    <cleanimps srcdir="${dirs.source}">
        <classpath refid="project.classpath"/>
        <cleanformat>
            <import   comment="Application Libraries"
                      package="com.networksByteDesign"/>
            <import   comment="Standard Java Libraries"
                      package="java"/>
            <import   comment="Extra Java Libraries"
                      package="javax"/>
            <import   comment="External Libraries" />
        </cleanformat>
    </cleanimps>
</target>


<!-- clean target -->
<target name="clean" description="Clean all system generated files.">
    <delete dir="${dirs.build}" />
</target>


<!-- unittest target -->
<target name="unittest"
        description="Run the unit tests for the source code.">
    <mkdir dir="${dirs.test}"/>
    <junit haltonfailure="no"
           printsummary="yes"
           failureproperty="unittestFailed">
        <classpath refid="project.classpath"/>
        <batchtest todir="${dirs.test}">
            <fileset dir="${dirs.build}">
```

```
                          <include name="com/**/*Test.class" />
                      </fileset>
                  </batchtest>
          </junit>


          <antcall target="unittestReport" />
          <antcall target="cleanupUnittest" />
          <fail if="unittestFailed" message="One or more unit tests failed."/>
      </target>


      <!-- cleanupUnittest target -->
      <target name="cleanupUnittest">
          <delete>
              <fileset dir="${dirs.temp}">
                  <include name="*${ant.project.name}.test" />
              </fileset>
          </delete>
      </target>


      <!-- javadoc target -->
      <target name="javadoc" description="Generates javadoc for the source.">
          <mkdir dir="${dirs.doc}"/>

          <javadoc destdir="${dirs.doc}">
              <classpath refid="project.classpath"/>
              <fileset dir="${dirs.build}">
                  <include name="**/*.java"/>
                  <exclude name="**/*Test.java"/>
              </fileset>
          </javadoc>
      </target>


      <!-- cvsInit target -->
      <target name="cvsInit">
          <available file="${user.home}/.cvspass"
                      property="cvsAlreadyLoggedIn" />

          <antcall target="cvsLogin" />
      </target>


      <!-- cvsLogin target -->
      <target name="cvsLogin" unless="cvsAlreadyLoggedIn">
```

```
    <requiredInput message="Please enter CVS password:"
                   addproperty="cvsPassword"
                   errorMessage=" You didn't enter your CVS password."/>


    <cvspass cvsroot=":local:/usr/local/cvsArchive"
             password="${cvsPassword}" />
</target>

<!-- cvsCheckout target -->
<target name="cvsCheckout" depends="cvsInit">

    <requiredInput message="Please enter CVS module:"
                   addproperty="cvsModule"
                   errorMessage="You didn't enter a CVS module." />

    <requiredInput message="Please enter working directory:"
                   addproperty="dirs.working"
                   errorMessage="You didn't enter a working directory"/>

    <mkdir dir="${dirs.working}" />

    <cvs package="${cvsModule}" dest="${dirs.working}" />
</target>

<!-- cvsUpdate target -->
<target name="cvsUpdate" depends="cvsInit">
    <cvs command="update" dest="${dirs.source}" />
</target>

<!-- cvsCommit target -->
<target name="cvsCommit" depends="cvsUpdate">
    <requiredInput message="Please enter your CVS comment:"
                   addproperty="cvsComment"
                   errorMessage=" You did not enter a CVS comment."/>
    <cvs command="commit -m ${cvsComment}" dest="${dirs.source}" />
</target>

<!-- cvsTag target -->
<target name="cvsTag" depends="cvsInit">
    <requiredInput message="Please enter your CVS tag:"
                   addproperty="cvsTag"
                   errorMessage=" You did not enter a CVS tag."/>
```

```
            <cvs command="tag ${cvsTag}" dest="${dirs.source}" />
    </target>

    <!-- cvsCheckoutTag target -->
    <target name="cvsCheckoutTag" depends="cvsInit">
        <requiredInput message="Please enter your CVS module:"
                       addproperty="cvsModule"
                       errorMessage=" You did not enter a CVS module."/>

        <requiredInput message="Please enter your CVS tag:"
                       addproperty="cvsTag"
                       errorMessage=" You did not enter a CVS tag."/>

        <requiredInput message="Please enter working directory:"
                       addproperty="dirs.working"
                       errorMessage="You didn't enter a working directory."
        />

        <mkdir dir="${dirs.working}"/>

        <cvs package="${cvsModule}" tag="${cvsTag}" dest="${dirs.working}"/>
    </target>

    <!-- backupTar target -->
    <target name="backupTar"
            description="Backs ups all source into a tar file.">

        <mkdir dir="${dirs.backup}" />

        <tstamp />
        <property name="backupFile"
                  value="${ant.project.name}_${DSTAMP}${TSTAMP}.tar.gz" />

        <tar tarfile="${dirs.backup}/${backupFile}"
             basedir="${dirs.source}" compression="gzip" />

        <echo message="Backup file ${backupFile} has been created." />

    </target>

    <!-- backupAdvancedInteractive target -->
    <target name="backupAdvancedInteractive"
```

```
            depends="backupTar"
            description="Moves backups to server with supplied login/pwd">

    <requiredInput message="Please enter ftp user id:"
                   addproperty="ftpUserID"
                   errorMessage=" You didn't enter your ftp user id."/>

    <requiredInput message="Please enter ftp password:"
                   addproperty="ftpPassword"
                   errorMessage=" You didn't enter your ftp password."/>

    <property name="ftpLogin" value="" />

    <antcall target="backupAdvancedInternal" />
</target>

<!-- backupAdvancedBackground target -->
<target name="backupAdvancedBackground"
        depends="backupTar"
        description="Moves backups to server with hardcoded login/pwd">

    <property name="ftpLogin"    value="" />
    <property name="ftpUserID"   value="cronus" />
    <property name="ftpPassword" value="f#8jW9t3s!" />

    <antcall target="backupAdvancedInternal" />
</target>

<!-- backupAdvancedInternal target -->
<target name="backupAdvancedInternal"
        if="ftpLogin">

    <ftp server="127.0.0.1" remotedir="ftpFiles"
         userid="${ftpUserID}" password="${ftpPassword}">
         <fileset dir="${dirs.backup}" />
    </ftp>

    <delete dir="${dirs.backup}" />
</target>

<!-- nightlyBuild target -->
<target name="nightlyBuild"
        description="Conducts the nightly build process">
```

```xml
        <mkdir dir="${dirs.nightly}" />
        <delete dir="${dirs.nightly}" />

        <cvs package="${ant.project.name}" dest="${dirs.nightly}" />

        <antcall target="clean" />
        <antcall target="compile" />
    </target>

    <!-- nightlyUnittest target -->
    <target name="nightlyUnittest"
            description="Run the nightly unit tests for the source code.">
        <mkdir dir="${dirs.test}"/>
        <junit haltonfailure="no"
               printsummary="yes"
               showoutput="yes"
               fork="yes"
               failureproperty="unittestFailed">
            <formatter type="xml" usefile="true" />
            <classpath refid="project.classpath"/>
            <batchtest todir="${dirs.test}">
                <fileset dir="${dirs.build}">
                    <include name="com/**/*Test.class" />
                </fileset>
            </batchtest>
        </junit>

        <antcall target="unittestReport" />
        <antcall target="cleanupUnittest" />
        <fail if="unittestFailed" message="One or more unit tests failed."/>
    </target>

    <!-- unittestReport target -->
    <target name="unittestReport">
        <junitreport todir="${dirs.test}">
            <fileset dir="${dirs.test}">
                <include name="TEST*.xml"/>
            </fileset>
            <report format="frames" todir="${dirs.test}"/>
        </junitreport>
    </target>
```

```xml
<!-- buildLogformat target -->
<target name="buildLogFormat">
    <xslt in="build.log" out="build.html" style="log.xsl"/>
</target>


<!-- format target -->
<target name="format" description="Reformats code to meet team standards">
    <jalopy fileformat="unix"
            convention="format.xml">
        <fileset dir="${dirs.source}" >
            <include name="**/*.java" />
        </fileset>
    </jalopy>
</target>


<!-- checkCode target -->
<target name="checkCode" description="Checks code for improper structure">
    <pmd verbose="true"
         rulesetfiles="rulesets/basic.xml,rulesets/design.xml"
         shortFilenames="true"
         failonerror="no">
        <formatter type="html" toFile="${dirs.build}/pmd_report.html"/>
        <fileset dir="${dirs.source}">
            <include name="**/*.java"/>
        </fileset>
    </pmd>
</target>


<!-- codeReview target -->
<target name="codeReview" description="Conduct a code review.">
    <checkstyle>
        <fileset dir="${dirs.source}" includes="**/*.java"/>

        <property key="checkstyle.javadoc.scope"
                  value="private"/>
        <property key="checkstyle.require.packagehtml"
                  value="false"/>
        <property key="checkstyle.require.version"
                  value="false"/>
        <property key="checkstyle.allow.noauthor"
                  value="false"/>
        <property key="checkstyle.javadoc.checkUnusedThrows"
```

```
                        value="false"/>
        <property key="checkstyle.pattern.member"
                  value="^[a-z][a-zA-Z0-9]*$"/>
        <property key="checkstyle.pattern.publicmember"
                  value="^f[A-Z][a-zA-Z0-9]*$"/>
        <property key="checkstyle.pattern.const"
                  value="^[A-Z](_?[A-Z0-9]+)*$"/>
        <property key="checkstyle.pattern.static"
                  value="^[a-z][a-zA-Z0-9]*$"/>
        <property key="checkstyle.pattern.parameter"
                  value="^[a-z][a-zA-Z0-9]*$"/>
        <property key="checkstyle.pattern.package"
                  value="^[a-z]+(\.[a-zA-Z_][a-zA-Z_0-9]*)*$"/>
        <property key="checkstyle.pattern.type"
                  value="^[A-Z][a-zA-Z0-9]*$"/>
        <property key="checkstyle.pattern.method"
                  value="^[a-z][a-zA-Z0-9]*$"/>
        <property key="checkstyle.pattern.localvar"
                  value="^[a-z][a-zA-Z0-9]*$"/>
        <property key="checkstyle.pattern.localfinalvar"
                  value="^[a-z][a-zA-Z0-9]*$"/>
        <property key="checkstyle.header.file"
                  value=""/>
        <property key="checkstyle.header.ignoreline"
                  value=""/>
        <property key="checkstyle.header.regexp"
                  value="false"/>
        <property key="checkstyle.ignore.imports"
                  value="false"/>
        <property key="checkstyle.illegal.imports"
                  value="sun"/>
        <property key="checkstyle.maxlinelen"
                  value="80"/>
        <property key="checkstyle.tab.width"
                  value="8"/>
        <property key="checkstyle.ignore.importlength"
                  value="false"/>
        <property key="checkstyle.ignore.maxlinelen"
                  value="^$"/>
        <property key="checkstyle.maxmethodlen"
                  value="150"/>
        <property key="checkstyle.maxconstructorlen"
                  value="150"/>
```

```
<property key="checkstyle.maxfilelen"
         value="2000"/>
<property key="checkstyle.maxparameters"
         value="7"/>
<property key="checkstyle.allow.tabs"
         value="false"/>
<property key="checkstyle.ignore.whitespace"
         value="false"/>
<property key="checkstyle.ignore.whitespace.cast"
         value="false"/>
<property key="checkstyle.paren.pad"
         value="nospace"/>
<property key="checkstyle.wrap.operator"
         value="nl"/>
<property key="checkstyle.ignore.public.in.interface"
         value="false"/>
<property key="checkstyle.allow.protected"
         value="false"/>
<property key="checkstyle.allow.package"
         value="false"/>
<property key="checkstyle.pattern.publicmember"
         value="^f[A-Z][a-zA-Z0-9]*$"/>
<property key="checkstyle.ignore.braces"
         value="true"/>
<property key="checkstyle.block.try"
         value="stmt"/>
<property key="checkstyle.block.catch"
         value="text"/>
<property key="checkstyle.block.finally"
         value="stmt"/>
<property key="checkstyle.lcurly.type"
         value="eol"/>
<property key="checkstyle.lcurly.method"
         value="eol"/>
<property key="checkstyle.lcurly.other"
         value="eol"/>
<property key="checkstyle.rcurly"
         value="same"/>
<property key="checkstyle.pattern.todo"
         value="TODO:"/>
<property key="checkstyle.ignore.longell"
         value="false"/>
```

```xml
                    <property key="checkstyle.illegal.instantiations"
                              value=""/>
            </checkstyle>
    </target>


    <!-- instrument target -->
    <target name="instrument">
        <mkdir dir="${dirs.build}/instrument"   />
        <mkdir dir="${dirs.build}/repository"   />

        <icontract srcdir="${dirs.source}"
                   excludes="**/*Test.java"
                   instrumentdir="${dirs.build}/instrument"
                   repositorydir="${dirs.build}/repository">
            <classpath refid="project.classpath"/>
        </icontract>
    </target>


    <!-- jdepend target -->
    <target name="jdepend">
        <jdepend outputfile="${dirs.build}/jdepend-report.xml" format="xml">
            <sourcespath>
                <pathelement location="${dirs.build}" />
            </sourcespath>
            <classpath location="${dirs.build}"/>
        </jdepend>

        <style basedir="${dirs.build}" destdir="${dirs.build}"
               includes="jdepend-report.xml"
               style="${ant.home}/etc/jdepend.xsl" />
    </target>


    <!-- cvsComments target -->
    <target name="cvsComments" depends="cvsInit">
        <mkdir dir="${dirs.build}"/>
        <tstamp />

        <cvschangelog dir="${dirs.source}"
                      destfile="${dirs.build}/cvsComments.xml"
                      daysinpast="1" />

        <style in="${dirs.build}/cvsComments.xml"
               out="${dirs.build}/cvsComments_${DSTAMP}.html"
```

```
                style="${ant.home}/etc/changelog.xsl">
            <param name="title"
                    expression="CVS Comments - ${TODAY}"/>
            <param name="module" expression="${dirs.source}"/>
        </style>
    </target>


    <!-- weeklyCVSReport target -->
    <target name="weeklyCVSReport" depends="cvsInit">
        <mkdir dir="${dirs.build}"/>
        <tstamp />

        <cvschangelog dir="${dirs.source}"
                    destfile="${dirs.build}/cvsComments.xml"
                    daysinpast="7"
                    usersfile="userMapping.lst" />

        <style in="${dirs.build}/cvsComments.xml"
                out="${dirs.build}/weeklyCVS_${DSTAMP}.html"
                style="${ant.home}/etc/changelog.xsl">
            <param name="title"
                    expression="Weekly CVS Report ending ${TODAY}"/>
            <param name="module" expression="${dirs.source}"/>
        </style>
    </target>

    <!-- releaseCVSReport target -->
    <target name="releaseCVSReport" depends="cvsInit">

        <mkdir dir="${dirs.build}"/>
        <tstamp />

        <requiredInput message="Please enter start date:"
                    addproperty="startDate"
                    errorMessage=" You didn't enter a start date."/>

        <requiredInput message="Please enter end date:"
                    addproperty="endDate"
                    errorMessage=" You didn't enter an end date."/>

        <requiredInput message="Please enter report title:"
                    addproperty="reportTitle"
                    errorMessage=" You didn't enter a report title."/>
```

```xml
        <cvschangelog dir="${dirs.source}"
                      destfile="${dirs.build}/cvsComments.xml"
                      start="${startDate}"
                      end="${endDate}"
                      usersfile="userMapping.lst" />

        <style in="${dirs.build}/cvsComments.xml"
               out="${dirs.build}/releaseCVS_${DSTAMP}.html"
               style="${ant.home}/etc/changelog.xsl">
            <param name="title"  expression="${reportTitle}"/>
            <param name="module" expression="${dirs.source}"/>
        </style>
    </target>


    <!-- cvsTagReport target -->
    <target name="cvsTagReport" depends="cvsInit">

        <requiredInput message="Please enter CVS module:"
                       addproperty="cvsModule"
                       errorMessage="You didn't enter your CVS module."/>

        <requiredInput message="Please enter first tag:"
                       addproperty="firstTag"
                       errorMessage="You didn't enter a CVS tag."/>

        <requiredInput message="Please enter second tag:"
                       addproperty="secondTag"
                       errorMessage="You didn't enter a second CVS tag."/>

        <cvstagdiff destfile="${dirs.build}/tagdiff.xml"
                    package="${cvsModule}"
                    startTag="${firstTag}"
                    endTag="${secondTag}" />

        <style in="${dirs.build}/tagdiff.xml"
               out="${dirs.build}/tagdiff_${firstTag}_${secondTag}.html"
               style="${ant.home}/etc/tagdiff.xsl">
            <param name="title"
                   expression="Comparison of: ${firstTag} and ${secondTag}"
            />
            <param name="module" expression="${dirs.source}"/>
        </style>
    </target>
```

```
<!-- smartBuild target -->
<target name="smartBuild" depends="cvsInit">

    <cvs command="update"
        dest="${dirs.source}"
        output="${dirs.build}/smartBuild.txt" />

    <loadfile property="filesChanged"
            srcFile="${dirs.build}/smartBuild.txt" />

    <condition property="mustCodegen">
        <contains string="${filesChanged}" substring=".codegen" />
    </condition>
</target>


<!-- remoteDeploy target -->
<target name="remoteDeploy" depends="remoteTransfer">
    <rant buildFile="/home/dist/Deploy.xml"
        soapURL="http://localhost:8080/rant/servlet/rpcrouter"
        target="deploy"/>
</target>



<!-- remoteTransfer target -->
<target name="remoteTransfer" depends="deploy">
    <tar tarfile="${ant.project.name}.tar.gz"
        basedir="."
        includes="${ant.project.name}.war"
        compression="gzip" />

    <requiredInput message="Please enter cronus ftp password:"
                addproperty="ftpPassword"
                errorMessage="You didn't enter the ftp password."/>

    <ftp server="127.0.0.1" remotedir="/home/dist" action="put"
        userid="cronus" password="${ftpPassword}">
        <fileset dir=".">
            <include name="deploy.xml"/>
            <include name="${ant.project.name}.tar.gz"/>
        </fileset>
    </ftp>
</target>
```

```
<!-- selectSql target -->
<target name="selectSql">
    <sql driver="oracle.jdbc.driver.OracleDriver"
        url="jdbc:oracle:thin:@127.0.0.1:1521:orcl"
        userid="system"
        password="testPassword"
        print="true"
        onerror="continue"
        output="output.txt">
    select TO_CHAR(SYSDATE) from dual;
    </sql>
</target>


<!-- loadData target -->
<target name="loadData" >
    <loadTask userid="system@127.0.0.1/testPassword"
            haltonfailure="false">
        <fileset dir=".">
            <include name="**/*.ctl"/>
        </fileset>
    </loadTask>
</target>


<!-- pipeline target -->
<target name="pipeline">
    <styler>
        <fileset dir="${dirs.source}/samples">
            <include name="*.sample"/>
        </fileset>

        <transform file="${dirs.source}/sample1.xsl" />
        <transform file="${dirs.source}/sample2.xsl" />
        <transform file="${dirs.source}/sample3.xsl" />
        <transform file="${dirs.source}/sample4.xsl" />
        <transform file="${dirs.source}/sample5.xsl" />

        <output dir="${dirs.build}"/>
    </styler>
</target>


<!-- stressor target -->
<target name="stressor">
```

```
    <mkdir dir="${dirs.test}"/>
    <junit haltonfailure="no"
           printsummary="yes"
           failureproperty="stressFailed">
        <classpath refid="project.classpath"/>
        <batchtest todir="${dirs.test}">
            <fileset dir="${dirs.build}">
                <include name="com/**/*StressTest.class" />
            </fileset>
        </batchtest>
    </junit>
</target>

<!-- stressTestLoop target -->
<target name="stressTestLoop">
    <script language="javascript"> <![CDATA[
        for (i=1; i<=10; i++)
        {
            stressor.execute();
            if(project.getProperty("stressFailed"))
            {
                break;
            }
        }
    ]]> </script>
</target>

<!-- stressTest target -->
<target name="stressTest" depends="stressTestLoop" if="stressFailed">
    <sound>
        <success source="drama.wav"    />
        <fail    source="drama.wav" />
    </sound>

    <mail from="${project.email}"
          tolist="${project.email}"
          subject="Stress test Failed"
          mailhost="mail.networksByteDesign.com"
          encoding="plain"/>
</target>
```

```xml
<!-- perfTest target -->
<target name="perfTest">
    <tempfile property="files.temp"
              prefix="perfTest"
              suffix=".xml"
              destdir="${dirs.temp}" />

    <echo message="${files.temp}" />
</target>

<!-- purgeFiles target -->
<target name="purgeFiles">
    <purge keep="5">
        <fileset dir="${dirs.temp}">
            <include name="**/perfTest*.xml" />
        </fileset>
</purge>
</target>

<!-- missingTests target -->
<target name="missingTests">
    <missingteststask>
        <mapper type="regexp" from="^(.*)Test\.java$$" to="\1.java"/>
        <testsfileset dir="${dirs.source}">
            <include name="**/*Test.java"/>
        </testsfileset>
        <filesfileset dir="${dirs.source}">
            <include name="**/*.java"/>
            <exclude name="**/*Test.java"/>
        </filesfileset>
    </missingteststask>
</target>
```

E

Tool Version

This appendix details the products and version numbers that the buildfiles and custom components were developed and tested with. At the time of the writing of this appendix, the latest available version of all of the tools was utilized.

Development and Testing Platforms

All of the code from this book was developed and tested on the following platforms:

- Mac OS X 10.2.5 running Ant 1.5.3 on Java 1.4.1

- Windows 2000 Professional running Ant 1.5.3 on Java 1.4.1

- Windows XP Home Edition running Ant 1.5.3 on Java 1.3.1

Tool Versions

The components listed in Table E.1 are all used as a part of this book. The version number of each tool that was tested with the build files in this book is listed in the table as well.

TABLE E.1   Versions of Tools Used in the Book

Tool	Version Number
JavaBeans Activation Framework	1.0.2
AntEater	0.9.15
BSF	2.2
Cactus	13-1.4b1
Checkstyle	2.4
CleanImports	1.0.5
CruiseControl	2.0.1
CVS	1.10
ESS-Model	2.1
GnuPG	1.2.1
iContract	0.3d2
Jakarta Tomcat	4.1.18
Jalopy	1.0b10
Java Mail	1.3
JBoss	3.0.4
JDepend	2.4
Jikes	1.17
JUnit	3.8.1
Log4j	1.2.7
Mocha	Beta 1
NetBeans	3.4.1
NetComponents	1.3.8
NoUnit	0.6
Oracle	9.0.1.0.0
PMD	1.02
Purge	20021015
Rant	0.1
Rhino	1.5R4
Styler	20020331
WebLogic	7.0
Xalan-Java	2.4.1
XDoclet	1.2.0 Beta 2
yGuard	1.1

Index

A

How can we make this index more useful? Email us at indexes@samspublishing.com

J–K

M